DIVINE HEALING:
THE YEARS OF EXPANSION,
1906–1930

DIVINE HEALING:
THE YEARS OF EXPANSION,
1906–1930

Theological Variation in the Transatlantic World

JAMES ROBINSON

PICKWICK *Publications* · Eugene, Oregon

DIVINE HEALING: THE YEARS OF EXPANSION, 1906–1930
Theological Variation in the Transatlantic World

Pickwick Publications
An Imprint of Wipf and Stock Publishers
199 W. 8th Ave., Suite 3
Eugene, OR 97401

www.wipfandstock.com

ISBN 13: 978-1-62032-408-0

Cataloguing-in-Publication data:

Robinson, James.

Divine healing: the years of expansion, 1906–1930 : theological variation in the transatlantic world / James Robinson

xii + 234 pp. ; 23 cm. Includes bibliographical references and index.

ISBN 13: 978-1-62032-851-4

1. Healing—Religious aspects—Christianity. 2. Pentecostalism. 3. Protestantism—20th century. I. Title.

BT732.5 R63 2014

Manufactured in the U.S.A.

To
Edith Mary Robinson

In the year of
Our Golden Wedding
(1963–2013)

It is God in his sovereign judgment that determines when the miraculous is to occur, and then how powerful and apparent the interventions should be. God does the calibrating in ways appropriate to the particular occasion.

Robert N. Wennberg, *Faith at the Edge.*

Contents

Preface

THE SEED FOR ENGAGING with the history of divine healing was sown while working on my doctoral thesis, which studied the first twenty years of the history of Pentecostalism in Ireland. It soon became clear that the movement did not emerge onto the historical stage in the first decade of the twentieth century without a past. I felt challenged to dispute the view of Donald Gee, a leading Pentecostal authority, that the new movement was a "spontaneous revival" that owed nothing to either outstanding personalities or religious leaders. Writing later, Donald Dayton, showed that by the closing decades of the nineteenth century some trends in popular Evangelicalism were only "a hairs-breadth from Pentecostalism." It soon became clear that divine healing played a sizeable part in opening hearts and minds to the charismatic spirituality that Pentecostalism came to embrace. The trilogy seeks to record and explain how the doctrine of divine healing came to play a significant part in the growth of the worldwide church into the twenty-first century.

It is some eight years since the project started. The original intention was to write a book that covered the period 1830–1930 but, Topsy-like, it just "grow'd"—hence the trilogy. This book concludes the task, which aspired to study the history of divine healing within the world of transatlantic Protestantism. The first volume to appear covers the years 1830–90, while the second concentrates on the period 1890–1906. The year 1906 is regarded as the putative date for the beginning of Pentecostalism as a movement, which in a number of ways has remained without precedence since the days of the early church. This volume brings the coverage up to 1930, by which time Pentecostalism had firmly established itself, thus making it certain that the ministry of healing, in all its diverse forms, will continue to be on the agenda of the global church. For those who are not familiar with the content of the first two books, the Introduction presents the main themes and personalities pertaining to the period 1830–1906. This is followed by a synopsis of the six chapters that bring the story up to the early 1930s.

Acknowledgments

I WORK AS AN independent researcher, so the long list of names that decorate the acknowledgement pages of most other books is absent here. It is, therefore, all the more reason for thanking those who have played a large part in my reaching this point.

Wipf & Stock have been splendid to work with. Not many publishers would have considered publishing a trilogy from a writer not formally engaged in academia. Robin Parry, the British editor, has been a great encourager, and helpfully decisive when called upon.

There are a number other books dealing with the subject that have proved an inspiration in setting a standard to which I could only aspire. One, in particular, I would pick out. It was written by Heather Curtis, under the title *Faith in the Great Physician: Suffering and Divine Healing in American Culture 1860–1900* (2007). One reviewer of the book was exact in stating that the author "had done both the historical guild and the church a great favor in so elegantly narrating the history of a movement that challenged the long-standing assumptions about the spiritual utility of corporal pain and, in so doing, remapped our imaginations and transformed our understanding of suffering." If the trilogy comes even within distance of such an encomium, it would be a reason for gratification.

I am deeply indebted to Caroline Stevenson for her proof-reading skills brought to my rather error-strewn drafts. She rarely, if ever, missed a semi-colon or quotation mark. Some of the style changes she suggested have sweetened the final text. Typical of her, she volunteered to undertake this arduous task. I hasten to add that the text as submitted is my responsibility.

The book is dedicated to my wife, Mary, in the year of our golden wedding anniversary. She has been exemplary in every way as wife and mother of our three married sons, and grandmother of our five grandchildren. Her prized contribution over the past eight years has been to keep the path clear for me to complete the trilogy.

Abbreviations

AF	*The Apostolic Faith*
AoG	Assemblies of God
CMA	Christian and Missionary Alliance
EE	*Elim Evangel*
IDPCM	*International Dictionary of Pentecostal and Charismatic Movements*
JEPTA	*Journal European Pentecostal Theological Association*
LH	*Leaves of Healing*
LRE	*Latter Rain Evangel*
MEC	Methodist Episcopal Church
NAE	National Association of Evangelicals
PMU	Pentecostal Missionary Union
RT	*Redemption Tidings*
TH	*Thy Healer*
WCC	World Council of Churches

Introduction

Tнis воок рicкs up where its two predecessors left off. To assist readers who may not be familiar with these works a résumé of their content is provided below, followed by a synopsis of this volume.

RÉSUMÉ: BACKGROUND 1830–1906

In the years 1830–35, the religious world of Britain was alerted to a charismatic revival that predated the Pentecostal movement by more than seventy years. For Mrs Oliphant, the biographer of Edward Irving, the Scottish Presbyterian divine, the revival was "an agitating and extraordinary chapter in the history of the modern church. . . . Almost every notable Christian man of the time took the matter into devout and anxious consideration." The almost unheard doctrine that Irving espoused was "the idea that disease itself was sin, and that no man with faith in his Lord ought to be overpowered by it." Irving's two churches in London witnessed a charismatic outburst between 1830 and 1835. Irving promulgated in essence the Pentecostal theology some eighty years before its spread from the Azusa Street revival in Los Angles. The spotlight then shifted to Mottlingen, a village in south-west Germany where the Lutheran pastor Johann Christoph Blumhardt labored. There, he was pitched into a case widely regarded as demonic possession that tested him to breaking point. The ministry of exorcism was followed by a revival in the surrounding district. The critical view taken by the regional Lutheran consistory of his healing ministry led to his decision to establish a healing home. It became the prototype of subsequent healing homes. Around the same time, over the border in Switzerland more such homes were established by Dorothea Trudel in a village on Lake Zurich. Her four homes there attracted visitors from both sides of the Atlantic.

While Blumhardt and Trudel were in the continental Pietistic tradition, a widely acknowledged coupling of perfectionist ideas and divine healing can be more clearly attributed to early Methodism in both Britain and America. The theology of a clean heart evinced the idea of a healthy body. One of the most important pioneers in the ministry of healing was the Methodist Ethan Allen (1813–1903) who earned the sobriquet "Father of Divine Healing." The perfectionist message was not confined to Methodism in America. William Edwin Boardman was one of the Americans who helped to advance the holiness/healing message in Britain. He played a notable part in promoting the "International Conference on Divine Healing and True Holiness," held in London in June 1885. In this venture he had the support of Elizabeth Baxter, the wife of the publisher of the *Christian Herald,* a periodical that played a major part in raising the profile of divine healing throughout Britain and Ireland. Elizabeth Baxter' edited the magazine *Thy Healer,* which carried the healing message to the English-speaking world.

In America, A. B. Simpson and A. J. Gordon were among the more gifted leaders to come to the fore in their advocacy of divine healing in the 1880s. Their writings remain still as major classical texts of the doctrine. Simpson encapsulated his teaching under four dominant motifs, presented as the fourfold gospel of Christ as Saviour, Sanctifier, Healer, and Coming King. Both Simpson and Gordon are representative of the power of the written word to spread the healing message. Gordon's fellow Bostonian, Charles Cullis, was a prolific publisher of healing literature. His publishing enterprise, the Willard Tract Repository, through its annual reports, books, and tracts, reached a worldwide audience conveying the message of holiness and healing. Between 1872 and 1892 twenty major titles on faith healing were published. It was through the reprint of works by or about Blumhardt and Trudel that the work of these continental pioneers became better known.

The 1890s saw a sharp decline in the impact of the message of divine healing. Christian Science, Spiritualism, and Theosophy were attracting both interest and increasing support. Also, the early pioneers were either ageing or dead. The revitalization of the healing theme owed much to the American Holiness movement with its roots in the mainstream Methodist Episcopal Church. Many ardent believers became increasingly perturbed by its liberally-inclined theological sophistication and middle class refinement that had little time for the older and formative Wesleyan emphasis on second-blessing perfectionism. While many remained loyal to the MEC, others became schismatic "come-outers" who established diverse fellowships, most in the 1890s. Not all, but a sizeable number of the new groups practiced divine healing. It was from this body of believers that many were drawn to form the nascent Pentecostal movement. From this new platform, they were free to unleash the full panoply of the *charismata* cited in 1 Corinthians 12.

Outside the Methodist tradition, there was an input from those with a Reformed Higher Life background, such as J. A. Dowie, A. T Pierson, R. A. Torrey and Carrie Judd Montgomery. Dowie was the best-known on this list. In 1901, he established on the shore of Lake Michigan a settlement known as Zion City. It was run on strict theocratic lines by a controlling Dowie, who was noted for his charismatic predisposition, anti-medical fulminations, and lavish claims to healing. His controversial career ended in ignominy but his legacy was far-reaching. Many healing evangelists could trace the inspiration for their ministry back to Zion, among them John G. Lake in South Africa, Gerrit Polman in the Netherlands, and indirectly Smith Wigglesworth in Britain. By contrast, Pierson and Torrey were not associated with the Pentecostal movement, and their teaching on healing was more guarded

The major developments in the history of divine healing prior to the Azusa Street revival in 1906 took place in America. The holiness message in Britain was largely defined by the Keswick Convention. A number of speakers who addressed the Keswick convention both favored and practiced divine healing. Donald Gee acknowledged that those who identified with the early Pentecostal movement were Christians who "had tasted a previous experience of the Spirit's grace and power in connection with the Holiness and Keswick Movements." Alexander Boddy, the father figure of British Pentecostalism was a regular attender. He was glad to see at the 1908 Keswick Convention the "faces we had looked in at the [first Pentecostal] Sunderland Convention."[1] Elizabeth Baxter addressed the women's meeting at Keswick. She was heavily involved with the Bethshan healing home in North London, which throughout the first half of 1880s was the hub of the healing movement in Britain. A number of prominent Pentecostal leaders had links with Bethshan. For one, Eleanor Crisp was appointed Principal of the women's training home of the Pentecostal Missionary Union.

SYNOPSIS: THE YEARS 1906–1930

The first chapter concentrates on the two men who were most closely associated with the formation of the Pentecostal movement, both in formulating its theological distinctives and initiating its denominational separateness. It was through Charles F. Parham and the students at his Holiness-based Bethel Bible School, Topeka, Kansas, that the conviction grew that speaking in tongues was the initial evidence of Spirit-baptism. This took place January 1901, and for a short time the school attracted attention, only to lose its initial impetus until revival broke out in Galena, Kansas, in 1903. Dramatic healings opened the door to a three-month revival, which restated his ministry, and increased the ranks in his expanding Apostolic Faith Movement. With the movement's extension into Houston, Texas, a short-term Bible school was located there. It was at the school that William Seymour first encountered Parham. After pastoring a number of Holiness missions, Seymour moved to Los Angeles in January 1906 to lead a black Holiness mission in Azusa Street, Los Angeles. In April, some members began speaking in tongues, and from that point news spread to attract a worldwide response. Meetings continued daily under Seymour's guidance, and for the next three years Azusa Street was an catalyst for the spread of global Pentecostalism. The chapter concludes with a review of the contribution made by the healing homes in the context of medical advance at the beginning of the century in America.

Chapter 2 considers the distinct theology of healing hammered out in America in the nascent Pentecostalism. Themes dealt with include the quest for power; the weight given to the longer ending of Mark 16:9–20, with its ramifications for the practice of snake-handing. Following these, the implications for divine healing arising from the Finished Work controversy are discussed. Contention over this issue is the basis for Kimberley Alexander's thesis, which postulates the idea that the practice of divine healing was expressed in two different ways. Her position is that those Pentecostals with a Wesleyan Holiness background differed in their theological understanding and practice of divine healing from those who took a Reformed /Higher Life view. The validity of this proposition is examined.

In chapters 3 and 4 the scene moves to Britain. It centers on the Anglican vicar, A. A. Boddy, the founding father of British Pentecostalism. He hosted the annual Whitsuntide Convention at Sunderland between 1908 and 1914, as well acting as the editor and publisher of the monthly periodical *Confidence* (1908–26). In the pre-war years he maintained

---

1. Gee, *Wind and Flame*, 3; Dayton, *The Theological Roots of Pentecostalism*, 176.

close links with Pentecostal leaders in Europe. His own healing ministry is examined first, before a survey of two other healing movements sponsored within Anglicanism. Three recognized models of divine healing—therapeutic, sacramental, and thaumaturgic—are then considered. How the application of the sacramental model was worked out in the life of Dorothy Kerin, noted for her much publicized healing in 1912, is examined. Chapter 4 deals with the contrasting ministries of two British healing evangelists, the Welsh George Jeffreys, and the Yorkshire-born Smith Wigglesworth. The former was the founder of the Elim Church in Britain, while the legacy of Wigglesworth continues to ripple throughout the worldwide church.

Chapter 5 switches back to America, and looks at developments in the ministry of healing into the 1930s. It was a period when heated debates were aroused by Fundamentalism in its conflictual exchange with Modernism and Pentecostalism. The charismatic healing ministry of F. F Bosworth, with its links to Paul Rader and William Branham, is examined. Though Fundamentalism was at loggerheads with much of Pentecostalism, some of its leading lights, notably W. B. Riley and J. Stratton Roach, engaged in the healing ministry. Their contribution is discussed. The chapter ends with the marked contribution of Aimee Semple McPherson capture in the two biographical titles devoted to her. One highlights her role in the "Making of Modern Pentecostalism," and, grander still, the other accentuates her contribution to the "Resurrection of Christian America." An explanation for her growing ambivalence towards the healing ministry is the main quest of this section.

The Conclusion seeks to challenge the view of the renowned Princeton theologian, B. B. Warfield, who in his *Counterfeit Miracles* (1918) wrote that any claims to post-apostolic miracles would be "without significance; mere occurrences with no universal meaning." The chapter summarizes trends in the present rapid growth of Christianity in the developing world, and Pentecostalism's part in contributing to its escalation. The important part played by healing in contributing to this growth is instanced. Three case studies, from Brazil, Ghana, and China, exemplify the role that healing plays in the rapid expansion of global Christianity, taking place almost entirely outside the advanced economies.

1

Healing in the Early American Pentecostal Movement

Two doctrines distinguished the early Pentecostals from the majority of other Christians, viz., speaking in tongues taken as the initial evidence of Spirit-baptism, and the prominent place given to divine healing. This contrast is less sharp today, an adjustment made explicable in part by the arrival of the Charismatic movement in the late 1950s. In the Pew survey *Spirit and POWER: A 10-Country Survey of Pentecostals* (2006) divine healing stood higher in a number of ways than tongues.[1] The data collected from the USA and the nine other countries selected from South America, Africa, and Asia revealed that in the USA 49 percent of Pentecostals claimed never to have spoken in tongues, while 62 percent claimed to have witnessed or experienced divine healing, as against 28 percent of other Christians. The same pattern was found in all ten countries. Other polls indicate that 70–80 percent of all Americans believe in divine healing. As shown throughout this study, divine healing has been practiced considerably longer than speaking in tongues in its distinctive Pentecostal understanding. The reason for this is obvious. Human suffering is endemic within the fallen creation, the source of an existential angst that searches unremittingly for a universal panacea. That search is of greater magnitude and intensity than tongue-speaking could summon. Both practices owed much to Holiness theology, with its stress on purity and power, in both its Wesleyan and Reformed Higher Life guises. The foundational leaders of the new Pentecostal movement in America almost invariably had a background in the Holiness movement, though considerable numbers of the latter were opposed to the upstart it had nourished in its womb. How the message and practice of divine healing was continued and shaped in its new Pentecostal setting is the challenge of this chapter.

TOWARDS AZUSA STREET REVIVAL: PARHAM, SEYMOUR, AND HEALING

Kansas at the end of the nineteenth century provided the background that was typical of the historical and socio-religious milieu in which the Holiness movement thrived. Such an environment, representative of much of the American Midwest, had as distinctive a part to play in the birth of Pentecostalism as that frequently given to California.[2] The

---

1. Anon. *Spirit and POWER*. Online

2. In Pentecostal historiography, Robert Anderson in his *Vision of the Disinherited* (1991) was the first to offer a comprehensive account of American Pentecostalism's origins in the socio-cultural setting of early twentieth-century America. He contended that the movement burst into recognition within "a group of

Middle West states had become from the middle of the century the bread basket of the transatlantic world. In good years farm incomes soared, while in the depression years of the 1890s the situation became grim. In response to their despair farmers formed local Farmers' Alliances that were more than sales cooperatives. Masonic-like, their lodges were hugely popular, especially their mass picnics that "drew hundreds of families into something like revivalist meetings."[3] Despairing of the two great national political parties, they went political in creating the People's Party, a radical alliance commonly known as the Populists. One of its leading figures advised a meeting, "What you farmers need to do is raise less corn and more Hell."[4] Root, in his thesis, has shown that Parham's sympathies were with the radicals, for example, in writing a glowing obituary for the prominent editor of *Appeal to Reason*, a socialist newspaper printed in Girand, Kansas.[5] It became clear that his sympathies lay with the anti-capitalist views and class antagonism of the Populists and Socialists.

Kansas was not only a farming state but for a short period became a leading centre for the mining of metals. The mining town of Galena, Kansas, was typical of the many settlements founded at the time. It was established in 1877 with the discovery of lead and zinc ores. For a few years it became one of the largest producers of these minerals in the world. Between 1890 and 1900 the population jumped from 2,496 to 10,514, a more than fourfold increase within a decade. In the early years the business was largely in the hands of small operators who had little or no capital. The mineral deposits were scattered and shallow in depth, thus providing conditions that "make a favourable locality for poor men to operate in [and] made rich by the stroke of a pick."[6] This period of the small, localized lease-system could not last in face of the incursion of national and foreign capital invested in purchasing large tracts of land and establishing a pyramiding of land leases and royalties that penalized the miner in the bottom layer of royalty payments. This was not the least of their problems. They had to face the hazards of collapsing roofs in the shallow tunnels, explosive hazards and, most seriously, disease in the form of lead poisoning silicosis that made them also susceptible to tuberculosis. Contagious diseases such as tuberculosis were transmitted rapidly throughout the poorly-housed camps scattered throughout the area. A recent convert, Howard A. Goss, recounted that in the center of his hometown Galena nearly every other building housed a saloon or brothel. Frequently on his way to work, he observed at least one dead man lying between the tent shacks where he had been thrown during the night.

The Ozark area attracted sizeable numbers of Scotch-Irish in the mid-nineteenth century. The American geographer Carl Sauer described them as "a restless frontier type

---

religiously inclined social and economic losers in an industrialising America [that] eschewed realistic solutions to their plight and instead sought comfort in Pentecostalism's rather unhealthy mixture of socially pessimistic millenarian thought and psychologically and socially debilitating tongues or ecstatic speech." Cerillo,"Beginnings of American Pentecostalism," 234–35.

3. Reynolds, *America*, 261.

4. Ibid., 262.

5. Root, "People's Religion," 131.

6. Ibid., 103 & 104.

[who] . . . in the main formed the advance guard of civilization on the outer margin of he frontier."[7] In 1903, Mary Arthur, an American citizen of Scotch-Irish descent, was a forty-one-year-old resident of Galena. Her husband was a prominent local businessman. She was an active member of Galena's Methodist Episcopal Church. Dark shadows were cast over her family by Mary's numerous and diffuse ailments. Her greatest distress lay with her eyes. Her right eye had been virtually blind from birth and the other eye was subject to spasms of sudden blindness. It was in August 1903 in Eldorado Springs, Missouri that she first encountered Charles Parham, then an itinerant Kansas preacher who described his message as "the apostolic faith" that claimed to rest on the contemporary restoration of New Testament Christianity. After prayer for her healing her health improved dramatically, whereupon she returned immediately to Galena, totally committed to Parham's message and ministry. Emboldened by her healing, she invited him to hold services in her home. The home, though large and commodious, soon proved to be too small for the numbers who attended. Eventually, a group of businessmen, not all of whom were Christian, approached her husband and told him "to get that man here, we need this very thing and we must have it. If you can't get him, we will go there."[8]

Why such insistence from the business class? Root identified a number of factors that helped to make the time ripe for his arrival in the town in October 1903. The town was going through a difficult time with the decline in production of lead and zinc, both faced by competition from more productive mines elsewhere in the region. By 1904 the population of the town had virtually halved. As the price of the ores dropped the mine operators agreed to shut down production to force the price up. As the closure strengthened, many miners became destitute. The one positive note struck was the message delivered by Parham of personal salvation, divine healing, and Spirit-baptism. Parham was in an advantageous position to strike the right note with his listeners in their alienation. The county in which the town was sited in almost all the elections in the 1890s voted for Populist candidates. As late as 1912, 25 percent of the county voted for the Socialist Party. Parham's anti-establishment and anti-elitist inclination served him well in catching the ear of his audiences. He was convinced that he could offer something of more substance than *ad hoc* political reform measures. A revival mood pervaded the area, particularly at Joplin just over the border in Missouri. A minister in the town associated the conversion of over 670 people with the end of the mining boom that allowed the residents to "give a little thought to religion."[9]

With the Arthur residence proving too small, Parham began meetings in a tent close to his hosts' home, but with the onset of winter and growing crowds the meetings moved to a large warehouse, improvised to become a "rude temple" that could hold around 2,000 people, and twice that number when two meetings were convened each day. The meetings were run on Pentecostal lines. A local paper reported that "the wicked are being forgiven and blessed, the blind are made to see, and cripples throw away their crutches as they nev-

7. Blethen, *Ulster and North America*, 155.

8. Root, "People's Religion," 102.

9. Ibid., 110–12.

er walked before." As well, some converts had spoken in tongues and many of the town's "best people" had vouched for Parham, proclaiming that the Spirit could enable converts to speak in languages they had never heard or learned.[10] At one meeting, a woman spoke for ten minutes in a language unfamiliar to all except for a member of the regional Pawnee tribe who understood "every word of the testimony."[11] Parham's stay in Galena stretched into the New Year. The watch-night service was among the most memorable. The *Galena Evening Times* estimated that 2,500 were present at its height while 400 people remained into the morning. One participant remembered that "business and professional men and families, as well as folk from all walks of life, remained at the altars until after sunup the next morning." At the same service there was a foot washing, still favored as a sacrament by some Holiness/Pentecostal churches, followed by the ordination of twelve persons to the ministry.[12] The meetings closed at the end of January after a three-month revival. It was estimated that over 875 people had been converted, over 1,000 healed, and several hundred had spoken in tongues.

Anyone not familiar with the history of Pentecostalism other than associating it with Azusa Street, Los Angeles in 1906, some three years *after* the events recorded here, will be surprised by its comprehensive expression at Galena. How Parham came to be involved in the healing ministry and the part he played in the doctrinal formulation of Pentecostalism is the burden of the following pages. The significance of the Galena episode for him in the history of the new movement will then be touched upon. The story can be divided into five parts. The first is his boyhood years from 1873 to 1891, the second his college years 1891–93, the third his ministry in the Methodist Episcopal Church 1893–95, the fourth his work as an independent Holiness evangelist 1896–98, and fifth the masterminding of the Bethel Healing Home 1898–1900. This brings the story up to 1901 and the seminal events at Topeka that laid the foundation for the classical Pentecostal movement.

Born in Iowa, Charles Fox Parham (1873–1929) was the fourth of five boys of a farming family that moved as pioneers to establish a homestead in Kansas in 1878. He grew up as a weak and sickly child, not strong enough to do the heavy work of the farm. From the age of six months he was taken with a fever that left him a childhood invalid. His ailments he described as "dreadful spasms and enlargement of the head," and "inflammatory rheumatism virtually tied [me] up in a knot."

Related problems hindered his growth between the age of nine and twelve. Despite the episodes of healing he claimed later for himself, he remained a frail figure throughout his life. A press report of the Galena revival described him as "a slight, spare man extremely delicate looking" with a pale and earnest face topped with a mass of brown hair covering his "remarkably shaped head." One of his supporters commented that during the mission there were evenings when he "looked so tired and worn he would scarcely look able for the night services."[13]

---

10. Ibid., 112.

11. Parham, *Life of Charles F. Parham*, 98.

12. Root, "People's Religion," 120–21.

13. Ibid., 97 & 94. Parham's medical history was laced with problems. His enlarged head in infancy was most likely a symptom of encephalitis, a viral infection that causes a blockage of the spinal fluid flowing

Prior to 1900 there were three occasions when he experienced physical healing that require to be set in context, with the proviso that "context" requires caution: some of his accounts, like most of his memories, tend to "exaggerate events as well as his own significance in them."[14] Parham dated his conversion to the age of twelve in response to the preaching of an itinerant Congregational preacher who conducted meetings in a local schoolhouse. This took place shortly after the death of his mother, which, most likely, opened him to religious influence. The funeral service was conducted by C. S. Bolton, the missionary of the CGGE (Church of God of the General Eldership) or Winebrenner church for the area. Later Bolton officiated at the marriage of Parham's widower father to Harriet Miller, a devout Methodist. The noted charismatic healing evangelist, Maria Woodworth-Etter, began her evangelistic work with the support of the Winebrenner church. Bolton later assisted Maria in Topeka before becoming pastor of the church there. Blumhofer suggests that Bolton's links with Maria and the Parhams may well have furthered in Parham "an inclination toward holiness themes and charismatic experience. . . . Such elements would later characterize his meetings."[15] Filled with zeal, the young convert for the first time in his life became a regular church-goer and eventually a Sunday School teacher. He held his first public meetings at the age of fifteen, and three years later he enrolled at Southwestern Kansas College, a Methodist-affiliated school where he spent two years of study punctuated by a sizeable commitment to "religious work" outside the college that resulted in a downgrade in his examination results.

His two years (1891–93) at the college were not particularly happy. As he stated, "it was not a good place to backslide, but I did." Reflection on his short experience of church life undermined his initial intention to enter the Methodist ministry: "With no special abiding place, its many starvation places and hard scrabble circuits, it was not nearly alluring as some other professions." A career in medicine appeared more inviting, a chimera he put down "to the wiles of the devil who tried to make me believe I could be a physician and a Christian too." When he was stricken by a recrudescent, severe attack of rheumatic fever, he attributed it to divine chastisement, tormented as he was by the thought of reneging on a promise he had made to God on his conversion that he would go to Africa as a missionary. While lying in a daze from an overdose of morphine, he overheard a prediction from a visiting doctor that his death was imminent. He sensed it was a prognosis that would be overturned because "some day I would have to surrender my arms of rebellion, and preach the everlasting gospel."

The next morning brought a shift in his thinking. He was struck by "all those wonderful lessons of how Jesus healed," that raised the question "why could He not do the same today?" He recalled that when the physician said he would last only a few days, "I

---

through the brain. The pain and weaknesses that he suffered in boyhood stemmed from rheumatic fever. The disease probably accounted for his stunted growth in boyhood and heart problems. In damaging the heart valves the condition creates an enlarged and weakened heart muscle. It is usually a lifetime affliction, lightened by periods of remission. His "sick headaches" of later days were most likely migraines. During times of stress his health deteriorated. At such times relief though prayer for healing acted as a precursor to new and positive directions in his ministry.

14. Blumhofer, *Assemblies of God*, 69.

15. Ibid., 69.

cried out to the Lord, that if He would let me go somewhere, someplace, where I would not have to take collections or beg for a living that I would preach if He would turn me loose." Then I tried to pray." Recovery was swift but not instantly complete. His ankles all but crippled him due, as he believed, to the stretching of the sinews by the months of rheumatism that left them as "though tin cans were tied to my ankles." For a while he had to learn to walk upon the sides of his feet rather than his ankles with his feet angled outwards. The complete healing took place after he renewed his commitment to ministry and to quit college. It took place one night while praying beneath a tree within the college campus: "[I]nstantly . . . the virtue of healing like a mighty electric current [passed] through my body, and my ankles were made whole like the man at the Beautiful Gate of the temple [Acts 3: 7–8]."[16]

For the next two years (1893–95) he started preaching despite having neither extensive formal training nor recognized license of ordination. He was assigned as a supply pastor to a Methodist Episcopal Church near Kansas City and preached on Sunday afternoons to another nearby congregation. Spiritually, they were lean years with only one conversion recorded. One of the themes preached was sanctification as a second definite work of grace. During 1893 he was befriended by the Thistlethwaites, a Quaker family, one of whose daughters, Sarah, he married in 1896. His wife's maternal grandfather, David Baker, persuaded Parham to accept the doctrine of conditional immortality which he held until 1902, after which he promulgated a view more akin to universalism.[17] It is probable that it was under the influence of Baker's holiness Quakerism that he came to reject water baptism for a time, and accept sanctification as a distinct second blessing. None of this went down well with his Methodist superiors, especially as he advised seekers not to be overly bothered about which church to support. His strong feelings against "the narrowness of sectarian churchism" reflected his temperamental aversion to received authority.[18] A rigorous take on holiness impelled him to reject any salary that was financed "by suppers and worldly entertainment."[19] Once the rupture with Methodism took place in 1896, he embarked on an itinerant evangelistic ministry in Kansas with a determination to work on faith lines as his means of financial support.

Kansas was a propitious state for a young newly married couple to evangelize on Holiness lines. The state threw up its fair share of religious prophets. John Brown's anti-slavery crusade in the 1850s was a major factor in the bloodshed over the issue that earned Kansas the tag "Bleeding Kansas". Carrie Nation's temperance campaigning at the turn of the century activated a spate of saloon wrecking. Alone or accompanied by hymn-singing women, she would march into a bar, and sing and pray while smashing bar fixtures and stock with a hatchet. Between 1900 and 1910 she was arrested some thirty times for "hatchetations", adding to the reputation of the state for producing an inordinate number of zealots. It also earned the epithet of "Holy" Kansas that underlined its strong puritanical streak. Folk-dancing was banned for kindergarten children and both tobacco

16. The quotations in the last three paragraphs are taken from Parham, *Life of Charles F. Parham*, 6–9.

17. Blumhofer, *Assemblies of God*, 73.

18. Parham, *Life of Charles F. Parham*, 23.

19. Ibid., 25.

and liquor sales were prohibited under laws that were among the earliest and most comprehensive in the country.

The term "Kansan ethos" has been ascribed in the late nineteenth century to its citizens, who revealed a "tendency to legislate morality as a substitution for tradition and custom."[20] The state was also a center for the radical Populist movement that was not slow to excoriate the mainstream churches for being insensitive to the plight of the downtrodden. Parham took a similar line. For him "the cry of socialism that is sweeping the world is the heart-cry of Jesus." He called on the churches "to descend from the fashion show" of social climbing because their failure to show "practical Christianity" had forced thousands of people to agitate for political reform. Where he differed from the reformers was to see their quest for universal brotherhood as of no "lasting benefit unless founded on . . . spiritual regeneration. If we could wield the prestige of the lodges and unions to the old-time religion of our fathers, we could do what they hope to do." [21] Goff makes the point that the idea of human efforts for justice being futile and God alone the defender of the weak and oppressed made religion, psychologically, "a tremendous source of POWER for the POWERLESS. It was from this insecure world that Charles Parham drew his formative thoughts and it was among others like him that his ministry, and the message of the Pentecostal movement, found an enthusiastic following."[22]

Charles F. Parham

The years 1896–98 marked another advance in Parham's conviction about divine healing. In these years the newly-weds started married life by spending part of their honeymoon in evangelistic efforts in Kansas. In the succeeding months numerous meetings were held in schoolhouses in scattered rural settings. Arduous winters with their fierce blizzards added to the privations they willingly faced. Their joy was compounded with the arrival of a baby son in September 1897, only to be short-lived, overcast as it was by "a cloud hung

---

20. Ibid., 22.

21. Parham, *Selected Sermons*, 2–3. Parham seems not to have appreciated the ministry of Charles M. Sheldon who accepted the call to the Central Congregational Church in Topeka in 1899. A leading figure in the Social Gospel movement, he sought to establish the Kingdom of God on earth here and now through social and political engagement. His most famous book *In His Steps* (1897) introduced the phrase "What would Jesus *do?*" in situations of need. Parham criticized Sheldon for not including an example of faith healing in the book because this would have been Jesus' response to disease (Goff, *Fields White Unto Harvest*, 1990, n. 43.).

22. Goff, *Fields White Unto Harvest*, 22.

low which seemed determined to steal away our joy."[23] Both the health of Parham and the new-born baby hung in the balance. The doctor diagnosed Parham's heart complaint was "in the worst form" and advised that he must give up preaching entirely. The baby "was gradually slipping away from us," an eventuality for which the doctor could provide no explanation. It was while he was praying for a sick neighbor that Parham was seized by the text "Physician, heal thyself." His prayer for himself found a biblical denouement in that "he was made every whit whole." It was a pivotal moment. When he returned home, he had reached the conclusion that "we would throw away all medicines, give up doctors and wholly trust Him as our Healer, and our baby too would be well." His health was soon restored, and shortly afterwards the infant began to thrive. "From that time," he averred, "we have not trusted in the arm of flesh in sickness, but in the POWER of God."

About the same time, Parham received word that his close friend, Ralph Gowel, had died. The young man had just been appointed a professor in the State University. In her grief, his mother died heart-broken a fortnight later. For Parham, the distress of the situation was heightened by the thought that they "might have lived if I had but told them of the POWER of Christ to heal." At that moment he made a vow "that 'Live or Die' I would preach this gospel of healing. . . . How much suffering it takes sometimes to bring the human heart to a depth of consecration, that our wills may be wholly yielded to, and His will can be wrought out in our lives!" Quickened by this pledge, the family moved to Ottawa, Kansas, from where he launched out on his first ministry in public on divine healing, one that till then had been practiced only sporadically and discreetly. He was now firmly committed to the doctrine that healing was in the atonement, and though he never claimed to have the gift of healing, his wife believed that he had received it, "so great was the manifestation of the POWER of God to heal, through him."[24]

One of the more striking healings was that of Mrs Ella Cook who suffered from dropsy [oedema]. It took place in the Salvation Army Hall, Ottawa, Kansas. The sufferer had been given up by physicians with only a slight possibility of living three days. Evoking a moment of high drama, Sarah Parham wrote:

> She was carried upstairs into our meetings. When prayer was offered the disease was instantly killed so that she fell to the floor as one dead, or like one from whom the fever had just left. The audience arose as a mob to punish us for her seeming death. Mr. Parham stepped beside her body and ordered the people to stand in their places as she was not dead, as a few minutes would prove. In a few moments she opened her eyes, smiled and we assisted her to her feet. She not only walked down the stairs alone, but walked for over a mile to her home, shouting and praising the Lord. People along the way followed to see what would take place. Neighbors came running in, and until three o'clock in the morning people were getting to God and others were wonderfully healed. Her recovery was complete.[25]

In another case a young woman, a consumptive, who had been given only two weeks to live by six doctors was prayed for. During the prayer, a tearing sensation passed through

23. Parham, *Life of Charles F. Parham*, 31.
24. Ibid., 33.
25. Ibid., 34.

her chest and she was completely healed. Her eyesight, which had been so poor that, without glasses, she could not recognize anyone across a small room, was also restored. So complete was her healing that she took up sewing for a living, and gave up her invalid's pension. Marriage and motherhood with several children followed.

Revitalized and keener than ever to advance the work, Parham relocated his growing family to Topeka, a booming city of some 30,000 people. It was here in its downtown area that he established Bethel Healing Home in 1898.[26] The building was a commodious structure with three floors. The ground floor furnished a large chapel that could seat 200, a public reading room, and a printing office. The second floor had fourteen bedrooms, while the third floor was an attic, used for sleeping when demand spilled over. Its core purpose was to provide homely comforts for those seeking healing, with prayer offered for both bodily and spiritual needs. By June 1899, over thirty visitors, which included one Roman Catholic, came in the quest for healing. In an average week there were two or three guests staying for about a fortnight. A wider social dimension also featured. Christian homes for orphan children were found, as well as work for the unemployed. Short courses offering instruction in "Bible truths," focusing on salvation, healing, sanctification, the Second Coming, and Spirit-baptism (Holiness style) were made available to "ministers and evangelists."

The new bi-monthly paper, *The Apostolic Faith*, was published for free and was rarely short of testimonies to healing in which Parham featured prominently. One of the most unusual accounts was that of a left arm lengthened by a full one and a half inches. As his reputation grew, inquisitive local citizens felt free to wander through the building in the hope of seeing a miraculous cure, possibly an exorcism. One exhibit on display was a bottle containing a cancerous tumor that attracted the attention of "doctors, lawyers, preachers, and infidels." The success of the enterprise stimulated others to set up healing homes in the surrounding area at Emporia, Ottawa, and Eskridge, both loosely affiliated to Bethel. Beside services organized on an interdenominational line with an occasional local guest speaker, Parham remained true to his egalitarian instincts in seeking out and assisting the underprivileged. Through serving as a trustee for the city's Industrial League, he became involved in a scheme to secure vacant plots of land for the deserving poor to grow vegetables. For a period of a few months, he organized a rescue mission facility for young lowly-paid working girls and prostitutes. This effort was among a number of well-intentioned projects that failed to achieve permanence. There was the "Helping Hand" effort to bring regular food and shelter to the poor that drew insufficient support to survive. A similar fate met his attempt to garner financial backing for a famine relief program in India organized state-wide throughout Kansas. Arguably, most shattering of all for the twenty-six-year-old Parham was the desertion of erstwhile supporters, financial and otherwise. In August 1899, frustrated he vented his anger against those "several worldly people who have withdrawn from the Mission because they could not stand the preaching against worldliness and the awful tendencies of the age."[27]

---

26. Healing homes are discussed in the excursus at the end of the chapter.

27. Goff, *Fields White Unto Harvest*, 50.

On top of such disappointments there was added responsibility with an increase in his family size to five, two of whom were born after their arrival in Topeka in 1898. Personal and mission finances were insufficient to sustain his diverse ministries. Any ideas Parham had for winning over all social classes to his revolutionary doctrine of divine health began to disintegrate. As had transpired in the past when greatly stressed, the exhausted young, ambitious evangelist and social reformer succumbed in late September 1899 to a nervous breakdown. It was at such times that he undertook a re-evaluation of his ministry. With the arrival in Topeka in February 1900 of one of the Shiloh-based teams recruited by Frank Sandford, he was able to delegate most of his responsibilities to two members of the team and create space for himself for reflection and prayer. Excited by what he saw of the ministry of the two men, he regained his energy and renewed a number of activities, none of which gathered any great momentum.

Following a visit to Topeka by Sandford in person, Parham decided to travel to enrol at Sandford's Holy Ghost and Us Bible College at Shiloh, Maine. He left his family with friends and committed Bethel to the charge of two Holiness ministers. On his way to Shiloh, he seized the opportunity to visit Zion and survey Dowie's signal ministry. Among other places to visit, he selected A. B. Simpson's Bible and Missionary Training Institute in Nyack, New York before reaching Shiloh in mid-July 1900. He spent six weeks at Shiloh and then accompanied Sandford to Winnipeg for revival services before returning home in late September. During the next few months events surrounding Parham were to prove to be among the most far-reaching in the church history of the twentieth century with the birth of the Pentecostal movement. One of the outcomes of the arrival of the new movement was the certainty that the ministry of divine healing would not only be perpetuated but also intensified. How this came about can only be summarized here as the topic is much wider than the healing ministry which is the main thrust of this work.[28]

On his return to Topeka, Parham discovered that Bethel was firmly in the control of the Holiness workers left in charge until his return. Rather than react with indignation, he was after his recent experiences, especially with Sanford, disposed to see the situation as a divine leading to change direction. He announced that he would open a new Bible School in the conviction that God would use it to initiate an end-time revival. The school was located in a large mansion on the south-western edge of Topeka. The building was built by E. R. Stone, a real estate agent, and then taken over by the American Bible Society when Stone lost his fortune as a real estate agent. It was spacious enough to accommodate some forty people, students and dependents, when classes began in mid-October. The school took as its model Sandford's Bible School in Maine, of which one of its students could say: "'Curriculum,' there is none: it is the Bible. 'Faculty,' there is none: it is the Holy Ghost."[29] When it came to the examination period at the end of term, the students were tested on the topics of repentance, justification, consecration, sanctification, and healing.[30] The one subject missing, the elephant in the room, was the omission of Spirit-baptism.

---

28. A readable account of early Pentecostalism is found in Robeck, *Azusa Street*.

29. Blumhofer, *Assemblies of God*, 78.

30. Parham, *Voice Crying*.

The latter was in the arena of serious debate since nearly all the students were experienced religious workers who, with their Holiness, second-blessing background, could claim to have already received the Baptism of the Holy Spirit. Despite their certitude, Parham had come to the conclusion that there was something lacking, defined by him as an experience "such as the disciples received of old, to make His saints today world-wide POWERS for good, to the end that this gospel might be preached to all the world as a witness."[31] He acknowledged that in his own life he had known the POWER of the Holy Spirit "to a wonderful degree for many years, and had such wonderful anointings that we were carried far beyond ourselves, many times for ten, fifteen and twenty minutes words of living truth flowed from our lips." The words may have by-passed his mind in their formation though he could receive them as "an interested listener." To him, such moments were not to be confused with Spirit-baptism "as many declared it to be."[32]

At this point, Parham was struggling to bring theological coherence to a set of convictions that he had embraced over recent months and years. At Bethel they were trying, as he put it, "to sink deeper into the things of God, and to obtain a more comprehensive view of the heights and depths, lengths and breadths of God's eternal purpose." His visits to Sandford's Shiloh and Dowie's Zion had stirred him greatly, but to his mind neither work had the final word. He wrote: "We visited institutions of deep religious thought, which were reported as having the POWER of the Holy Ghost; yet these all failed to tally with the account in Acts." None of their leaders were "really enjoying the POWER of a personal Pentecost." This led him to the conclusion that his own experience of "wonderful anointings" was comparable, if not better, than that of others. Even so, this was not enough to diminish his conviction that God had more in store, indeed a special baptism of the Holy Ghost.[33] This line of thinking had been promoted by Benjamin Hardin Irwin (b. 1854), an itinerant Holiness evangelist who operated in Kansas and neighboring states in the period 1892–95. In 1895, Irwin's ministry was radically changed when he experienced a "baptism of fire" as a third blessing separate from sanctification. On the strength of this radical doctrine, Irwin began organizing Fire-Baptized Holiness Associations (FBHA), starting with Iowa in 1895. Not content with the "fire" blessing, he added baptisms of "dynamite," "lyddite," and "oxidite," dubbed by critics "chemical jargon," and derided as the "pathetic pursuit of this religious rainbow's end."[34]

This view that all Christians should seek a special Spirit-baptism was but one in the ferment of ideas that seized Parham. Others were his immersion in premillennialism that harmonized with the concept that Christ's second coming would be preceded by a global revival. The analogy of the "Latter Rain" was frequently employed to suggest the ripening of a vast harvest of souls which would immediately precede the *parousia*. He foresaw three measures that would feature in such an end-time revival. One depended on a new para-

31. Ibid., 33.

32. Ibid., 31.

33. Jacobsen, *Thinking in the Spirit*, 24.

34. Synan, *The Holiness-Pentecostal Tradition*, 57. Irwin took on board the premise of John Fletcher, Wesley's chosen successor, that many "effusions" or "baptisms" might be necessary in the progress to perfection of the believer.

digm of Christian unity that captured his imagination during his times with Sandford. It was a unity that came about not through ecclesial statecraft, but one led by the Holy Spirit "into all truth, was free from the human restraints of denominationalism and energized for world conquest."[35] His visit to Zion and the impression formed by Dowie's ministry and string of divine healings confirmed his view on the role of miracles in evangelization. Believing in the imminence of Christ's return, Parham was acutely aware of the problem the multiplicity of languages posed for the global spread of the gospel message. He came to the conclusion that at least some people would be specially gifted by God with the miraculous ability to speak foreign languages without specific training—hence the epithets "missionary tongues" or *xenolalia*. The concept of missionary tongues for those like Parham was no mere Will-o'-the-wisp, an elusive guiding principle. There were recent precedents of persons suddenly receiving the capacity to preach in other languages. In 1881, a missionary to India, Miss C. M. Reade, testified to the Spirit's giving her the "gift of speaking Hindustani" to enable her to preach without a translator. Similar reports came from Jonathan Goforth, the famed Canadian Presbyterian missionary to China, as well as W. P. Buncombe, an Anglican serving in Japan. Though it was possible that Parham was not aware of these particular reports there were others that heartened him.

One whose story was familiar to him was that of the young Jennie Glassey, who became a missionary to Sierra Leone. During her preparation to leave America in 1898, an article appeared in Sandford's *Tongues of Fire* that detailed her reputed xenolalic gifting: "Sister Glassey has at different times spoken while in the Spirit, in Greek, French, Latin, German, Hebrew, Italian, Japanese, Chinese, and several African dialects, words and sentences given her by the Holy Ghost. She has also written many letters of the Greek and Hebrew alphabet. Words in as many as six of these languages have been recognized as such by one who has studied classics, thus proving the genuineness of God's gifts to our sister."[36] In the May 1899 edition of the *Apostolic Faith*, Parham reprinted a brief account of her receiving "the African dialect in one night while in the Spirit in 1895, but could read and write, translate and sing the language while out of the trance or in a normal condition, and can until now. Hundreds of people can testify to the fact, both saint and sinner, who heard her use the language. She was also tested in Liverpool and Jerusalem."[37] It was incidents like these that moved him to reproduce the article in *Tongues of Fire* the sentence, "He who said, 'They shall speak with new tongues' is proving his words true, thus enabling one like Sister Glassey to preach the 'everlasting gospel' to any soul on this globe, with the necessary language at her disposal."[38]

Such were the unresolved issues brought together at the Bethel Bible School, issues in which Parham was desirous to see some kind of breakthrough that would knit together the threads of his thoughts. The one missing piece of the jigsaw was the means by which the end-time global revival could speed across the earth, expedited by miracles of healing. The current Holiness experience of Spirit-baptism had proved, to his mind incom-

---

35. McGee, *Miracles, Missions,* 74.

36. Gleason, Willard. "Notes from My Journal *Fire.*" Online.

37. Goff, *Fields White Unto Harvest,* 73.

38. Gleason, "Notes from My Journal," 107.

plete, lacking in the galvanizing power of the Spirit. A heaven-sent endowment similar to that received on the day of Pentecost would provide the missing piece. On that historic day the polyglot hearers were constrained to ask "How hear we every man in our own tongue, wherein we were born" (Acts 2:8 KJV). It now seems clear Parham had reached the conclusion that speaking in tongues was the initial evidence of Spirit-baptism before he opened the Bethel Bible School. Years later, he admitted:

> I had felt for years that any missionary going to the foreign field should preach in the language of the natives. That if God ever equipped His ministers in that way, He could do it today. That if Balaam's mule could stop in the middle of the road and give the first preacher that went out for money a 'bawling out' in Arabic [then] anybody today ought to be able to preach in any language of the world if they have horse sense enough to let God use their tongue and throat. . . . I believed our experience should tally exactly with the Bible, and neither sanctification nor the anointing that abideth taught by Stephen Merritt and others tallied with the 2nd chapter of Acts.[39]

By this stage he was persuaded that he was God's instrument to actuate the second Pentecost of the Spirit. It was with this aim in mind that he established Bethel Gospel School. Indeed, in April 1900, he reported that a "Brother and Sister Hamaker" were tarrying in the Bethel Healing Home for Christ "to give them an heathen tongue, and then they will proceed to the missionary field."[40]

The role of the Bible School changed from that of a healing home to its becoming the center from which a redefined mode of Spirit-baptism would emanate, one that would fuel the end-time mission to the ends of the earth. In short, all so blessed would become "instant missionaries."[41] As one of the students, Agnes Ozman, recalled they had been encouraged to seek for a new outpouring of the Spirit and that "it was our privilege to have it fulfilled to us here and now."[42] Though the students had been encouraged to think on these lines, they showed signs of obtuseness. In her biography *What God Hath Wrought* (1921) Ozman admitted: "I did not know that I would speak in tongues when I received the Holy Ghost for I did not know it was Bible. But after I received the Holy Spirit speaking in tongues, it was revealed to me that I had the promise of the Father."[43] It was to help his students to sort out their thinking on Spirit-baptism that over the New Year period Parham left them for three days to attend to a teaching engagement in the Topeka Free Methodist Church. He asked them to search diligently for "the Bible evidence of the baptism of the Holy Ghost that we might go before the world with something that was indisputable because it tallied absolutely with the Word."[44]

---

39. Parham, *Life of Charles F. Parham*, 51–52. Stephen Merritt (1775–1845) was among the earliest advocates of entire sanctification, a state of perfection considered by its advocates to be instantly available, a view Parham shared with Phoebe Palmer. The "anointing that abideth" (1 John 2:27 KJV) refers more to the process whereby the Spirit's indwelling in the believer's life promotes holiness in act and thought.

40. Goff, "Initial Tongues." In McGee, *Initial Evidence*, 64.

41 Ibid., 65.

42. Faupel. *Everlasting Gospel*, 175.

43. Ibid., 175.

44. Parham, *Life of Charles F. Parham*, 52.

The breakthrough finally arrived within the period December 31, 1900 to January 3, 1901, the imprecision reflecting the disparate accounts of the whole episode. The precise details of what happened on the eventful evening are somewhat confused. Parham was not there at the time, and his account does not fully harmonize with Ozman's report, but the point on which all agreed was that Ozman had received the baptism of the Holy Spirit and had at the same time been granted the miraculous power to speak in a number of foreign languages, to which was added their sealing as members of Christ's bride.[45] Soon Parham and the other students at the school shared the same experience. Together they became convinced that these events heralded the start of the predicted end-time revival; it was beginning with them. Parham explained: "In the close of the age, God proposes to send forth men and women preaching in languages they know not a word of, which when interpreted the hearers will know is truly a message from God. . . . This is truly the acme of inspiration, prayed for every Sabbath and desired by all true ministers of God."[46] The long-term implications of this novel teaching for healing will be reflected on later subsequent to the events at Azusa Street in 1906.

The linking in 1900 of Spirit-baptism with speaking in tongues as its initial evidence found only a limited favorable response outside Parham's narrow circle. Trouble started almost immediately. A young Bethel student of only a few weeks' residence, S. J. Riggins, denounced the institution as a "fake" and the tongues speakers as "crazy." He informed the local press that he had tried to persuade the others to leave the place as "they were under the influence of evil."[47] Other trials followed thick and fast so that the next few years were among the most difficult in their married life. Success in bringing the message to different locations was only fitful. In March 1901, personal tragedy struck with the death of their year-old son. On return to Topeka with the expectation of picking up the reins of the Bible School, they found the building had been sold as a roadhouse, only to be burned to the ground a few months later. A small core of students followed him to Kansas City. Among the students who drifted away was Agnes Ozman who returned to city missionary work. In 1906, she heard about the Azusa Street revival, and identified with the new movement.

The Parhams were left with a sense of abandonment, bereft of live-in companionship but for Sarah's sister. "Both the pulpit and the press sought to utterly destroy our place and

---

45. In his interpretation of Eph 1:13, those baptized in the Spirit were sealed, which meant they would be spared the end-time tribulation and would return to assist Christ in his rule in the millennial kingdom. Both this idea of the "seal" and xenolalic competence faded., making the evidential nature of tongues as witness to Spirit-baptism the core doctrine to define Pentecostalism.

Goff postulated that the Bethel community mistook *glossolalia* for *xenoglossa* because its members were simply not qualified to make a linguistic assessment: "What seems to have occurred was that certain language-like patterns—and possibly even some words—did resemble known foreign language. Through a phenomenon called *cryptomnesia*, words and sounds previously heard are stored in the subconscious mind without any apparent effort at retention. Then, in a moment of intense stress, the language-like forms emerge though they are seemingly unknown to the speaker" (McGee, *Initial Evidence*, 67). Wacker explains the phenomenon more in terms of "ideology dictating behavior. Everything in the culture conspired to encourage Pentecostals to find ways to birth and then legitimate the practice" (Wacker, *Heaven Below*, 48).

46. Parham, *Voice Crying in the Wilderness*, 31.

47. Martin, *Topeka Outpouring*, 95–96.

prestige," he wrote, "until my wife, her sister and myself seemed to stand alone."[48] Sarah in looking back on this period described how they were "hated, despised, and counted as nought, for weeks and weeks never knowing where our next meal would come from."[49] Their situation was so perilous that an aunt, distressed by press reports and fearing that her niece had lost her mind, appeared on the scene to rescue the children. During their domicile in Lawrence, Kansas, there was minimal response to the new message about evidential tongues, its hearers conveying to the Parhams that "it was not the POWER of God that enabled us to speak in tongues."[50] It was at this time that Parham published *A Voice Crying in the Wilderness*, a title reflective of a lone prophet giving voice in a spiritual wasteland. One lesson he did learn from a mission he conducted in Nevada, MO, was the way to "rebuke fanaticism." Seemingly, he witnessed some "fleshly manifestations, and [the] giving out of messages we had not witnessed before."[51] The charge of fanaticism was one taken seriously by Parham. Of the events in early January 1901, he insisted that "the propriety and decency of the conduct of each member of the Bible School won the warmest comment from many visitors."[52] Riggins, on the other hand, wearing different spectacles, asserted that the students "had been led to this extreme through their fanaticism."[53]

It was at this point that Galena came to the rescue as Parham shifted his emphasis back to healing. The Galena episode in 1903 stands roughly at the mid-point period of Parham's greatest contribution to classical Pentecostalism. That period can be defined as lying between the events at Bethel Bible College, Topeka, Kansas, in January 1901 and the takeover bid for Zion City in 1907. The failed coup to seize Zion, followed by an unproven sodomy charge, was the prelude to his decline into relative obscurity. Galena was preceded by his summer mission to El Dorado Springs, MO, a popular spa center where people gathered from across the country. Parham and his workers stood at the corner of the park where steps led down to the springs. "People came by the hundreds to hear the message," he reported, "and many were healed. . . . Our home was continually filled with the sick and suffering and God manifested His mighty POWER."[54] Among the callers was Mary Arthur, who conveyed her invitation to Parham to bring his message to Galena, the outcome of which was outlined above. Mary Parham exulted in the dramatic change in their fortune at Galena: "We had experienced our years of trials and testings and now the time had come when God was going to visit his people in mercy and the Holy Spirit again to be poured out."[55]

The *Cincinnati Enquirer and Joplin News Herald* summed up the impact of Parham's three-month campaign in Galena in his assessment that nothing in recent years had occurred that "awakened the interest, excited the comment or mystified the people of this

48. Blumhofer, *Assemblies of God*, 86.
49. Anderson, *Vision of the Disinherited*, 58.
50. Parham, *Life of Charles F. Parham*, 86.
51. Parham, *Voice Crying in the Wilderness*, 87.
52. Parham, *Life of Charles F. Parham*, 55.
53. Martin, *Topeka Outpouring*, 97.
54. Parham, *Life of Charles F. Parham*, 55.
55. Ibid., 91.

region" as those stirred by the commonly referred to "Divine Healer."[56] Healing more than speaking in tongues captured the attention of Galena, important as *glossolalia* was in shaping the theology of nascent Pentecostalism. It was the means that turned the tide and led him to be considered by some "with almost superstitious awe."[57] What people found striking was the fact that healing was not confined to "an ignorant, uneducated class of people" but was broadened to include "some of the most conservative, intelligent persons, not only here, but within a radius of over a hundred miles."[58] None of this ministry was conducted to the neglect of the full Pentecostal message. The paper observed that the "followers receive what they term 'the Pentecost' and are enabled to speak in foreign tongues." One woman who spoke for ten minutes in tongues discovered that the language had been recognized by a Pawnee American Indian from the nearby reservation who indicated that she "was speaking in the language of his tribe and he could understand every word of her testimony."[59]

It was within the orbit of Galena that Parham sent out bands of devoted workers recruited in the town to spread the message of the Apostolic Faith. As a result of these campaigns, several Apostolic Faith missions and house meetings were established in the Tri-State District. In 1904 at Keelville, Kansas, the first frame church was built specifically as a Pentecostal assembly. In the spring of 1905 another effective field was opened to Parham in the boom-towns of the Houston-Galveston area, which sprang up overnight following the Spindletop oil strike that proved to be the most productive oil field in the world. The find changed the future of Texas and soon made the United States the world's leading oil producer. In July 1905 some two dozen adherents of the Apostolic Faith Movement set out to "lay siege" on Houston, visiting homes and jails during the day. In the evenings Parham, clad in the robes of a bishop, marched through the streets at the head of his Palestinian-costumed retinue as a means to attract the curious to his meetings.

As in Galena, the dramatic healing of a well-known woman made the headlines. In this case it was Mrs J. M. Dulaney, the wife of a prominent lawyer in Houston. The victim of a street car accident in 1902, the onset of paralysis restricted her to life in a wheel-chair, and left her with no hope of recovery through medical intervention. The highly publicized lawsuit that followed raised her public profile. Brought up in a Catholic home, she had never read the Bible before she heard Parham preach in Market Square on 4 August 1905. She recognized him as the man who had appeared in a vision before she first met him. During the day before the vision she had prayed for God either to take her or send someone to heal her. At a service a few days later, and accompanied by her husband, she was prayed for by two women from Parham's party who, as reported in the press, placed their hands upon her: "In a short time Mrs Dulaney arose from her chair and walked in a state of ecstatic joy, shouting, clapping her hands, and praising the Lord for restoration."[60] The permanence of her healing was confirmed in a letter to the Parhams from a correspon-

---

56. Ibid., 95.
57. Ibid., 98.
58. Ibid.
59. Ibid.
60. Goff, *Fields White Unto Harvest*, 97.

dent in California, written sometime in the second decade. It was written while attending an Apostolic Faith camp meeting and passed on the information that "Sister Dulaney . . . is here and how she loves to minister to the suffering ones on the camp grounds."[61]

By the fall of 1905, the ranks of workers had swelled and with their fanning out in evangelistic bands into surrounding states the Apostolic Faith movement began to take off, with directors appointed for individual states, as the work became viable. His policy this time was to remain separate and not seek the support of other Holiness groups of whatever description as had been his policy hitherto. In December 1905, he began to use the title "Projector of the Apostolic Faith Movement." In the same month, he rented a large, two-storey house in Houston to launch a ten-week Bible School for training the additional number of workers needed to "firmly establish this great growing work in Texas." The school ran on similar lines to Bethel, but with the innovative policy of teaching by the Holy Spirit directly through "prophecy," and through "messages" in tongues and interpretation. Among the students was thirty-six-year-old William Seymour, an African-American Holiness evangelist who seems to have used Houston as a base for his itinerant ministry.[62]

ENTER W. J. SEYMOUR

William Joseph Seymour (1870–1922) was the first of four children born to parents who had been slaves. He was brought up in Centerville, Louisiana. When William was aged fourteen, his father was shot dead in the so-called "Battle of Loreauville" in a factional fight within the Republican Party over black voting rights.[63] For the ten years following the murder William labored on the lumber and sawmill side of a local plantation. In 1895 he moved to Indianapolis, where he worked as a hotel waiter. There he joined the Methodist Episcopal Church for a short period, before associating with smaller progressive interracial fellowships. In 1900 he moved to Cincinnati, possibly because the lines of segregation were beginning to harden in Indianapolis. With racial attitudes increasing in sourness even within the more liberal mainstream denominations, he associated with smaller Holiness groups, such as the Evening Light Saints, and probably God's Bible School and Missionary Training Home operated by Martin Wells Knapp, author of *Lightning Bolts from Pentecostal Skies* (1898).[64] It

William J. Seymour

---

61. Parham, *Life of Charles F. Parham*, 240.

62. Sanders, *William Joseph Seymour*, 58.

63 Ibid., 34–35.

64. On the importance of Knapp, see Robinson, *Divine Healing: 1890–1906*, 204–8.

was during his time in the city that Seymour contracted smallpox. While confined to bed, he had a dream that he would be healed if he was prepared to preach the gospel. Resolved to obey the call, he was healed almost completely, except for a loss of sight in his left eye from corneal ulcerations that forced him to wear a glass eye for the remainder of his life. In 1903 he set out for Houston in search of lost relatives.

While in Houston, Seymour associated himself with a black mission that was founded and led by Lucy Farrow. A widow, she was a niece of Frederick Douglass, a towering figure in the anti-slavery crusade. She made a big impression on Parham, who engaged her as a governess for his sizeable family when they returned to Kansas in August 1905. Farrow convinced Seymour of his suitability to pastor her church while she was away. It was during her stay in Kansas that she entered the Pentecostal experience. When she returned home in October, she encouraged Seymour to attend Parham's planned Bible School. This presented Parham with the problem of negotiating the rigid local segregation laws, which he circumvented by allowing Seymour to listen to the lectures while seated outside the open door to the classroom. Elsewhere, a member of the black Holiness community, Neeley Terry, was on a family visit from Los Angeles to Houston. Her mission work had just lost its leader and, having seen Seymour in action, she persuaded the Houston leadership to release Seymour to serve as their associate pastor in California. Parham's intention for Seymour's future clashed with this proposal. He saw him as a worker among "those of his own color" in Texas once he had received his personal Spirit-baptism. He was unable to convince Seymour, who left for California in January 1906, meeting with Alma White in Denver en route.[65]

Los Angeles at the time was a city predominantly of whites. It counted around 100 churches in the Holiness tradition, most of them driven by news of the Welsh Revival to prayer and fasting for a similar breakthrough in their city. Seymour's time with the mission with which Neely Terry was associated was short-lived. At this stage, he considered himself as under the leadership of Parham and an advocate of the Apostolic Faith message, which meant that his preaching of Spirit-baptism evidenced by tongues did not go down well with a company of people who felt this teaching debased their personal experience of sanctification that needed no physical evidence. He found the doors padlocked against him, and the membership split on the issue. A couple, the Lees, sympathetic to his cause, invited him to their home for prayer meetings and on 9 April 1906 Edward Lee spoke in tongues. Three days later Seymour received the experience that he preached.

A localized revival broke out with crowds swelling around the house. Healings were among the manifestations witnessed. Premises at 312 Azusa Street were rented. Originally built as an African Methodist Episcopal Church, the building was abandoned after a fire and turned into horse stables on the ground floor and tenement apartments on the upper floor. Located in a run-down district, it was one of the least churchy settings imaginable, yet eminently suitable for its largely marginalized clientele. Within a month of its opening, the place was bulging with people as news spread. At high points, around 350 worshipers were jammed into the two-storied building with a motley crowd of seekers

65. Ibid., 35–45 for Alma White.

and hecklers gathering outside. Services were held three times every day of the week for three consecutive years. The mission's newspaper *The Apostolic Faith,* with its worldwide circulation of 50,000 copies in the years 1906–8, ensured that the message rippled to the far-flung outposts of Holiness missionary endeavour, notably India.[66] The San Francisco earthquake, which struck on the 18 April and caused 10,000 deaths, added an apocalyptic edge to the ferment of debate about the Second Coming.

At the helm in all this excitement was Seymour, who adopted a distinct nondirective leadership style, in a way not dissimilar to Evan Roberts during the 1904–5 Welsh Revival. He thought of himself as not controlling the revival, so much as serving it.[67] His preaching was simple without the taint of flamboyance, yet powerful. Described by William Durham, pastor of Chicago's North Avenue Baptist church, as the "meekest man" he had ever met, he was quite prepared to share with others his modest pulpit made of shoe crates. Nothing was planned, orders of service never contemplated, silence and uproarious shouts alternated haphazardly. One seeker paying his first visit to the mission described the scene: "Prayer and worship were everywhere. The altar was filled with seekers; some kneeling; others prone on the floor; some were speaking in tongues. Everyone was doing something, all seemingly were lost in God."[68] Bartleman was so moved on one occasion that he described the atmosphere as "almost too sacred and holy to attempt to minister in. . . . Like the priests in the Tabernacle of old we could not minister for the glory"—an image drawn from 2 Chr 5: 14.[69] Seymour often worked his way through the throng laying hands on people to receive some manifestation of the Spirit, whether tongues, prophecy or healing. Yet it was from this unprepossessing setting, led by nobodies, that a revolutionary spirituality was launched. Its import was not immediately apparent.

By the end of 1906, critics described the events of the previous month as "of small moment", and even Carrie Judd Montgomery's husband showed himself less than enthralled by his comment that "there is no real revival as a whole in Los Angeles, but only here and there a little company who are trusting God fully and receiving a rich experience of his grace."[70] Nevertheless, it does not stretch historical outcome outlandishly to liken the impact of the Azusa event to Luther pinning his Ninety-Five Theses on the door of Wittenberg castle church, or to Wesley's heart-warming experience at Aldersgate Street chapel, all seemingly minor acts yet of profound historical moment. Harvey Cox saw the dramatic advance of Pentecostalism as nothing less than "the reshaping of religion in the twenty-first century." [71] Henry Van Dusen opined that it was the harbinger of "a revolution comparable in importance with the establishment of the original church and with

---

66. For Pentecostalism in India, see Anderson, *Spreading Fires,* 77–101. An outbreak of tongues preceded those at Azusa Street at the Mukti welfare mission in India for widows and orphans established by Pandita Rambai.

67. Dorries, "William J. Seymour." In McClymond, *Encyclopaedia,* 395.

68. Owens, *Speak to the Rock,* 74.

69. Bartleman, *Azusa Street,* 69.

70. Robeck, "Azusa Street Revival," in *IDPCM,* 345–46.

71. The subtitle of Cox, *Fire from Heaven.*

the Protestant Reformation."[72] If the theology of Pentecostalism was honed in Houston in 1901, the Azusa Street Revival was the spot from which it was launched.

Azusa's direct impact was remarkably short-lived. The earliest chronicler of the revival, Frank Bartleman, was of the opinion that "'Azusa' began to fail the Lord early in her history."[73] There were only two periods when the number of regular worshipers topped more than a couple of hundred. The first was 1906–8 followed by a major dip between 1909 and part of 1911, when there were only a dozen blacks in attendance and no whites before numbers picked up in a short burst. The fact that Pentecostalism did not need a Rome, Canterbury, even a Geneva, is a reflection that, then as now, it travels well. The early Pentecostals made such an impact on the people who heard them as to make their message their own and then pass it on. By 1908 the movement had planted itself in fifty countries.[74] Cox sought to uncover the staying power of the new movement at a time when the forces of secularization were beginning to amass, pitting "the culture of technical rationality" against the fumbling conservatism of the churches. As for Pentecostals, "they rebelled against the creeds but retained the mystery . . . abolished hierarchies but kept ecstasy . . . rejected both scientism *and* traditionalism. They returned to the raw inner core of human spirituality and thus provided just the new kind of 'religious space' many people needed."[75]

Pentecostals had a high sense of calling in believing that they had a vital part to play in heralding the consummation of the age. Theirs was to be the vanguard of the Latter Rain when the vigor, gifting and governance of the early church would be reinstituted in preparation for the parousia.

The approach taken by the Azusa Mission was that it was to be undenominational and nonsectarian: "We believe in unity with Christ's people everywhere. . . . It is the old-time apostolic assembly, the same old teaching of 1900 years ago. It is new to the world in these last days, but its teaching and doctrine is as old as the New Testament."[76] That the gift of tongues had been restored to complete the panoply of charisms in 1 Cor 12: 8–10 was for Pentecostals clear evidence that the gospel of the kingdom would be "preached to the entire world for a witness unto all nations, and then shall the end come" (Matt 24:14). The unscriptural baggage accumulated by the Christian church in the intervening centuries would be swept away. Denominational hierarchies, for one, would be cleared to off-stage thus alleviating the gap between clergy and congregation as the Spirit initiated a new freedom. For Bartleman, such freedom would save the renewed church from becoming "entangled again in a yoke of ecclesiastical bondage."[77] The virtual binitarianism of much conventional Christianity would give way to a trinitarianism that gave the work of the Holy Spirit a restatement of the message and deeds of the primitive church.

72. Van Dusen (1897–1975) was a leading world churchman.

73. Bartleman, *Azusa Street*, 68.

74. For a short, but illuminating, account of the rapid and successful spread of the movement, see Maxwell,. "'Networks and Niches." In Hunter, *Azusa Street Revival and Its Legacy*, 127–40.

75. Cox, *Fire from Heaven*, 105.

76. *AF*, Oct-Jan., 1908, 2/2.

77. Bartleman, *Azusa Street*, 68.

In an article Seymour unearthed new terms for the role of the Spirit and Christ, viz., bishop, chairman, and archbishop that denied church leaders personal grandeur. The article, entitled "The Holy Spirit: Bishop of the Church," declared that no religious assembly is legal without His presence and His transaction. . . . The first thing in every assembly is to see He, the Holy Ghost is installed as the chairman." Working a similar vein he hailed "Christ is the archbishop of these assemblies." For Pentecostals, church history revealed that God was apt to do "a new thing" (Isa 43:19). An early issue of *The Apostolic Faith* expressed the conviction that "all along the ages men have been preaching a partial Gospel, [but] God has from time to time raised up men to bring back the truth to the church.[78] He raised up Luther to bring back to the world the doctrine of justification by faith. He raised up another reformer in John Wesley to establish Bible Holiness in the church. Then He raised up Dr. Cullis who brought back to the world the wonderful doctrine of divine healing. Now He is bringing back the Pentecostal Baptism to the church."[79]

The sense Pentecostals had of themselves as a people called to a special destiny, a new spiritual aristocracy, antagonized many of their contemporaries.[80] In the war of words, Pentecostals in turn were referred to as "the scum of society" and their religion demeaned as fit only for blacks and poor whites. The earliest report in the *Los Angeles Times* of the meetings that it described as held in "a tumble-down shack [and led by] an old colored exhorter" related that "the devotees of the weird doctrine practice the most fanatical rites, preach the wildest theories and work themselves into a state of mad excitement. . . . Night is made hideous in the neighborhood by the howlings of the worshipers."[81] Little wonder that in June 1906, the Los Angeles Ministerial Association filed a formal, though unsuccessful, complaint with the city authorities against the Azusa Mission for disturbing the peace and calling for its closure.

The prolonged worship and emotional fervor that marked the earliest days were not sustainable. Careful reading of *The Apostolic Faith* indicates conflict brewing between Parham and Seymour. In the first issue a letter "from Brother Chas. Parham, who is God's leader in the Apostolic Faith Movement" was quoted. In it Parham wrote: "I rejoice in God over you all, my children, though I have never seen you. . . . Keep together in unity till I come, then in a grand meeting let all prepare for the outside fields."[82] Within three months, a notice in *The Apostolic Faith* revealed a darkening of mood: "Some are asking if Dr. [*sic*] Chas. F. Parham is the leader of this movement. We can answer, no he is not the leader of this movement of Azusa Mission. We thought of having him to be our leader and so stated in our paper, before waiting on the Lord."[83] It did not help matters that Parham was engaged elsewhere when the first outpouring took place in April 1906.

It is clear that Parham regarded Seymour as his protégé, and both regarded the Azusa Mission as an extension of the Apostolic Faith Movement. It was in seeking to further the

---

78. *AF*, June-Sept,, 1907, 3/1 &2.

79. *AF*, Oct. 1906, 1/1. For Cullis, see Robinson, *Divine Healing, 1830–1890*, 165–72.

80. Nicol, *Pentecostals*, 79.

81. Bartleman, *Azusa Street*, 175.

82. *AF*, Sept. 1906, 1/1

83. *AF*, Dec. 1906, 1/1.

interests of his movement that Parham was unable to spend time Los Angeles when the revival started. His delay in not reaching Azusa Street until October resulted in part from a lengthy visit to Zion City when he attempted to wrest control of Dowie's empire from Glenn Voliva.[84] When he finally arrived in Los Angeles, what was expected to be a blessing turned out to be nothing short of a disaster that led to the irreconcilable rift between the two men. The breakup was the beginning of the end to Parham's prominence within the nascent Pentecostal movement. It also presaged the imminent decline of the Azusa Street Mission, though without impairment to its iconic status.[85] Bartleman's aphorism is pertinent to the expansion of the movement from other satellite foci, "A charge of dynamite does not produce the finished product. But it does set loose the stones that later stand as monuments."[86]

When Parham arrived in Los Angeles in October 1906, he was eagerly welcomed. However, from his first setting foot in the building in Azusa Street he was clearly disturbed by what he saw. It is difficult to work out which of two incidents upset him the more as they were mingled. Was it the scenes of emotional excess, or the mixing of the races? "Men and women," he wrote, "whites and blacks knelt together or fell across one another; frequently a white woman, perhaps of wealth and culture, could be seen thrown back into the arms of a 'buck nigger,' and held tightly thus as she shivered and shook in freak imitation of Pentecost. Horrible, awful, shame!" Such behavior he likened to that of a "darkly revival." When he addressed his first meeting, he assailed his hearers for engaging in "animism," declaring "God is sick at his stomach."[87] With such an onslaught it is not surprising that Seymour and the racially mixed body of elders failed to appreciate Parham's rebuff. They believed that one of the greatest blessings of the Pentecostal experience was the breaking down of racial barriers, picked out as a supreme work of the Holy Spirit. Bartleman, sharing the elation of the earliest days, rejoiced that far more white than black people were in attendance, a sure sign that "the 'color line' was washed away in the blood of Christ."[88]

When Parham was asked to leave and never come back, he opened a rival mission across town. It helped to redraw the color line by siphoning off 200 to 300 white followers for a short time. Finally, he left Los Angeles for good. Any ambition to lead a united movement was soon to be shattered within months. In late January 1907, the *Waukegan Daily Sun* reported that Parham had been served with a warrant for his arrest during a stay in Zion City. The matter became public in July when he and a younger man were arrested in Texas on the charge of sodomy. In denying the charge, Parham suggested he had been framed by a resentful Glenn Voliva, the then leader of the Zion community suspicious of a takeover by Parham. No indictment was filed and the case was dropped. However, the fact that rumors had been widespread for months before the threat of legal proceedings convinced many that the charge was substantive. He continued with a modest work

84. For this incident, see Robinson, *Divine Healing, 1890–1906*, 85.

85. Robins, *Pentecostalism in America*, 27–28.

86. Bartleman, *Azusa Street*, 68.

87. Goff, *Fields White Unto Harvest*, 131.

88. Bartleman, *Azusa Street*, 54.

that remained limited largely to the Tri-State area up to his death twenty years later. He dropped below the radar of serious Pentecostal history until the 1960s when the arrival of the Charismatic movement renewed an interest in the roots of modern charismaticism, and a cadre of able scholars of the movement engaged in research into its origins.

When it came to the test of leadership, Parham showed a lack of spiritual and emotional maturity, unable to rise above his churlish attitude to rival leadership and his culturally ingrained racism. His early socialist sympathies for the underdog were over-ridden by an Anglo-Israelism that bred a sense of racial superiority as captured in his statement, "The Saxon Conquest of Great Britain, (today coupled with the United States) of nearly all the world proves the Scriptures: they were to be the 'head and not the tails of nations.'"[89] His image was not improved by his admiration for many leaders of the reorganized Ku Klux Klan. As the Pentecostal movement sought to balance spiritual experience with doctrinal orthodoxy, he challenged it by his long-held support of conditional immortality, and an increasing indulgence in idiosyncratic interpretations of Scripture. One example was his advocacy of an eighth day creation, whereby the Adamic race was created on the eighth day that followed on the tail of an initial race formed on the sixth day. Intermarriage between the two races, he believed, brought trouble to the earth in Noah's time from which he was rescued not because he was a just man but rather from his "pedigree without mixed blood." Miscegenation, he believed, would cause similar distress in America by introducing many diseases and wiping "the mixed bloods off the face of the earth."[90]

The Azusa Street Mission also was not spared from seeing its influence drain away. Dissension among key people played a large part in eroding the work of the Mission. Three women—two white, Florence Crawford and Clara Lum, and one black, Jeannie Moore Evans—played a prominent part in the history of the Mission. Serious problems arose when Seymour married Evans in May 1908, an event that Nelson described as "the turning point of Seymour's influence."[91] Evans acted as pianist, worship leader, and exhorter at the services. The marriage, unannounced and held in private, stunned many members. Clara Lum was joint editor with Crawford of *The Apostolic Faith*. Responsible for recording in shorthand the numerous testimonies given during the services, she felt betrayed by the marriage. Like many others, she saw it as a step that undermined the strongly held doctrine of the imminence of the Second Coming.

Clara Lum's opposition was that of a betrayed lover. Seemingly she and Seymour had entertained the idea of marriage, only to be put off by a ministerial friend, C. H. Mason, who deemed such a mixed marriage would stir jaundiced controversy and cause schism. Florence Crawford had a different reason for dissent. She was convinced that marriage, with its family responsibilities, was detrimental to the sense of urgency required for the last days. Both women finished up in Portland, Oregon where a separate Apostolic Faith Mission was established. Fatally for Seymour, they took with them the only copies of the

---

89. Parham, *Voice Crying in the Wilderness*, 106.

90. Nelson, "For Such a Time," 242, n.156.

91. Ibid., 217. See also Espinosa, "Ordinary Prophet," 51–52.

national and international mailing lists of *The Apostolic Faith*. With a circulation of 50,000 copies and a worldwide distribution, the loss of the paper was a body blow for Seymour and Azusa Street. With editorial expertise gone, the link to the revival had gone and with it any sense of coherence within the new movement.

A more overtly theological issue triggered another serious disruption. The dynamic, youthful pastor of Chicago's North Avenue Mission, William H. Durham (1873–1912) made claim to his Spirit-baptism during a visit to the Azusa Street Mission in March 1907. On his return to Chicago, he engaged in a Pentecostal ministry that was of revival proportions. Aimee Semple, before her second marriage to Harold McPherson, was instantly healed of a broken ankle through Durham's ministration in January 1910.[92] In 1910, Durham introduced the Reformed as against the Wesleyan Holiness view on sanctification when the latter was the more dominant within American Pentecostalism at the time. Durham's "Finished Work" teaching denied the doctrine of entire sanctification as a second work of grace in the believer prior to the third stage of Spirit-baptism. He did not accept the need for the second, usually instantaneous, blessing of sanctification. Instead, he proposed that sanctification began at conversion and was progressive throughout the believer's life. When he purposely brought this message to Los Angeles in 1911, it was accepted in a number of quarters but not in Azusa Street where the three-stage position was the lynchpin doctrine. Spirit-baptism was a heritage only for the sanctified ("the clean vessel"). It was an ironic twist when Seymour locked Durham from the Mission, an act that was reminiscent of the treatment Seymour had received five years previously. About two-thirds of Seymour's flock left and were presented with a choice of twelve or so Pentecostal missions in Los Angeles where the Finished Work doctrine was preached. This division, as will be shown in the next chapter, was to have a significant effect on the theology and practice of divine healing in the movement.

---

92. Chicago became one leading centers for worldwide Pentecostalism, notably as the mother church for Italian assemblies in Italy and South America.

Excursus: Healing Homes in Their Medical Context

D ESPITE THE PLETHORA OF curative agencies at the turn of the century there still remained room for the practitioners of divine healing to expose their own advantages. Relevant to the issue of contemporary medicine is the fact that the American Medical Association, founded in 1847, was in the 1890s weak and in need of reorganization. It was generally recognized that there were too many ill-equipped doctors. The newly constituted Council on Medical Education, formed in 1904, was charged to improve the academic requirements for medical schools. Up to that point, many schools had inadequate entrance requirements and many were run as profit-making bodies.[1] Medicine was not the only body that was in need of reform. The inventor, Thomas Edison, spoke for many in the Protestant middle class when he declared, "Our production, our factory laws, our charities, our relations between capital and labor, our distribution—all wrong, out of gear. We've stumbled along for a while, trying to run a new civilization in old ways, but we've got to start to make this world over." So pervasive was this upbeat mood, the label "Progressive Era" was given to the period between the Depression of 1893 and World War. It ushered in a period of marked social activism and political reform. It was a time of major reform that saw the introduction of universal suffrage, and the desire to clean up the party political machines.

A related theme was the push to achieve greater efficiency in all sectors of society by identifying outmoded ways that needed modernizing, particularly through the application of science to human affairs. Medicine felt the full impact of this trend with the publication in 1910 of the *Flexner Report*, sponsored by the Carnegie Foundation. The report estimated that 60 percent of medical schools were not up to the required standard. Its findings about the state of medicine in Kansas found that of the four medical schools "none is at this time satisfactory." It called for the national scrapping of local small medical schools, many of them run for profit, with poor facilities that bespoke their minimal capital investment. The President of Harvard, Charles Eliot (1869–1902), argued that entrance requirements were so low that anybody could "walk into a medical school from the street."[2] The Report recommended higher qualifications for entry to university medical departments. The initial outcome of the Report saw the number of medical graduates drop from 4,400 to 2,000 with their training restricted to thirty-one university departments.

The last third of the nineteenth century was the period that witnessed an increasingly complex understanding of human anatomy and physiology. New findings began

---

1. Peterson, "Major Events." In Ward, *Foundations*, 22.

2. Flexner, *Medical Education*, 22.

to overturn traditional medical views of human nature, and increasingly the profession found itself at odds with conservative Christianity. Such a conflict has a long history. For centuries it was the religious establishment that regulated and controlled the practice of medicine. In the Middle Ages this control was so complete that the church was the official body that issued medical licenses to physicians, many of whom were monks or priests.[3] The general belief was that physical and mental disorders resulted from spiritual forces and had to be dealt with on spiritual terms. It was within this conceptual framework that in 1487 the persecution and burning of witches was sanctioned. The majority of such women suffered chronic mental illness and their ordeal lasted till 1782 when the last witch was decapitated. Over the last 500 years the power of the church has waned and that of medical science has increased, at least until recent times with signs of an accommodation becoming acceptable.[4] Bishop Henley Henson, the liberal Bishop of Durham (1920–39), was acutely aware of the conflict and praised the medical profession for being "justly jealous of anything that might lead to a return of that baleful confusion between religious beliefs and curative science which once worked so ill."[5] The Bishop reckoned that the association of disease with sin had the effect of subordinating medicine to theology, and "thereby of hindering the advance of science." When the profession showed suspicion of the church's ministration to the sick, then, he conjectured, it may be in response to "the meddlesome and unintelligent procedure of the church in the past."[6] Such comments were entirely consonant with the whole spirit of the *Flexner Report* that held, "Science, once embraced, will conquer the whole. . . . There is no logical justification for the invocation of names or creeds."[7]

During the period of this study the breach between the contesting viewpoints was widening, though without a convincing resolution. What Schoepflin wrote about Christian Science is for the most part applicable to other therapies dismissed by the medical profession:

> Primarily understood in terms of various mechanical, chemical, and electrical models, for many physicians the body came to eclipse the soul in importance. But Christians still claimed to possess authoritative knowledge regarding human nature; and the will, with its seat the soul, continued to figure prominently in their view. . . . Religious healers thrived in Progressive Era America in part because they undermined this mechanical human by appealing to the *still-strong popular belief* that the ontological, if not the immediate, cause of disease lay in a fallen human nature. Healing therefore required some ministry to the broken soul of humanity and not just dosing of the material body.[8]

3. The Lateran Council in 1215 ordered that all physicians before considering treatment should induce patients to confess their sins, and only when the cure of the soul had been secured could the affliction be given attention. The rule was enforced by denying the rites of the church to any physician who failed to follow procedure.

4. Based on Koenig, *Handbook*, 3–4. This book reviews research dealing with the relationship between religion and a variety of mental and physical illnesses.

5. Henson, *Notes on Spiritual Healing*, 182.

6. Ibid., 175.

7. Flexner, *Medical Education*, 161 & 157.

8. Schoepflin, *Christian Science*, 128. (Emphasis added)

The issue revealed competing worldviews. Modernizing physicians sensed competition could imperil advances in the scientific understanding of the human body and mind, and their growing prerogative over them. Faced with this threat they sought to undermine the appeal of metaphysical and religious healers by asserting that such practitioners could cure only functional, not organic disorders, while their healing techniques were explicable by suggestion and updated versions of mesmerism. Taking an opposing view, some Christian doctors reacted against the trend their discipline was taking. At one extreme was the Edinburgh-trained doctor David Traherne, who believed so fervently in divine healing that he came to the conviction that "the occupation of a medical practitioner was an unscriptural one" that he gave it up after thirty years, despite the fact "it was the only means of livelihood familiar to me."[9] Others, who took a less extreme view, nevertheless were unhappy with the current trend in medicine and reacted to it by integrating elements of what later became termed "holistic medicine" into their practice. One physician from Grand Forks, Dakota, decried the secularization of medicine and the failure of the church in challenging it. He indicted the "arid waste of Protestant teachings [that] caused us to lose the idea of the belief of God's illimitable power and mercy," a charge that could not be levelled at the radical healers.[10] With them there was an expansive growth in the number of healing homes.

Parham, of course, was not alone in setting up a healing home as has been shown from the instances of Dowie at Zion City, Sandford at Shiloh, and Carrie Judd at Faith Rest Cottage, Buffalo. Such homes became a recognizable part of the contemporary religious landscape. Seen in purely economic terms their growth in numbers can be understood in the market terms of supply and demand. It is a market where demand is virtually insatiable and continues to outstrip supply. The rapid growth of Christian Science, Spiritualism, and other therapeutic alternatives such as chiropractic (reputably begun in 1895) mopped up a considerable amount of the pressure.[11] Orthodox medicine was just beginning to make some significant advance through its scientific approach but was distant from the heights of scientific and technical sophistication reached a century later. One medical historian of the period noted that "the average physician had only a hazy notion of etiology, and he prescribed largely for such symptoms as fevers, coughs, diarrheas, consumptions, and sore throats. The treatment itself was often hit or miss. While dosage was moderating, quinine, aconite, opium, alcohol, mercury, strychnine, arsenic, and other potentially dangerous drugs still formed the basis of *materia medica*."[12] Untried and open to quackery, patent medicines flooded the market and were readily purchasable by direct mail.

---

9. Treharne, *Healing*, Preface.

10. Schoepflin, *Christian Science*, 130.

11. The number of medical journal articles dealing with Christian Science jumped from around eighteen in 1890–94 to a peak of about 170 during 1900–1904. By 1910–14 it had fallen to around forty, a reflection of the sense of threat between the profession and spiritually-based therapies (Schoepflin, *Christian Science*, 11). "The case of chiropractic has far-reaching implications for understanding the interconnectedness of scientific, metaphysical and evangelical practices." For the teasing out of this remark, see Brown, "Chiropractic and Christianity," 145–81.

12. Goff, *Fields White Unto Harvest*, 41.

One advantage divine healing had over doctors, patent medicines, and most alter-native therapies was that its rationale precluded any entrepreneurial spirit that aspired primarily to increase profitability. The *Flexner Report* was not slow to condemn the commercial spirit that imbued some medical schools: "The advertising methods of the commercially successful schools are amazing. Not infrequently advertising costs more than laboratories. The school catalogues abound in exaggeration, misstatement, and half-truths. The deans of these institutions occasionally know more about modern advertising than about modern medical teaching."[13] The medical profession took it for granted that Christian Scientists attracted so many patients because their usual fee was one dollar a treatment despite the fact that no outlay for medical requisites was involved. By contrast, healing homes established on faith lines were rarely free from financial strain, largely because the motivation behind the healing home was for the most part far removed from the calculus of the market place. It is on this point that any recourse to economic theory falls apart. High fees were also a sticking point with Parham in his criticism of the medical profession. With the increase in their training and rising status, physicians were in a posi-tion to increase their earning power and elevate their social standing in society. Superior treatment was fine for the better-off, but presented a barrier for the poorer majority that led to a sense of disaffection with doctors and an enticement to seek help outside the medical profession.

Parham had a poor view of the state of medicine. In his view "the fact still remains that after 4000 years of practice—humanity willingly laying herself upon the altar to be doped, blistered, bled and dissected—medical science has gained little more than has the Bible recorded of her, that they have sought out many ways of relieving pain. While the fatal diseases that have existed are fatal still; and medical science stands with fettered hands in the presence of consumption, catarrh, cancers, fevers, and many other diseases."[14] Goff makes the astute observation that for a faith healing preacher to bring a charge of quackery against doctors may seem incredible to us in a world of widespread technical sophistication, "but in an age suspicious of the advancement of medical science, Parham captured the attention of quite a few." Alienation from the profession was most keenly felt by those least able to meet the doctor's fee. Parham allied himself with this class when he insisted that "the principal relief from medical science is pocket book relief." [15]

Parham's skepticism about medicine went deeper than querying the success of particular treatments. Medicine like all disciplines had, for him, to be measured against Scripture. On that score, he aped Dowie in ferocity by contending that in both Testaments medical science and its practitioners are in league with "those guilty of vilest sins against God and humanity. The word invariably translated in the English is sorcerer; in the Hebrew (*Kasaph*); in the Greek (*Pharmakas*), signifying a concoctor of drugs and poisons. So to-day the principle (*sic*) drugs are poisons."[16] Medicine was arraigned as "this octopus-god

---

13. *Flexner Report*, 19.

14. Parham, Charles F. *A Voice Crying in the Wilderness*. Baxter Springs, KS: Apostolic faith Bible College, 1910, 41.

15. Goff, *Fields White Unto Harvest*, 42.

16. Parham, *Voice*, 41.

Moloch" from which many people are turning to "osteopathy, Christian Science, hypnotic and magnetic healing. These are fast displacing the power of medical science whose coercive power and execution of compulsory laws begin to wane."[17] Parham admonished his readers that if they would give as much time in prayer and thanking God as that given in studying what doctor, drug or patent medicine should be tried next, then they would "not only get healed, but stay healed." Even stronger was the claim that "the more proficient in relieving pain a system becomes, the more anti-Christian is its influence; for man has ever been prone to wander to seek help from every source . . . before he will humble himself . . . and accept the deliverance freely purchased for him at Calvary."[18] For him and likeminded others among the radicals, the physical body pertained to the Lord, and the Lord was the sole restorer of the body. Anything or anyone other was an intrusion.

Faith healing differed from all the other therapies, whether orthodox/scientific or alternative. In the latter group can be counted such therapies as the hygienic, diet, botanic/eclectic, homeopathic, hydropathic, electric, mesmeric/magnetic, chiropractic, and osteopathic.[19] Such options were not simple purveyors of uncomplicated remedies, but can be thought of more as medical sectarian schools, each with its own metaphysical understanding of nature and disease. In their writings the prose can take on a religious tone, often with allusion to biblical themes. The editor of one health journal that promoted a particular dietary regimen went as far as to state that "our views [if] carried fully into practice, by strictly observing the physical, moral and intellectual laws of our being—sinless in every respect—would constitute the Millennium."[20] These curative agencies were categorized in the *Flexner Report* as "sectarian medicine," which prior to the placing of medicine on a scientific basis was inevitable. But with the advance of scientific medicine they had, for Flexner, become indefensible because "there is no logical justification for the invocation of names or creeds, for the segregation from the larger body of established truth of any particular set of truths or supposed truths as especially precious."[21] The *Report* came down hard on homeopathy, osteopathy and eclectic medicine, the last specializing in botanical remedies. They were accused of being "self-contradictory" in that in their training institutions they integrated metaphysical ideas with scientific methodology, with the result they "violate scientific quality."[22]

In their own subclass can be placed the more overtly, religiously-rooted cures associated with Christian Science, New Thought, Spiritualism, and Theosophy, a grouping to which the "faith-cure" was commonly assigned, much to the dismay of all who upheld the cause of divine healing. Where the latter differed from all other systems was its total reliance on biblical witness that preempted an appeal to any other source. Their interpretation of Scripture could and was keenly contested by fellow believers but not their source.

17. As a god worshiped by the Phoenicians, Moloch was associated with propitiatory child sacrifice by parents (Jer 32:35). In modern English the name refers to anything/person demanding a costly sacrifice.

18. Parham, *Voice*, 40.

19. For an account of some of these see Gevitz, *Other Healers*, and Fuller, *Alternative Medicine* .

20. Albanese, *Republic of the Mind*, 127.

21. *Flexner Report*, 157.

22. Ibid.,157.

There was no sharper critic than B. B. Warfield, who from Princeton's lofty eminence of Calvinist cessationism confessed

> to being chilled when we hear of such things as "religious faith and prayer" being looked upon as therapeutic agents for the cure of disease, and administered to patients as such. We are frankly shocked at the coupling, together of faith and paregoric, prayer and podophyllin in a single comprehensive pharmacopoeia. We are too accustomed to thinking of faith and prayer as terminating on God, and finding their response in His gracious activities, to feel comfortable when they are turned back on themselves and—while still, no doubt, addressed to God—used as instruments for moving man.[23]

His disquiet stretched even to the Emmanuel movement when he asked what it had to offer "which was not offered in the old Faith-Houses–say, Zeller's House in Mannedorf—except a very much thinner religion and a more advanced medical science?"[24]

In contradistinction to conventional medical practice and other alternative therapies the spirit that informed faith homes instanced at Mannedorf was captured in verse written by Elizabeth Baker (1849–1915) who with her sisters opened their Elim Faith Home in Rochester, NY, in 1895. Such homes focussed on what A. J. Gordon called "God's direct and supernatural action upon the body of the sufferer," a charge versified artlessly by Baker:[25]

> *This rest-home by the way,*
> *I need not call it "home."*
> *'Tis but Thy guest-house, night and day,*
> *Where pilgrims go and come.*
>
> *For it is Thine, not mine,*
> *And therefore is no care.*
> *Yet I must do my best with Thine*
> *To make it bright and fair.*
>
> *To make it bright and sweet*
> *For Thee and Thine alway,*
> *A resting-place for weary feet,*
> *To speed them on Thy way.*[26]

By operating on a worldview that embraced the supernatural, the founders of faith homes were marginal to the ongoing debate raging around science and medicine. Not entirely so, however, because it was necessary to distinguish the homes from hospitals, in part to avoid the possibility of litigation over medical negligence or malpractice. Such sacred

---

23. Warfield, *Counterfeit Miracles*, 203. "Paregoric" and "Podophyllin" were plant-derived purgatives.

24. Ibid., 203. The Emmanuel movement is discussed in chapter 5. The faith work at Mannedorf, Switzerland, was established by Dorothea Trudel in the 1840s and continued by Samuel Zeller after her death in 1862. (See Robinson, *Divine Healing, 1830–90*, 70–87).

25. Curtis, "Acting Faith." 151.

26. Blumhofer, "Life on Faith Lines", 12. Baker later became the leader of the Elim Tabernacle, a Pentecostal work, though she refused ordination on the gender issue. The words "no care" (sixth line) hardly represent the reported times of acute financial stringency at her Elim Faith Home.

spaces cocooned residents from the indifference or misgivings dominant in the prevailing culture. The homes fostered an unworldly life of intimate spirituality, one that allowed an unhurried quest for meditation and instruction in the life of holiness and faith. Parham, in describing the facilities of Bethel, spoke of "our office, where daily the sick and sinful may consult as to their spiritual and physical welfare, . . . a reading room, where all kinds of helpful literature can be found, and where amidst the flowers a quiet hour or two can be spent, . . . the printing room where busy hands prepare the messages of 'glad tidings and great joy' to send to our dear friends outside of the city."[27] Many, if not most, homes were started and then run on faith lines, in many cases taking George Mueller and his faith orphanages as a template. Cullis could affirm, "I never charged a person a dollar in my life for praying for them."[28]

A sizeable number of faith homes were founded by women despite the fact that they themselves opposed the ordination of women to the time-honored ministry of the church. Women, in particular, for whom ministerial status was denied, seized the opportunity presented by the caring nature of such homes to exercise and enhance their gifts. Among their number were Lucy Lake Osborn's Home for Incurables in Brooklyn, NY, Mother Moise's Home in St. Louis, IL, and Mrs Dora Dudley's Home in Grand Rapids, MI. Curtis summarized the sense of liberation the healing home inspired, particularly in women, who formed the majority of boarders: "Separated from skeptical critics and pessimistic doctors, as well as from the responsibilities and cultural pressures that characterized their everyday worlds, guests at faith homes were surrounded instead with believers who persuaded them to abandon modes of thinking and acting that kept them bedridden, to embrace the promises of healing contained in the Bible, and to adopt a manner of living that linked holiness with the energetic pursuit of purity and service, rather than with the resigned endurance of bodily affliction."[29]

The generalizations made in the previous paragraph can be exemplified in the Bethel Healing Home. The home served not only its guests but also reached out to the local community. The intent was that the home would become an ecumenical center, able to draw support from all Topeka's churches. A guest observed that hardly a day passed that someone did not drop in for prayer for their healing. They included "consumptives, dyspeptics, cripples, and people with almost every known disease most of whom "always get a spiritual uplift."[30] Boarders were expected to make a contribution, four to seven dollars a week, with discrete arrangements made with the impoverished. Praying for the sick was regarded as a gospel entitlement, and an enactment not to be sullied by running it as a profit-making business. Testimonies paid tribute to the spiritual atmosphere about the place. One spoke of "comforts and informality of home life" to which she added "that spirit of cheerfulness and consideration for others which reveals the Christ life within seeking earnestly to realize that ideal life." Another, during her six-week stay, failed "to discover anything that is not of God in the life of the occupants. Everything moves in

27. Faupel, *Everlasting Gospel*, 163.

28. Curtis, *Faith in the Great Physician*, 151.

29. Curtis, "Houses of Healing," 611.

30. Parham, *Life of Charles F. Parham*, 46.

peace and harmony; and love prevails everywhere." Another testified to receiving such spiritual uplift that "the Bible is a new book to me."[31]

Faith homes formed communities of saints and could function much as a church, though with a floating membership. For many guests the sacramental rites such as laying-on of hands, anointing and communion held a hallowed place in their hearts. Pentecostals grew to refer to communion as "God's Medicine."[32] An article in *Confidence* in 1915 carried the title *The Lord's Supper: Medicine for his Children.* The author wrote of a thrice-repeated dream when "I had a conversation with my Lord regarding His Supper." The message he was requested "to pass on to God's children" came as an illumination: "I can see now that if we are sick or afflicted in any way and will partake of the bread and wine in faith, we must be healed . . . if we are living in obedience to the will of God in other ways."[33]

For many Pentecostals, during communion believers are brought into God's presence and can expect to receive "spiritual nourishment for their souls and medicine for their physical bodies."[34] Parham took the position that in the sacrificial death of Christ, his body and the blood served two different ends, viz., healing and forgiveness respectively: "The blood was for the cleansing of the sin, [while] his perfect body was broken for our imperfect bodies . . . to bring us to perfect health." Exegetically, this reading was a take on Isa 53:5/Matt 8:17, which propounded a dichotomy between the elements that was widely accepted in Pentecostal settings, lending a pristine depth of meaning to the communion service.[35] Communion at Bethel Healing Home was normally held on Sunday afternoon following the delivery of a healing homily. An elderly lady resident in her account of the schedule for Easter Sunday 1899 noted that at the service "several sisters claimed healing. . . . God's presence was manifested in great power and healing work was done."[36] Another guest noted that before the distribution of the elements, "Brother Parham gave some convincing thoughts, showing definitely that healing was in the atonement."[37]

Financial problems often lurked behind the scenes at Bethel. On one occasion when he arrived home, exhausted by a hard day of ministering to the sick and attending the death bed of the President of the Santa Fe Railroad, Parham had to face the problem that there was "not a cent" to pay the rent due the next day. The next morning an Irish visitor from the east coast who was familiar with Parham's work among the poor called, and told him, "Last night, between eleven and twelve o'clock (being the hour that I had prayed) I was suddenly awakened with the thought of you and your work; no sleep came to me until I had promised to bring you this." The "this" was a check for forty dollars, "the exact sum of to pay the rent."[38] Stories of food being supplied when the family table was empty and bills being met by monetary gifts just at the exact time of need, all relayed the same mes-

---

31. Ibid., 42–43 & 46.

32. Tomberlin, *Pentecostal Sacraments,* 178.

33. *Confidence,* April 1915, 70.

34. Tomberlin, *Pentecostal Sacraments,* 178.

35. Parham, *Life of Charles F. Parham,* 40.

36. Ibid., 44.

37. Ibid., 40.

38. Ibid., 47.

sage that "He is faithful who has promised." Living on the edge—socially, religiously, and financially—Holiness/Pentecostal people ventured into improbable situations that invited God to display his faithfulness.

Faith homes were not without their critics. Among the more prominent was James Monroe Buckley (1836–1920), described by his biographer as unquestionably the most potent individual leader in the Methodist Episcopal Church in his roles of pastor, administrator and editor of *The Christian Advocate*, the MEC's leading periodical.[39] The biography described Buckley's book *Faith Healing, Christian Science and Kindred Phenomena* (1892) as "thoroughly rationalistic," then tellingly added that Buckley had "probably not said the last word . . . on occult psychic questions."[40] In his book Buckley alleged that "families have been split over the doctrine taught in some Faith-Homes that friends who do not believe this truth are to be separated from [others] because of the weakening effect of their disbelief upon faith."[41] A heartrending letter to that effect had reached him from a man whose mother and sister were in residence at a faith-institution of New York, "refusing all intercourse with their friends, and neglecting obvious duties of life."

A similar complaint was brought against those women who had been persuaded to leave husbands and parents only to find themselves pressurized into giving thousands of dollars, on the ground that "the Lord had need of the money."[42] He fumed against those faith institutions that declared they were entirely by faith and use "subtle sophistry" in raising money. By contrast, others who had failed to raise sufficient financial support had "suffered the agonies of death. Some have starved, others have been relieved by benevolent Christian friends, and still others have been taken to asylums for the insane. Similar wrecks are to be found all through the land, dazzled and deceived by the careers of a few persons who have succeeded in getting their enterprises under way and enjoy a monopoly of their limited method of obtaining revenues." He, conceded, nevertheless, that some of those who were successful in the healing ministry were "doubtless as sincere men and women as ever lived." [43]

Buckley's wider views must take into account the fact that he believed passionately that any incentive to female autonomy would only prove ruinous to society. As recorded in his biography, he held that "however refined, vital and distinctive may be the legitimate sphere of woman yet . . . it is eternally distinctive from the sphere divinely designed for man."[44] It is doubtful if he ever engaged with any women who had found healing through their stay in a home. If he had, he might have come across some who could testify to their healing enabling them to fulfill the domestic duties that they were unable to fulfill by the nature of their complaint. In their case, their healing in releasing them to engage in domestic activity buttressed, rather than destabilized, conventional gender ideologies.

---

39. Mains, *Buckley*, 11.

40. Ibid., 174. The biography appeared some twenty-five years after the publication of Buckley's book.

41. Buckley *Faith Healing, Christian Science*, 57.

42. Ibid., 57.

43. Buckley," Faith Healing and Kindred Phenomena," 786.

44. Mains, *Monroe Buckley*, 186.

For others, their healing was more transformative than a lapse into domesticity. Carrie Bates was one such who received "the blessing of healing from the Lord" during her stay at Carrie Judd's Faith-Rest Cottage in March of 1884. Her restoration to health enabled her to embark on mission work in New York City, follow a three-year course of study at the New York Missionary Training College, and serve as matron at a faith-home for a summer. Five and a half years later, she parted from her family circle to engage in missionary work in India until her death in 1909. For women like her, Curtis concludes, their sojourn "in houses of healing facilitated internal transformations that prompted them to bump up against, stretch, and even to overstep the medical and cultural norms that characterized women as naturally and necessarily weak, passive, domestic, and sick."[45] For women, not all cultural restrictions were diminished. Missionary work had become an established route for women to engage in full-time Christian ministry. Notwithstanding such advance, essentialist ideas of the female nature remained to discourage their full participation in civic life and deter their criticism of all the powers that helped make them sick in the first place.[46] "Invoking the Great Physician," concludes Heather Curtis, "ultimately involved the acceptance, rather than the resolution, of the perplexing paradoxes and inscrutable enigmas that arise whenever human beings confront the mystery of bodily affliction and embrace the hope of divine healing."[47]

45. Curtis, "Houses of Healing," 610.

46. Porterfield, Amanda. "Forum on Sacred Spaces," 595.

47. Curtis, *Faith in the Great Physician*, 209.

2

Theology of Healing in Early American Pentecostalism

THE GREAT HISTORIAN OF the Pentecostal movement Walter Hollenweger maintained that the heart and core of Pentecostal reality is to be found in the first five or ten years of the movement.[1] The Dominican John Orme Mills was clear that what defined the Pentecostal revival in the United States was not that people spoke in tongues: "No, what was arresting about those first twentieth-century Pentecostals was their conviction that the new pouring-out of God's Holy Spirit on them had empowered them to share fully the life of the church of the apostles, the 'church of Pentecost.' . . . The charismatic manifestations emerging among them—tongues, healing, exorcism, prophecy—they interpreted as signs that they were bringing in the 'last times.'"[2] It was in the earliest years that Pentecostal message, its ethos, dynamism, and tensions were beginning to be defined. Even on the question of the evidential nature of tongues complete assent was not reached, and it has rarely been endorsed within the later Charismatic Renewal.

Seymour came to differ with Parham on the issue of tongues. He believed that the revival was a sign of divine approval of racial unity, and the movement had more to do with the eradication of racism, and "the achievement of unity in the body of Christ than the formal criterion of *glossolalia* as evidence of Spirit baptism."[3] Seymour insisted that love was as certain as tongues as a sign of Spirit-baptism. Without love, which necessitated an end to racial prejudice, tongues were insufficient as sign of Spirit-baptism, an experience he saw more as "an added blessing or impartation of grace" than an essential element of post-conversion gifting.[4] His was a doctrine formulated through frustration with the pertinacity of racial prejudice within Spirit-baptized ranks. In 1915 he published a book, short-titled *Doctrines and Disciplines*, for members of the Mission. One of the tenets shows his shift in understanding of the initial evidence issue. It starts with the statement that all believers should be given the opportunity to encounter God through the Holy Spirit in such a way as to be transformed and empowered for a life of service. The result of such an encounter "will be an expression of the 'Bible evidence' that this has taken place. . . . Markings of this journey include miracles, healings, dreams and visions,

---

1. Chan, *Pentecostal Theology*, 6.

2. Land, *Pentecostal Spirituality*, 62.

3. Sanders, *Saints in Exile*, 32.

4. Alexander, *Black Fire*, 130.

and charisms ranging from prophecy and speaking in tongues to administration."[5] For him, healings can stand as but one evidential sign of Spirit-baptism or, to use his term, "transformation."

Dayton suggested that perhaps even more characteristic of Pentecostalism than the doctrine of Spirit-baptism is "its celebration of miracles of divine healing as part of God's salvation and as evidence of divine power in the church."[6] Wacker reckoned that over the years the doctrine and practice of divine healing "has been the enduring backbone of the Pentecostal tradition."[7] The Pentecostal movement in essence piggybacked on the nineteenth-century Holiness movement, drawn particularly to healing as that movement's one salient charismatic manifestation. As Land pointed out, within the nineteenth-century Holiness movement "the whole range of gifts of the Spirit was seen as rare, occurring only here and there, without eschatological significance or import for the understanding of the Christian life, nature of the church, and missionary witness."[8] In the same vein, Warfield remarked that the sizeable minority who did promote the healing message failed to meet the objection that "if you insist that miracles are possible in this age, then you must logically admit that such miracles as raising the dead [and] speaking in tongues are still possible."[9] Pentecostals undermined Warfield's argument by being unfazed by the expectation of both tongues and resuscitation. The early Pentecostal healing evangelist Levi Lupton reported that during a summer camp "some of the over-zealous ones believed that all things done by the Apostles, even the rising of the dead, would be accomplished by the gathering."

A question that has to be answered is whether or not the early Pentecostals brought anything different or fresh to the ministry of divine healing. Stated otherwise, how far did Pentecostalism conform to the three features that distinguished the earlier Holiness understanding of divine healing. The three issues were: (i) the role of the atonement in healing; (ii) the weight given to faith; (iii) the question of medical intervention. Each of these components will be examined to assess the degree of conformity between the early Pentecostalism of Parham and Seymour's Azusa Street as expressed in *The Apostolic Faith*, and its Holiness progenitor.

(i) The earlier healing apologetic had no stronger advocate than A. B. Simpson. For him, "redemption finds its center in the cross of our Lord Jesus Christ. There we must look for the fundamental principle of divine healing. . . . Our healing becomes a great redemption right that we simply claim as our purchased inheritance through the blood of His Cross." Parham was equally convinced: "Healing is as certainly purchased in the atonement of Jesus Christ as salvation. To be healed you don't have to travel to some shrine . . . nor is it necessary that two or three agree in your case; healing is obtained like conversion, by

---

5. Seymour, "Divine Mandate." In Hunter, *Azusa Street Revival*, 363–64.

6. Dayton, *Theological Roots*, 115.

7. Wacker, "The Pentecostal Tradition." In Numbers, *Caring and Curing*, 515–16.

8. Land, *Pentecostal Spirituality*, 95.

9. Warfield, *Counterfeit Miracles*, 168.

faith in the atonement of Jesus Christ."[10] Seymour's article in the very first issue of *The Apostolic Faith* was equally adamant: "Sickness and disease are destroyed through the precious atonement of Jesus. O how we ought to honor the stripes of Jesus, for 'with his stripes we are healed.' . . . Not only is the atonement for the sanctification of our souls, but also for the sanctification of our bodies from inherited disease."

For Seymour, the atonement was all-encompassing in its virtues: "We that are the messengers of this precious atonement ought to preach all of it, justification, sanctification, healing, the baptism with the Holy Spirit, and signs following."[11] In an article in *The Apostolic Faith* addressed to those seeking healing, the writer reminded readers that "Jesus bore our sicknesses. Through him we are entitled to the healing of soul and body. The sacrifice on Calvary was for our bodies as well as our souls. Oh, let us honor the atonement of Jesus. . . . Healing is a part of our inheritance in Christ, purchased by the Blood."[12] Steven Land, writing of the early Pentecostals, noted that for them "Calvary was not only a specific historical event but also a testimony and focus for daily life. From the blood of Christ's atonement, as was said over and over, all benefits flow. . . . Everybody became a witness to Calvary and his or her own crucifixion with Christ, the biblical Pentecost and a personal Pentecost, and the healings of the disciples and his or her own healing."[13]

(ii) The major role of faith in the healing ministry of Christ made it indispensable in any ministry of healing. Intrinsic to A. B. Simpson's teaching on divine healing is the identification of healing with the atonement, thereby elevating it to a "great redemption right," something God-given to be appropriated by faith. Such faith he described as "the great lost lever."[14] When Florence Crawford wrote an article in her Portland version of *The Apostolic Faith* carrying the title "To Those Seeking for Healing," she admonished her readers: "Doubt is sin. . . . Doubt and fear will destroy every bit of faith in your soul."[15] It was a sentiment much on the lines of Carrie Judd's assertion that "Doubt is fatal to faith."[16] Parham remonstrated against those hearing good news from their doctor about making a recovery "begin to rejoice in your healing; But when God says, 'I am the Lord that healeth thee,' you begin to make excuses because you do not believe what God says. Polite indeed to man; to God most rude."[17] Seymour answered his own question, "Does the Lord Jesus provide healing for everybody?" with the positive response, "Yes; for all those that have faith in Him."[18]

---

10. Parham, *Voice Crying,* 48 & 47.

11. *AF*, Sept. 1906, 2, col. 1.

12. AF (Portland), Vol. 13 in *The Apostolic Faith: The Original Azusa Street Editions 1–13 plus Editions 19 & 20 from Portland, Oregon.* CD-ROM. Revival Library @ http://www.revival-library.org/library/libi-aries.htlill.

13. Land, *Pentecostal Spirituality,* 73.

14. Van de Walle, "A Man for His Season," 217.

15. *AF* (Portland), Vol. 20 in "*The Apostolic Faith*: 20." CD-ROM.

16. Hardesty, *Faith Cure,* 96.

17. Parham, *Voice Crying,* 47.

18. *AF*, Oct-Jan 1908, 2, col. 2.

Counter to such certitude, *The Apostolic Faith* as early as 1910 was issuing "qualifications, explanations and retractions" of extreme statements being voiced by "hyper-faith
healers"—a reference to those who indulged in an over-realized eschatology, which claims
for the present life what pertains to the future life. Experience proved that the claim made
in the first issue of *The Apostolic Faith* that God "will heal every case" was overdrawn, as
was the expectation that *xenolalia* would solve the language problem in missionary work.
This gift was so minimally actualized as to lead to its demise by the mid-1910s. Wiser
Pentecostal leadership, recurrently concerned about the possibility of self-gratification,
counterfeit claims and spiritualist deception being entertained in their churches, sought
to counter such fears. Seymour, for one, preached that "where a church is very gifted, the
only safeguard from deceptive spirits is by rightly dividing the Word of God, to keep out
fanaticism. . . . God wants everything to be balanced by the Word of God."[19]

Though the term "faith" cannot be avoided in any discussion of healing that looks to
Scripture as its datum, the emphasis placed on it by the Pentecostals quoted here would
appear to be less than its Holiness predecessors urged. They were familiar with the no-
menclature of "faith-cure" and "faith healing" adopted by their predecessors in the final
third of the nineteenth century before "divine healing" became widely accepted. When
Carrie Judd titled her first book *The Prayer of Faith* and her new periodical *Triumphs of
Faith* she was signaling the importance of faith, not least in healing. Reasons for the lesser
stress on the term "faith" can be ascribed to a number of factors. The role of faith in healing came readily to Pentecostals for whom it was an inbuilt requisite. Also, Pentecostals
came with a strengthened certitude about healing in the knowledge that it was but one
of the gifts of the Spirit that were being reinstated, a circumstance vouched for by the
upsurge of tongues, and they one of the lesser gifts. Also, the experience of Spirit-baptism
was a veritable gestalt of blessings that could erupt unpredictably. No better description of
a briskness that left little place or time for the itemization of an *ordo salutis* could be given
than that recounted in the first issue of *The Apostolic Faith*: "In about an hour and a half, a
young man was converted, sanctified, and baptized with the Holy Ghost, and spoke with
tongues. He was also healed from consumption. . . . He has received many tongues, also
the gift of prophecy, and writing in a number of foreign languages, and has a call to the
foreign field."[20] By any standard, this cascade was of breakneck proportion though, as an
experiential succession, it threatened to devalue the realities it claimed.

(iii) While figures like A. B. Simpson and Andrew Murray modified their reluctance to
allow medical intervention, the earliest Pentecostals strongly affirmed the incompatibility
of faith and medicine. As shown above, Parham, besides dropping medicine in all its
forms, gave up his life insurance provision, since to retain it would be inconsistent with
a position of trusting God for life while at the same time making provision for death.
The Apostolic Faith testified that "canes, crutches, medicine bottles, and glasses are being
thrown aside as God heals. That is the safe way. No need to keep an old crutch or medicine

19. *AF*, Jan 1908, 3/col. 1. One "line" discouraged by Seymour because it was not found in Scripture was
the writing of automatic messages in tongues. It smacked too much of Spiritualism.

20. *AF*, Sept 1906, 1, col. 3.

bottle of any kind around after God heals you. Some, in keeping some such appliance as a souvenir, have been tempted to use them again and have lost their healing."[21] Posing the question whether it is wrong to take medicine, Seymour responded: "Medicine is for unbelievers, but the remedy for the saints of God we will find in Jas. 5:14. . . . If Christ's bride, his body, were a mass of disease; it would look as if He had gone out of business and we would have to get the doctors to help him out. But we do not need a doctor to help Christ heal his body."[22] A male sufferer testified to the superiority of divine healing over medical treatment. He had been diagnosed with cancer of the stomach three years previously. After spending over $12,000 on medical care, he was given up by the profession. He linked his healing to his own prayers. When he met with his doctors subsequent to his healing they were astonished because they assumed he had died. They invited him to attend a major medical conference held in his hometown of Los Angeles. "I gave my testimony," he related, " before the assembly of doctors, and the three doctors who had counseled over my case vouched for me and told what condition they found me in, and gave me up to die and how miraculously I had been healed."[23] It was a scenario reminiscent of the woman with the issue of blood who "had spent all that she had" on many physicians (Mark 5:26).

That the two movements, radical Holiness and Pentecostalism, were broadly of a common mind on healing bears out Wacker's view that despite some peculiarities of emphasis and institutional history, the two traditions shared a great deal, especially during the years discussed here: "Both tended to represent God in anthropomorphic terms. Both stressed the infallibility of Scripture, the ready availability of miracles, the healing of the body, the omnipresence of demons, and the imminence of the Lord's return. More basically, the world-views of the two proved to be virtually identical: ahistorical, supernaturalist, primitivist, apocalyptic, biblicist, and pious."[24] What separated them was not the three-blessing idea. That doctrine had been articulated beforehand in radical evangelical circles for several decades. Rather, the determining factor, "the dynamite in the crevice," was Pentecostals' uncompromising insistence on tongues as evidence of the third blessing of Spirit-baptism.

THE QUEST FOR POWER

Various writers have sought to identify the underlying motifs and the centrally organizing beliefs that define Pentecostalism. As implied above, the evidential nature of tongues for Spirit-baptism is too narrow to be representative of the heart of the movement. William Faupel was on stronger grounds in suggesting that the eschatological expectation of the Second Coming was the motivating force behind the rapid growth of Pentecostalism. On the other hand, Peter Althouse places the emphasis elsewhere in postulating that the basic concept that defines the movement is that of "power." These three key convictions,

---

21. Ibid., 2, col. 4.
22. *AF*, Oct-Jan 1908: Feb-March 1907, 6, col. 2.
23. *AF* (Portland), No. 13.
24. Wacker, "Travail of a Broken Family," 26.

of course, hang together. The expected soon return of Christ called for the intense missionary effort that gave rise to the need for the gift of tongues, hence the early acceptance of its xenolaliac mode. The early church was faced with a similar demand to go into all the world. The disciples were forbidden by Christ to move out from Jerusalem "until ye be endued with power from on high." In his departing words they were told they would "receive power, after the Holy Ghost is come upon you" (Luke 24:49; Acts 1:8 KJV). Althouse noted that the early Pentecostals referred to power as much as, and sometimes more than, the doctrine of speaking in tongues: "Once baptized by the Spirit, Pentecostals believed they had received personal power to perform miraculous and non-miraculous feats for God, in imitation of the charismatic Christ. . . . A cosmology of power and empowerment was at play in early Pentecostalism, which created an atmosphere where the Pentecostal utilized a hermeneutic of power to interpret life. The Spirit-led life of the Pentecostal was a quest for power."[25] It was in this area of "power" that Pentecostalism showed its debt to the wider Holiness movement.

Practically all the hymns of the early Pentecostal movement were written by Holiness writers celebrating the second blessing as both a cleansing and an enduement of power. The cry of "Back to Pentecost" found its popular expression in gospel songs and hymns by such Holiness advocates as Charles G. Gabriel in his composition "Pentecostal Power":

> Lord, as of old at Pentecost
> Thou didst Thy power display,
> With cleansing, purifying flame,
> Descend on us today.
>   *Refrain:*
> Lord, send the old-time power, the Pentecostal power!
> Thy flood-gates of blessing on us throw open wide!
> Lord, send the old-time power, the Pentecostal power,
> That sinners be converted and Thy name glorified!

Mrs. C. H. Morris (1862–1929) presented a similar theme in her "Another Pentecost," the first verse of which read:

> We have today the power which they had at Pentecost
> Just the very same power (x2)
> This our heritage in Jesus, e'en the blessed Holy Ghost
> Just the very same power (x2)

The British Pentecostal teacher, Donald Gee (1891–1966) acknowledged that one of the most abiding and beautiful links with the older Holiness movement remained in the special hymns produced by writers such as Mrs C. H. Morris, "whose hymns have been enthusiastically adopted by the Pentecostal Movement all over the world." He pointed to R. A. Torrey, the Higher Life advocate, as among the first to give the teaching of Spirit-baptism "a new, and certainly more scriptural and doctrinally correct, emphasis on the line of 'power from on high,' especially for service and witness (Acts 1: 8)."[26]

---

25. Ibid., 12
26. Gee, *Wind and Flame*, 4.

In the previous chapter W. B. Godbey was alluded to for his witness to the growing acceptance of the healing message inside the American Holiness movement. Within the period c. 1860–90, he recorded that there was a shift from the situation when there was "no light on divine healing" to one when it had become "so common as to be no longer a matter of controversy." Others witnessed to the same fact and its association with divine power. Seth Cook Rees (1854–1933), a leading figure in the radical Holiness movement, gave the title "The Power of the Lord is Present to Heal the Sick" to one chapter in his book *The Ideal Pentecostal Church* (1897). In it, he argued that healing should not be neglected out of a fear of fanaticism: "Let us then help each other's faith. It is much more Christ-like than to break off the heads of the tender shoots of trust in God and his power and willingness to heal."[27] He concluded that the strength of the ideal Pentecostal Church was "the Holy Ghost himself," coming into the church by coming into individual members and so "purifies, electrifies and endues her with power."[28] Another leading figure in the movement, John P. Brooks (1826–1915), in his *Divine Church* (1891) maintained that one of the marks of the true church was the "power of miracle" that was intended to be "a reassertion of the original gifts [and] a permanent investiture."[29]

Pentecostals followed Dowie, more so than the wider Holiness movement, in rooting healing in a more distinctly pneumatological than soteriological/redemptive vein. For them, as Dayton pointed out, healing became "more a manifestation of Pentecostal 'power' and an evidence of 'God also bearing witness with them, both by signs and wonders, and by manifold powers [miracles] and by gifts of the Holy Spirit [Heb. 2:4].'"[30] Armed with the testimony of the evidential sign of tongues, Pentecostals luxuriated in the unlocking of the panoply of charismatic gifts. When Parham was quizzed about his denial that Wesley had received "the Baptism," he responded, "Exactly . . . he may have enjoyed a mighty anointing, [but] the power of this Pentecostal Baptism of the Holy Spirit is a different thing entirely."[31] This statement lent weight to Dieter's contention that while the Holiness constituency generally saw itself as a movement developing within the historic church, "the Pentecostal movement came to regard itself as a *de novo* act of God."[32] For Parham, there had to be a clearance of the present dead churches, a threat he voiced with his hallmark vitriol: "With fire and sword, the masses will utterly destroy the modern churches with vengeance, for they will be permitted of God to punish them for their pride, pomp, deadness, dearth and unfaithfulness."[33]

Some correspondents to *The Apostolic Faith* were so enraptured with their experience of Spirit-baptism that the readiest word they found to describe it was "power." One participant rejoiced: "There is such power in the preaching of the Word in the Spirit that people are shaken on the benches. Coming to the altar, many fall prostrate under the

27. Dayton, *Theological Roots*, 135.

28. Dieter, "Primitivism," 89.

29. Ibid., 86.

30. Dayton *Theological Roots*, 137.

31. Goff, *Fields White Unto Harvest*, 79.

32. Dieter, "Primitivism," 80.

33. Anderson, *Vision of the Disinherited*, 214.

power of God, and often come out speaking in tongues. Sometimes the power falls on people and they are wrought upon by the Spirit during testimony or preaching and receive Bible experiences." One man from Minneapolis used the term four times in three sentences: "The *power* becomes stronger and the Spirit speaks plainer and more mightily. The *power* of God streams through my whole body, (I suppose the healing *power*.) I have fallen on the floor through the mighty *power* coming upon me."[34]

The first Pentecostal assembly in Canada was established by the Yorkshire-born couple, James and Ellen Hebden. It was reported in *The Apostolic Faith* that they "began praying for more power to heal the sick and cast out demons. The Lord said to Mrs. Hebden, 'Tongues, tongues.' She answered, 'No, Lord, not tongues, but power, power.' The Spirit was grieved. Then she replied, 'Anything, Lord, tongues or anything.' Soon after this, the power came upon this yielded woman and she began to speak in an unknown language."[35] Healing was frequently associated with physical excitation. When Garr prayed for a woman she "immediately shouted that she was healed. I felt the healing power flow into her body." One other reader, who sent for an anointed handkerchief, wrote that as soon as she had opened the letter containing one "such power went through my whole being as I have never felt before, and I praise Him, I feel the healing balm just now go through soul and body."

When the healing evangelist, Mattie Crawford, was ministering at Colorado Springs in a home, she found a man lying on his back, shaking violently with his feet thrashing wildly. His wife and other helpers were throwing water over him in an attempt to lower his temperature. "But," in Crawford's telling, "we told them it was the power of God, and they must leave him alone." The onlookers surmised that the man, who had a known heart condition, was dying, but Crawford and those with her kept on singing and holding on in prayer till he came through: "While we were singing, the daughter of this same man arose, came to the altar and fell under the power. The fire spread over the house, God working in a wondrous way. Some said it was the power of God, others said we were hypnotizing the people, and that was what made them fall. The whole country was stirred, and many heard the last-day message of the outpouring of the Holy Spirit to prepare the people for the coming of the Lord."[36] To non-Pentecostals, such a scene was nothing less than a rash escapade that could have gone badly wrong. In this instance, what seemed like a miracle could have been interpreted as a complex psychosomatic response, which happened on this occasion to turn out favorably. By contrast, to Pentecostals it was yet another instance of the mustard seed of faith fulfilling the promise to remove mountains, a confirmation that every promise of Scripture was to be claimed, and sealed by a positive outcome.

Such extracts show that the power repeatedly described was that of a visceral and conspicuous nature, more wind and earthquake than still small voice (1 Kgs 19:12). The first flush of Pentecostalism revealed its penchant for a *theologia gloriae*, and its failure to

34. *AF*, December 1906, 4, col. 1.

35. *AF*, January 1907, 4, col. 4. The couple, after an abortive missionary visit to Jamaica, arrived in Toronto in late 1904. In May 1906 they opened the East End Mission work. The three-storey building was intended at first for use as a healing home.

36. Crawford, Mattie. *On Mule Back*, 28–29.

envision a *theologia crucis*. Parham's contention that "we can walk through this world of disease and be immune . . . without it touching you" makes the point.[37] E. W. Kenyon in his first book *The Father and His Family* (1916) pronounced: "You have as much right to demand healing as you have to demand the cashing of a check at a bank where you have a deposit."[38] Given such conviction about healing for the faith-dependent sufferers, blame for the persistence of their illnesses must lie with them. Lillian Yeomans, drawing on her experience as a physician who had witnessed patients refusing prescribed medication, wrote: "If we are not healed, we must look to the cause in ourselves. It must be that we have not taken [God's Word] according to instructions."[39]

Many of the radical healers of the nineteenth century had drawn a similar conclusion, though most came to temper it once reality checked in. Wacker recognized that the propensity to blame the victim was implicit in the work of Simpson and other nineteenth-century writers, but it remained for Pentecostals to make it painfully explicit: "For better or worse, the blame-the-victim theory of illness soon became a hallmark of the Pentecostal understanding of the human condition."[40] Tom Smail, writing at the end of the twentieth century, warned fellow charismatics that "we can easily come to see ourselves as living in a world of supernatural power that leads us from triumph to triumph where the weak, desolate sufferer of Calvary has ceased to dominate the scene."[41]

Martin Percy is more scathing in sensing in much charismaticism "a capacity for self-validation by internal reference from one dogma to another." Such self-validation can give rise to what he called "power knowledge," a created discourse that can speak of the world and the experiences of individuals, yet without really being connected to reality. "[Thus,] sin, liberalism, demons and malign spirits are blamed for failures and for the insanity of the world, whilst the Spirit accounts for the wisdom of the believers. In this scheme it is not difficult to understand how a complete world-view that expresses so much madness is in fact seen as sanity to those who are 'in the know'; nothing can break this circle, not even reality."[42]

Though Donald Gee, who earned the sobriquet "apostle of balance," did not address this particular criticism, he, nevertheless, made a case for the necessity of a certain form of extremism. Though he acknowledged that truth is not to be found in extremes, he also contended that "we desperately need to recognize that revivals are never launched without someone going to an extreme. . . . There HAS to be an extremism to move things. . . . Miracles of healing occur when faith refuses to be logical, and blinds itself to arguments based on plenty of contrary experience, and more 'balanced' teaching." His own view was that "we need extremism for a miracle of healing, but we need balanced sanity for health. We need extreme fervor to launch a movement, but we need the repudiation of extremes to save it from self-destruction. It takes Pentecostal genius to know when and where an

---

37. Parham, *Divine Health*. 10.

38. Simmons, *Kenyon*, 275, n. 188.

39. Yeomans, *Healing Treasury*, 332.

40. Wacker, Grant. "The Pentecostal Tradition," 522.

41. Smail, "The Cross and the Spirit," 57.

42. Percy, *Words*, 70 & 151.

extreme doctrine or practice must be modified to a more balanced view and where, on the other hand, the broad lines of truth must be temporarily narrowed into an extreme emphasis upon one point to ensure a dynamic powerful enough to move things for God."[43] His own views on divine healing and those others of like mind, arguably exemplars of "Pentecostal genius," will be dealt with in a subsequent chapter.

THE LONGER ENDING OF MARK

Another pointer to understanding the Pentecostal experience was the weight placed on the longer ending of Mark 16:9–20, most particularly vv. 17–18 with their reference to exorcism, *glossolalia*, serpent handling, poison-drinking and "the laying of hands on sick people, and they will get well" (NIV). Kimberley Alexander in her work on Pentecostal healing was surprised at the preponderant usage of this text, in contrast to its almost complete absence from the nineteenth-century healing movement's biblical lexicon. She found in the Scripture index of *The Church of God Evangel* (1910–19) that twenty-six references to Matt 28:18–20, sixteen references to Acts 1:8, and seventy-five to Mark 16:9–20 were listed. A similar comparison of those texts cited in *The Apostolic Faith* from September 1906–May 1908 reveals that there were three references to the Matthew text, five to the Acts text, and twenty references to the Markan text.[44] One potent reason for the downplaying of the Markan passage in pre-Pentecostal literature was the almost complete, contemporary absence of the phenomena listed in the passage to substantiate them at the time. Even the knowledgeable Holiness commentator, W. B. Godbey, had not considered the text because of the questions surrounding its canonical status. Despite such a doubt, the two verses within the disputed ending with their promise of signs that followed "those who believe" became a prime proof text for what Pentecostals considered was a new and powerful work of God. The Pentecostal missionary and pastor, John G. Lake, was adamant that the signs specified in Mark 16:14–18 were "God's eternal trademark, issued by the Son of God, and sealed in His own blood."[45]

Pentecostal writers were aware of the controversy about the ending of Mark's Gospel but viewed the reliability of the text through the lens of their personal experience.[46] Excerpts from *The Latter Rain Evangel* give some indication of the weight given to the Mark 16 passage. Alma Doering, a Mennonite missionary with Holiness sympathies,

43. Gee, Donald. "Extremes are Sometimes Necessary," 9. He drew attention to incidents in the NT that raised the charge of insanity. In Mark 3:21, Christ's own kinsmen thought he had gone mad. In Acts 2 the disciples gave an impression of drunken men. Paul protested to Festus that he was not insane, and sought to convince the Corinthian church that "if we are out of our mind, it is for the sake of God" (2 Cor 5:13).

44. Alexander, "'And the Signs Are Following,'" 150.

45. Savige, "King James Bible Only Position." Online.

46. Some scholarly types in the movement took an interest in the earliest codices of the New Testament. Arthur Frodsham saw it as hugely significant that in 1906 the Azusa Street event coincided with the purchase in Egypt of the *Washington Codex (Codex W, Freer Gospels)*, by C. L. Freer, who donated it to the University of Michigan. He savored the fact that the codex is "one of the earliest known, and free from later corrections, and it contains the last twelve verses in Mark 16. It was discovered at the very time it was needed." He took the fanciful view that God had kept the manuscripts hidden throughout the intervening centuries to authenticate the arrival of the Pentecostal movement (Frodsham, "The Sixteenth Chapter of Mark," 9).

wrote in 1914 from Berlin of a failed attempt to poison a fellow missionary Walter Herr in the Congo. His recovery was attributed to "prayer-burdens in the homeland", adding that "this is not the first healing from poisoning, according to Mark 16:18, I might record."[47] When R. A. Torrey was asked in the hearing of a Pentecostal pastor why, if the Bible was inspired, "didn't we see Mark 16: 17 fulfilled today," he replied: "God is doing it today. I could stand here for hours and tell you of the healings I have witnessed as a result of the operation of the power of God, and we have speaking in tongues today."[48]

J. M. Perkins, a retired Pentecostal missionary to Liberia, recalled the help he received from a young African after the death of his wife. The young man, named Jasper Toe, soon after he began to preach, was frequently called upon to pray for the sick. Once, when requested to pray for a woman given up to die, he with a few others went into her room. After singing a hymn and reading Mark 16:17, he said, "I cannot do anything myself but God will honor His word." While praying for the woman, he "received a mighty baptism and spoke in another language." In the morning, the woman informed him in her broken English, "My sick leave me night-time. In the morning I got up and throw away my cane and walk about myself where I like."[49] The redoubtable English missionary, W. T. P. Burton, wrote in a letter penned en route by ship to South Africa that he had a long talk with "a dear old P. B. [Plymouth Brother] on the Lord for the body." Such were his powers of persuasion that before the end of the day the brother "had received and was preaching Mark 16:15–18 and James 5:14"—a feat of some rarity.

One of the longer accounts of missionary work was the script of a talk given in the Stone Church in October 1915 by William Wallace Simpson (1869–1961), a pioneer missionary to China. Simpson, after his training at A. B. Simpson's Missionary Training Institute, set out for China in 1892 in the company of other Christian and Missionary Alliance (CMA) colleagues. Encouraged and instructed by the legendary J. Hudson Taylor, he and a companion headed for Tibet, considered by some in missionary circles to be the "uttermost" part of the earth. On his return to America in 1899, he reported to colleagues that he felt himself to be a failure as a missionary because, in his own words, "I couldn't point to a single case in which the Lord had worked with me and confirmed the Word with signs following." Disheartened, he remarked: "Now some people want to cut out the last part of Mark 16. There was a time when it would have pleased me very much if it could have been proved beyond the shadow of a doubt that this didn't belong to the original Gospel of Mark." He traced his sense of failure to the response the Chinese and Tibetans made to their reading of biblical miracles. They would say, "Your book is all right but you do not live up to it." They held in regard the teachers of the Confucian classics and the Koran, because for them "the book is the book, and the man is the man," whereas for Christians "Your book is all right, but you lay it aside. . . . There is a great difference between the man and the book."[50]

---

47. *LRE*, January 1914, 2.

48. *LRE*, July 1918, 17.

49. *LRE*, April 1919, 13.

50. *LRE*, November 1915, 2.

After his return to China, he learned in 1908 of the Pentecostal revival through the pages of the periodical *A Cloud of Witnesses to Pentecost in India*. His reading convinced him of the reason for his sense of failure: "It was simply this: I had not received the baptism in the Holy Spirit." It was another four years before he received Spirit-baptism at a missionary convention in China. In 1915, on his return home he was forced to resign from the CMA, subsequently to join the Assemblies of God. He told his hearers at the Stone Church: "Since the evening of May 5, 1912, the sixteenth [verse] of Mark has been realized in my life and in my service as a missionary in China. . . . From the time I received this baptism, May, 1912, until the end of June, 1915 . . . I have preached in at least twenty places in China, ten places in the province of Kansu on the border of Tibet, and ten places in four other provinces in China, and every place the Lord has worked with me and confirmed His Word with signs following."[51]

SERPENT HANDLING IN APPALACHIA

George Went Hensley (c. 1880–1955) is generally credited with popularizing the practice of snake handling. A native of rural Appalachia, he experienced conversion around 1908. Almost immediately, he traveled through the southeastern states, preaching a strict Holiness-Pentecostalism. He grew concerned that not all the signs itemized in Mark 16:17–18 were being practiced. Tongues and healing were clearly evident but the taking up of serpents was quietly ignored. He had a fascination with snake handling that went back to his boyhood when the phenomenon commonly featured in revivals that broke out periodically in the 1890s in coal mining camps in West Virginia. Both snake and fire handling were restricted to the backward and culturally isolated regions of Appalachia and the Ozarks, places where such customs were sanctioned by time-honored folkways.[52] It was in this setting that Hensley first witnessed serpent handling almost twenty years before he was to pick up his first serpent at White Oak Mountain in Tennessee.

The person who influenced him greatly in his youth was the prophetess Nancy Kleinleck, who built a reputation for her handling of rattlesnakes and copperheads as she practiced and preached "the signs of Mark 16."[53] When Hensley handled his first serpent nineteen years later, it was the memory of Kleinleck that kindled his drive to obey Mark 16.[54] Emboldened by the certainty that the fivefold signs in the passage were in fact commands that believers must obey, he felt his eternal security rested on obedience to them, not least the taking up of serpents. In an interview given in later life, he recounted the story of his climbing White Oak Mountain to pray for a resolution to his spiritual struggle at the time. The story continued: "In a great rocky gap in the mountainside he found what he sought, a large rattlesnake. He approached the reptile and, disregarding its buzzing, blood-chilling warning, knelt a few feet away from it and prayed loudly into the sky for God to remove his fear and to anoint him with 'the power.' Then suddenly with a shout

51. Ibid., 4.

52. Anderson, *Vision of the Disinherited*, 93.

53. Morrow, *Handling Serpents*, 4.

54. Hood, *Them That Believe*, 43.

he leaped forward and grasped the reptile and held it in trembling hands."[55] Energized by the experience, he launched into his first evangelistic effort in his own community of Grasshopper Valley, proclaiming that believers should obey all that Jesus had commanded, including the handling of serpents.

By 1914 Hensley had attracted the attention of leaders in the Church of God through his evangelistic efforts that took him to a number of its churches. One notable revival erupted in the South Cleveland Church of God tabernacle, during which snake handling took place. By that time General Overseer, A. J. Tomlinson had returned to Cleveland from his church travels in time to witness the revival. Impressed by what he saw, Tomlinson wrote favorable editorials in the denominational *Evangel*. Besides reports of divine healing in the periodical, there was one article about scoffers who, in response to Hensley's preaching, had brought a rattlesnake and copperheads to the services to challenge the faith of the snake handlers in the expectation of unmasking them. As none of the handlers was harmed, many unbelievers were convinced enough to seek salvation. Tomlinson, too, was persuaded that serpent handling should be considered as one of the attested Pentecostal signs, provided it was given neither undue emphasis nor pushed to extreme limits. Another pressure on him was the in-house concern being voiced about the stuttering growth of the denomination.

The events at the South Cleveland revival soon persuaded the leadership of the Church of God that the literal taking up of venomous serpents was as much a legitimate a Pentecostal sign as speaking in tongues, exorcism, and healing. For them, there was no good theological reason why serpent handing should be distinguished from the other gift-signs. The KJV rendering of Mark 16:17 ("These signs *shall* follow them that believe") was read as a literal authoritative command that had the effect of making serpent handling mandatory. To believe otherwise was to be "in the house of some selfish opinion."[56] The licensing of Hensley as a minister of the Church of God in 1915 attested to the widespread, if not complete, acceptance of the doctrine within the Church of God.

Reports of serpent handling in the *Evangel* died out completely only after 1935, with most appearing in 1921 when thirteen were printed. Tennessee, Alabama and North Carolina, in that order, were the top three states as the source of published accounts. Of the 105 persons named in the reports, fifty-eight were either licensed or future ministers of the denomination. Seven of the ministers became State Overseers, of which Tomlinson was one. However, Tomlinson's days with the Church of God were to come to a tarnished end. His autocratic ways, and the charge against him of mishandling church funds led to his departure in 1923, and the founding of yet another sect.

Hensley's departure was even more offbeat. He resigned his ministerial credentials in 1922 for unstated family reasons, and proceeded to lapse into his pre-conversion ways. He separated from his wife Amanda in 1922, reportedly after an incident in which he was involved in a drunken brawl with a neighbor. This was followed by imprisonment in 1923 for moonshining. His second marriage produced five children, and proved acrimonious,

55. Ibid., 43.
56. Ibid., 62.

impaired by frequent unemployment and the mistreatment of his wife. The couple were divorced in 1943. The following year he married a widow with ten children, soon followed by divorce and remarriage to a fourth wife. The frequent absences from his first three households marked the periods when he engaged in recurrent evangelistic work that only added to the families' sense of abandonment. He died, like many of his supporters, from a rattlesnake bite, the last of 400 he had subjected himself to during his seventy-five years of life.

From the late 1920s onwards, the Church of God gradually shifted its position on serpent handling as injuries and deaths increased. This led to those who supported the ritual being marginalized, and ultimately forming independent sects. No other major Pentecostal body other than Tomlinson's much smaller splinter sect, the Church of God of Prophecy, took up the practice. With growing social acceptance and swelling membership, the Church of God (Cleveland) played down snake handing, exorcism, and more ecstatic forms of worship that began to lose their appeal and were seen as a hindrance to numerical growth. Articles critical of serpent handling bred an increasing sense of animus towards the practice. The writer of one such article bemoaned the situation in which

> many have gone into rank fanaticism, and false teaching, bringing reproach on the Church and disgust to intelligent people over the handling of serpents. . . . When it comes to using the Church of God as a medium to advertise snake shows it is absurd and ridiculous. I have seen a few of these displays undertaken in the spirit of boasting men, and when bitten by the poisonous reptiles, severe sickness and sometimes death has resulted. And again it has caused much suffering to the victims, and many times [it] has taken much prayer to save life, then we are made a laughing stock to the world and a reproach for the cause.

Other denominations opposed the practice, none more strongly than E. N. Bell, a leading figure in the AoG, who commented that Mark 16:18 "does not mean that we are to become snake chasers, nor that we should wilfully and knowingly take up poisonous snakes." He cited the episode when Jesus was tempted to jump from the pinnacle of the temple with the promise that "angels *shall* bear thee up in their hands." In the same way, he argued, as it was not God's will to test his own promises, so "it is not His will for us purposely to pick up venomous snakes, to try thereby to work a miracle to convince unbelievers."[57] The serpent-handling sign is apposite only "when in the path of duty a child of God accidentally is bitten by a snake," as Paul was in Malta. In that situation, "God promises it shall not hurt him, if he by faith lays hold of this promise to true believers."[58]

The snake-handling tradition, however, has yet to be eradicated despite legal restriction. It still remains as a live option in a few dissident sects in Appalachia.[59] A report in

57. Ibid., 72.

58. Bell, "Questions and Answers," 5.

59. Although most Appalachian states have outlawed snake handling, it remains legal though rare in West Virginia. Even so, it was reported in 2013 that the young pastor of a church at La Follette, TN, is "part of a new generation of serpent-handling Christians who are revitalizing a century-old faith tradition in Tennessee. These younger believers welcome visitors and use Facebook to promote their often misunderstood—and illegal—version of Christianity. They want to show the beauty and power of their extreme form of spirituality. And they hope eventually to reverse a state ban on handling snakes in church" (*Washington*

the *Huffington Post* showed a photograph of forty-four-year-old Pastor Mark Wolford who died after a rattlesnake bit him on the thigh during an outdoor service in May 2012. His father passed away in similar circumstances some thirty years earlier. Unlike many other preachers in this tradition, the son embraced publicity, welcoming journalists and photographers, even taking some on snake hunts as he tried to revive interest in his particular faith. It was also alleged that he had on occasion ingested poisons, such as strychnine. Ralph Hood, Professor of Psychology at the University of Tennessee, whose major book on the topic has been cited here, knew him well, and had witnessed him being bitten by a copperhead about six years previously. His analysis of Wolford's death was in line with his book *Them That Believe*. Hood maintained his friend would want people to remember him as "a Christian who was living his beliefs and being obedient. . . . Serpent handling was only a small part of that. He was trying to revitalize a strong tradition that doesn't make a distinction between beliefs and practices. A common misunderstanding is that handlers believe they can't get bit, or it won't kill them. What they'll tell you is, 'No one will get out of this alive.' They'll also tell you it's not a question of how you live; it's a question of how you die. This is how he would have wanted to die."[60]

Snake-handling in Appalachia

For Wolford's family, his death was accepted as something that he knew was coming and something that was ultimately God's will. "His faith is what took him home," said his sister. For them, his death was an affirmation of the "Signs Following" tradition. Theirs was nothing more than an explanation carried to an extreme limit that underpinned Pentecostalism from its beginning, and explains much of its rationale. A doctrine or custom is not recognized as authoritative unless it can be traced back to its primal source, the biblical record of the Lord and His apostles.[61] But then, as David Ford commented, those who "take the Bible as a set of propositions, that can be grasped without attending to their literary forms and contexts, are likely to think and write theology very differently from those who do not."[62]

In the backwoods of Appalachia scholarly sensitivity was at a premium. The subtleties of scholarship, occupied with such abstractions as genre, context, and socio-rhetorical criticism, were not for Appalachian backwoodsman. Literalism was and remains their stock hermeneutic. Theirs was, and is, "an interpretive community," a concept that stems

Post, January 16, 2013. Online: http://www.washingtonpost.com/national/on-faith).

60. Smith, "Pastor Mark Wolford." Online.

61. Anderson, *Vision of the Disinherited*, 92.

62. Ford, *Future of Christian Theology*, 202.

from *reader-response theory* identified with Stanley Fish (b. 1938), American literary critic. His theory propounds that any text does not have meaning outside of a set of cultural assumptions brought to it by the reader. Meaning is not something interpreted from the text; it is an event that happens between the words and the reader's mind. In short, "interpretation is the art of constructing, and not the art of construing."[63] Fish claims that we all are part of an interpretive community that shares in reading texts in a particular way. Because we cannot escape our interpretive community, we can never really know its limits. Clearly, serpent handlers and Barthians belong to different interpretive communities. If, as Fish holds, the question "What does this text *mean*" should be replaced by "What does this text *do*," then the issue can become acutely important. Two imagined scenarios make the point. A mature Pentecostal academic theologian receives kudos for her ground-breaking thesis on the Markan ending. In the other, a young Appalachian pastor dies an agonizing death from serpent venom in the belief that he was living out the same passage.

THE FINISHED WORK CONTROVERSY AND HEALING

Early Pentecostalism was a high-energy religion, quite unsettled and unsettling. Jacobsen described it as a movement that "was never united enough to fragment."[64] Wilson's *aperçu* still holds that in Pentecostalism "every generation is the first generation," to which can be added: "By almost any standard, Pentecostalism presently is not what Charles Fox Parham or any of his successors has pronounced it to be, but rather what contemporary Brazilians, Koreans, and Africans demonstrate that it actually is."[65] The various schisms that emerged reflected the process of defining and systematizing practices and beliefs as the movement grew. The difficulty in finding cohesion lay in part in the fact that participants came into the Pentecostal experience from diverse denominational traditions that carried a legacy of theological contention among them. It grew from the confluence of diverse theological currents awash in the transatlantic world toward the close of the nineteenth century, such as the differing Wesleyan-Holiness and Keswick/Higher Life positions on sanctification, premillennialism, divine healing, and restorationist ideas on reclaiming the power and authority of the primitive church. It was never going to be straightforward to blend these five elements with the new doctrine of tongues-evidenced Spirit-baptism into a coherent whole, acceptable to all. Bartleman was not the first to admit that matters of doctrine proved to be "a great battle. Many were too dogmatic at Azusa."[66] When he returned to Los Angeles after the split between Seymour and Parham, he found that many of the new missions that had sprouted from his previous visit "had fought each other almost to a standstill. . . . A cold, hard-hearted zeal, and human enthusiasm, had taken the place of divine love."[67]

63. Macy, *Dictionary of Critical Theory*, 130.
64. Jacobsen, *Thinking in the Spirit*, 134.
65. Bergunder, "Constructing Pentecostalism," 67.
66. Bartleman, *Azusa Street*, 101.
67. Ibid., 143.

The period 1910–18 produced a number of conflicts within the new Pentecostal movement that led to the emergence of three distinct theological streams:

1. Wesleyan-Holiness Pentecostalism stressed the need for three separate and distinct spiritual experiences that featured in the normative path to spiritual maturity, viz., conversion, sanctification, and tongues-evidenced Spirit-baptism.

2. Finished Work Pentecostalism held that full salvation involved only two distinct experiences, regeneration, which incorporated growth in personal holiness, and tongues-evidenced Spirit-baptism.

3. Jesus-only, or Oneness, Pentecostalism developed from a dispute over the proper formula used in water baptism that rejected the Trinitarian understanding of the Godhead. Their modalist doctrine (one God in the three modes of presentation as Father, Son, and Spirit) treats the three persons of the Trinity as different manifestations of the one God. Oneness doctrine preserves the formula of baptizing in the name of Jesus alone. The relevant texts are Acts 2:38, 8:16, and 10:48, in which baptism is in the name of Jesus, *contra* Matt 28:19.

Doctrinal differences were not the only cause of disunity. Racial tensions and social/cultural divisions, in some cases regionally located, also played a sizeable part.

It was the growing conflict between the first two groups above that are of interest in this study because the positions they took had a bearing on their understanding and practice of healing. So argues Kimberly Ervin Alexander in her doctoral thesis, published under the title *Pentecostal Healing: Models in Theology and Practice* (2006). To understand her argument, which is fresh and exploratory, it is essential to have a grasp of the broader theological issues at stake.

Up to 1910 the majority of American Pentecostals adhered to the three-stage doctrine. Pristine Pentecostalism is better considered as a renewal than a revival movement, as those who entered the Pentecostal experience were seasoned adherents, drawn largely from a Wesleyan Holiness background. They were burdened by a sense that something was missing in their spiritual journey.

Parham is representative of those Wesleyans who made the transition from the two to three stage models with the arrival of Pentecostal. The initial two-stage model followed John Wesley's understanding of salvation with its emphasis on the "two grand branches" of justification and sanctification. Sanctification is characterized in Charles Wesley's hymn as the freedom "from actual and from inbred sin" that washes out the "deep original stain." Holiness radicals believed this entailed a distinct experience subsequent to justification. This second experience was frequently equated with Spirit-baptism, though without a distinctive, confirming manifestation.

As described earlier, Parham, post-1900, initiated the teaching of a third-stage crisis of Spirit-baptism with tongues as its evidential sign. The second stage could not be dropped because "a clean heart" was regarded as a prerequisite for Spirit-baptism. While the second stage was for radical cleansing, the third was an empowering experience for service and witness, as well as a prelude to wider charismatic gifting. This teaching was common to all the earliest Pentecostal groups—the Church of God in Christ, the Church of God, and the Pentecostal Holiness Church, all rooted in the Holiness revivalism of the previous century. Most were largely confined to the south-eastern states. Both the Azusa Street mission and the Apostolic Faith centres, under the leadership of Parham and Florence Crawford respectively, were also of this stamp.

As the decade progressed, however, increasing numbers of Pentecostals came from a non-Wesleyan background that was shaped by the teaching found in Keswick and Reformed circles. While some went along with the eradicationist, second work teaching, the majority rejected it. The Chicago area became the leading center from which this non-Wesleyan Pentecostalism expanded, during the Pentecostal ministries of William Hammer Piper (1868–1911) at the Stone Church, and William H. Durham (1873–1912) at the North Avenue Mission. Pentecostalism in Chicago had a different feel about it compared to the seminal days of Azusa Street. Creech highlighted the differences: "In terms of ethos, prominent Chicago Pentecostals of Anglo or old-stock descent displayed a lower-middle/middle-class urban sensibility consistent with their CMA, Dowie, and evangelical backgrounds."[68]

The first definitive work of Pentecostal theology had its origin in a course of lectures given at the Stone Church by David W. Myland (1858–1943), and published under the title *Latter Rain Covenant* (1910). Chicago soon became a major center for the global dissemination of the Pentecostal message through its periodicals, and its location as a transport hub at the center of the country. Piper's *The Latter Rain Evangel* and Durham's *The Pentecostal Testimony*, combined with tracts, pamphlets and books emanating from their churches, gave the city a prominence greater than that of Los Angeles in the promulgation of the Pentecostal cause in the course of the second decade. Because of its hub position most people traveling across America changed trains in Chicago. This allowed the churches to host conventions and entertain missionaries on their way to foreign lands.

William Durham

In contrast to Parham's OAFM [Old Apostolic Faith Movement] leadership, Chicago's Pentecostal leaders were generally positive about education, less given to voicing racist remarks, and more engaged in socially benevolent activity. Moreover, Durham's church demonstrated a good deal of ethnic diversity. Such contrasts help to explain why Parham sensed a threat to his own claim as "Projector" of the movement, and why he accused Piper of being influenced by a "spiritualistic medium" in his congregation. However, it was Durham who became his *bête noire*. It was at a convention in Chicago in 1910 that Durham first publicly began preaching the Reformed view on sanctification that became known as the "Finished Work" doctrine, which found no place for a distinct second work of sanctification. Instead, he argued that when one lays claim

68. Creech, "Visions of Glory," 416.

to the benefits of the cross at conversion one appropriates also sanctification. In this he was following such verses as Rom 6:6, which assure believers that the "old self *was* crucified with [Christ] so that the body of sin might be rendered powerless, that we should no longer be slaves to sin." In union with Christ and through the power of the Spirit, the obedient Christian is enabled to grow in greater conformity to the Christ-like life. In effect, Durham reduced the three-stage Pentecostal position to two-stage Pentecostalism by combining justification and sanctification into a unified whole, and at the same time maintaining Spirit-baptism as a second and subsequent experience of empowerment.

That the differences between the two viewpoints were far from trivial is illustrated in the reaction to Durham when he introduced the concept of the Finished Work in 1910. When he brought this message to Los Angeles in 1910, he was in a combative frame of mind, prepared to hail the doctrine as "by far the most important teaching in the Bible. . . . We knew it would mean the loss of friendship with all who did not see it."[69] To bring the message to Azusa Street was deliberately provocative, knowing that the three-stage position was a lynchpin doctrine. It was an ironic twist when Seymour locked out Durham, a replay of the treatment Seymour had received five years earlier at other hands. About two-thirds of Seymour's flock left and were presented with a choice of twelve or so other Pentecostal mission churches where the Finished Work doctrine was preached. J. H. King, the founder and first bishop of the [Wesleyan] Pentecostal Holiness Church, dubbed Durham's doctrine "Satan's big gun."[70]

No less threatening was the assault on Durham by an incensed woman who lunged at him with her hat pin while he was preaching, an assault that morphed subsequently into her eventual acceptance of the doctrine she had shunned. As for Parham, he declared that the teaching only afforded a refuge for "back-slidden, unsanctified experiences [that stirred up] a fleshly animalism, similar to the working up of the power in the old-fashioned Negro camp-meeting."[71] Conceding that both interpretations could not be right, he prayed for God to demonstrate the truth through the death of either Durham or himself, whichever one was in error. Unfortunately, Durham died six months later. Weakened by tuberculosis, he had caught a head-cold in Chicago that developed into pneumonia and other complications. Parham tasted the sweet flavor of vindication.

Durham had been similarly denunciatory of three-stage adherents: "They take it for granted that they are perfect, neglect to continually seek for a fuller knowledge of God . . . become confirmed babies or spiritual dwarfs, yet all the time claiming . . . to be in a state of grace unknown to many. Every church and Holiness movement needs a radical purging of these things. The Pentecostal movement will have to be purged from them, before it will be the burning and shining light in the world."[72] So strongly did he feel about the issue that his stand on the Finished Work principle, and not Spirit-baptism, became the central focus of his theology. That the rift rumbled on into the post-World War II years comes out in the reminiscences of Vinson Synan (b. 1934), distinguished Pentecostal scholar, who

69. Craig, *William Seymour*, 214.
70. Clayton, "Significance of Durham," 32.
71. Parham, *Everlasting Gospel*, 118–19.
72. Jacobsen, *Thinking in the Spirit*, 152.

was reared in the Wesleyan Holiness tradition. He recalled that as a youth "sermons bristled with denunciations of such perceived false teachings as 'Finished Work,' 'Russellism,' [Jehovah Witness] and 'Jesus Only.'" The gist he picked up was that the Finished Work people "had abandoned sanctification as a second blessing and were too worldly."[73]

When Alexander Boddy addressed the congregation at Durham's Stone Church in September 1912, he described the effect of the controversy he had seen in his recent visit to California: "I found the Pentecostal people in Los Angeles were just about tired of shaking fists at one another, and beginning to want to shake hands instead; they were getting very much disgusted at all this division and wondered how it had ever come about." Whilst there, he had drafted a resolution that was fully endorsed by the large congregation. It contained the pledge, "Recognizing the great need of unity in the Body of the Lord . . . we by the help and grace of our Lord do undertake individually and collectively to refrain from condemning one another on the matter of the question known . . . as the 'Finished Work OF CHRIST.'"[74] He submitted the same resolution to all the centers he visited.

THE ALEXANDER THESIS

Kimberly Alexander in her *Pentecostal Healing* contends that the doctrinal differences between the Wesleyan Pentecostal and the Reformed Pentecostal/ Finished Work streams played a significant part in the theology and practice of divine healing during the period 1906–23, sufficient to furnish two distinct models of Pentecostal healing. The work is exploratory in that its thesis opens new ground, thus adding to the list of ways that reveal the anything-but monolithic nature of early Pentecostalism. It draws extensively from the Pentecostal periodical literature published during first seventeen years of the movement. Her own roots are in the Pentecostal Holiness Church and the Church of God (Cleveland, Tennessee), placing her within three-stage Wesleyan Pentecostal tradition. In his review of the book, Vinson Synan was somewhat hasty to describe her treatment of Finished Work views as "fair and balanced," and as a book of theology and history "there are very few questions about her research and conclusions."[75]

On the Reformed Pentecostal side, Frank Macchia recognizes that "Alexander is convinced the healing doctrine which convinced Pentecostalism sits firmly within a Wesleyan soteriology." He insisted that he had no intention in his "quarrel" with the book to take anything away from its excellence or the validity of the models, but "only to give some indication of the exciting debate that her book is sure to inspire."[76] Synan reckoned the thesis could open up "new avenues of debate and research." Five years on, there is little evidence of such debate. Could it be that any remaining tensions between the two parties would at this stage exhibit, in Freud's phrase, the "narcissism of minor differences."[77]

73. Synan, *Eyewitness Remembers*, 28 & 33.

74. *LRE*, October, 1912, 6.

75. Synan, "Pentecostal Healing," 347.

76. Macchia, "Pentecostal Healing," 145–46.

77. Vinson Synan was instrumental in the founding in 1970 of the Society for Pentecostal Studies which publishes *Pneuma*. It attracts scholars from all quarters who have an involvement or interest in Pneumatology.

After all, both sides concurred on the same basic lineaments of the healing doctrine—the centrality of the atonement, the place of faith and a wariness of medical intervention. The differences lie in the detail of their understanding of these strands. Also, there has been a softening of positions over the years, notably towards doctors and medicines, crudely dismissed by Dowie respectively as "butchers" and "poisons." The AOG theologian Stanley Horton expressed his opinion that the AOG leaders and scholars "are now able to talk more freely and cordially with those of Pentecostal Holiness persuasion."[78]

The essence of Alexander's argument, expanded in the following paragraphs, is that the early proponents of the Finished Work position contextualized the efficacy of healing within the atoning work of the cross, while Wesleyan Pentecostalism set it in a more sweeping framework. In essence, the first tied healing back to the cross, the other saw healing as a foreshadowing of the future restitution of all things. The grounds for the distinction can be traced back to their view of the Trinity. For Wesleyan Pentecostals, the love that binds in mutuality the Triune Godhead is shared with the whole created order. The perfect scenario is primal Eden where Adam communes with the Creator in the cool of the day, an evocative picture of wholeness and *shalom*. The Fall, by perverting creation, introduced the spiritual and physical ills that have subjected the creation to frustration and judgment. That humanity could be restored is implied in the promise that Satan would be defeated by Christ, "the seed of the woman." The atoning work of Jesus was the divine answer to the spoliation wrought by the Fall, reversing its effects not only of sin but also its concomitant of suffering.

In contrast, Alexander posits the view that in Finished Work soteriology the roles of the Triune Godhead "were less intimate and more juridical. The Father had passed a sentence of judgment and death upon humanity because of the sin of Adam. Therefore, the role of the Father was more accurately described as Judge."[79] In the Genesis account of the Fall, the focus falls on human guilt and condemnation, with humanity subjected to the penalty of sin, and the collateral damage of disease and death. The remedy could only be found in a judicial act which would reverse the sentence by the atoning death of Christ. This decisive act was complete, final and eternal in its effect, so decisive as to push its soteriological expression towards "an extreme Christocentrism."[80] Neither the life of Jesus nor his resurrection had any apparent salvific effect. It was primarily a judicial or forensic view of atonement, the merit of which was made available to humanity in justification, sanctification and healing—all on the same ground of the cross. Though Durham said little about healing in relation to his Finished Work position, others in the Reformed tradition made the claim that healing, like salvation, was won for all in the atonement. Salvation and healing were effected on the same grounds of promise and gift. One simply reckoned it done, thereby resisting illness by denying the symptoms: "Just as one reckoned that their salvation was accomplished on the cross, so one looked back to the cross and reckoned his/her healing accomplished."[81] As a confirmation or proof of

---

78. Dieter, *Five Views on Sanctification*, 52.

79. Alexander, *Pentecostal Healing*, 210.

80. Ibid., 210.

81. Ibid., 212.

the completed work, healing was to be anticipated when prayer was offered for the sick. Therefore, to wait for assurance of healing before testifying to it denoted a lack of belief.

Wesleyan Pentecostals discerned in the Incarnation the beginning of what Irenaeus (c. 185) called the recapitulation of humanity, whereby all that was lost in the Fall will be regained. The recapitulation is seen in the Spirit's work in ushering in the Kingdom, at times with demonstrable inbreakings of power through a sign such as healing. Each healing is an anticipatory witness to the final resurrection: "Just as speaking in tongues was thought to signify that the immanent-transcendent God had filled the human vessel, the healing of the sick signified that the Spirit of Life had broken into the cursed and fallen world. Restoration to health, while still wrapped in mortality, was viewed as a quickening of the mortal body, and a foretaste of the life in the age to come."[82] This vision in bringing a more generous dimension to the ministry of the Spirit is a feature that Alexander found missing in Finished Work periodicals. On the other hand, she found in Wesleyan Pentecostalism literature "a rediscovery of the ancient understanding of salvation as a healing from sickness, of which the atonement is but only one component along with incarnation, resurrection, Pentecost, and the future new creation."[83] On the Reformed side, signs of the Spirit's activity were interpreted as manifestations of a work already completed, whether speaking in tongues, healing or exorcism. All such signs bore witness to the completion of the redemptive work of the cross.

Wesleyan Pentecostals understood grace in the more Eastern Christian sense of divine power working in the earth, the church and in believers up to the time when they are removed from the very presence of sin. Salvation thus becomes an all-inclusive term that covers the journey of faith from conversion to glorification. In holding such a progressive view of the Christian life, Wesleyan-Pentecostal lifestyle could be defined as a life of ongoing worship through prayer, praise, lament, song, testimony and sacramental acts in the manner that rehearsed the worship of heaven: "Every act of the believer in community was an act of worship, an encounter with God, whereby one received more and more grace. Like other forms of ministry, the ministry of healing was an act of worship, where offering was made to God and where healing grace was imparted."[84] The Reformed position was less overarching in that it viewed grace in a juridical sense, primarily as pardon. In Macchia's summation, Alexander "regards this soteriology as oriented towards a forensic and legal atonement theory that replaces a transformative growth in grace with a more static identification with Christ. Healing in this context is frequently claimed as an accomplished fact rather than an experiential or eschatological goal, thus leaving little room for an understanding of healing as a metaphor of salvation."[85] Thus, the Reformed Pentecostal focus on the cross could be said to render healing less open to "a therapeutic and transformative understanding of the Christian life."[86]

82. Ibid., 204.
83. Macchia, "Pentecostal Healing," 146.
84. Ibid., 203.
85. Ibid., 146.
86. Ibid.

Both sides contended that healing was received by faith. For Wesleyan Pentecostals, such faith looked forward to the promise, not backward to the accomplishment of the cross. They were more disposed to think in terms of faithfulness/fidelity than faith as a prescription. In living a life of faithfulness toward God, and savoring his grace, then one could trust him for healing: "The ultimate question was 'Are you faithful?' In the test of faithfulness, one could even have to face illness. In this case, the test was to continue to abide, trusting God fully."[87] Absence of healing was not regarded as defeat or a failure to exercise faith. In this, Wesleyan Pentecostals followed closely John Wesley who acknowledged that "God has a bias towards healing without making healing simply an end in itself. Emotional and physical health is itself a means toward a much greater end, which is the Christian life of holiness."[88] Persistence in prayer was not to be regarded as of little avail if it does not achieve its end because, in the sovereign will of God, healing may be either delayed or never actualized; rather such prayer could play a therapeutic and transformative part in the believer's life. With such a holistic understanding, faith sat easily with both the living and the dying. The one topic on which both camps agreed was that faith in the Great Physician precluded medical encroachment. To act otherwise would be a betrayal of trust in God. Medical expertise was fine for the unbeliever, though healing by such expediency should not be confused with divine healing.

For those in the Finished Work stream, faith for healing was paired with that for salvation in that both were dependent on the merit of the finished work of Christ, by whose stripes healing comes. This stream broadened its virtue by believing that one could claim the "blood" for healing, even though symptoms lingered. Thus, faith became an all-important choice of the will that acted on the premise that healing had already taken place; hence the origin of the concept of "acting faith" that repudiated any negative thinking evoked by protracted illness. Giving in to sickness by owning up to symptoms only showed a lack of faith. Accompanying this kind of faith-claim was the invocation of the name of Jesus in such formulistic phrases as "in the name of Jesus" or "in Jesus' name" when praying over the sick. Death was something to be resisted and denied, an outlook made slightly more plausible by the prevalent belief that the Lord's return was imminent. Tension was created when a community faced the death or protracted illness of a member because it raised a question about the supplicant's lack of faith.

Wesleyan Pentecostals, drawing on early Methodist tradition, saw healing in sacramental terms, in the sense that healing of the stricken body was a direct manifestation of the divine presence in and through the materiality of human flesh. The prayer of faith was viewed as movement toward God, anticipating an inbreaking of the Spirit and a transformative gift of grace. This prayer most often took place at the altar: "For these Pentecostals, the altar, an area sometimes designated in the space between the pulpit and the congregation, was the place where one met with God. . . . In the worship setting, whether formal church services or informal prayer meetings in homes, the sick were anointed with oil, in obedience to James 5. This sacramental anointing signified the work of the Holy Spirit

---

87. Alexander, *Pentecostal Healing*, 204

88. Knight, "God's Faithfulness," 89.

in the gift of healing."[89] In keeping with a sacramental understanding, hands were laid on the sick to convey the idea of a transference of the Spirit from one believer to the next, or from God through another believer: "These Pentecostals, without arrogance, apparently believed that 'healing virtue' could be transferred through human touch," though they were slow to claim possession of the gift healing. Even when the sick person was unavoidably absent, prayers were offered as a ministry of the whole church.[90] Often in this situation a handkerchief, following Acts 19:11, was prayed over and anointed before dispatch. Loath as they were to make claims of the gift of healing, Wesleyan Pentecostals regarded the ministry of healing to be a major component of the Pentecostal minister's calling. If healing was needed, then the Spirit would gift that minister, or indeed any Spirit-filled believer, with gifts of healings. The itinerant healing evangelist did not feature within the Wesleyan Pentecostal stream during the period of Alexander's study, a potent reflection of the communal, "sacramental" understanding of divine healing.

In Reformed Pentecostal circles the name of Jesus was often accompanied by sacramental acts such as anointing with oil or laying on of hands, signs that pointed back to the work of Christ on the cross. Faith-claim supplication in the name of Jesus was taken as a mandate for restoration of health, regardless of time and place. Because Finished Work theology did not necessarily call for more than an individual's attitude of faith, it opened the way for healing evangelism to operate in a parachurch settings, administered even by an evangelist without accreditation by any recognized and responsible body. The mobility of the healing evangelist introduced a shorter, more urgent, route to healing. Following biblical precedent, such as Peter with the cripple at the temple gate (Acts 3:6), it was a theology that called for an instantaneous work. The literature emanating from this source lacked discussion of healing at the altar: "It would not be expected that one would need a place for seeking a transformative experience if one simply looked back to what had already been accomplished and reckoned it done. Probably . . . they understood the cross to be the altar, once and for all."[91] If there was a typical space, it was to be found in a queue standing in the "healing line" that allowed only the briefest of encounters, as opposed to kneeling expectantly at the altar,

Such is the case argued by Alexander, presented here with brevity that scarcely does it justice. Two issues remain for further examination. First, the Alexander thesis will be subjected to a short appraisal as to the strength of its central thesis. Second, the healing practice of the two schools of thought will be modeled before speculating how the ministry of healing might have fared if the Finished Work position had not become dominant.

Appraisal

Kimberly Alexander's religious roots are in the Pentecostal Holiness Church, and the Church of God (Cleveland, Tennessee), both of which reflect the Wesleyan Pentecostal

89. Alexander, *Pentecostal Healing*, 206.

90. Ibid., 206. Alexander was surprised at the lack of discussion of spiritual gifts, especially the gift of healing, in Pentecostal discourse in the period of her study (226).

91. Ibid., 214.

tradition. Synan commended her "fair and balanced treatment of Finished Work and Oneness views on healing. . . . As a book of theology and history, there are very few questions about her research and conclusions."[92] Others are prepared to challenge such a bland assessment. Frank Macchia makes the case for Durham's position on the Finished Work issue being more sympathetic to Wesleyan views than Alexander allowed. He maintains that the atoning work of the cross extends across a wider spectrum of Pentecostal experience and can accommodate, albeit in some tension, the Wesleyan *ordo solutis*.[93] Jennifer Miskov writes of Alexander's "heavily" Wesleyan-Holiness perspective in her doctorate study of the theology of Carrie Judd Montgomery that subsumes a spirited defense of the soteriology behind Finished Work teaching.[94] For one, she regards Alexander's view on the logic of the Finished Work position, with its presupposition that healing should be instantaneous, as too sweeping. In general, for Miskov, Alexander is "greatly biased by her Wesleyan Holiness Pentecostal background."[95]

Miskov, contests Alexander's claim that the two streams interpreted signs such as healing differently, with Wesleyan Pentecostals interpreting them as witness to the inbreaking of the kingdom, against the Finished Work position that sees such signs as pointing to the outworking of the atonement. In response, she poses a number of questions that aim to replace the future/backward dichotomy with an alternative idea, labeled here as one of "coherent purpose." She asks: "What if these signs were shown so that people were able to serve God more effectively in the future? What if it was not an either/or question [about the] 'inbreaking Kingdom' or 'signs of a work already finished,' but rather if they were signs that came because of a work already finished for the purpose of breaking into the Kingdom in their present realities?" Miskov sees Carrie Judd Montgomery as one who blended the Wesleyan and Finished Work streams in that she believed the battle with Satan necessitated an inbreaking of the kingdom, exemplified in this quotation: "Thus shall we glorify the Father. Soul and body filled with the abounding life and health of Jesus Christ, we shall go forth strong in His might to proclaim 'deliverance to the captives' whom Satan hath bound. Then shall they indeed realize that the Kingdom of God hath come nigh unto them."[96]

Macchia detects a failure on Alexander's part in her taking too narrow a view of the Finished Work concept. He maintains that Durham did not intend the forensic notion of the atonement to be confined to making the believer complete in Christ with little or no bearing on live Christian experience: "The cross was not an abstract event that reconciles God to humanity totally apart from us but rather an all-sufficient power for regeneration, sanctification, healing, and empowered (Spirit-baptized) witness in that it had the resurrection and Pentecost at its horizon as parts of a seamless flow of events by which the Spirit is mediated."[97] It was his view that early Wesleyan Pentecostals "separated

92 Synan, "Pentecostal Healing," 347.

93. Macchia, "Pentecost as the Power," 3.

94. Miskov, "Life on Wings," 247.

95. Ibid., 227.

96. Ibid., 249–50.

97 Macchia, "Pentecost as the Power," 3.

sanctification from Spirit-baptism by defining sanctification narrowly and negatively as a cleansing or a separation from sin. Sanctification, however, is also positively a consecration unto God in preparation for a holy task, as it was for the Old Testament prophets and Jesus of Nazareth. As an aspect of the life of discipleship to which we are consecrated and called, sanctification involves a transformation by the Spirit of God into the very image of Christ 'from glory to glory' (2 Cor. 3:18)."[98] In effect, the distinction between sanctification and Spirit-baptism can be maintained only through a reductionist understanding of sanctification as an inward cleansing and of Spirit baptism as an outward empowerment for Christian service. For Macchia, this distinction between the two is more semantic than substantial. He cites Seymour in holding that Spirit-baptism is the gift of power "upon the sanctified, cleansed life," a veritable baptism that "fills us with divine love" —a view kindred to John Wesley's concept of the denouement of the transformed life attaining "perfect love."[99] By contrast, the standard Reformed view on sanctification is to subsume it under the growth of holiness in the regenerated life, and also to reject the doctrine held in Pentecostalism that Spirit-baptism is a distinct, subsequent experience to conversion.

Macchia, however, is prepared to accept that the Western legal theory of atonement must be transcended if Pentecostalism is to nourish a soteriological vision adequate to its healing practices. Indications of how that "vision" can be realized are captured in his groundbreaking work *Baptized in the Spirit* (2006). In it, the redemptive work of Christ is set in a boundlessly wide context: "Signs were at the very substance of his mission to inaugurate the reign of God in the world and to overthrow the reign of death, sin, and the devil. Such a victory is not reducible to the inner recesses of the religious or moral imagination but grants a foretaste of the renewal of creation in extraordinary signs of redemption, healing, and reconciliation. Only in a redemptive context can the religious imagination or the Christian moral life gain theological significance."[100] Macchia gives due recognition to the cosmic conflict or *Christus Victor* understanding of the atonement that was revived with the publication in 1930 of Gustaf Aulen's book of that title. Aulen sought to reclaim the "classic" or "dramatic" view of the atonement, which, he maintained, was the dominant view held in the first thousand years of Christian history. It is "dramatic" in the sense that it sees the atonement as a cosmic drama in which God in Christ does battle with the powers of evil and gains the victory over them. Macchia, in citing Aulen favorably, gives evidence that this theory of the atonement adds an extra dimension to the forensic view that defines the soteriology of the Reformed and Lutheran traditions.

Macchia's main dispute, however, with *Pentecostal Healing* is its portrayal of Wesleyan soteriology as more or less dominant throughout global Pentecostalism. To counter this notion he draws attention to the influence that the Lutheran pastor Johann Christoph Blumhardt (1805–80) had on European Pentecostalism with its roots in Reformed soteriology. From his doctoral study of the Blumhardts, father and son, he acknowledges that J. C. Blumhardt made much of the idea of the "inbreaking of the kingdom," giving

---

98. Macchia, "The Kingdom and the Power." In Welker, *Work of the Spirit*, 122.

99. Ibid., 122.

100. Macchia, *Baptized in the Spirit*, 146.

it a centrality and force possibly unequaled within his Pietist background. Healings, for Blumhardt, reveal that "the entire person, in body and soul, should be liberated from the power of darkness. With healings, Jesus showed that he inaugurated the Kingdom of God."[101] The failure of the post-apostolic church, Blumhardt concluded, had thwarted the universal outpouring of the Spirit but he expected that such an inbreaking of the kingdom would take place before the *parousia*, and the world would then witness a renewal of apostolic power. In effect, ideas about the present inbreaking of the kingdom and eschatological expectation are not exclusive to the Wesleyan Pentecostal tradition.

Faupel has shown that an upbringing in a religious tradition, though important, did not hinder individuals on this issue from accepting a different viewpoint from the one they were brought up in.[102] He cites Charles Mason, nurtured in the Baptist Reformed tradition, yet becoming a pastor in the Wesleyan Church of God in Christ.[103] On the other hand, despite his position as General Secretary of the AoG, the denominational progenitor of the Finished Work position, nevertheless retained his belief in the Wesleyan eradicationist "second work" doctrine throughout his life. Faupel comes to the conclusion that "a complex set of conditions in each case determined the direction an individual or a group would take. The ego factor was certainly present. Racial prejudice and regional bias were clearly in evidence. Religious predisposition is apparent. In the final analysis, however, no examination of the Finished Work doctrine is adequate without coming to terms with the theological significance of Durham's message."[104]

If statistics are anything to go by, the Finished Work stream became dominant in the USA, with, on one estimate, four out of five adherents numbered within its ranks by the year 2000. Such vigorous growth can, in part, be explained, by the fact that it carried a greater appeal to the wide band of evangelical Christians who entered into the Pentecostal experience, finding its doctrine of sanctification more in accord with their own convictions. Such dominance probably extends now to the global scale with the result that the heat of early controversy has cooled down. Synan in his favorable review opined that scholars mostly "have always assumed that there were no significant differences between second blessing 'Wesleyan' and the more Reformed/'Baptistic' Pentecostal theology and practice in the area of divine healing."

Outcome

What remains to be addressed is the longer-term outcome of the issues raised so far. Alexander is persuaded that healing practice fell into two major streams, and was of "enormous importance." If this were so, it is unusual that it has not raised more academic exchange. The differences can be elucidated if the practice of healing within each stream is modeled on the information summarized above. What is offered here is in the form

---

101. Macchia, *Spirituality and Social Liberation*, 74.

102. Faupel, "William H. Durham." In Jongeneel, *Pentecost, Mission and Ecumenism*, 90.

103 Ibid., 89. Charles H Mason (1866–1961) was a leading figure in Afro-Pentecostalism and founder of the Church of God in Christ (COGIC). Martin Luther King preached his last sermon from Mason's pulpit in Memphis.

104. Ibid., 90.

of a model, or idealization, that would characterize the practice of healing in Wesleyan Pentecostal and Finished Work settings.

In the former, healing would be limited largely to the setting of the local church and would be in the hands of the leaders, some of whom would be women. (Indeed, the itinerant healing evangelist was altogether absent from this stream during its first seventeen years.) The sufferer would move to the altar, the space between the pulpit area and the front seats. Prayer would be offered within a communal setting, with the whole church body sharing in its own way in intercession. Anointing with oil and the laying on of hands would be customary and, on occasion, be extended to a handkerchief for forwarding to a distant supplicant. Healing would be interpreted as a breakthrough of the kingdom of God in its manifest power. Expectation of healing would be tempered by an emphasis on the sovereign will of God that would help to breed a spirit of repose. A realistic attitude would be taken to persistent illness without recourse to the notion, of "acting faith," thus freeing the sick person from a sense of guilt. Because healing would be confined more to the local church, there would be an emphasis on sustained pastoral care. Suffering and death would be assuaged by the inward assurance that neither has the final say. The whole could well be a picture of how divine healing is practiced in many Neo-Pentecostal/ Charismatic churches throughout the globe at the present time.

The Finished Work model would highlight a number of contrasting features. Prayer within the assembled church would be unhesitating in its claim for healing, believing that the atoning death of Christ and the victory over Satan had made it available to those who took hold of the finished work of the cross in faith. Sometimes the force of prayer for healing would be expressed as "pleading the blood. Where the Wesleyan position would place emphasis on God's freedom to choose as to how and when to act, the Reformed view would lay stress on God's being bound by his intrinsic faithfulness to fulfil his promises.[105] They would insist that, if God promised healing, he would remain true to his promise, stirring a high expectation of it being instantaneous. Some believers from this tradition would foster an over-realized eschatology to the extent that death could be resisted. If healing was not forthcoming, two strategies would be adopted. One would encourage the sick person to believe that healing had been activated, and not give in to symptom or doubt. The other would question the depth of faith in the sufferer. Critics would not be slow to point out that this left the person with a burden of guilt for lacking sufficient faith. With its more individualist ethos, Finished Work Pentecostalism would be expected to give greater freedom for the ministry of the freelance healing evangelist, both men and women—such as that which came to the fore in the 1920s and soared in the 1950–60s. The large tent pitched for a limited period, and the healing line and a scatter of bodies lying prone "under the power" at the front would come to provide iconic images of such gatherings.

That healing in Finished Work tradition could be practiced irrespective of locale or setting is a pivotal distinction. It swings the door wide open for healing revivalists to reveal, in Harrell's phrase, their "whole curious world of hullaboo and hope."[106] In many

105. Knight, "Love and Freedom," 57–67.
106. Harrell, *All Things Are Possible*, 4.

cases, it was the impact of their itinerant ministry that lay behind the rapid spread of the healing message from the 1920s onwards, reaching a peak in the immediate post-war years. The evangelists ranged widely, often not answerable directly to any supervisory authority, and heavily dependent for their financial support on claims to sustained healings to draw the crowds. A few turned out to be spiritual hustlers and showmen who made a living by shady practices. Most, however, encouraged their listeners to attach themselves to more settled ministries that played their part in stabilizing the Pentecostal cause not only across the continent, but globally. Harrell observed that the revival "contributed to the growth of organized Pentecostal churches abroad in the 1959s and 1960s. . . . The burst of independent mission work—remarkably vital in contrast to the sluggish and impoverished mission programs of most denominations—resulted in stunning growth for world-wide Pentecostalism."[107]

Alexander's thesis poses an intriguing question: would the theology and practice of divine healing, and Pentecostal growth, have been significantly different if the Finished Work doctrine had not become dominant? Any assessment can only be speculative, but a brief look at American church history may help to shed some light on the question. In some ways, the healing evangelists were reminiscent of the Methodist circuit riders who were among the early trailblazers of early nineteenth-century Second Great Revival (c. 1795–c. 1835). Active on the advancing frontier, and operating within a democratic and populist culture, they were not tightly bound by regulatory structures and strictures. It was in these years that American Methodism grew at an exponential rate, accounting for 34 percent of the total church membership in 1850. Baptist congregational autonomy, allied to the exertions of its unpaid preacher-farmers forming local gatherings, brought about growth in numbers to form 20 percent of all churchgoers in 1850.

By contrast, mainstream denominations, notably Anglicanism and Presbyterianism, in statistical terms, limped behind. Mobility did not feature so greatly with them, characterized as they were by well-educated clergy in settled pastorates. This dip back into history might well apply to the healing evangelists working within the Finished Work tradition. If, as Alexander discovered, the itinerant healing evangelist was apparently altogether absent from the Wesleyan Pentecostal stream for at least its first seventeen years, the possibly follows that the Pentecostal movement would not have made the numerical advance that it did from the mid-1920s. "Itinerancy is the life of Methodism," opined one long-term evangelist around 1850, "Destroy this, and you will destroy Methodism."[108] Subsequent chapters in this book will indicate the sizable contribution that healing has made to the numerical growth of Pentecostalism throughout its history.

The idea that Wesleyan-Pentecostalism, sacramentally attuned, ecclesiology was less open to an individualistic, entrepreneurial spirit may have some relevance to modern times. This consideration is particularly apt with the advent of some of the televangelism that promotes the controversial prosperity gospel, the seeds of which Alexander detected in Finished Work literature. The charge has been brought that Pentecostalism's belief in the miraculous has laid it open to exploitation, making "the televangelist showmanship,

---

107. Ibid., 94.
108. Wigger, *Taking Heaven*, 34.

entertainment, and miracle-working" comparable to the snake oil salesmen of former days.[109] This raises some related questions: Would the cult of celebrity surrounding some modern ministries have been curtailed if the Wesleyan model had overruled all others? If it had, would the practice of divine healing, particularly as conveyed in much of the modern media, have been less fevered, more local church-based, and more modest in the expectations it arouses? Interesting as they may be, such questions cannot be neatly answered because possible causal links have become much too tenuous over time. However, what Kimberly Alexander has done is enough to suggest that things may have been different, and for this her work is to be commended.

109. Stewart, *Handbook of Pentecostal Christianity*, 205–6.

3

The Diverse Healing Scene in Britain

BACKGROUND OF BODDY

WITHIN A YEAR OF the Azusa Street event, Pentecostalism put down its first shoots in the British Isles. The Rev. Alexander Alfred Boddy (1854–1930) played a major part in its introduction. William Kay viewed that the formative years of the Pentecostal movement in Britain "were providentially in Boddy's hands. What he taught, and the way he taught it, was to become normative and those problems which he faced were, by and large, similar to those that recurred in future years."[1]

Something of his background as an Anglican minister helps to explain his role as the "father" of the movement in Britain. Boddy was born in 1854, the third son of James Alfred Boddy, rector of St. Thomas Church, Manchester. Before studying Theology at University College, Durham, he was articled for a short time to a firm of solicitors in Manchester. In 1881, he was ordained by J. B. Lightfoot, the scholarly Bishop of Durham, and was appointed curate to All Saints, Sunderland in 1884. After two years, he was given full charge of the church where he was to minister for the next thirty-eight years. In 1891 he married Mary Pollock, who was to prove a strong influence on him. Boddy was enlivened by news of the Welsh Revival, and made the decision to see it on the ground in December 1904. On return, he was inspired to start a prayer meeting for revival: "A little circle of earnest young men met night after night in prayer in my vestry for further revival—for a great outpouring of the Holy Spirit."[2] During the visit of T. B. Barratt from Oslo during August/September 1907, the Boddy women, Mary and daughters Mary and Jane, received their Spirit-baptism in the Pentecostal mode of evidential tongues.[3] Boddy had to wait until December, and took great delight in informing Mrs Penn-Lewis that "I am the 50th here to receive the sign of tongues (Pentecost means 'Fiftieth'). Seven have been thus blessed this weekend."[4]

---

1. Kay, *Inside Story*, 25.

2. Wakefield. *Alexander Boddy*, 77.

3. T. B. Barratt, English-born, founded the Oslo City Mission in 1904. During a visit to New York in 1906, he learned of the revival at Azusa Street, and was Spirit-baptized in November, 1906. An ardent proponent of the doctrine, he introduced Pentecostalism to Western Europe from his base in Norway.

4. Wakefield, *Boddy*, 89.

Boddy's Spirit-baptism came to enshrine Sunderland forever in the hearts of the early Pentecostal believers in Britain. It was there that he instigated and publicized the annual Whitsun Conventions, starting in June 1908, until 1914. Gee, in his assessment of the impact of the Conventions observed:

> From the point of view of the early history of the Pentecostal movement in the British Isles the Sunderland Conventions must occupy the supreme place of importance.... Their importance . . . was not in their size but in their formative influence in attracting and helping to mould not only the immediate leaders of the multitudinous little Pentecostal meetings which were springing up all over the land, but the younger men who were destined to become the leaders of the Movement when it came to years of maturity.[5]

Besides the Conventions, he published and edited the monthly periodical *Confidence* that ran from April 1908 until 1926, 141 issues in all. The magazine quickly established itself as the authentic voice of the new movement in Britain. With articles presenting and defining Pentecostal teaching as well as full reports of conference sermons and snippets of news of events and personalities, it was an avidly-awaited publication each month in the homes of many Pentecostal believers. By these two means, convention and periodical, and his own respected authority, Boddy bestowed a firm, though benign, leadership over the early movement.

The importance of the leadership of Pentecostalism in the British Isles lying in the hands of Boddy cannot be overemphasized. It meant that Pentecostalism did not come as some strange new cult associated with some charismatic guru-figure, but with a vicar of the established church. That by itself did not necessarily ensure it respectability, but it meant that it could not be easily dismissed. When he stated his mind that if the church "will not receive this [Pentecostal] blessing from the Lord, or if it hinders me from spreading it abroad, then I shall consider my position as a member of the C. of E.," he never had any serious cause to exercise such consideration. If anything, in the final years of his ministry spent in the coal-mining village of Pittington, his Anglicanism came to the fore more than his Pentecostalism. Without Boddy's standing, there was always the possibility that a mix of external hostility, fanaticism, low calibre leadership and doctrinal zaniness might have proved sufficiently damaging to kill off the young sapling. Theological aberration and behavioral excess were a constant threat. With his legal and theological background, he proved a perfect foil to the excesses that threatened the infant movement. The magazine earned him such regard that the standing of *Confidence* as the unofficial voice of the movement in the British Isles remained undisputed for its first ten years.

BODDY'S HEALING MINISTRY

Boddy's interest in divine healing was roused by the recovery of his wife from chronic bronchial asthma in 1899. Mary Boddy was the daughter of an Anglican clergyman who, like Boddy, was warm towards Keswickian spirituality. She suffered health problems almost from the beginning of their marriage, exacerbated by serious atmospheric pollutants

---

5. Gee: *Wind and Flame*, 37.

belched from the chimneys of the nearby industrial plant. Three different doctors told her she
would never get well if she continued to live in
such conditions.[6] Her search in the Scriptures
as to what was God's will in the matter of divine
healing led to her conviction that health was
one of the blessings in the atonement. The verse
in John 5:40 ("Ye will not come to me that ye
may have life") struck her with sudden force: "At
once I thought this is just what I have been doing, searching the Scriptures, instead of taking
Life from Christ Himself. I then and there told
the Lord I would take his life for my body and if
His Life were in me, I was whole for no disease
can be in Him."[7] Twelve years later, she could
affirm that "since that time I have not taken
any medicine or been kept indoors by weather.
Once I had a severe attack of influenza, but in
one day it entirely disappeared, and whenever
I am threatened with cold or any other attack, I

Rev. A. A. Boddy

always get the victory by resting on the fact that the Living Saviour is within me, and able
to save to the uttermost."[8]

Their daughter Jane, in a short memoir of her parents, recalled the impact of her
mother's healing:

> [It] led to my father's great interest in Spiritual Healing. Mother soon discovered
> that she had the gift of healing and was often called upon to pray with the sick and
> to lay her hands on them. My father did not have this gift but he used the service of
> Anointing the Sick frequently and was a pioneer in the movement towards Spiritual
> Healing that has grown during this century. In our family, we rarely saw a doctor.
> If we were sick, father would anoint and my mother lay her hands on us for healing
> and we accepted this as the normal procedure. Although my father had not the gift
> of healing, his simple prayers and faith, and his compassion helped many.[9]

That, Mary Boddy, two years before Azusa Street, was ripe for a Pentecostal-type experience comes out in letter she wrote in reply to a correspondent. She stated: "Last September
[1904] the power of God came upon me wonderfully and shook my whole frame, but I
think I was a little afraid then of the *full*-Baptism. . . . He sends so many to me for help,

6. Boddy described the church at Roker as the "smoke smitten Church of All Saints, with the Vicarage,
adjoining some busy ironworks."

7. *Confidence*, September 1910, 211.

8. Ibid., *Confidence*, September 1910, 216.

9. The typescript is in the Donald Gee Pentecostal and Charismatic Research Center, Mattersey, near
Doncaster. When the piece was written (c. 1970), Jane was known as Mother Joanna Mary CR. (the Anglican
Community of the Resurrection at Grahamstown, South Africa).

and I quite think the same signs should follow now as in apostolic days."[10] In a subsequent letter she mentioned that "after a time of great filling . . . God used me to heal two people and two others were visibly anointed with the Holy Ghost." Her article "Divine Health and Healing in Jesus," which appeared in the May 1908 edition of *Confidence,* was given a wider circulation when distributed as a leaflet. For the last sixteen years of her life she was an invalid, but continued to minister to the sick both in Sunderland and Pittington.[11]

In the introduction to his wife's article in *Confidence,* Boddy stressed that "whenever the 'Pentecostal Baptism' is received, this question [of divine healing] becomes prominent"; otherwise he expressed it thus on another occasion: "Pentecost and Divine Healing are closely united together."[12] Soon after his wife's healing, they held a meeting once a week "for the teaching of Divine Life for Spirit, Soul and Body." His tract, *Health in Christ,* published soon after, helped to raise the profile of the subject. The booklet, he announced, "brought the writer in touch with a very large circle who trusted the teachers in All Saints Vicarage, because they had been blessed by the messages given."[13] In a letter a hospital nurse wrote of her healing of a chronic heart/lung problem, indicating that the pamphlet proved for her "such a help and blessing that I long for others to read it with the same result."[14] In 1910, Boddy addressed two clerical groups, both groups doubtless hesitant about, if not downright hostile to, the new movement. The first was a paper written for the Durham Junior Clergy Society and the second was prepared for the Sunderland Church Missionary Society (CMS) clergy. The second paper carried the title "The Missionary's Supernatural Outfit," in which he challenged his hearers to think about the gift of healing.

As recorded, Boddy told his clerical colleagues: "If anyone should expect to be used in the healing of the sick it is the missionary in heathen lands. . . . A native doctor, working in North India, said to me, 'It is really most difficult to answer some of these people when they show us these passages [on healing] and say, Why do you not do as your Book says?'"[15] In contradistinction, he pointed out that modern missionaries carry with them

> ant-proof packing-cases and camping out necessaries to which might be added medicine chests and supplies of insect powder. . . . [We] sometimes wonder how St. Paul and his fellow workers in the heat and discomforts of Asia Minor, Greece, or Syria did without some of our modern appliances. . . . The Lord needs to-day missionaries, men and women in the apostolic succession with the apostolic equipment—the gifts of the Spirit, men who in His name shall lay hands upon the sick and they shall recover, who in that Almighty Name shall cast out demons and they shall go.[16]

10. Wakefield, *Alexander Boddy,* 78–79.

11. Mary suffered severely from arthritis and was forced to sit when addressing the Sunderland Conference.

12. *Confidence,* June 1908, 18.

13. Ibid., August 1908, 195.

14. Boddy: *A Vicar's Testimony,* Online.

15. *Confidence,* March 1910, 71.

16. Ibid., March 1910, 70.

It was a challenge reminiscent of Edward Irving's protest against the missionary societies of his day, only Irving's attack was more about their physical sustenance by faith rather than healing. It was one of Boddy's consistent themes that "God is doing wonders, marvels, in these last days. . . . The Lord is restoring the gifts of the Church, and many in this land have, in measure, the gift of healing."[17]

Boddy's theology of healing was essentially that formulated by the radical healers in the nineteenth-century Holiness movement. His thinking was kindred to that of A. B. Simpson with whom there was a mutuality of great respect. During a visit to America in 1909, he was invited by Simpson for lunch at the CMA center at Nyack. He declared his host "a real help to myself and to many. His sermons every week in the [CMA] paper are always spiritual and helpful."[18] On leaving, Simpson invited him to preach at the Tabernacle the next time he was in New York. Two years later, Boddy was able to entertain Simpson at Sunderland: "We had the joy of happy fellowship with him in All Saints' Vicarage, and at Pastor Scroggie's home."[19] Boddy's *Health in Christ* booklet differs hardly at all from that of the nineteenth-century radical healers. This can be seen in the prayer of affirmation and trust printed in *Confidence* as a help to those seeking healing on their own. After its publication, he received letters from readers from all parts of the world who had been healed whilst reading the booklet and meditating on the prayer. The prayer reads:

A SOLEMN ACT OF TRUST

1. Blessed Lord, I am by nature a sin stained fallen being, liable to succumb to all the attacks of the enemy.

2. Thou hast died for me, and I in Thee. I accept Thy full salvation again. On the Cross I was crucified in Thee with my affections and lusts. I am therefore dead unto sin (in Thee, Oh Christ) and alive unto God (in Thee).

3. Thou *hast saved me* - body, soul and spirit. Thou hast borne all my sicknesses. With Thy stripes I am healed. Thou art the Lord that healeth me.

4. Once more I definitely trust Thee for Divine Health, I accept deliverance from this present attack, and from this moment, whatever the apparent symptoms may seem to indicate, I hold fast to my union with Thee. If the Son has set me free, then am I free indeed. Thou art my Life. "No longer I, but Christ liveth in me." I praise Thee that I am saved to the uttermost, body, soul, and spirit. Therefore, I can praise Him for complete healing.

5. I recognize that these symptoms (however trying) are entirely from the enemy, and in the Name of Jesus I rebuke him, and place myself under the precious Blood of my Saviour. I take the Holy Ghost of God to make my faith strong. I praise Thee now for complete victory over the enemy. Whatever I feel or see, Jesus is Victor! Hallelujah![20]

17. Ibid., June 1908, 18.

18. Ibid., September 1909, 199.

19. Ibid., April 1911, 88. W. Graham. Scroggie (1877–1958) was pastor of the neighboring Bethesda Free Church in Sunderland. He gave acclaimed Bible readings on twelve occasions at the Keswick Convention.

20. Ibid., December 1913, 236.

The prayer is in accord with the teaching of the radical healers in a number of ways: It underpins the healing power in the atonement (point 3), and "under the precious Blood" (5). It upholds the role of faith (4 and 6), to the point of the sufferer dismissing "apparent" symptoms. The holistic nature of salvation is maintained (3) with healing of the body one facet of it. Holiness is taken as the prerequisite (2) for the cleansing and healing power/ life of Christ to be continually operative (4). No concession is made to the use of medical means. The call is to "hold fast" (4) despite the continuing symptoms, to "rebuke" the "enemy" and offer praise for the "complete victory" (6) over the evil one. The prayer ends with the, perhaps consciously, Blumhardtan flourish of "Jesus is Victor."[21]

Boddy at the beginning took a qualified absolutist position on the use of medical intervention for those seeking healing. As Taylor has pointed out, Boddy, "in inculcating a high view of divine healing . . . inevitably gives the impression of holding a low view of medical aid, though he is often at pains not to give this impression."[22] One of his strongest cautions against medical intervention is found in *Health in Christ*: "But there must be no unbelief. . . . If when the elders have departed from the anointing service the sick person fails to perseveringly act out his faith; or if any unbelieving Christian in the household by half-heartedness succeeds in discouraging the sick one, there will be no continuance of the work begun. Again, if there is any deception or keeping back on the part of the sick person, God will not heal."[23] However, he recognized that "only a few patients out of hundreds have faith enough to lean only on the Lord. It must be Holy-Ghost-given Faith, and Spirit-given Light." It was for this reason "Christian doctors and nurses are a great blessing to those who have not faith enough to go to Headquarters." While, in these cases, one gladly prays for a blessing on those providing medical attention, "one cannot feel that this is the best way, or the way for those whom the Lord has taught deeper truths, but it is still the way for these."[24] He found it necessary to provide practical guidance to those troubled and indecisive about their condition:

WARNING

No one should give up the doctor or medicine unless fully convinced that the Lord not only can, but has healed. Giving up taking medicine, or dismissing the painstaking, skilful doctor, does not necessarily show perfect trust in Christ. You may ask God to bless the medicine and the skill of the doctor, and trust to that, but this is altogether different from trusting Christ for His Spiritual Health. It is the way, however, for you until you are sure of the better way.[25]

---

21. See Robinson, *Divine Healing 1830–1890*, 56, for the background to the "Jesus is Victor" exclamation of Lutheran Pastor, Johann Christoph Blumhardt, uttered after an exorcism in 1853.

22. Taylor, "A Historical Perspective," 58.

23. *Confidence*, August 1910, 178.

24. Ibid., 8 & 9.

25. Ibid., August 1910, 178.

Still, the conscientious believer is left in a quandary in a situation that carried a sense of failure in seeking medical help that placed them among those not following "the method of the Apostolic Church."[26]

The absolutist view on divine healing has always to face the stern test of personal suffering and the heartache borne by members of family and friends of the sick one. The Boddys were not unfamiliar to such grief. Their only son, James, in the Royal Flying Corps from 1916, had a leg amputated after being shot down over France in 1917. He underwent twenty-seven operations and was at death's door on at least three occasions before resuming work with an artificial limb. Some of their missionary friends in the PMU (Pentecostal Missionary Union) died on the mission field of blood poisoning and influenza in two cases, and a married couple was forced to return home from the effects of blackwater fever.[27] Mary was stricken with rheumatoid arthritis for the last sixteen years of her life, the last six years of which were spent in Pittington village. During those final years she required the assistance of Miss Newton as her resident nurse/companion. Writing of 1923, she recalled "the past year has not been a year of tremendous power, but a year of tremendous weakness—a year of helplessness." The failure to receive her personal healing, and at the same time witness healings in the vicarage when she prayed for locals, exacted a reorientation of her thinking:

> We must get our views of divine healing changed. Praise God for every relief from pain, but it is *Life* we need. . . . Not one word Jesus has ever said to me has failed. [God] has life abundant—life that will produce new desires, new habits. We try to get new desires before we have new life. But we need *Life, Life, Life.* . . . We have had the idea that if we were filled with the Holy Ghost we should become powerful. Power is good; we have realised power in a measure; but God wants us to be vessels, willing to let our thoughts be consumed. . . . Many do not understand that the Baptism of the Holy Ghost is a baptism of *fire,* the utter demolishing of everything contrary to God in us—a baptism into death, a baptism in which we shall disappear and Christ shall take our place.[28]

The realization reached was that, whereas healing is a sign of God's power working *for* us, the purpose of Spirit-baptism is to allow God to work *in* us—a retreat from an outward sign to the more elevated inward working of the Spirit. When Mary's arthritis started, and despite her short periods of remission, she realized that though "a quick deliverance is beautiful . . . patient endurance which perfects and strengthens the faith in God is not exercised in a short trial." Additional to this insight, she accepted that "the justice of God must be satisfied by allowing our Accuser to try us on every point, so that he also finds that Christ in us is a great reality."[29] In her last article in *Confidence*, a note of accommoda-

26. Ibid., January 1910, 8 & 9 and December 1913, 232.

27. The PMU was formed in 1909 under the leadership of Cecil Polhill with Boddy a member of its Council,

28. *Confidence*, January- March 1924, 118–19.

29. Ibid., January 1914, 12. Of her times of relief from pain, she wrote that "up to a certain point the severest symptoms of rheumatoid arthritis were allowed, but His life was manifest in a wonderful way, for no trouble of the internal organs was allowed, and wonderful strength given for work such as correspondence, meetings, Bible Classes, and a gracious continuance of being allowed to be an instrument for healing."

tion to medical intervention appeared when she maintained that "there is no reason why the doctors, and those who are 'called' and obey the 'urge' to help their fellow-sufferers, should not work together."[30] In a letter sent to a friend after her death, Boddy wrote, "My beloved one to the last expected to be healed"—a comment neatly summed up by Taylor, "Such were the tensions and frustrated hopes often engendered by Pentecostalism's emphasis on health and wholeness."[31]

Boddy had his own concessions that modified a strict absolutist interpretation of divine healing. When his daughter Jane stated that her family "rarely" saw a doctor, she implied they sometimes consulted one. Boddy declared his admiration for the profession many times because they "with hospitals and scientific appliances will be necessary until the end of the Great Tribulation for all who cannot go directly to the Lord of Life for help."[32] He accepted that God "may allow us to be chastened for a season for our profit," though only up to the point of repentance and obedience because "the Father . . . will not continue to allow the enemy cruelly to punish us."[33] As for apparent failures, he believed that "behind such, unknown to us, there was a good reason for delay, or what seemed to be failure." While recognizing that in "many cases where full healing was not manifested at once, yet gradually but surely the healing came," he could never bring himself to say that healing might never come.

On the other hand, at the first Sunderland Conference, Boddy warned against any temptation to exaggerate in giving testimony to divine healing. In order to give God glory, his people sometimes may be tempted to go a little beyond their experience.[34] One other area of concern was a failure to show love by "unkind criticism and judging [when] so often . . . sickness is attributed to disobedience, going out of God's will. Friends, shall we remember that many of these dear ones are devoted children of God, who would rather die than willingly go out of God's will but above all, let us not forget that we are putting them under the bondage of law again."[35] It is clear that this statement was aimed to counter a prevalent view in some circles that there was a direct link between sickness and personalized sin—Dowie and Wigglesworth were two who held such a view.

ALTERNATIVE ANGLICAN HEALING MODELS

As shown, there was a widening of sympathies towards alternative forms of healing by both Boddys as they reached the final decades of their lives. Mary showed a decided recognition of the work of psychologists numbered among "the great army of scientific men . . . who are giving their lives to this great subject of healing and the power of mind. . . . The psychologist can do a great deal by suggestion. . . . Autosuggestion and suggestion have their place in this work. . . . There is no reason why the doctors, and those who

30. Ibid., May 1925, 167.

31. Taylor, "A Historical Perspective," 70.

32. *Confidence*, January 1910, 8.

33. Ibid., January 1910, 11.

34. Ibid., June 1908, 18.

35. Ibid., August 1911, 181.

are 'called' and obey the 'urge' to help their fellow-sufferers, should not work together."[36] She also recognized the environmental dimension to public health by drawing attention to the recent decline in the death rate attributable to "the sanitary conditions of towns and villages being vastly improved," with the suggestion that further improvement would follow once the housing condition had been more drastically dealt with. Even so, she maintained, there will always be a place for divine healing on the lines she had practiced for the previous quarter of a century: "[Though] a clever surgeon and physician can do almost anything with the human body, specialising in its various parts, [yet] the spirit and soul are beyond their power, and that is where the spiritual healing is needed."[37] Boddy, too, softened his views on healing with increasing age. It is almost inevitable that the aging process, with its greater exposure to illnesses, would temper his mindset. With the move to Pittington, away from the heavy industrial fumes of Sunderland, he began to feel the benefits of clean air. He wrote of the change: "For the first time for a number of winters I have not been laid aside with bronchitis and asthma, but have gone on with my duties through these months feeling stronger and better than in those last days beside the ironworks in Fulwell Road, Sunderland."[38]

By this stage, his leadership role in the growing Pentecostal movement had declined in the aftermath of the Great War. The war brought about the termination of the Sunderland Convention and caused a breach between, on one hand, Boddy and Cecil Polhill, who both supported the war and those younger men who suffered for their stand as conscientious objectors.[39] The view of the direction the movement should take began to split. Martin Robinson, however, maintains that Boddy's vision, one shared by Polhill, was always that "of an interdenominational revival within the church. . . . Their emphasis was always on Pentecostal mission abroad and Christian evangelical fellowship at home."[40] Both men remained, throughout their lives, faithful members of the Anglican Communion, a factor that contributed to the declining influence of both men once a new breed of leaders arose, most of whom identified with the new Pentecostal denominations.

The thinking of these new leaders, swayed in many cases by considerations of social class and Free Church background, ran on different lines: "It was easy," wrote a Pentecostal historian, "for Mr Boddy and Mr Polhill from the shelter of parsonage and country mansion, to suggest that their followers should be baptised in the Holy Spirit and remain in their churches. It was by no means so easy for those who had entered the Pentecostal blessing to follow their advice. The movement met with almost universal ridicule and hostility. The resolute determination Mr Boddy and Mr Polhill to remain in the Anglican Communion left the newly-established Pentecostal groups without any overall direction

---

36. Ibid., May 1925, 166 & 167.

37. Ibid., May 1925, 166.

38. Ibid., April 1923, 86.

39. Cecil Polhill was one of the noted "Cambridge Seven" missionaries who set out for China in 1885. He inherited the family estate in 1903. Following a trip to China, he arrived in Los Angeles in 1908, where he received his Spirit-baptism. A widower, he used his social position and finances to promote the Pentecostal cause, notably through the PMU (Pentecostal Missionary Union) and financially supporting *Confidence*.

40. Robinson, "The Charismatic Anglican," 121.

at a time when these meetings were beset with difficulties and problems."[41] If anything, in the final years in the village of Pittington, Boddy's Anglicanism came more to the fore than his Pentecostalism, a circumstance that was to have a bearing on his respect for other modes of healing.

The early decades of the new century saw new movements, notably within the Anglican Communion, arise that aimed to reconcile the claims of medicine and spirituality. Pressure for new thinking on this issue arose from a number of sources. These included doubts raised by those critical of the theology and practice of the radical healing movement; a perceived threat that the medical profession would monopolize the care of the sick and deprive the church of one of its historic ministries; the need to counteract the rising tide of anti-supernaturalism, correlative with the progress of scientism, marked by advances in the understanding of functional disorders and psychosomatic diagnoses that challenged long-held views on the causation of diseases.

How all this related to God's agency in the world of rapid change became a matter of keen debate when narrowed down to the test case of healing. Four basic positions were taken on this issue in the early part of the twentieth century, the first of which bypasses any discussion here because of its cessationist slant. It is exemplified by Henley Henson, Bishop of Durham, in an article in *The Hibbert Journal*. The healing of disease, to him, "is the incommunicable task of the physician. . . . Religious acts take their place in the healing process [only] as potent instruments of suggestion. Spiritual Healing means no more, and no less, than mental [psychological] healing." In this scheme, the place where the clergyman's duty is unquestionable is limited to "the sphere of conscience."[42] By dealing with the troubled conscience, the clergy may assist the patient to benefit from the efforts of the doctor. The remaining three positions—respectively the therapeutic, the sacramental and the thaumaturgic—were more positive in granting a greater role to the spiritual, and were less fulsome in their affirmation of the medical profession, though to varying degrees. The three positions were not so clear cut that they did not share some significant insights among them.

At the expense of pre-empting a conclusion, an attempt will be made to show that Boddy, despite his advocacy of the thaumaturgic model, was not entirely dismissive of the other two, as they were practiced within his own Anglican communion. In this he was joined by his wife. Mary Boddy in the last article she wrote for *Confidence* declared, "We must get our views of divine healing changed."[43] If anything, his sympathies widened with age, thereby anticipating some of the more mindful thinking of the present day.

The Therapeutic Model

The most celebrated examples of the therapeutic model were the Emmanuel Movement in America and the Guild of Health in England. Episcopal priests, Elwood Worcester and Samuel McComb, established a clinic at the Emmanuel Episcopal Church, Boston, which

41. Missen, *The Sound of a Going*, 6.
42. Henson, "Spiritual Healing," 399 & 395.
43. *Confidence*, January-March 1924, 119.

lasted twenty-three years and provided both medical and psychological services. Elwood Worcester (1862–1940), after completing his studies at the General Theological Seminary of the Episcopal Church, New York, spent three years at the University of Leipzig. After an initial year devoted to classical studies, he spent two years studying with Franz Delitzsch, foremost Hebraist of the day, and Wilhelm Wundt, a pioneer in the new science of psychology.[44] In his autobiography, Worcester wrote that the liberal German academic tradition, "tends to weaken and remove the false opposition which has grown up between the things of the mind and the things of the Spirit," a conclusion that was the inspiration for much of his later work.

Worcester envisioned a ministry of healing based on a scientific model shaped by the best of modern medical theory and the fruits of recent critical studies of the New Testament. Worcester apprehended that the growth of modern knowledge had revealed that "many nervous disorders have their main root in the moral region. . . . The sense of some moral fault unpurged by penitence creates a dissociation of consciousness which in turn may lead to hysteria, and hysteria, as we know, can simulate almost any disease and turn life into a prolonged wretchedness. . . . If then the representatives of Christ to-day are to speak the healing and reconciling word, they must first understand more of the relations between abnormal states of mind or soul and the reflections of these states in the physical organism."[45] It was on this basis that the Emmanuel Movement introduced a psychologically-centered approach to religious healing as a mission of the church. His base was the Anglican Emmanuel Church in Boston in the period 1904–29, followed by years committed to independent psychotherapeutic practice.

Much store was laid by the Movement on the subconscious mind as the link between the individual and God, and the role of suggestion in conditioning it. Worcester believed that Christianity, shorn of its superstitious accretions "has ideas and emotions which can release psychic forces strong enough to create a unified state of mind in which inhibitions, weaknesses, and disharmonies incline to disappear, with consequent beneficial reaction to the physical organism."[46] Suggestion played a key role in treatment by helping believers to understand and perform acts of faith. Therapy worked towards putting patients into a relaxed and receptive mood in the belief, as Worcester maintained, that when the human spirit was in this state, then "a higher Spirit, the Spirit of all goodness enters into us, takes possession of us and leads us in better ways."[47] In individual counseling sessions, ministers and other trained assistants sought to make patients open-minded about faith and healing by formulating, in simple and positive form, suggestions, for example, that their pain was diminishing; that sleep would certainly return; that doubt would change to certainty.[48] One outcome of the movement was its formative part in the work of Alcoholics

44. Wundt is best known for establishing in Leipzig the first psychology laboratory, generally considered the beginning of Psychology as a field of science, separate from philosophy and physiology.

45. Worcester, *Religion and Medicine,* 351.

46. White, *Unsettled Minds,* 188.

47. Ibid., 190.

48. Ibid., 189.

Anonymous. Their church-based courses attracted many alcoholics and reached a high percentage of success in their treatment.[49]

Samuel McComb (1864–1928) was involved directly with the Emmanuel movement when he became assistant to Worcester between 1905 and 1916, after which he became rector of the American Episcopal Church in Nice, France. He was born and educated in Londonderry, Northern Ireland, and studied theology at Oxford. Like his clerical colleague, McComb put great effort into explaining and promoting the work of the Emmanuel movement by means of pamphlets and their best-selling book *Religion and Medicine* (1908). Both men embarked on lecture tours that took them to several American and European cities. Early in 1908, the Archbishop of Canterbury, Randall Davidson, invited Worcester to discuss his work before a committee composed of members of the Pan-Anglican assembly. Unable to accept the invitation, Worcester requested that McComb attend in his place.

Although he did not win the committee's formal endorsement of the Boston program, McComb persuaded the members of the potential virtues of a clerical/medical alliance. A report in the *New York Times* recounted his talk to the full committee. The journalist wrote that on hearing a bell signaling his allotted thirty minutes had come to an end, McComb attempted to stop talking, but "the audience wouldn't let him. The whole assembly rose to its feet and from every quarter there were cries of 'Go On! Go On!'"[50] Addresses at various London churches and to several meetings of doctors and ministers followed. As in America, press coverage of these events was wide, and shortly before he departed for Boston a similar movement, known as the Church and Medical Union, was established in London.

Two years later, McComb appeared in London before a Committee of Inquiry made up of Anglican representatives from the clerical and medical professions "to discuss the asserted results and the rapid development of 'Spiritual' and 'Faith' healing movements."[51] In his evidence McComb emphasized that the work of Emmanuel was under strict medical control. While it aimed to combine the forces of religion with the results of scientific psychotherapy, the latter had a "weakness" in not being scientific enough by "not recognizing the psychological value of religious faith in certain instances."[52]

The Emmanuel method, he suggested, differed from conventional psychotherapy by its belief in the "healing forces of religion and in the value of an ethical discipline of the will."[53] It worked on the basis that the discoveries of medical science are as much a revelation of the divine will as the Ten Commandments or the Sermon on the Mount. Pressed by the Committee, McComb explained that the theory operated "by suggestion

49. Clinebell, *Understanding and Counseling*, ch. 6.

50. *New York Times*, 22 November, 1908.

51. The committee eventually produced its report, Anon., *Spiritual Healing: A Report of a Clerical and Medical Committee* Two of the best known clerics on the committee were the Broad churchmen, W. R. Inge, Dean of St. Paul's, London, and Hensley Henson, Dean of Durham (1912–18), before becoming Bishop of Durham (1920–39).

52 Ibid., 42.

53 Ibid., 43.

upon a spiritual influence in the man, who is thus lifted by an outsider through psychic energies, which he cannot himself arouse. The Divine Spirit is the ultimate cause, but the approximate cause might be called suggestion."[54] For this reason treatment was confined to functional cases, while those suffering from organic conditions were left to professional medical care. Only about 40 percent of persons applying for treatment was treated, and that on the advice of a doctor.

The nearest British equivalent of the Emmanuel Movement's therapeutic model was the Guild of Health. The Guild was formed in 1905 by three young Anglican clerics, Percy Dearmer, Conrad Noel, and Harold Anson, who aimed to arouse the whole church to a fresh recognition of the holistic nature of the Christian message.[55] In his autobiography *Looking Forward*, Anson wrote that the motivation behind the formation of the Guild rested on his conviction that "if this gospel of health were indeed the teaching of Jesus, then there was need of a mission both to the Church and to the medical profession. . . . Very few doctors realised how intimately these two provinces [soul and body] were connected, and how quickly the health of the one reacted upon that of the other."[56] In *Spiritual Healing* (1923), he recommended that every clerical healer should have some knowledge of psychology, otherwise "his powers as a healer will be very much restricted, and may even be completely nullified."[57] He found that a considerable number of people whose physical sufferings were religious or behavioral in origin turned against clerical advisers because they could receive more enlightened advice from practitioners in psychology "who are not hampered by an unfortunate ecclesiastical tradition."[58] It was Anson's ambition that the Guild should not be confined to Anglicans in seeing it more a means to serve the cause of reunion. In the event, Free Churchmen were reluctant to engage while Anglo-Catholics and the Mothers' Union were equally cool. The majority of psychologists looked on the work of the Guild as "at best unnecessary, and at the worst, positively dangerous."[59] His main battles, Anson found, were against those Christians who held the view that pain was the means of spiritual victories. Though he did not wish to deny entirely that pain might serve that function, he dissented from the still prevalent view that "disease ought to be the normal way of spiritual education."

In holding his therapeutic view of healing, Anson was more or less at one with Henson and the majority of the Committee of Inquiry. The Committee's Report reached the conclusion that the physical results of "faith" or "spiritual" healing are essentially not different from those of mental healing or healing by suggestion by recognizing that religious affirmation may often prove to be the most potent form of suggestion. It concluded that healings claimed by faith are usually permanently effective only in cases of

54. Ibid., 44–45

55. Percy Dearmer was the author of *Body and Soul* (1909). Conrad Noel in 1911 became a founding member of the British Socialist Party. He was more identified with the sacramental mode than Anson.

56. Anson, *Looking Forward*, 174.

57. Anson, *Spiritual Healing*, 112.

58. Ibid., 116. Presumably by "unfortunate tradition," Anson was referring to the role that institutionalized religion expected of the sick believer, as stated in the last two sentences of this paragraph.

59. Anson, *Looking Forward*, 207 & 208.

"functional" disorders. Claims for organic healing are so disputable that they cannot be taken into account. Those seeking healing at the hands of healers should be warned not to delay seeking medical advice. The Committee strongly deprecated treatment of disease "by irresponsible and unqualified persons."[60] At the same time, it was keen to promote co-operation between the two professions on the lines of the therapeutic model.

The Report revealed a sharp division within the group of nineteen witnesses interviewed by the panel. Only one, the Right Hon., the Earl of Sandwich, strongly maintained that spiritual healing allowed for "direct, external divine interposition above the ordinary laws of nature [the thaumaturgic understanding].[61] Other witnesses defined spiritual healing as one in which "religious rites such as the laying on of hands, unction and prayer" featured [the sacramental understanding].[62] The Committee had little time for the thaumaturgic position and warned that those who resorted to such "healers" were denying themselves medical treatment designed to arrest organic disease. Those healers who claim to exercise "gifts of a special character" owe their effective exercise to their power of suggestion.[63]

It comes as no surprise that proponents of the radical healing message were less than enamoured by the tone of the report of the Committee of Inquiry. When the local press approached Boddy to comment on the report, the journalist received a surprisingly objective analysis, without Boddy making any concession to opponents of the thaumaturgic position. He submitted that even the ordinary Sunday congregation was scarcely attuned to the topic of divine healing: "It needs an inner circle of those who are earnestly seeking a return to apostolic usages and faith, and this means that there is a heavy price to pay for loyalty to the standard given to us in the New Testament." Asked how he differed from the attitude of the Committee of Inquiry as to his degree of co-operation with doctors, he replied, "The apostles did not attempt co-operation with the medical profession when they worked the miracles recorded. They possessed an infectious confidence in the unbounded supernatural power of the Founder of their faith, and there was such a response as staggered their opposers." Asked about his view on the effectiveness of methods other than the one he advocated, Boddy pointed out that it was given only to a limited number of the sick to seek divine healing without any human intervention.

As for others who sought healing by more conventional means, Boddy declared, "We never wish to undervalue the splendid work of doctors and nurses. We gladly join in prayer with those who have committed themselves into the doctor's hands. . . . The doctor receives quite naturally a large share of the credit. Divine healing, as we teach it, is the miraculous intervention of the supernatural in response to simple trust, that trust resting on distinct promises in the Christian Scriptures."[64] The reply was classic Boddy in his resolute stand on the primacy of direct divine intervention, at the same time forbearing of those unable or unwilling to attain the uncompromising faith position. There is good

---

60. Anson, *Spiritual Healing*, 18.

61. On Sandwich, see Robinson, *Divine Healing 1890–1906*, 157–62.

62. Ibid., 11–12.

63. Ibid., 16.

64. *Confidence*, June 1914, 111.

reason to believe that in his latter years his views moderated. That would appear to be true of Mary Boddy, when in 1925 she could see no reason why the parson and physician "should not work together."

She conceded that auto-suggestion had its place in healing. By this stage, she began to employ the widely-used, less contentious term "spiritual healing" on the holistic grounds that such healing lifts the whole concept to "a much higher plane than any other healing, for it permeates the whole man—spirit, soul and body." Authentic spiritual healing is more comprehensive than bodily cure in that it includes "all that we mean by life in its richest measure." It raises people to the position that God intends them to be—"a child of God, a great brotherhood—unity of spirit, unity of love, unity in soul, and all this wondrous vitality expressing itself through a healthy body, for health is wholeness, holiness."[65]

Boddy, in general, was not entirely happy with the trend towards the use of psychotherapy in Christian healing, believing that "we find our psychology in the Word of God. The great loving wisdom and Mind of God has given us certain laws, which if we break, he has warned us what will be the result." He allowed that "students of psychology are finding out the facts" in uncovering the reality of evil and evil thoughts that "have their immediate effect on our spirit and soul and body."[66] On a visit to America in 1912, he approved of a lawyer who had been a Methodist preacher "but had imbibed too much psychology and higher criticism and now want[ed] to be rid of it."[67] On the other hand, he commended *Faith and Suggestion* (1912) by Dr. Edwin Ash, described as "a mental therapist who [has] written a most valuable book based on the miracle of Miss Dorothy Kerin."[68] Chapter 7 of the book carried the title "The Sub-Conscious Mind," and chapter 9 "The Spiritual Beyond—A Problem of the Sub-Conscious Mind."[69]

Mary Boddy, for her part, was prepared to use the concept subconscious in an article addressing the problem of discerning the credibility of some prophecies and glossolalic utterances. She was relieved "to think that many false 'messages' were produced by the [speaker's] own heart, or subconscious mind, therefore it is a relief to find it is not demon possession, though undoubtedly it is one of the 'snares of the devil.'"[70] Ash's book was undoubtedly well thumbed by the Boddys and this particular reflection may well have been inspired by a quotation from William James' *Varieties of Religious Experience* (1905) quoted in Ash's book. James wrote of the sub-conscious (his "subliminal region") as harboring "the springs of all our obscurely motivated passions, impulses, likes, dislikes, and prejudices . . . in general all our non-rational operations come from it." That *Faith & Suggestion* was, to Boddy's mind, "valuable" owed much to Ash's attempt to show that

65. *Confidence*, May 1925, 167.

66. *Confidence*, January–March, 1919, 8.

67. Ibid., November, 1912, 251.

68. The Kerin healing will be dealt with below.

69. *Confidence*, June 1912, 131. Ash was a prolific author of psycho-therapeutic studies that included *and Mind and Health: The Mental Factor and Suggestion in Treatment with Special Reference to Neurasthenia and Other Common Nervous Disorders* (1910), *Nerves and the Nervous* (1911) and *The Problem of Nervous Breakdown* (1919)

70. *Confidence*, 15 December, 1908, 14.

"mystical experience and psychic healing . . . have reached a position which is neither incompatible with the teachings of the New Testament [or] any of the systems which rely on non-physical principles for their efficacy."[71] Ash followed James in his position that "*if there be* higher spiritual agencies that can directly touch us, the psychological condition of their doing so *might be* our possession of a sub-conscious region which alone should yield access to them. . . . If the grace of God miraculously operates, it probably operates through the subliminal door."[72] Ash's attempt to find a place for the direct "touch" of spiritual agencies, doubtless, gratified Boddy. Thus, it can be shown that Boddy, though wary of the psychologizing of divine healing—more so than his wife—was not entirely dismissive of it, insofar as it distanced itself from the mechanistic reductionism that explained healing in purely physical or deterministic terms.

Boddy, in his stance on healing and psychology, was probably not prepared to go as far as Herbert Pakenham Walsh (1871–1959), the nephew of his Irish clerical colleague, Thomas Hackett.[73] Walsh was appointed first Bishop of Assam when a new diocese was created out of the diocese of Calcutta. In an article he was asked to contribute to divine healing he pointed out that he had been "constantly using the ministry of healing," and had kept a careful record of all cases.[74] He admitted to having have read widely on the subject. Walsh's article acknowledged the relevance of the current discussion raised by "the remarkable experiments in mental healing or psycho-therapeutics, and in psycho-analysis." His interest in the topic reflected the emergence of mental therapeutics, which owed much to the psychoanalytic theories of Sigmund Freud, Carl Gustav Jung and Alfred Adler. Walsh showed his interest in these developments by the questions he put to himself: "Is there any real basal distinction between mental healing and what is called spiritual or divine healing? Is healing in the name of Christ only a higher form of suggestion, and the same in essence as the healing by faith in an idol, a fetish, a charm, a medicine, a doctor?"[75]

In his search for an answer to these questions, Walsh disclosed that he was encouraged by the ministry of the Anglican healing evangelist J. M Hickson, whose travels in India, China, and Japan had forced fellow missionaries to ask whether it was the Lord's will today to "confirm the word by signs following [Mark 16:20]" in the manner of the primitive church. In looking through the records of those involved with the Hickson missions, he had spotted evidence of remarkable and sudden cures, "including total blindness, deafness, and dumbness from birth, also of many gradual cures, and above all of spiritual blessing both to the sick and to those who prayed with them."[76] His own conclusion was that "God is leading us back at this time to the rediscovery of an almost forgotten truth, and the recapture of a great and wonderful power." This power, he believed, is closely

71. "Psychic healing" in this and similar contexts should be considered as healing through working of the mind through sub/unconscious process and the power of suggestion.

72. Ash, *Faith and Suggestion*, 139.

73. The possibility of Boddy having a personal link with Walsh is explored below.

74. Walsh. "Divine Healing," 96.

75. Ibid., 97.

76. Ibid.

connected "with that class of phenomena we call 'psychic' power," and that it followed natural laws.

This conclusion did not in the least cause Walsh to think that healing consequently was less divine, or less supernatural. He drew an analogy with conversion in that both are equally a work of the Spirit, yet has been shown "by masters of psychology to follow natural laws, and the more we know of such natural laws, the more we can co-operate with the Spirit of God in effecting it." Any difference in kind or degree between "mind" and "faith" healing was for him "unimportant." Of greater consequence were the different outcomes when measured "by their fruits"—the test that William James advocated in his pragmatic theory of truth.[77] In essence, the difference lay in the fact that whereas mental healing does not produce spiritual fruits, healing by faith in God issues in a "fuller life of the spirit as well as of the body." Walsh was much less wary than Boddy about the ramifications of the new psychology. As men of scholarly bent, both had to face the perennial challenge of finding a harmonization of biblical truth with relevant new insights engendered by the expansion of knowledge in the medical sciences. They were prepared, even if minimally, to take from the new psychology such insights that could be made to serve as a defense for divine healing. The concept of the "subconscious", as discussed above, is a case in point.[78]

The Sacramental Model

It is to be expected that Boddy would be closer, though with some reservation, to the views of the advocates of the sacramental option in that both looked foremost to scriptural warrant for unction, the anointing with oil of the sick. Of the two biblical texts that refer to this unction, Mark 6:13 and Jas 5:13–16, Father F. W. Puller of the Anglican Society of St John the Evangelist, (usually referred to as the Cowley Priests), regarded the James passage as the more important of the two.[79] Puller's initial intent in writing his *Anointing the Sick* (1910) was to controvert the Catholic position of reading the James passage in terms of extreme unction, thus limiting it to the dying rather than the restoration of the ailing. In the book, he considered the witness of the early church fathers, and the liturgies of the early Latin and Greek liturgies. Historically, the anointing of the sick featured recurrently in the first seven centuries of the Christian church when recovery from illness was generally expected to follow the act of anointing. From the early Middle Ages, however, the rite became increasingly tied to the whole penitential system, and this

77. Ibid., 101–2. Philosophical pragmatism can trace its beginning to a talk given by William James at Berkeley, California in 1901, from where it spread rapidly to the wider American culture. It holds that the meaning of a belief is to be found in its fruits, not its roots: "It is results, not origins that matter" (Richardson, *William James*, 377).

78. William James was in favor of mind cure in that it has made "an unprecedently great use of the subconscious life" and its results were incontrovertible. He regarded the placebo effect as a true rather than a pseudo cure.

79. Puller, *Anointing the Sick*, 9. In 1883, Puller was in Africa and given charge of a congregation of Black African Christians who had earlier been converted to Pentecostal ways, but then felt a desire to join the Anglican Church. Puller found their worship unusual, but, recognizing that it echoed aspects of the early church, he allowed the church to remain Pentecostal and Anglican. DeArteaga, "A Wedge into Cessationism." Online.

led to its becoming confined to individuals at the approach of death. With the rise of the Oxford Movement, and Anglo-Catholicism in general from the mid-nineteenth century in England, pressure was increasingly exerted for the revival of the church's sacramental heritage. This was shown by its preoccupation with matters such as patristic and liturgical scholarship, apostolic succession, the elevation of the bread and wine for adoration and ascetic holiness.

Puller urged that new prayers should be introduced into the Book of Common Prayer for the consecration of the oil used and its administration. By so doing, he unfolded the labyrinthine nature of church tradition in its healing ministry. He suggested that the compilers would do well to study, *inter alia*, "the Ethiopic Church Order, the Verona fragments, Serapion's Sacramentary and also the form for blessing *Oleum Simplex* in the *Rituale Romanum*."[80] The final chapter of the book argued for its title, "On the Desirability of Reviving in the Church of England at the Present Time the Use of the Primitive Rite of Anointing the Sick." Hensley Henson gave Puller's plea short shrift in expostulating that to revive long-abandoned practices, miraculous effects "could not follow unless at the same time there could be revived in the minds of the people the beliefs and assumptions which once gave to those practices their meaning and potency—their crude demonology, the childish literalism, the abject fear, the preposterous science, the debased sacramentalism, scarcely superior to the fetish-worship of Africa; these lie behind the exorcisms, unctions, and the benedictions of the Church in the early centuries and in the Middle Ages."[81]

Puller's appeal to Mark 6:13 and Jas 5:13–16 was also sharply dismissed. The James passage, to Henson's mind, seemed to imply the sanctioning of a practice in the early church, rather than the formal introduction of a perpetual ministry. The visitation and anointing of the sick by elders, he maintained, "were familiar procedures among the Jews, and were naturally carried over from the synagogue to the church," and could well have been limited to Jewish Christians. To clothe elders, therefore, with sacerdotal authority in the administration of the sacrament of unction was "an anachronism."[82] Such a dismissive rebuff demonstrated Henson's biting polemic that aimed to rescue the church, as he feared, from returning wilfully to the beliefs and methods of a primitive and superstitious past. In this he was joined by the Dean of St. Paul's, W. R. Inge, who protested against any sanctioning of "the craze for miracle-mongering [that was] part of a widespread recrudescence of superstition among the half educated."[83]

Sacramentalists held a high view of the place of the sacraments in the ministry of healing. Their theology made them sensitive to the interpenetration of the spiritual and the material worlds, whereby spiritual reality finds expression in a tangible or visual form. The Incarnation is the most comprehensive expression of such interpenetration.[84] The

---

80. Ibid., 309.

81. Henson. "Spiritual Healing," 398–99.

82. Ibid. 391–92.

83. Mews, "Revival of Spiritual Healing, 1982, 304.

84. See the classic statement in 1 John:1:1–3. The Word of life "seen with our eyes . . . looked at, and our hands have touched."

incarnational principle has its counterpart in the sacraments of the Eucharist (wine and bread) and Baptism (water) and Unction (oil), the benefits of which become available when approached in the right manner, and engaged in sincere intention. When such conditions are met, then the due performance of the act is deemed normally to convey divine grace. Such a view offers a framework for the continuation of divine activity in healing with the conveyance of divine succor through anointing with oil and the laying on of hands.[85] Evelyn Frost in her classic study of Christian healing from this sacramental/liturgical angle, expressed it with precision: "The sacraments are the means by which the nature of the old order becomes interpenetrated and hence transformed by [the new order]. . . . The church, then, in Holy Unction, has been entrusted with a sacrament which exists *primarily* for the sick in body and mind."[86] At the Anglican Conference on "Spiritual Healing," Father J. G. FitzGerald, Community of the Resurrection, Mirfield, Yorkshire, expressed the view that healing is "the extension of the Incarnate Life in the Church."[87] With this understanding of the body of Christ, the incarnational dimension of the Christian message, with its acute sense of divine "presence," played a central role in the High Church understanding of spiritual healing.

The Guild of St. Raphael was formed in 1915, when the High Church members of Anson's Guild of Health withdrew after it sought to expand beyond its Anglican roots. Another sticking point was the Guild of Health's commitment to the alignment of religion with medicine and psychology, while less emphasis given to sacramental grace. The Guild of St. Raphael accentuated healing as mediated through the priesthood and the sacraments, without undue regard to the claims of modern psychology and, unlike the Emmanuel movement, did not limit itself to functional disorders. Its declared object was to forward a healing ministry both "by sacramental means and by intercessory prayer, until the Church, as a whole, accepts Divine Healing as part of its normal work." The Guild started under the patronage of the two Archbishops and thirty English diocesan bishops as well as twenty-five overseas bishops. It adopted three measures: To prepare the sick for all ministries of healing by teaching the need for repentance and faith; to make use of the sacrament of Holy Unction and the rite of Laying on of Hands for healing; to bring to the aid of the Ministry of Healing the power of intercession, individual and corporate, and the other spiritual forces of Meditation and Silence.[88] The administration of Holy Unction was confined to the priesthood, and then only after careful preparation of the patient that included teaching on the nature of repentance and faith. The Laying on of Hands, not being a sacrament, could be administered by lay members of the Guild under the direction of a priest or member of the Guild, and with the approval of the bishop of the diocese.

That the issue of unction was a pressing one for some readers of *Confidence* is hinted at in an article published in 1922. A letter writer wanted to know, with reference to Jas 5:14, what "form of procedure" Boddy used when anointing with oil.[89] Boddy acknowl-

85 For the incarnational shift at the time see Worrall, *Making of the English Church*, 110–12.

86. Frost, *Christian Healing*, 330 (emphasis added).

87. Anon. *Spiritual Healing: Report of a Clerical and Medical Committee*, 39.

88. Weatherhead, *Psychology, Religion and Healing*, 224.

89. *Confidence*, April–June, 1922, 21.

edged that "it is admittedly a help with some to have their anointing in Church," thinking perhaps of those from a High Church background. He made reference to a booklet that enclosed an order of service for healing that he considered some might find helpful. The booklet was written by Herbert Pakenham Walsh (1871–1951), the first Bishop of Assam, India, to whom reference was made above. It is of some relevance that Walsh was the son of Bishop William Pakenham Walsh. The Bishop's second wife was Annie Frances Hackett, the daughter of the vicar of St. James's, Bray, Co. Dublin. The second Mrs Walsh was the sister of Thomas Edmund Hackett (1850–1939), who followed his father as incumbent of St James. Thomas Hackett retired in 1903 but his spiritual journey was not complete. After a Keswick-type experience c. 1906, he attended the first Pentecostal Sunderland Conference in 1907. It is likely that he received his Spirit-baptism there. If that were so, he would have been the first Irish person to receive his Spirit-baptism in the classical Pentecostal understanding. It is eminently probable that with the friendship of Boddy and Hackett, the latter would have drawn attention to his nephew's booklet. It carried the title *Divine Healing* (1921), and ended with the sixteen-page text of "A Service of Anointing." Whether Boddy used Walsh's liturgy is not clear, though possibly not, because he confessed that he felt it "rather long. " Despite that, he was prepared to recommend it to the writer of the letter.

Boddy made it clear that for individuals seeking healing it was preferable, if the sufferer was physically able, to meet in the Vicarage and not in the church. Ceremonial propriety was deliberately downplayed to keep faith with his evangelical churchmanship: "No robes[,] . . . [t]he sick one kneeling perhaps at the dining room table." A tiny bottle of olive oil was ready, though he felt the need to explain that "only half a dozen drops or so were used," as if to underscore evangelical minimalism. The ministration to the sick person began with family and friends kneeling, and the elder standing and seeking God "for the promised Presence." The Jas 5:13–16 passage was then read, followed by the supplicant making confession of sins (v. 16). On one occasion a sufferer's "trouble instantly disappeared" after his/her confession was made. In Boddy's account, the elder then

> rebukes the sickness, and all the evil powers behind the disease, (Luke 4: 39), next placing the sufferer under the Precious Blood for cleansing. . . . Also [for] protection from all evil powers and for victory (Rev. 12:11). Thus the sick one is prepared to receive the Blessed Quickening Spirit, the Lord, and Giver of Life and Health, the Holy Ghost Himself. [Then], pouring a few drops of olive oil into his left palm, the Elder prays that God will graciously sanctify the oil, and that He will use it as a channel of spiritual blessing to the sufferer for Christ's sake. . . . Then with a finger of his right hand dipped into the oil, he touches the forehead in the 'Name of the Lord,' and then in the full name of the Trinity, placing his left hand with the oil in it on the head of the sufferer, with such oil as remains. As in Mk. 16:18, he lays on both his hands, and asks that the hands of Christ—the Pierced Hands—may also rest on the sick one to impart His Life. . . . Then he asks the person to thank God and praise, and praise.[90]

The act concludes with the Aaronic Blessing, with the patient still kneeling the elder again placed his hands upon the head of the believer.

90. Ibid., 22.

The whole procedure clearly was liturgically structured, sensitive to scriptural guidance and vindication, strongly affirming of the merits of the shed blood and the power of the Spirit, with an allusion to the sacramental efficacy of unction, expressed in the prayer that "God will graciously sanctify the oil, and He will use it as a channel of spiritual blessing." The article was written in 1922, but he let it be known that the procedure outlined above had been followed since 1892. The more Pentecostal elements in the ceremony come out in the call for the patient "to thank God and praise and praise," an act assuredly prolonged and volumetrically vibrant. Such was the sense of blessing on these occasions that he could report that "some at this service have received a Baptism of the Holy Ghost, when they came for healing."

Two episodes in Boddy's life are recorded in *Confidence,* where contact was made with healers with Anglo-Catholic sympathies, viz., John Maillard and Dorothy Kerin.

John Maillard

In 1922, during one of his frequent visits to London, Boddy took the opportunity to attend a healing service at St. Mark's Church, Marylebone Road, London. There, the Rev. John Maillard held a weekly healing service every Thursday afternoon. Possibly unknown to himself, Maillard may well have been distantly related to his namesake Marie Maillard (1680–1731), who with many others escaped with her parents to London following the persecution of French Protestants (Huguenots). Some of them brought a millenarian and prophetic tradition and were known as the French Prophets. They attracted English followers, one of whom, John Lacy, suggested that the miracles that they brought with them were "but the first stage of a new Pentecostal outpouring of the Holy Spirit."[91] Marie, at the age of thirteen, was instantly healed from congenital lameness while reading in her Bible the story of the "palsied" man in Mark 2:1–12. Her cure attracted widespread attention, from such dignitaries as the Lord Mayor of London, three bishops and four surgeons sent by Queen Mary. Jane Shaw contends that Marie's cure took place at a significant moment in the history of science in England when the philosophical debate on miracles was about to be launched. A spate of similar miracles followed, notably among women, many of whose stories were published. One Baptist minister, who put a positive spin on the whole affair, saw the cure of Marie as part of the "'miraculous effusion' that would usher in the new age, the coming of the kingdom of Jesus Christ." Such expectation had to await a greater measure of fulfilment in the period of this study.

Maillard, in his early twenties, displayed an active social conscience before coming to the conclusion that the majority of reforms were just tinkering with problems, with little sense of spiritual need or direction. His desire to engage in Christian mission took him to Kelham Theological College, the center for the Anglo-Catholic Society of the Sacred Mission (SSM).[92] Ordination took place in 1910, followed by a curacy in the dockland area of Poplar, East London. During his first year he came into contact with J. M. Hickson on his visits to the parish. This provided Maillard with his introduction to the healing ministry as playing a key part in the mission of the church. He accompanied

---

91. Garrett. *Spirit Possession,* 45.

92. Maillard, *Healing Faith and Practice,* 27.

Hickson on his visits to the homes of the poor and sick, and co-operated with him in his healing services. One of the most remarkable healings was that of a young girl who was left crippled by infantile paralysis and had to wear a surgical boot and irons. Her healing was "perfect."[93] When Maillard wrote *The Sacrament of Healing* (1925), its Foreword was penned by Hickson who disclosed that he had followed the writer's ministry in the East End of London "with deep interest," especially since the two had worked together in visiting the sick in their homes. Occasionally, the two men conducted healing services together. One such occasion was February 1926 when they conducted a "spiritual healing mission" in St. Anne's Cathedral, Belfast, followed by a Thanksgiving Service two months later.[94] About 600 persons had been prayed for on the initial visit, after which the organizers had received 112 letters that testified to the benefits received, a selection being read at the Thanksgiving Service.

Mallard's call to engage fully in the ministry of healing was confirmed in the chapel of the Poplar church, while awaiting an opportunity to report to the vicar on his morning visits round the parish. The small chapel had been set aside for the needs of the sick and suffering to receive the Eucharist. While waiting, he was struck by the idea that if Jesus were on earth again, he could heal all the sick to whom he had administered communion that morning. What happened next was of a visionary moment. He saw laid out on stretchers and couches a multitude of diseased people, and standing in the midst of them the figure of a man with his back turned and motionless. It suddenly became clear that the man had his hands tied behind its back. Then slowly turning, the man looked "earnestly and sorrowfully" at him before fading away. Whereupon, Maillard, retreated to his own room, where his prayer for an interpretation of the vision "came swiftly":

> The figure I saw standing in the midst of the sufferers was Christ . . . longing to impart healing to them all, but unable to do so because his hands were tied by the unbelief of those who professed to be His followers. I cried, "Lord, let me loose thy hands" . . . and a voice seemed to say, "I cannot use my hands now as when I was in the world. . . . Will you trust me and let me use yours?" Then overcome by emotion . . . I said, "Lord, take me" . . . there came a deep peace and a strong resolve to my soul. . . . I knew God had called me into fellowship with Him for this ministry of divine healing, and I dared not disobey Him.

With the support of the vicar a week-long healing mission was held in the church that witnessed, on a smaller scale, exactly what Maillard had seen in the vision. From then on, he was enabled to move forward, in his own words "with confidence, assurance and singleness of purpose in the ministry of divine healing . . . depending upon God, who has wonderfully manifested his power with signs following." From 1926 he devoted himself to establishing the interdenominational "Prayer Healing Fellowship," which claimed to have over nine thousand prayer helpers, divided into groups, each of which prayed for four or five people every day. In 1937, he became the first warden of Milton Abbey Healing Sanctuary, Dorset, before moving to Bournemouth as warden of the Healing Life Mission.

93. Maillard, *Healing in the Name of Jesus*, 20.
94. *Northern Whig*, 10 April 1926, 9.

While at Milton Abbey, it is known that he was in correspondence with the English war poet and novelist, Siegfried Sassoon, in response to a request for prayer.

Maillard was a man of intense spirituality, to whom the unseen world was the supreme reality. In this, he believed he followed Christ who "came to set us captives free from the bondage of material things and our material thoughts about them." That the "presence of Christ" was a critical motif in his ministry was attested to in his remark that "the center of my interest is the Presence of Christ in our midst today."[95] There was nothing finer that the church can do, he believed, than return to its ancient mission of healing: "There it will come face to face with the living Christ. . . . There it will enjoy the conscious realisation of his Presence."[96] Work among the sick and suffering was but "serving Christ in the consciousness of his Presence among us, and serving the sufferers for his sake."[97] Central to his thinking was the Eucharist because it is there that "in a real and spiritual sense Jesus Christ is indeed present."[98] The service is germane to "the bodily life of God's child, for the sacrament is heavenly food for body and soul, and divinely nourishes the whole being. That this Communion is from Christ Himself is sufficient, for us, to guarantee its divine nature and its power. . . . In denying the supernatural element of the Holy Communion we deprive it of all potency for good in the 'strengthening and refreshing' of body and soul." With growing numbers experiencing healing in making their communion, he could envisage the day when receiving communion "will become the great healing service of the church in the revival which is already taking place."[99]

When Boddy attended a healing service conducted by Maillard, referred to earlier, he found the church well filled with "a devout congregation." The service was quite formal, and when it came to ministering directly to those seeking prayer, Maillard in his surplice moved from the lectern to the front pews where the sick were sitting:

> The female sufferers had white handkerchiefs or veils on their heads. He prayed for each and anointed each, the people all continuing in silent prayer. After the females, the male sufferers. With his hand on the head of the sick one he said words like these: "With this Sacred Oil I anoint thy body for healing in the name of the Father, and of the Son and of the Holy Ghost. Amen. I ask our Lord to give thee the inward and invisible anointing of thy soul in the power of the Holy Ghost." When he had anointed all he recited the Anaphora, "Lift up your hearts" and they all answered, "We lift them up unto the Lord," and so he followed on with the words from the Prayer Book.

Boddy took the opportunity to have a heart-to-heart talk with Maillard at the house that had been given to him by a well-wisher who had been healed under his ministry. Boddy found him to be "a strong character." His reaction to the service could be described as mildly supportive in acknowledging that "it had been good to be there. There was an element of great reality in it all. . . . I do not know whether any were healed at the service,

---

95. Ibid., 26.
96. Ibid., 30.
97. Ibid., 34.
98. Maillard, *Sacrament of Healing*, 31.
99. Ibid., 33–34.

but the spiritual side is emphasised—to get a touch from the Lord Himself."[100] That he was not overly moved is revealed in his remark that "this is the sort of service which appeals to 'advanced' Church people of a reverent cast of mind."[101] This remark can be taken to imply that its appeal was more attuned to persons with High Church sympathies and devoted observers of Anglican Formularies. Their meeting highlighted their two traditions—Boddy's unembellished Anglicanism, and Maillard's more rarefied High Churchmanship.

DOROTHY KERIN

Dorothy Kerin belonged more distinctly to the mystical tradition than Maillard. In his preface to one of her biographies, Donald Coggin, retired Archbishop of Canterbury, wrote that "her life, her 'spirituality' and her work are set [in the book] against the background of the mystical tradition of the church, and the parallels with other visionaries are of great interest."[102] Certainly, her healing was the most publicized of its sort in England in the years leading up to World War I. The healing took place in her home at Herne Hill, London on the 18th February, 1912 at 9.30 p.m. Earlier, she had shown no detectable pulse for eight minutes, when suddenly and dramatically the sixteen people in the room witnessed her rising up and walking steadily across the room, perfectly healed. The London *Evening News* reported the facts without comment. The following day the *Daily Chronicle* printed an interview with her doctor who admitted that "she got well, but how she got better I don't know."[103] The *Daily Mirror* printed a photograph of her in her garden under the heading FIRST TIME OUT OF DOORS FOR FIVE YEARS. Dorothy gave numerous interviews and was examined by other doctors. Crowds of journalists and the general public poured into her street for days blocking the road outside the home. Such large numbers made it necessary for her to withdraw to quieter surroundings.

Her background and the events leading up to Dorothy's healing presented no hint of her later prominence. She was the second of five children, for whom the shock at the death of her father when she was aged twelve may have contributed to a deterioration of her health. Three years later she succumbed to diphtheria and for the next seven years she was more or less a permanent invalid, and confined to bed when tuberculosis was diagnosed. Thus, her adolescent years were denied the normal process of socialization, a lack that lent her a certain naivety and emotional vulnerability when she first entered the demanding world of adulthood. By the end of 1911, aged twenty-two, she was near to death with advanced tuberculosis and diabetes. She lay unconscious for long periods, and when conscious her emaciated body was racked by pain.

In January 1912, haemorrhaging occurred frequently, and she became both blind and deaf while the dread diagnosis at the time of tubercular meningitis was made. Her physician warned her mother that there was no hope of recovery. In the two weeks before her healing, she was semi-comatose, during which she had different reassuring visionary experiences in which angels featured. The angelic visitation ended when, in her account,

---

100. *Confidence*, October-December 1922, 58.

101. *Confidence*, October-December 1922, 57.

102. Maddocks, *Vision of Dorothy Kerin*, xi.

103. Ibid., 20.

a "great light came all around me, and an angel took my hands in his and said, 'Dorothy, your sufferings are over. Get up and walk.'"[104] To the amazement of those gathered around her, all "looking very frightened and some clutching each other", she sat up and said "I am well; I must get up and walk." Though having been unable to walk for five years, she got out of bed unassisted, "not the least bit shaky," and descended two flights of stairs to the larder. There, she reported, were "the materials for a real meal of meat and pudding . . . the first solid food I had been able to digest for years." The following morning, her family and friends were amazed to see that her body was in a perfectly normal condition: "I was quite plump, my bones being covered with firm, healthy flesh—all this in the space of twelve hours."[105]

Dorothy left her home four days after her restoration to stay in the home of Dr. Edwin Ash, who took her under his wing for six weeks. Ash seized the opportunity to extend his on-going study of the interrelationship of psychotherapy and spirituality. As he put it in *Faith & Suggestion*, "Here was an opportunity for debating, in full light of scientific investigation and objective fact, the old problems of Mind and Spirit, Suggestion or Faith, Material or Spiritual."[106] Dorothy's version of the invitation, one she gladly accepted, was that it was extended for her to receive necessary rest and quiet. One biographer, however, expressed the view that, for Dorothy, her stay must have been a totally disagreeable experience:

> Dr Ash subjected Dorothy to many hours of painful cross-examination. He was trying to prove that the sudden healing was the result of a supernormal experience, which could be analysed between visionary and dream states of consciousness. He questioned her frequently. Had she read books about religious people, for example St Teresa? Did she know about a mystic play, called *The Miracle*? Did she know there had been a faith-healing mission in her neighbourhood? He asked intrusive questions about the services and prayers that had taken place in her sick room. Throughout these weeks of questioning, Dorothy affirmed, "My healing came direct from God, and from God alone; to Him be the glory."[107]

Though Ash's sympathies lay with finding a place for the "spiritual" dimension, this conclusion did not stretch much further than the tame verdict that "one finds it difficult to neglect the spiritual, as distinct from the mental, aspects of such problems."[108] Any resolution, therefore, of the issues surrounding Dorothy's healing, had to await the test of time: "Her future may perhaps be the witness of their inner meaning."[109] On this pragmatic test,

104. Kerin, *Living Touch*, 11.

105. Ibid., 13.

106. Ash, *Faith & Suggestion*, xiii.

107. Ernest, Johanna. *Dorothy Kerin: Her Ministry of Healing*. Online. Saint Teresa was a prominent Spanish nun. In 1559, she believed that Jesus Christ presented himself to her in bodily form, though invisible, the first in a sequence that lasted for over two years. The drama *The Miracle*, translated from the German, opened in London in 1911. Written by Karl Vollmolle and directed by Max Reinhardt, noted Austrian theatre manager, it was an immediate success. The play retold the old legend of a nun in the Middle Ages who has several mystical adventures. During her absence, the statue of the Virgin Mary in the convent's chapel comes to life and takes the nun's place in the convent.

108. Ash, *Faith & Suggestion*, 142.

109. Ibid., 142.

Dorothy's later remarkable ministry did stand the test of time and came to play a seminal part in the ministry of healing within Anglicanism. Cuthbert Beardsley, the energetic Bishop of Coventry (1956–76), described her among those "who have borne their special witness to the power of the supernatural. . . . Her ministry is one of the most significant features of our day."[110] For twenty-six years (1954–80) the bishop was the spiritual Warden of the Burrswood Fellowship that provided support for the Burrswood Christian Healing Center in Kent, founded by Dorothy, which continues its work up to the present.

It was during her stay with the Ash family that Dorothy had a vision that defined the future course of her life. This vision took place on 11 March 1912 after she was awakened out of sleep by a voice calling her name. When she sat up, she saw at the foot of the bed the face of a beautiful woman holding a lily. Coming closer to her, the woman spoke: "Dorothy, you are quite well now. God has brought you back to use you for a great and privileged work. In your prayers and faith many sick shall you heal; comfort the sorrowing and give faith to the faithless. Many rebuffs will you have, but remember you are thrice blessed: His grace is sufficient for thee. He will never leave thee." After making the sign of the cross over her with her lily, the figure disappeared. When she awoke in the morning, the room was still full of the scent of the lily.

In an article penned for *The Weekly Budget*, she disclosed that "how these things are going to be brought into practice has not been revealed to me yet." It took seventeen years to pass before she entered her defining ministry. The period 1912–29 has been described as the years of preparation that ended when she opened in 1929 her first residential home of healing. St. Raphael Home became part of an enlarged complex known as Chapel House, in Ealing, London. In 1948 she established Burrswood, a large residential healing center at Tunbridge Wells, Kent, which lives on as a forty-bed licensed Hospital with extensive outpatient facilities. These are proclaimed to offer "excellence in interdisciplinary healthcare, where hurting and broken people discover the love of Christ in action."[111]

The years of preparation had phases of longer-term consequence. Dorothy's letters reveal that she lived at many different addresses, though for long periods she was a house guest of the Rev. Dr. Richard Langford-James and his wife. Langford-James was one of the few Anglican priests in England at the time who was well-versed in mystical and ascetical theology. During this time, Dorothy had full access not only to his extensive library, but she also had to face his quite rigid and demanding spiritual direction. He became to her the father figure she lacked since the death of her natural father when she was a girl of thirteen. The vicarage had a chapel of the Blessed Sacrament on an upper floor where all the niceties of Anglo-Catholic practice were observed.[112] This was probably the period of her greatest mystical encounters, when she went through phases of spiritual development such as those described in the writings of St. John of the Cross.[113] She had conversations with the Devil and visions of the Virgin Mary and the Holy Family at Bethlehem. During

110. Ross, *Dorothy*, 5 & 6.

111. Anon. "Burrswood: Christian Hospital." Online.

112. Furlong, *Burrswood*, 36.

113. St. John of the Cross (1542–91), Spanish writer whose treatises on the mystical life direct attention to the purifying of the soul for transformation and participation in God.

Bishop of Rochester, Dorothy, Bishop of Coventry

the Great War, she had out-of-body experiences, finding herself among the terrors of trench warfare at the Front in France ministering to the dying soldiers. At this time also, during the Feast of the Immaculate Conception in 1915, she became the first Anglican known to have manifested the stigmata, which persisted painfully for months. Langford-Jones invited fellow-priests and trusted friends to witness the marks, a fact that was kept confidential at her wish until after her death. Throughout these years her general health at times deteriorated. Such times were distinguished as occasions of redemptive suffering that was "offered perhaps in some tiny way as a drop in the filling up of the cup [of suffering]."[114] The guiding hand of Langford-Jones confirmed her in the Anglo-Catholicism of her upbringing, though not at the expense of wider sympathies. During her first overseas mission in 1959 to Sweden, her biographer noted that "the sight of an Anglo-Catholic speaking from the pulpit of a Lutheran stronghold, interpreted by a member of the Salvation Army, was for many an inspiring event."[115]

Incidents such as these, bizarre as they are to the prevailing mindset, came into wider circulation with her book *The Living Touch*. It was first published in 1914, in part to put right "inaccuracies and exaggerations" that had been spreading since her healing two years previously. Ever since, it has rarely been out of print. The favorable reaction to her story from the four distinguished personages named below helps to disabuse any easy idea that her experiences were little more than the reveries of a deluded mind given to hallucinatory bouts. Of the three men, one was a member of the House of Lords and the other two were distinguished scientists, honored for their eminence in science by being elected FRS (Fellow Royal Society). In later editions, the Preface to the book was

---

114. Kerin, *Fulfilling*, 46. The biblical reference is to Col 1:24: "I fill up in my flesh what is still lacking in regard to Christ's afflictions, for the sake of his body which is the church."

115. Arnold, *Dorothy Kerin*, 205.

provided by Lord Daryngton (Herbert Pike Pease), who was elected MP (Member of Parliament) for Darlington (1908–23) and ennobled in 1923. For thirty-two years he was President of the Church Army, an Anglican society of lay evangelists, somewhat similar to the Salvation Army. The book, he wrote, was in his judgment "a truthful account, with corroborating evidence, of probably the most remarkable miracle of modern times."

One other member of the nobility who took an interest in Dorothy was Lady Henry Somerset (1851–1921), the separated wife of Lord Somerset whose homosexual proclivities broke their marriage. She came to wide public recognition when she was elected President of the British Women's Temperance Association.[116] Her involvement in the ministry of healing stretched back to 1903 when she was invited by J. M. Hickson to join the committee of his Society of Emmanuel, a year after the formation of the Guild of Health. In November 1912, she invited Dorothy to one of her palatial properties in Surrey. During her stay Dorothy had several visions of the Virgin Mary. In one of them "the Blessed Virgin held a large shiny cross, which she placed on my knees, and said, 'Always by prayer and faith, but this must come first,' pointing to the cross."[117]

Daryngton illustrated the impact of *The Living Touch* by inserting a quotation from G. F. C. Searle (1864–1954) in the Preface. Searle had been elected a Fellow of the Royal Society (FRS) in 1905 for his work in experimental physics carried out at the prestigious Cavendish Laboratory, Cambridge, where he claimed to have had more Nobel Prize winners as his pupils than any other man. The quotation read: "For about seven years, I went through a dark time of nervous and physical weakness, with a complete breakdown in 1910. At the end of 1914, there came into my hands Miss Dorothy Kerin's little book, *The Living Touch*. . . . It opened my eyes, as they have never been opened before, to the present-day power of the living God. . . . As an immediate result, all the old weakness left me, and I was well."

The other FRS was Sir Alister Hardy (1896–1985), a distinguished zoologist, and investigator of religious experience. In the latter pursuit, he founded and became director of the Religious Research Unit at Oxford that subsequently extended to Princeton. He wrote the Foreword to Johanna Ernest's biography of Dorothy Kerin, making it clear that, though he called himself a Christian, he was far from being an orthodox one. Even so, he described *The Living Touch* that he had read during the Great War a "remarkable little volume," regarding it as one of "the spiritual classics."[118] To show how much he agreed with a statement she made on prayer, he cited it approvingly in his Gifford Lecture, later published as *The Divine Flame* (1966). Dorothy was mentioned in his book *The Spiritual Nature of Man* (1979), in his reference to prominent figures who gave witness to experiencing visions and hearing voices. The list included Socrates, Saint Francis, Saint Joan of Arc, Luther, Swedenborg, and Blake. He continued: "In our own day we have had the

---

116. Under her strong leadership, she saw BWTA membership increase to make it a social and political force. In 1903, she left public life and devoted herself to establishing the "Colony for Women Inebriates" at Reigate, Surrey.

117. Ernest, *Life of Dorothy Kerin*. 57.

118. Ibid., xiv.

striking testimony of both phenomena in the remarkable life . . . of the late Miss Dorothy Kerin."[119]

As might be expected, Boddy moved quickly to make contact with Dorothy. Those items in her story that disturbed mainstream Christians were neither unfamiliar nor unprecedented to the editor of *Confidence*. Visionary occurrences and angelic visitations featured at times in Pentecostal worship. One of the earliest references to a vision was that experienced by a new convert in the All Saints Parish Hall, Sunderland, in October 1907. The man testified to the "Blessed Lord Himself" standing before him "just ready to put his loving arms around me."[120] He claimed to have seen and conversed with his two younger sisters and brother who had died a few years earlier. During a visit he paid to Oslo early in 1909, Boddy described the scene in "a very bare low mission-room" where boys and girls between seven and twelve years old "were seeing visions and speaking in tongues. . . . A bright lad cried out with intense vehemence, 'Oh, I see the house of Satan thrust down.'"[121]

One of the most reported of visions was one of Christ seen in the Island Place Mission Hall, Llanelli, South Wales, in July, 1914. While Stephen Jeffreys was preaching, on the wall behind him there appeared a lamb's face that remained clearly visible for about a quarter of an hour, and then morphed into the face thought to be of Christ. The vision remained on the wall for many hours and was seen by hundreds of people who came to behold it. J. W. Adams, the Vicar of Wall Parish Church, Lichfield, Staffs, investigated the incident assiduously and was satisfied of its credibility.[122] That said, a cautionary note on such phenomena was issued by a correspondent to *Confidence* from Nova Scotia: "Visions and dreams are sweet, but the [written] Word is mighty. . . . I have seen some fail on that point."[123]

Visions in which angels appeared also were recorded. In a letter from Bournemouth, the writer spoke of his vision of Calvary where beside the cross "stood an angel."[124] From South Africa, J. G. Lake related that at "a children's meeting a choir of angels appeared (angel children) and sang 'Suffer little children to come unto Me.'"[125] The most reported of angelic appearances emanated from Boddy, who had ministered to troops on the battlefront in France during the Great War. Testimonies to what took place after the much-publicized Angel of Mons episode were printed in *Confidence*.[126] A "Pentecostal brother" who served as a stretcher-bearer in the King's Royal Rifles spoke of angels "visiting our

119. Hardy, *Spiritual Nature of Man*, 37.

120. *Confidence*, 15 August, 1908, 6.

121. Ibid., March, 1909, 59.

122. Gee, *Wind and Flame*, 91–92. Also, Adams *Miracles Today*, 14–21.

123. *Confidence*, 15 August 1908, 14.

124. Ibid., March 1909, 61.

125. Ibid., August, 1909. Bournemouth was the town where the first purpose-built Pentecostal church in Britain was erected in November, 1908.

126. The unattributed article in *Wikipedia* on the Angel(s) of Mons presents it as "a popular legend about a group of angels who supposedly protected members of the British army in the Battle of Mons at the outset of World War I. The story is fictitious, developed through a combination of a patriotic short story by Arthur Machen, rumors, mass hysteria, and urban legend, claimed visions after the battle and also possibly deliberately seeded propaganda."

men" over the trenches near Ypres, Belgium. Speaking of his own experience, he told of his comrades in the trench "forming one line of prayer," then once the shelling ceased "we all saw a host of angels and talked about them." Another time, he saw an angel flying with a trumpet in his mouth.[127] In an attempt to prove the authenticity of these accounts, appended to the soldier's letter were ten questions put to him and his response. Question 9 read, "Where did this vision of the angel with the trumpet take place? [Reply]: At Labrick at 9 o'clock, the 7th December [1915]." Such baffling reports helped to ensure that Boddy and Dorothy would not be dismissive of like manifestations out of hand.

The first mention in *Confidence* of the Kerin healing was found in the March 1912 edition. It was a reprint from the *Christian Herald* under the heading "A Girl's Miracle-exclaiming Cure." At the Whitsun Annual Conference in Sunderland in June, Boddy retailed the same story. In a footnote to the printed report he added that he had a long talk with Dorothy and, at the same time, recommended Ash's *Faith & Suggestion: Including an Account of the Remarkable Experiences of Dorothy Kerin*. In the January 1913 edition of *Confidence,* he wrote that "everyone should read this booklet," a reference to the sixteen-page pamphlet by J. Logan Thompson, the Baptist minister who took Dorothy to his family home after her stay with Dr Ash. Without loss of time, Thompson published her story under the title *London's Modern Miracle*. It had a wide circulation outside Britain, the Swedish edition, in particular, forging a close link with that country.

In the April 1913 edition of *Confidence*, Boddy again referred to Dorothy, pronouncing: "We do not know a more wonderful miracle since the days of the Apostles, nor one which the Lord has allowed to be so fully verified by the medical profession." The May 1913 edition brought the news that Dorothy was currently spending some time with the Boddys and had given "her testimony with blessed effect" at some sessions of that year's Whitsun Conference. However, it was not until the following Conference that a significant fact became public knowledge. At the closing meeting, it was recorded that "Miss Dorothy Kerin [told] how she received the Baptism of the Holy Ghost at All Saint's Vicarage twelve months ago." In an extended tour of America in the early autumn of 1914, Boddy took the opportunity to meet A. B. Simpson, "a friend of 25 years standing." Invited to give an address on "Divine Health and Healing," he concluded by telling of "our dear Sister Dorothy Kerin's baptism in the Spirit with the sign of tongues."[128]

Dorothy gave her own account of the 1913 Sunderland Convention. After the Bishop of Durham, Handley Moule, had given permission, she was asked by Boddy to speak at All Saints on the first Sunday after Trinity. She recalled the occasion:

> I stood on the chancel steps, facing the congregation, and had begun to speak, when I was seized with a dreadful faintness, and felt as though I was falling into a black pit. I realised my danger, and was just able to breathe out the word "Jesus," when two great bright angels appeared, one on each side, supporting me. It seemed as if they put words into my mouth, and when I had finished speaking there was a great hush, and I found myself safely back in the choir stalls. How I got there I do not know,

127. *Confidence*, January 1916, 7.
128. Ibid., October, 1914, 183–84.

for I did not feel my feet touch the ground. Almost everyone in the church felt His presence, and two were healed.[129]

In the *Living Touch* edition, 1919, there is a footnote to this passage: "I now see definitely that it was a mistake." What to make of this statement will be considered below.

A vignette of Dorothy's stay of several weeks with the Boddys is presented in Marina Chavchavadze's biography of Dorothy. Marina was an aristocrat of Georgian extraction, who at the age of fourteen escaped at gunpoint with her mother from the Bolsheviks. She was to prove a devoted helper to Dorothy, then to Burrswood from 1930 for the next fifty-five years. Marina's biography recounts the picture that Jane, the younger of the two Boddy teenage daughters, painted of Dorothy's visit:

> I remember very well my first sight of her, in a cream serge suit and a white fur, with a small white felt hat to match, though she usually wore blue. She looked like a school girl though she was older than my sister and I. She settled down as one of us and she was always full of fun and entered into everything with zest. She soon tired and often we would find her curled up fast asleep on her bed. . . . She and my mother had much in common spiritually and I can picture her sitting on a low stool beside my mother's chair, having a very serious conversation. When my sister and I last saw Dorothy in 1960, she said: "I learned so much from your mother, and you two are the last remaining links with those days."[130]

The two women had much in common. Mary, too, ministered healing and administered the laying on of hands privately.

Marina, in the post-1960s, was often asked whether Dorothy would have joined the Charismatic Renewal had she still been alive, whether she prayed in tongues and whether she practiced the healing of memories. Her response was, "I am convinced she would have loved the joy, praise and thanksgiving when offered in true worship. I am equally sure that today she would have been in the forefront of the spiritual renewal. Dorothy did not speak in tongues, but this gift was not unknown to her according to some Swedish friends who told me that she had prayed in tongues when she shared their Pentecostal worship. As to the healing of memories, she did not need to learn any methods, as she was guided entirely by her Lord."[131] Marina then added an observation, which might have had a bearing on Dorothy's remark about her experience at the Sunderland conven¬tion being "definitely a mistake."

The problem with the statement is to what the "it" refers. Johanna Ernest took it to mean that it was a mistake "to have spoken at that time." This conjecture leaves unresolved the question as to *why* "it" was a mistake at that particular point in time. Could it be in some way related to her situation in 1919? By then, Dorothy had been based in the Langford-James vicarage for almost four years. The Chavchavadze biography contains Marina's personal appraisal: "Over the years I have seen [Dorothy's] potential powers for

---

129. Kerin, *Living Touch,* 22–23.

130. Chavchavadze, *Dorothy Kerin As I Knew Her,* 4. Jane Boddy became Mother Joanna Mary of the Community of the Resurrection in South Africa.

131. Ibid., 55. The healing of memories featured greatly in the ministry of Agnes Sanford, about whom see below.

expressing herself which Dr. Langford-James unwittingly suppressed during her early years by his Victorian disciplines. When we talked, I often saw Dorothy's eyes light up with enthusiasm—she was not Irish [her father] for nothing—and she would start singing a favourite hymn or a song of praise with gusto. We all noticed how she gradually moved from the set Anglo-Catholic formulae towards a middle-of-the-road Anglican worship. I am sure that today she would have moved with the times by keeping true [non-Roman?] Eucharistic worship intact."[132] Langford-James, her first mentor, was among the strictest of Anglo-Catholics, and demanded from Dorothy total obedience to his decisions. Later in their acquaintance, he suggested that she take as her Rule the vows of poverty, chastity and obedience, to which she acceded.

Dorothy was a strong-willed young woman, and obedience did not come easily to her. There were occasions when Langford-James had to reproach her for laxity in the observance of her Rule. In temperament, she "possessed a sparkling wit and naturally happy disposition . . . in every respect a magnificent and fascinating personality. All her friends of either sex had a tendency to fall in love with her."[133] Such was the view of another of her biographers, Dorothy Musgrave Arnold, who came to know her in her Burrswood days. It is of little wonder that, for a spirited person such as Dorothy, to imbibe the spiritual/mystical discipline known as the Dark Night of the Soul led her to think she was going mad.[134] Her split with Langford-James was precipitated by a young American clergyman who had been in correspondence with her for some time. In the summer of 1929 he traveled across the Atlantic in the hope of inducing her to marry him. He was aware of her vow of celibacy, though he considered the vows taken years before more as a private affair. When he approached Dorothy with his proposal, she reminded him that she had "vowed to live my life in God's service in holy chastity, poverty and obedience." Realizing this was her final decision, he strode across the lawn to speak to Langford-James. A long, heated argument ensued, during which "the American priest told his Anglican brother how wrongly he thought he had acted in allowing his young ward to make such vows for life, and that for his part he felt convinced that it was to do the work of the Devil to continue to keep hidden between the four walls of his Vicarage such a rare and precious soul whom God had endowed with so great a charismatic gift."[135] Shortly afterwards, Dorothy returned to live with her mother, making it quite clear that she was now convinced that God was calling her to serve him in the wider world.

The possibility remains that Dorothy was thwarted from a nascent sympathy for Pentecostalism by the dominating influence of her spiritual director, even if done from the best of motives. In his notes Langford-James observed that, under his direction,

132. Ibid., 55.

133. Arnold. *Dorothy Kerin*, 46.

134. Ibid., 60. The term "Dark Night of the Soul" is used for a spiritual crisis in a journey towards union with God as described by Saint John of the Cross. Typically, spiritual disciplines such as prayer become extremely difficult and unrewarding for an extended period of time. Feelings of abandonment by God are common. Such a process is seen as a purgation of the soul, cleansing it of all self-interest, preparing the way for interior purity and union with God.

135. Arnold, *Dorothy Kerin*, 64. Dorothy's maternal instinct is exhibited by her adopting nine war-orphaned babies between 1941 and 1942.

Dorothy "had learnt to be more discerning and less obliging in the sense of putting herself at the mercy of the sentimentalism of her friends."[136] When he first met her he found her anxious not to hurt feelings with a display of natural affection. He sought to moderate that side of her personality by cultivating a deeper sense of interiority. In Arnold's assessment, Dorothy's former manner of life, which allowed expression of her breezy temperament, "dissipated" under the Langford-James regime.[137] Her affections became increasingly rooted in the disciplines of the Langford-James' household. The price of giving up her freedom was her periods of restiveness and spiritual darkness. One of the last entries in the Langford-James' diary of his tutelage contained the admission, "It is quite certain that some mistakes have been made by me."[138] On the other hand, Dorothy, writing some thirty years after her departure from the Vicarage, was able to state, "I owe much to his wise guidance, and to his care for the development of my spiritual life. For this I am profoundly grateful."[139]

Dorothy's theological sympathies lay with the High Church tradition from her earliest years, something of which Boddy would have been aware. It is possible that the "mistake" surrounding the indeterminate "it" was the whole Sunderland experience interpreted through the stringent eyes of her spiritual tutor. Under the four years of his constraining influence, it would be understandable that any tug she might have felt towards Pentecostal spirituality would have waned under the intensity of his Catholic scrupulosity. When the Langford-James family, with Dorothy, moved to a new parish with a strong "Protestant" tradition, considerable friction was aroused, in Arnold's phrase, by his "extreme Catholic views and practices."[140] So, for him, any attraction to a different spirituality by Dorothy would have been judged a lack of discernment on her part, an exemplification, in his words, of putting herself at "the mercy of the sentimentalism of her friends."[141]

The passing of time has revealed that any antithesis of charismatic and Catholic spirituality is not inescapable. The Charismatic Renewal movement of the 1960s demonstrated that Catholicism in all its forms and Pentecostalism are not diametrically opposed. Agnes Sanford (1897–1982) is a case in point. The child of American Presbyterian missionaries to China, she married an Episcopal priest in 1923. After she was freed of long-standing depression, her ministry of healing blossomed with the publication of *The Healing Light* (1947). Around 1953–54, she received the gift of tongues, and became one of the foremost proponents of the Charismatic Renewal within the historic churches. Her teaching/healing ministry gave considerable weight to the sacramental dimension. She and Dorothy met only once, and that cursorily, at Burrswood. Later, after Dorothy's death, Agnes stayed at the center for a short spell and spoke to the community "with her usual inspired teaching, spiced with humor."[142] It was through contact with her at a summer

136. Ibid., 45.

137. Ibid., 48.

138. Ibid., 65.

139. Kerin, *Fulfilling*, 22.

140. Arnold, *Dorothy Kerin*, 61.

141. Ibid., 45.

142. Chavchavadze, *Dorothy Kerin*, 70.

retreat in 1967 that Francis MacNutt, at the time a Roman Catholic priest, found himself in the position where "Mrs Sanford and two other friends prayed over me that I might receive [the] unfolding of the Spirit and the release of all the gifts. As she prayed, she shared a prophecy that the Lord would work through me in bringing healing prayer back to the Catholic Church."[143] Stevens Heckscher, an Anglican Benedictine, brought the two women together in an article when he wrote, "My own Anglican tradition is less careful [than Eastern Orthodox] with its saints. Among these I would include the American Agnes Sanford and Dorothy Kerin. Both of these early-to-mid-twentieth century women were pioneers, each in her country, of their Church's healing ministry."[144]

Alister McGrath gives good reason why the Charismatic and Sacramental/Liturgical traditions have something in common that is not shared with the Reformed tradition. The former two insist that the divine may be encountered in the secular realm. Both Zwingli's Zürich and Calvin's Geneva conceived the world as one where the "spiritual/sacred" cannot be directly encountered but are known indirectly, primarily in a logocentric manner, through reading the Bible and sermons.[145] Such a development can be seen as the tendency to "desacralize" the world, and leave nature "disenchanted." It can be argued that it no accident that the two centers of early Calvinism—Geneva and Edinburgh—were to become beacons of Enlightenment rationalism two centuries later. The "resacralization" ethos of Pentecostalism affirms that Christ may be experienced at the present moment and has the power to heal and transform people and communities both at the point and moment of their need. There is an insistence "upon the universal accessibility of the divine."[146] The scorn that Bishop Henson poured upon Puller's plea for recognition of spiritual healing in the Book of Common Prayer arose from his fear that it would be a regressive step "remythologization," an objectionable signal of cultural death and the certain debasement of religion and "the recrudescence of medievalism in the ecclesiastical world.[147] His attitude to Pentecostalism, on this show, would have been, if anything, harsher.

The Thaumaturgical Model

James Moore Hickson (1876–1933) can be taken as more representative of the thaumaturgical (Gk: "wonder-working") mode, though with sacramental overtones. The Australian academic, Mark Henderson, places him firmly in the Anglo-Catholic tradition, declaring that his career as a charismatic healer "was underpinned, funded and shaped by his attachment to Anglo-Catholic attempts at church renewal in the 1920s."[148] This assertion will be weighed up below. What is known is that by the early 1920s Hickson had become, in Mullin's assessment, "arguably the most famous proponent of Christian healing in the

143. MacNutt, *Nearly Perfect Crime*, 225.

144. Heckscher,. "Dorothy Kerin," 20.

145. McGrath, *Christianity's Dangerous Idea*, 264.

146. Ibid., 427 & 428.

147. Henson, *Notes on Spiritual Healing*, xxiii & 16.

148. Hutchinson, "The Worcester Circle." Online.

English-speaking world."[149] Born in Australia, the sixth of thirteen children, into a family that often prayed for the sick, Hickson witnessed his first healing at the age of fourteen. Two of his cousins were healed instantly when he prayed for them. His mother encouraged him in the use of his special gift. Between 1882 and 1890 he used the gift when the occasion presented itself through prayer and the laying on of hands. Sometimes healing was received at a distance, with sufferers unaware that they were being prayed for. At the same time, he was pursuing a career in banking.

In 1900 a change in direction took place when his wife's uncle, a doctor, pressed him to come to London and minister healing to a young British officer who had been grievously wounded in the Boer War. He recorded:

> I went and laid my hands on [the officer] in silent prayer. In a few moments all pain had left him and he made a very rapid recovery. The doctor said to me afterwards: "You have no right to be doing anything else, with such a gift of the Spirit," and in a strange way it was borne in upon me that God was calling me to dedicate my life to His Healing Ministry. From that time I have done nothing else, and I have made it my life's work to try to revive in the Church this part of her ministry, which has been lying in abeyance for so long.[150]

On the doctor's advice, he decided to acquire a medical training, enough to gain a basic understanding of anatomy and physiology. It was something he found useful at times, especially when working with doctors. Much of the time up to 1919 was given to speaking on the subject and healing missions. Numerous addresses were given at theological colleges, conferences, and meetings of clergy such as the pan-Anglican Congress in London in 1908. A number of missions were held in the East End of London, during which he first met John Maillard, as well as in other parts of England.

In his autobiographical introduction to *Heal the Sick*, Hickson alluded to his part in founding the Society of Emmanuel in 1905 in England, and his role as its President. Its committee was composed of people drawn from polite society. It included, among others, Bishop Mylne, late Bishop of Bombay and present Suffragan Bishop of Worcester, as its vice-president, together with Adelaine Duchess of Bedford, Countess Beauchamp, Mrs Edward Trotter, Mrs Dickin, Rev. Maurice Bell, Rev. George Trevelyan, W. M. Wroughton, Lady Somerset, and Lady Mosley.[151] Such names and rank bear out Hensley Henson's observation, and foreboding, that the "new doctrine" of spiritual healing had "invaded the religious world recently, and gained in the Church of England considerable patronage and support."[152] Hickson provided no background to explain how such a collection of prominent, High Church, worthies came to be connected to a cause that had for its first aim "to develop the Divine gifts left to His Church by the Master, especially the gift of healing by prayer and laying on of hands, with the object of using these Divine gifts not only for the healing of the body, but as a means of drawing the souls of men nearer to God." Mark

---

149. Ibid., 237.

150. Hickson, *Heal the Sick*, 7.

151. Ibid., 8. As indicated above, Lady Somerset had links with Dorothy Kerin.

152. Henson, *Spiritual Healing*, xxiv.

Hutchinson has pieced together the complex background to the founding of the Society, of which only the bare bones can be presented here. The story fixes round his intriguing concept of the "Worcester Circle," which had for its leading players Charles Gore, and Louis George Mylne. Gore was appointed Bishop of Worcester in 1902 and, when the new diocese of Birmingham was formed largely through his efforts, became its first bishop in 1905. A personal friend of Gore, Mylne, following his retirement as Bishop of Bombay, was appointed rector of Alvechurch (1905–17) in the Worcester diocese.

Charles Gore (1853–1932), a lifelong Anglo-Catholic, was one of the leading church-men of his generation. Radical in his socio-political views and a stalwart for church re-form, he argued that it was almost impossible for an established church to be salt and leaven. In a sermon preached in 1906 he stated that while the early church spoke for the poor, the Church of England, despite many efforts, was not the church of the people. "What we need," he proclaimed, is "to make our religion more real, more full of power, and more attractive." This required a "deeper apprehension of the presence and activity of the Holy Spirit of God," a plea that he elucidated more fully in his book *The Holy Spirit and the Church: The Reconstruction of Belief* (1924). He drew the following lesson from Paul's first letter to the church at Corinth, noting that

> the enthusiastic cultivation of ecstatic gifts in a public assembly of the Church, this "liturgy of the Spirit" was a very highly valued part of public worship at Corinth and very likely elsewhere. . . . The Corinthian meetings afforded an opportunity for unofficial persons to exercise spiritual gifts. We cannot help wondering whether the ordinary excuses for officialism were not allowed too lightly to abolish them. We recall the revivalist meetings and free prayer meetings which before and after the Reformation the Church has frowned upon, but which, with all their admitted ex-cesses and absurdities, have nourished and exhibited a real and intense spirituality. We assent to St. Paul's demand that such manifestations of the Spirit should be kept within the bounds of Church order, but it is difficult to restrain the feeling that in one form or another they ought never to have been abandoned, and that a good deal of the freedom of the Spirit was lost, when they ceased to hold their place among the methods of the Church, and only officials of the Church could lead the public worship.[153]

To carry out his quest for a dynamic "church for the people" he needed to cultivate a sup-port base of like minded persons. When the rectorship of Alvechurch became available, it was to Mylne that he turned.

Scottish-born Louis Mylne (1843–1941) was for a time a tutor at Keble College, Oxford. The College was established in memory of John Keble (1792–1866), a founding member of the Tractarian Movement, which sought to recover the Catholic heritage of the Church of England. He moved in Anglo-Catholic circles, among whom was Percy Dearmer whose *Body and Soul* (1909) was a text for sacramental healing. Mylne's involve-ment in missionary work in India led to his appointment as Bishop of Bombay during the years 1876–97. One truth his missionary experience had impressed on him was that "work on Apostolic methods . . . is what will give Apostolic results." On his return to

---

153. Hutchinson, "The Worcester Circle." Online.

parish work in England, Mylne met with Hickson at a time of family heartache. His son, stricken by tetanus, had been given up by his doctor, only to be restored to complete health after Hickson had laid hands on him.

This event, to Hutchinson's mind, turned Mylne's thought to the opportunity to add a new dimension of apostolic method to the mix of mission outreach. It was a key moment for both men. For Mylne, by introducing Hickson to the Worcester Circle the profile of healing would be raised, and outreach to the outsider quickened. For Hickson, the introduction to Mylne was his gateway to the circle of the influential socially and religiously active Anglo-Catholic elite. Their involvement in the Society of Emmanuel confirmed his calling to the healing ministry, and raised his profile as a healer. Mylne's close relationship with Gore was critical because Gore needed the support of socially-minded High Church Anglicans for his restructuring of the church in the Birmingham diocese to make it more a church of the people. It was an assessment that had the full sympathy of Hickson who felt strongly that the healing ministry "gives to the church a point of contact with the 'man on the street' which nothing else can give," and provides a reminder that God is still active, using it as a means "to unite all communions of the Church of Christ."[154]

Another facet to the story is that, possibly through the good offices of Mylne, Hickson met with the Bishop of London apropos the ministry of healing. Three years later the Archbishop of Canterbury, Randall Davidson, was so impressed by Hickson's volume *The Healing of Christ in his Church* (1908) that he gave copies of it to all the bishops attending the current Lambeth Conference. In being recognized in the higher circles of Anglicanism, Hickson opened the door to the practice healing in a thaumaturgic direction to a degree that neither Boddy nor Polhill could have attained. Henson, for one, was alarmed by such developments: "It appears that the Church of the Future is to include Spiritualism, Socialism, and Faith-healing in its Gospel and every conceivable variety of spiritual exercise in its worship. . . . The prospect is not attractive."[155] Henson had every reason to hold such a view; such was the demand for exotic religion in the era of the "roar-

James M. Hickson

ing twenties." The impact of WWI lingered on as families sought to make contact with the war dead. Some folk sought healing at the hands of Spiritualist practitioners, the best known of whom included Harry Edwards and Estelle Roberts. In 1920 and 1922, Sadhu Sunder Singh brought his own brand of healing exoticism to Britain.[156] Also, the "new psychology" played a part in the relief of cases of wartime shell shock, in some cases to the

154. Mullin, *Miracles*, 241.

155. Mews, "Revival of Spiritual Healing," 315–16.

156. Sahdu Sunder Singh (1889–1929), often described as the "Apostle of India, was known for his endurance and supernatural deeds.

point of dramatic cure. There was sufficient evidence at the time for L. W. Grensted to announce, "The age of miracles had come again."[157]

As noted earlier, Hutchinson placed Hickson firmly in the Anglo-Catholic camp because almost every step in his career as a charismatic healer "was underpinned, funded and shaped by his attachment to Anglo-Catholic attempts at church renewal in the 1920s."[158] What this paragraph and the following seek to do is to make the case for a thaumaturgical edge to his ministry of healing, albeit in a sacramental contextual relationship. Henson, in his diary, wrote that Hickson's book *Heal the Sick* (1924), full as it was of commendations from Anglican bishops in the overseas territories he visited, only provided evidence "of the general surrender of the Anglican hierarchy to this wave of thaumaturgic literalism."[159] Other pieces of evidence would suggest that his practice of healing had a thaumaturgic flavor. Anson described Hickson as among those healers who were aiming to revive the "atmosphere of Galilee," the setting where many healings were an integral part of the wonders and signs recorded in the Gospels (cf. Acts 2:22).

Mullin is of the opinion that, of the three models of healing, Hickson fitted best with the thaumaturgic, in that he recognized the gift as one promised in 1 Corinthians 12, where healing is listed among the gifts of the Spirit.[160] We need never "have any doubt or scruple about receiving healing through an earthly healer," Hickson wrote to assure dithering sufferers that to some "has been given the gift of healing by the Spirit. It is an institution of God Himself for the restoration of those who are sick."[161] Like earlier proponents of this model, he believed that the gift of healing operated "frequently in the early church, less frequently through the Christian Ages, and was currently being renewed."

That he was not alone in the healing ministry is attested to by Hickson's mention of the frequency of reports of healing aired "at the present time." This is almost certainly a reference to the Pentecostal healing evangelists of the stamp of Smith Wigglesworth and the brothers Stephen and George Jeffreys. Hickson was close to the position taken by Pentecostals, though diversified by an added sacramental affinity, and lack of inhibition about co-operation with the medical profession. His calling was to work within the Anglican Communion in its global extension. There was little emphasis placed on the atonement, and more leverage given to the Incarnation: "The truth of the Incarnation is the rock on which our Lord's ministry is founded."[162] He pointed to the fact that persons of great faith had been known to receive healing "directly from Christ in the Holy Communion."[163]

---

157. Mews, "Revival of Spiritual Healing," 317. Canon L. W. Grensted was one of the foremost psychologists in the Church of England; Oriel Professor of the Philosophy of the Christian Religion; member of the Archbishop's Committee on Doctrine and on Spiritual Healing.

158. Hutchinson, "Worcester Circle."

159. Mews, "Revival of Spiritual Healing," 306–7.

160. Mullin, *Miracles*, 240.

161. Hickson, *Revival of the Gifts of Healing*. Online, 27.

162. Hickson, *The Healing of Christ*, 14.

163. Ibid., 8.

While recognizing that God grants requests for healing in answer to personal and united prayer, and through Holy Communion, Hickson was clear that "God has ordained special means by which he imparts healing," through the charismatic gifting of lay people as much as clerics. In his healing services, this was visibly instanced when he preceded the bishop or priest in the laying on of hands as they passed down the line of supplicants. What seemed to disturb those senior clerics who were otherwise supportive of the ministry of healing was the size of the crowds attracted to his healing services in the early 1920s. Fear of populist immoderation, popularly associated with religious sects, was uppermost in the mind of the church authorities. The Brampton Lecturer in 1930 opined that "the great danger of missions of healing is that by their very prestige and by their impressive setting they act with immense power along these lines [i.e., crudities of mere suggestion]. They attract and profoundly affect hysterics of all kinds."[164] George Bell, the Bishop of Chichester, approved of healing services in parish churches in his diocese so long as they were held under strict conditions and limited in scale. Arthur Winnington-Ingram, Bishop of London, told Henson that in his diocese he had requested Hickson to confine himself to laying hands "on a few folk quietly," and was vexed at reports of mass turnouts at healing services in the Bradford area, Yorkshire, in 1924. The Archbishop of York, Cosmo Lang, encouraged the local Bishop to support the York mission but hoped that it would be possible to avoid "attracting large over-emotional crowds."[165]

The upholders of the Anglican ethos of moderation clearly sensed a threat that called for a rethink on the whole issue of spiritual healing. With Hickson in their sights, the upshot was that both the American and English Anglican churches established Commissions on the question in the wake of the popular excitement raised by healing, with Hickson in their sights.[166] Meanwhile, the Society of Emmanuel was dissolved in 1921 as it considered itself to have achieved its object as Hickson explained: "Inasmuch as I was then holding healing missions throughout the world in cathedrals and churches, and therefore guilds and societies for healing were superfluous and unnecessary. Our work was for the revival of this ministry in the Church and no other organization should be needed." The reports of the Commissions, however, turned out to be not quite so sanguine.

Both the British and American medical establishments proved lukewarm on the Commission's report. Its reviewer in the *British Medical Journal* pronounced it "nebulous," and likely to "cause disappointment not only to the enthusiastic supporters of what is called spiritual healing, but also to those who may have looked forward to a reasoned statement on the matter."[167] The Report granted that "sometimes a special gift of healing seems to be bestowed on a particular person." Nevertheless, it recommended that attendances at healing services be restricted to the patient and one or two close Christian friends, and a small group of selected Christian people who had previously met for prayer and discussion on the whole theme of religion and healing.[168] The American main report,

---

164. Weatherhead, *Psychology*, 204. The lectures were delivered by L. W. Grensted.

165. Mews, "Revival of Spiritual Healing," 326–27.

166. Mullin, *Miracles*, 240.

167. Anon. "Spiritual Healing in the English Church," 120.

168. Weatherhead, *Psychology*, 208.

published in 1931, also largely limited healing in clerical hands to the therapeutic mode, finding little or no place for the use of consecrated oil or the gift of healing.

It was not until the 1920s that Hickson became an internationally known. Between 1921 and 1924 he conducted healing services and missions in North America, Egypt, Ceylon (now Sri Lanka), India, Burma, Malaysia, China , Japan, the Philippines, Palestine, South Africa, Rhodesia (now Zimbabwe), Australia, and New Zealand. He began a tour of the United States in 1919, visiting over thirty-three cites from Boston to San Francisco, preaching in their Episcopal churches. In May 1920, he returned to New York where his ministry found favor with William Manning, rector of one of the wealthiest and most prestigious churches in the country. Trinity Church in Wall Street saw throngs exceeding a thousand people pass through its doors, many of them crowding to the altar for the laying on of hands. One newspaper reported that "about 700 invalids were admitted yesterday to Trinity Episcopal Chapel near Broadway. . . . The doors of the church were opened at 9 o'clock and the church was filled in a few minutes. . . . Many of the visitors were apparently persons of means and drove up in automobiles. Mr Hickson gave special attention to each person, and this required several minutes in some cases. Then each individual knelt with Dr. Manning for prayer. Every day a clergyman will stand by Mr Hickson to give spiritual comfort."[169] Delighted with the response, Hickson rejoiced "that to America has been given this sacred trust of reviving the ministry of healing."[170] Manning's backing had the effect, as one journalist at the time observed, of opening "the most exclusive religious edifices in America" for Hickson, thus raising the profile of faith healing to a large constituency hitherto unimpressed by the practice.

In the wake of Hickson's tour, individual clergymen introduced healing services into their churches on a regular basis, and national societies dedicated to the teaching and practice of spiritual healing flourished. In 1919, the Rev. Franklin Cole Sherman, an Episcopal minister in Cleveland, founded the American Guild of Health, modeled on the English version. In addition, the General Convention of the Episcopal Church was persuaded by Manning to establish a commission to investigate the question of faith healing. It was a move such as this that played a part in persuading Randall Davidson to establish a similar colloquy for the English Church, as mentioned above. Such events, in Mullin's words, allowed "the social, cultural, and intellectual status of the Church of England [to legitimatize] a discussion of the question of faith healing on both sides of the Atlantic."[171] Indeed, even advocates in the Pentecostal tradition were prepared to acknowledge the importance of Hickson, and Anglican participation in healing. The American healing evangelist, Fred F. Bosworth, cited Hickson and the American Episcopal Commission's report to lend weight to his own views on the subject. Surprisingly, Bosworth chose to quote from Hickson an opinion rarely, if ever, aired in Pentecostal circles: "Spiritual healing is sacramental. It is the extension through the members of His mystical body of His own incarnate life."[172]

169. *New York Times*, 4 May 1920.

170. Cunningham, "Ministry of Healing," 195.

171. Mullin, *Miracles*, 238.

172. Bosworth, *Christ the Healer*, 38.

In other distinct ways Hickson showed his thaumaturgic colors. Unlike the church authorities, he was not against large healing missions so long as there was "nothing sensational, no excitement; just a simple address, a hymn, and then the quiet laying on of hands accompanied with earnest prayer and followed by the Church's blessing given by the priest."[173] By 1925, while still drawing crowds, he was aggrieved that "so much is being said at the present time to prejudice the public against healing missions," citing as evidence the Commission report emanating from Lambeth Conference in 1920, which stated: "On account of the immense importance that we attach to the spiritual preparation of the individual . . . we are not prepared to give any encouragement to public missions of healing."[174] Headlines such as the following in the *Yorkshire Evening Argus* in October 1924 did not sit easily with such Anglican reserve: WOMAN THROWS AWAY HER CRUTCHES; CRIPPLE WHO PUSHED HER BATH CHAIR; THREE FURTHER FAITH CURES; FERVOUR AT FRIZINGHALL.[175] Another paper reported that the church at Frizinghall, near Bradford, "was reminiscent of a casualty clearing station behind the front line of a Flanders battlefield, with nurses in blue and white dresses . . . flitting hither and thither." During this service, clergy from all over the deanery were flanked either side of the altar praying for the sick during the three hours of the service.

Throughout his ministry, Hickson presented leading churchmen with a poser. When Archbishop Randall Davidson invited him to Lambeth Palace in March 1909, he found him "to talk a certain amount of nonsense together with a good deal of shrewd common-sense." He became aghast, however, when Hickson told him that he sent handkerchiefs, over which he had prayed, to the sick who lived at a distance (following Acts 19:11–12). Such an act was confined largely to Pentecostals. Surprisingly, two of Hickson's sternest critics, Anson and Henson, were prepared to relent on some aspects of his ministry. When Dean Inge was gunning for Hickson to be shown up as a charlatan, Anson, fearful of liberalism's point-blank skepticism over the whole healing issue ,wrote to Archbishop Garbett: "Hickson and Pastor Jeffries (*sic*, George Jeffreys) . . . are, I suspect, quite as reliable as the average disciple in Galilee or the holy women!" The remark implied that to entertain doubts about the healing ministries of Hickson and Jeffreys was to endanger the veracity of the thaumaturgic narratives of the New Testament.[176] For his part, Henson was prepared to concede that Hickson may have possessed the specific gift of healing: "With Mr Hickson's exercise of the faith-healers' gift, which he appears to possess, I am not concerned. If he is wise he will exercise it with caution." His objection was directed to Hickson's call for the church to revive the ministry of physical healing that the healer alleged had been "lying in abeyance so long." As bishop, Henson believed that he owed it to the church to declare his deliberative judgement, namely that "the Christian ministry is not charged, and cannot wisely concern itself with the healing of disease."

173. Hickson, *Heal the Sick*, 59. This is the description of the healing services held at St. Matthew's Church in Poona, India. It is typical of all his services.

174. Weatherhead, *Psychology, Religion and Healing*, 208.

175. Mews, Stuart: "Revival of Spiritual Healing," 302–3.

176 Ibid., 330.

The question remains as to how Boddy regarded the growing emphasis placed on spiritual healing in the Anglican community. As to be expected, he identified most closely with Hickson, described by one newspaper as a man having "nothing ascetic in his appearance, for he is a thickly built man who might pass for a prosperous tradesman." Boddy took an opportunity to meet him in London at his home near Hyde Park. In paying tribute to his "loyal devotion to his Saviour," he referred to his belief "in the help which angels gave him in his work. He believes in angel ministry, but that they are under the direction of the Lord." He found him a man with "a great gift of quiet, simple speech, readily understood by the plain folk." Considerable space was given to accounts of Hickson's missions recorded in the editions of *Confidence* issued in the 1920s, vying for coverage with those of Smith Wigglesworth and the Jeffreys brothers. Considerable attention was given to the "unusual mission" in the parish Church of Frizinghall, Yorkshire, alluded to earlier, where for three days the church was filled with 400 sick people seeking healing.[177] The mission, Boddy reported, was held with the approval and personal co-operation of Dr Perowne, the Bishop of Bradford. It followed after Hickson's successful overseas ministry, notably in his Australian homeland.

Such was the success overseas that the Archbishops and Bishops in Australia wrote a lengthy letter to their fellow churchmen in Britain commending Hickson's efforts. In all his services in the USA, Palestine, India, South Africa, Australia, and New Zealand, the relevant bishops had not only commissioned him, but had personally supported him and given the blessing to each patient. Though Bishop Perowne acted likewise, Boddy bewailed that Britain, by comparison, "is very slow to move. Some of us have followed closely the wonderful scenes which occurred in nearly all the cathedrals throughout the United States and in the Colonies."[178] A related question was posed in an earlier edition of *Confidence*, "Is it not strange that England seems to be one of the most unbelieving countries as to divine healing? Brother Wigglesworth in Switzerland, Sweden, Denmark, Norway, is mightily used. Mr Hickson had every cathedral he visited in the States crowded to the doors and out into the streets; but we are very slow in our own dear country to lay hold of the Great Healer."[179]

After the five-year period (1918–24) of his global travels, Hickson finally returned to Britain and, for the next three years, diversified the nature of his ministry by regular visits to hospitals, sanatoriums, mental institutions, private homes, and schools for the disabled. Boddy was sufficiently impressed to give notice in *Confidence* of Hickson's weekly healing services held in St Michael and All Angels Church, Paddington, London. Readers were informed that services began at 11.15 a.m. and those wishing to attend had to obtain beforehand a card of admission. If the sufferer was under the care of a doctor, written

177. For a full account of the Bradford mission and changing Anglican views on spiritual healing, see Mews, "Revival of Spiritual Healing," 299–332.

178. *Confidence*, November-December 1924, 152–57.

179. *Confidence*, April–June 1921, 27. In several of the places he visited, Hickson's meetings often came within days or weeks of meetings held by Smith Wigglesworth or Aimee Semple McPherson, a circumstance that led some to be convinced that the crossing of denominational and cultural lines was confirmation of divine intention. Hickson estimated that in the missions across America, he had laid hands on at least 200,000 people.

consent had to be forwarded allowing the journey to the church to be taken, together with a diagnosis of the complaint. As well, a letter from a clergyman stating that the case had been investigated, and the sufferer had received due preparation.[180] By this time Hickson had distanced himself from the storms of well-nigh two decades. His legacy lay in the impetus he brought to the doctrine and practice of divine healing within the worldwide Anglican Communion. It was a task that Boddy could not fulfil because his attention was divided between the nascent Pentecostal movement and his dutiful commitment to Anglicanism, a balance that tilted to the latter in his declining years. Hickson's thauma-turgic/sacramentalist ministry of healing was to the worldwide Anglican Communion, while Boddy maintained a faithful parish ministry. Boddy made no claim to the gift of healing, Hickson ministered on the understanding that he had been divinely gifted, and was called to exercise the gift.

---

180. *Confidence*, November-December 1924, 152.

4

Two British Healing Evangelists

THE JEFFREYS BROTHERS, GEORGE and Stephen, have been described as ranking "among the greatest British evangelists and exponents of Pentecostalism in the twentieth century."[1] George Jeffreys was the founder of the Elim Pentecostal Church, while Stephen played a leading role in the early years of the Assemblies of God, the two denominations forming the largest Pentecostal churches in the British Isles. Attention here will be devoted to George as a healing evangelist, rather than as the undisputed leader of Elim until 1934. From then onwards, contention over matters of church government led ultimately to his break with Elim in 1940 and the emergence of the breakaway Bible-Pattern Church.[2] Smith Wigglesworth at the age of forty-eight was hardly known outside his hometown of Bradford, Yorkshire. By the time of his death forty years later, he was widely known throughout the world from the fabled accounts of answered prayers for healing. The distinctive features of his robust healing evangelism are examined here, and their influence on current healing methodologies assessed. The two men contrasted greatly in personality, ministry, and in the nature of their legacy but shared a common purpose to "expect great things from God; attempt great things for God."[3]

GEORGE JEFFREYS

George Jeffreys (1889–1962) was the eighth child in a mining family at Maesteg, South Wales. His mother was the daughter of a Baptist minister, though the family belonged to the local Welsh Congregational Church. Like many miners at the time, his father died prematurely from lung disease when George was six years old. The deprivations of their upbringing led to only three of the sons living beyond their thirties. The three favored with comparative longevity, Stephen, George and William, all became preachers. George was converted at the age of fifteen during the Welsh Revival in November 1904. At the time, he worked in the local Co-operative Store as an errand boy. George's frail health made his mother determined that he would not go down the mine where the more robust Stephen worked. Both brothers were converted under the preaching of their own minister, Glasnant Jones, who became for George the father he never knew. Of the youth-

---

1. Larsen, *Biographical Dictionary of Evangelicals*, 332.
2. An accessible treatment of is found in Cartwright. *Great Evangelists*, 133–59.
3. Saying attributed to William Carey (1792), pioneer Baptist missionary to India.

ful Jeffreys, ones revealed: "I was privileged to give him his early religious tuition and a splendid scholar he was. Superior to the other lads, there was character in his face: I knew he was a 'chosen vessel.'"[4]

Pentecostalism came to the Welsh valleys through the visit of Moncur Niblock to the English Congregational Church in the Ebbw Vale district in the last quarter of 1907. The brothers were at first opposed to the new movement. The Spirit-baptism experience of Stephen's son, Edward, while on holiday in 1910, was the catalyst for uncle and father to take the issue seriously. Shortly after, George was baptized by immersion, and before long he received both Spirit-baptism and healing. From childhood, Jeffreys carried a consciousness that he was "called to preach the Gospel. . . . There was no other purpose in life for me if I could not preach."[5] However, there was a problem. Since birth he suffered from facial paralysis as well as a speech impediment. He later spoke of his complete healing one Sunday morning at "exactly nine o'clock" while praying with Stephen's family: "I received such an inflow of Divine life that I can only liken the experience to being charged with electricity. . . . From that day I have never had the least symptoms of the old trouble."[6] The healing was for him the outward confirmation of his call and provided for him "a witness within to the faithfulness of God's word."[7] As he saw it, if his calling were to be an evangelist, then he would be a healing evangelist with a passionate conviction born out of his own deliverance: "The difficulty with opposers to this truth [of divine healing] is that they consult people about these experiences who have never known them."[8]

Jeffreys heartfelt need for training to fulfil his ambition was met by Cecil Polhill who, on a visit to South Wales and ever on the lookout for promising candidates, met Jeffreys. He urged him to leave the Co-op store, and provided the financial backing for him to study "as a candidate for foreign service" at the PMU School at Preston.[9] It turned out that he was not to stay there more than a few months, leaving in response to a call from Stephen to help in a mission in Wales. This mission was to have a profound effect on the direction of the brothers' lives in that it brought them to the notice of the wider evangelical constituency. The Keswick mouthpiece, *The Life of Faith*, in its 5 February 1913 issue, held out the tantalizing possibility of a replay of the Welsh Revival. Mention was made of *glossolalia* and specific healings, and the success of the meetings held the prospect for one writer that "in a week or two, possibly, Stephen Jeffreys will be considered another Evan Roberts." A correspondent writing to Boddy described the services as being in the mould of those in the 1904–5 Revival: "The meetings are left perfectly free and open, and the Holy Spirit just seems to bear us along—prayers, singing and speaking all interspersed. . . . We all do as we are moved and yet there is no confusion, no extravagance."[10]

4. Boulton, *Ministry of the Miraculous*, 11.

5. Jeffreys, *Healing Rays*, 56–57.

6. Ibid., 57.

7. Landau, *God Is My Adventure*, 134.

8. Jeffreys, *Healing Rays*, 58.

9. *Confidence*, October 1912, 237. See Hocken, "Cecil Polhill," 124.

10. *Confidence*, February 1913, 28.

The publicity given to the missions held early in 1913 began to lend recognition of the two brothers at national level. It led to numerous requests for them to conduct missions throughout Britain and lifted them from the parochialism of the Welsh valleys onto the wider national stage. There is no clear indication that George ever engaged regularly in formal study again after his brief stay at Preston. He was, in effect, an autodidact in biblical and theological matters, a circumstance that probably contributed to the assurance and conviction that marked his preaching and his tenacity in matters of principle and private judgement. He was not schooled to engage in cultured equivocation. His longest serving colleague and pianist, A. W. Edsor, told Landau c. 1935 that Jeffreys "only reads books on religious subjects. Practically only the Bible, which he studies constantly. He is not interested in the theatre, art and politics. At least I have never heard him talk about them in the six years that I have been with him. His spiritual mission occupies all his attention, all his thoughts."[11]

The *Life of Faith* articles led to the initial contact between Jeffreys and Boddy. Elated by the reports from South Wales, Boddy set out in February 1913 to visit a mission conducted by the Jeffreys brothers in rural Radnorshire. They had a "long heart-to-heart talk" where the view was expressed by both brothers "that the Lord needs evangelists in Pentecostal work today. There are many teachers and would-be teachers, but few evangelists. The Lord is giving an answer through this Revival to the criticism that the Pentecostal people are not interested in Evangelistic work, and only seek to have good times."[12] In the short period November 1912–May 1913 a dramatic transformation took place in the fortunes of George Jeffreys. At the age of twenty-four, he found himself lifted from the obscurity of mining village life in South Wales to center stage at the shrine of British Pentecostalism at Sunderland. Within a few short months of the visit by Boddy to Penybont, he was addressing the annual International Pentecostal Conference over the Whitsun period in Sunderland. With Boddy in the chair, he gave brief gospel messages each evening following the other speakers, who included Smith Wigglesworth, Jonathan Paul, and Gerrit Polman. The latter two were the founder-leaders of German and Dutch Pentecostalism respectively. Within a period of six months, Jeffreys was to meet the leaders of the international movement as well as fellow students at the Pentecostal Missionary Union school at Preston, who would come to be numbered among the next generation of leaders. They included pioneer missionaries, W. P. F. Burton and James Salter, and two who would later join him in the Elim movement, R. E. Darragh and E. J. Phillips.

During the May 1913 Sunderland Conference, a Belfast visitor was so impressed by the young preacher that he invited him to Ireland. It was the beginning of Jeffreys' engagement with the island that led to the formation of the Elim Evangelistic Band by a group of young men in Monaghan in 1915. In 1918, the group changed its name to the Elim Pentecostal Alliance to meet the legal requirement for its Council to become a property-owning body. By the end of 1919, Elim had sixteen male full-time workers and one female, Margaret Streight. As Jeffreys and the evangelistic team won converts to the

11. Landau, *God Is My Adventure*, 35–36.
12. *Confidence*, March 1913, 48.

Pentecostal cause, they met with such stiff opposition that, as Edsor pointed out, Jeffreys "established churches for the converts believing these fundamental [Pentecostal] truths because, as a general rule, they were not preached wholly in other denominations; hence the inevitable formation of the Elim movement under his leadership in 1915."[13] It was not until 1921 that the first Elim church to be formed outside Ireland was established in England. Between 1924 and 1934, Jeffreys was at the peak of his powers and achieved national press coverage, fame in Europe, and acclaim in parts of America. Assisted by his small team, he conducted some of the largest and most successful evangelistic missions throughout the British Isles since the time of Wesley, with the added distinction that divine healing was proclaimed and practiced. The Birmingham campaign recorded 10,000 converts though, here as elsewhere, there was a large discrepancy between those making a profession of faith and the number who joined the new assemblies formed as an outcome of the mission.

In a reissue of Jeffreys' book on divine healing, *Healing Rays* (1935), the publisher pointed out the role of the author in pioneering in Britain the "Foursquare Gospel," the *leitmotif* in which Christ is proclaimed as Saviour, Healer, Baptiser in the Spirit, and Coming King.[14] Jeffreys' evangelistic outreach was often likened to the missions mounted by Moody and Sankey, followed later by those of R. A. Torrey. This was notably so during the Birmingham campaign when the Bingley Hall was filled, a campaigning feat that had been accomplished previously only by the American evangelists. Pentecostals put his success down, above all else, to his anointing by the Spirit, but that alone would mask the natural attributes of Jeffreys as well as the meticulous planning by his team behind the scenes. Gee drew attention to his natural gifts: "He had a voice like music, with sufficient Welsh intonation to add an inimitable charm. His platform personality at times was magnetic. His face was appealing. Although lacking academic training, he possessed a natural refinement that made him acceptable in all circles. He presented his message with a logical appeal and a note of authority that was compelling."[15]

Hollenweger, equally positive in his assessment of both Jeffreys brothers, commented: "[They] possessed

George Jeffreys

13. Edsor, "*Set Your House in Order*," 42.

14. A. B. Simpson first coined the term "Foursquare" in 1890 to convey the *leitmotif* of his Christian and Missionary Alliance. Elim followed the precedent set by Aimee Semple McPherson who incorporated the motto in the name of the Angelus Temple—the "International Church of the Foursquare Gospel"—except that she had replaced Simpson's reference to "sanctifier" with "Baptiser [in the Holy Spirit]"—a shift that pointed more to the role of the Spirit in pneumatological manifestation than a focus on personal sanctity.

15. Gee, *These Men I Knew*, 49.

extraordinary natural talents, such as the Pentecostal movement, in Europe at least, has scarcely ever produced since. These talents did not consist of 'American gimmickry.' By simple, powerful and logically-structured addresses, they captured the minds and hearts of audiences thousands strong."[16] The poet John Betjeman, before his sacking as the film critic of the *Evening Standard*, wrote the article "The Foursquare Gospellers" for the paper. He described Jeffreys as "a man with a pale face, black hair bristling with electrical energy, and dark shining eyes." His preaching was not delivered in "the even intonation of a learned Anglican prelate giving a reasoned discourse to a temperate congregation. He uses reason, but his speech is flamed about: the audience is gradually carried away."[17] In the weekly *Picture Post* an article by A. L. Lloyd, and illustrated by photographs taken by Bert Hardy, carried the headline "A Prophet Holds a Revival Meeting."[18] The first feature that struck Lloyd about Jeffreys was his "quietness and modesty."[19] There was none of "the Bible-thumping and capers of the conventional hot-gospeller. . . . His appeal, say his followers, is to the will, not to the emotions." It was these qualities that increased his attraction to some of the well-healed members of society. Among them was Professor D. L. Savory, who penned a brief "Appreciation" for a later edition of *Healing Rays*, praising it for "its profound knowledge and interpretation of Scripture."[20]

Another factor contributing to Jeffreys' success was the organizational flair of his small team of four men. The campaigns were meticulously planned with venues carefully chosen, some requiring tickets to be purchased beforehand. Care was taken to avoid "extravagances and excrescences," a phrase seemingly picked up from an article in *Confidence*.[21] The huge Easter Conventions in the Royal Albert Hall were carefully staged spectacles—"more sacred dramaturgy than camp meeting revival."[22] Many drawn to the major events arrived by special trains and hired coaches. Even before arriving at the venue, the opportunity for personal evangelism was taken. A ticket collector on coming into a compartment on the so-called "Glory train" was amazed to find everyone on their knees praying. The report in the *Daily Telegraph* of the 1928 Easter Convention indicated that this was the first time in the history of the Royal Albert Hall that a baptismal service had taken place there. Around 1,000 converts, out of 10,000 present, were totally immersed in the tank by Jeffreys. The platform was decked like "a veritable arboretum. There were roses, lilies of the valley, palms, firs, ferns and rhododendrons peeping out from a bower of green. Here was fixed the baptismal pool, the encircling garniture of grass, over-

16. Hollenweger, *Pentecostals*, 199.

17. *Evening Standard*, 3 September 1936.

18. *Picture Post* was the pioneer British photojournalistic magazine published in the period 1938–57. In the 1940s, Lloyd was its leading journalist and Bert Hardy its best-known photojournalist.

19. *Picture Post*, 11 May 1946.

20. Sir Douglas Savory (1878–1969) was Professor of French and Roman Philology from 1909 to 1941 at Queen's University, Belfast. From 1940 to 1955 he represented the University as a Unionist member of the House of Commons.

21. *Confidence*, August 1910, 196. In this article that traced the short history of Pentecostalism in the British Isles, Jeffreys felt able to state that "extravagances and excrescences are dying down."

22. Walker, *On Revival*, 143.

hanging flowers giving a delightful touch of rustic freshness and beauty. When joining in the hymns people from all parts of the hall rose to their feet, waved hymn sheets and programmes and sang with ecstatic feeling."[23]

One supportive journalist grandiloquently gushed over the baptismal scene: "Lilies bowed their heads, and sweet-scented roses whispered sweet words of comfort and encouragement as each candidate passed down the steps into the water. . . . Our beloved Principal stood clad in full vestments in the centre of the running stream which bubbled and gurgled joyfully as it ebbed and flowed in a wonderful system of drainage."[24] Backing the whole event was the 2000-voice Crusader choir. The Good Friday afternoon service was "glorified with the rendering of *Messiah* by the Royal Choral Society." Less up-market were the Swiss yodellers on the program at Crystal Palace in 1936. Something of the flamboyance of Aimee Semple McPherson had evidently rubbed off on the Revival Party. At the same time, a decorous pragmatism guided its major decisions and restrained it from going overboard.[25] In 1926, Aimee McPherson preached at the Easter Convention in the Royal Albert Hall. The media attention she attracted caused Elim considerable discomfiture. For W. G. Hathaway, the relationship with McPherson "undoubtedly emboldened Jeffreys for the more dramatic occasions. However, the media love for her more sensational style caused Elim embarrassment when she visited again." [26]

The extensive press coverage, both national and regional, was a major factor in drawing large crowds to the campaign meetings. The style of worship and, especially, the ministry to the sick raised the whole profile of the Pentecostal movement to a level it had never attained in its previous twenty-years-history. Indeed, the publicity was so new and eye-catching that Gee was of the opinion that, "in popular conception the whole movement began with George and Stephen Jeffreys."[27] Edsor, one of Jeffreys' stoutest defenders, felt that "generally speaking, the Revivalist had a good press through the whole of his remarkable career." A report in the popular *Daily Express* related to the mission in St. Andrew's Hall, Glasgow where 1,400 people professed conversions and "hundreds have testified to faith healing. . . . Scores of people, blind, paralysed, deaf, suffering from all forms of 'incurable' maladies, have been brought to the meetings to join in prayer for healing. Crowds have been turned away when the place was filled."[28] Of course, this free publicity would have waned if nothing out of the ordinary had taken place. Testimonies from those dramatically healed were crucial to the authenticity of any supernatural claims. Florence Munday, the first person to be baptized in the Albert Hall in 1928, not only testified to

23. Quoted in *EE*, 1 May 1928, 135.

24. *EE*, 1 May 1928, 133. The flow was to represent the River Jordan.

25. Warrington, *Pentecostal Perspectives*, 18. There can be little doubt that if McPherson had not reappeared after her alleged kidnapping in 1926, Jeffreys would have been under considerable pressure to become her successor at the Angelus Temple where, during his visit to California in 1924, he "had thrilled American audiences with his powerful oratory and prayers." Blumhofer, *Restoring the Faith*, 279.

26. Hathaway was Elim's Field Superintendent for most of the period 1926 to 1950. His role was to oversee the activities of ministers and churches.

27. Gee, *Wind and Flame*, 140.

28. Edsor, "*Set Your House in Order*," 50–51.

healing when George Jeffreys prayed for her, but described an out-of-body experience in which she observed her tubercular knee being remade. The following year, the knee-cap was medically confirmed as normal. The *Elim Evangel* carried an elated report that "on Easter Monday,1929, the Harley Street specialist who was specially consulted as to the completeness of the cure made a thorough examination of Miss Munday, and certified as follows: "There is not a trace of tuberculosis in the body anywhere. The knee-cap is normal in every particular, and perfect in every movement."[29]

Undoubtedly, the inter-war captivation of the paranormal, notably spiritualism, ensured substantial press coverage. Mary Beverley, a spiritualist suffering shoulder pains, heard a voice saying "see the healing doctor." When Jeffreys touched her, the pain disappeared. "The success of Pentecostal healing campaigns," as Randall observed, "was related to wider religious phenomena in the inter-war period."[30] The mission held in the Winter Garden, Eastbourne, in May 1928 was reported in the *Elim Evangel* to have witnessed over one thousand conversions. True to its standing as a "select watering place" on the English south coast, it attracted "soldiers and sailors of the highest rank; authors and penmen not a few, and among them one of the most eminent in England—in the world."[31] The celebrated writer was no other than Sir Arthur Conan Doyle, best known for his detective novels featuring Sherlock Holmes. Though a medical man steeped in empirical reasoning, and the creator of a super-rational detective, he was one of the leading proponents of Spiritualism. The 1920s were dominated for him by a world crusade to evangelize for Spiritualism, resulting in most of his last books, including *The Wanderings of a Spiritualist* (1921), *The History of Spiritualism* (1926), and *Pheneas Speaks: Direct Spirit Communications in the Family Circle* (1927).[32] It can be assumed that his involvement in the supernatural attracted his interest without any change of mind.

One person of rank who was strongly influenced during the campaign was the wife of the distinguished soldier, Lt. Gen. Sir Herbert Campbell Holman (1869–1949), who after conspicuous service in the First Great War was knighted in 1920. Lady Holman suffered from an eye condition. After seeking prayer for healing during the mission, she found that she no longer needed the use of spectacles, a circumstance that led her to become a supporter of the Revival Party. In 1935, their daughter, Joan Holman, married James McWhirter, a member of the Revival Party between 1920 and 1936. He acted as Jeffreys' campaign organizer, with responsibility for public relations during the years of the great city-wide missions. Of the Eastbourne mission, he wrote that "more than usual 'top drawer' people came to the meetings as a result of the healing of a titled lady whose case got into the National Dailies"—a story he may well have fed them.[33]

Gee agreed with Randall in assessing Jeffreys' prominence when he wrote "the times were propitious," without providing any further elaboration.[34] Cultural historians

29. *EE*, 11 April 1930, 229.

30. Randall, *Evangelical Experiences,* 225. Most of this paragraph has drawn largely from this page.

31. EE, 15 June 1928, 184.

32. Edwards, "Doyle, Sir Arthur Ignatius Conan (1859–1930)," *Oxford Dictionary of National Biography.*

33. Robinson. "James McWhirter: Pentecostal Ecumenist" 87–98.

34. Gee: *These Men I Knew,* 50.

see much of the inter-war period as one characterized by a pervasive mood of insecurity and a lost sense of direction, an epoch the poet and essayist W. H. Auden called the "Age of Anxiety."[35] Richard Overy presented the intellectual history of Britain between the two World Wars as "the Morbid Age."[36] A reviewer described a pamphlet (1925) by Bertrand Russell on the future of science as "utter pessimism." There were, argues Overy, solid reasons for this reaction: "Physicists exploded the balanced Newtonian universe; biologists exposed the power of genetic inheritance and the possibility of degeneration; psychologists suggested that rational modern man was a chaos of instincts and urges within; chemists and engineers promised a new material environment, but also produced modern weapons of terrible destructive power; social science argued that the existing capitalist social system was corrupt and insupportable."[37] Various remedies were put forward, whether utopian politics of right or left, a planned economy, world government and eugenic engineering. To this list, Overy added revealingly "moral and religious revival."

By any reckoning, Christianity was at too low ebb to rise to the challenge. Stephen Neill described evangelicalism as being "reduced to a level of less repute and less influence in the Anglican world than at any time in the preceding 150 years."[38] It was estimated that only 3 percent of Anglican ordinands were evangelical. As for the Free Churches they had lost "the sense of daring, of desire to scale the heights of national life or to convert the world."[39] Barclay identified three movements that pressed for the renewal of spiritual life but ultimately conformed to liberal thinking. The best known was the Oxford Movement (from 1938 known as Moral Rearmament) founded by Frank Buchman, who had been powerfully impacted by the 1908 Keswick Convention.[40] All three moved progressively away from the biblical stance associated with conservative evangelicalism. Even the Keswick Convention became embattled for a time. The chairman of its Council, Stuart Holden, vicar of St. Paul's, Portman Square, London, was pre-eminent in the affairs of the Convention in the 1920s. He was a man of great personal charisma who lightened the tone of the Convention, but in the end "nearly wrecked it."[41] A widening split between conservative and liberal evangelicals caused one of the older stalwarts, Charles Inwood,

---

35. Wasserstein, *Barbarism & Civilisation*, 240.

36. Overy, *Morbid Age*, 2009, 4. Psychoanalysis with its probing of the unconscious mind revealed, stated Jung: "What was once a sheltering haven [the recesses of the rational mind] has become a cesspit." (164)

37. The economist J. M. Keynes observed that if the crisis deepened "gold-standard capitalism will be shaken to its foundation." A Cambridge colleague in 1932 believed that everyone was waiting for the crisis to develop into "universal anarchy and war."

38. Barclay, *Evangelicalism in Britain*, 17.

39. Hastings, *History of English Christianity 1920–1990*, 263. The Congregationalist, Nathaniel Micklem, said of the new Manual for Ministers that it was "careful to say nothing that might offend the least believing member of any congregation."

40. The other two groups were Methodist (The Fellowship of the Kingdom) and Anglican (Anglican Evangelical Group Movement).

41. Pollock, *Keswick Story*, 145. Some Keswick supporters were fearful of what they saw as Holden's social radicalism, his desire for control of the Convention and his openness to commend modernist authors.

to declare at a Council meeting, "Brethren, we are on the edge of a precipice."[42] The launch of the Cromer Conference on the Norfolk coast in 1928 as a liberal alternative to Keswick demonstrated the seriousness of the rift.

The sense of a void in the religious life of the nation at the time applied particularly to the working class. It could be argued that the Great War was a turning point, especially among men, in the loss of religious faith. As the historian Hugh McLeod observed: "For millions of working-class families [Sunday became] a day for digging the garden, visiting relatives, or snoozing over the *News of the World*."[43] While some smaller and more traditional movements stalled, others saw steady growth. The Salvation Army fell into the first category. After its initial *phase of enthusiastic mobilisation* it passed into *the period of organisation* (early 1890s–early 1930s). It was a period of reutilization and formalization during which numerous "'aberrations' such as belief in faith-healing and millennial tendencies were finally eschewed, and a more flexible and accommodative system of social teaching was developed."[44] By contrast, the Brethren movement in Scotland found the inter-war period "relatively favourable for the formation of assemblies, [taking] advantage of factors, such as the troubled social and economic conditions of the period."[45]

What the Jeffreys brothers introduced, in the words of Neil Hudson, was "a world-accommodating religion, operating in the aftermath of the First World War in the midst of a society exhibiting a general lack of confidence in traditional church life. George Jeffreys presented himself as an evangelist who could offer people the certainties they craved and create a church context that was new. In short, he presented a revitalised form of fundamentalist Christianity."[46] Hudson identified three particular changes in British society that were incorporated by Jeffreys into the alternative world that he helped to create. They were increased mobility, women's emancipation and the popularity of music. Thus, by adapting the world to the cause of Elim, "Jeffreys allowed people to experience the benefits of the changes in society whilst retaining a safe Christian environment."[47] By contrast, the leadership of the Anglican Church sought to engage with the industrial world by calling a Conference on Christian Politics, Economics and Citizenship (COPEC) under the chairmanship of Archbishop Temple in April 1924. One contributor, Lord Aberdeen (Church of Scotland), emphasized the importance of folk-dancing as the way forward.[48] The religious mainstream urge to engage with the ills of society raised the profile of the "social gospel" that inevitably led to a fresh approach to liturgy and theology. The new Anglican hymnal *Songs of Praise* (1925) led one commentator to refer to its "non-sectarian type of Christianity," expressed in its "modernist approach to sacramentalism, its liberal attitudes to other religions and its benignly immanentist theology which made it attractive to those in the post-war period who were impatient of creeds, dogmas, religions and social divi-

42. Ibid., 156.

43. Brown, *Religion and Society*, 27.

44. Robertson, "The Salvation Army." In Wilson, *Sects and Society in Britain*, 50.

45. Dickson, *Brethren in Scotland*, 190.

46. Hudson. "Schism and its Aftermath," 111.

47. Ibid., 111.

48. Robbins, *England, Ireland, Scotland, Wales*, 181–88.

sions, and traditional language about 'sin.'"[49] Jeffreys beat a different drum that drew the crowds in the barren years.

Barely noticed and dimly recognized by the religious establishment, the Jeffreys brothers were creating their own revivalist waves. The period 1925–35 was one of genuine expansion for the Elim movement with a steady increase in the number of assemblies. In 1928 there were seventy churches and by 1934 another 108 were added. Backing this growth was a substantial infrastructure centred on the headquarters at Clapham, London, where the Elim Bible College and Elim Bible Correspondence College also were sited— both of which met the demand for a supply of pastors and lay preachers. The Crusaders, Elim's vibrant youth movement that attracted 4000 members in the latter half of the 1920s, were used in house-to-house campaigns. The London Crusader Choir numbered almost 2000 young people at the 1928 Easter convention. It presented "a picture that can never be forgotten," cheered the *Elim Evangel*, "one of the greatest choirs of redeemed young people that has ever sung the praises of the Lord."[50] W. H. Stuart-Fox, vicar of St. Saviour's, Crouch Hill, enthused that the same Easter Monday service gave "the lie to the devil's rumour that is damping down the fire of religious enthusiasm in so many hearts, that religion in this country is a spent force, and that this nation is ripening for apostasy." Here was a choir "eschewing the common enchantments of youth . . . the recruits of a mighty crusade to lead this nation back from its helpless drifting, through false religious leadership, to a gospel which stands foursquare on the infallible Scriptures."[51]

As Hudson pointed out, the songs and choruses that were sung in the rallies "reflected an earlier taste in music, often that of the music hall or the more restrained rhythm of the waltz. Utilized to induce a bright, cheerful mood into a meeting, they provided a rhythmical rejoinder to the newer, perceptibly more dangerous rhythm of jazz. These songs, important to Pentecostals in expressing their corporate faith, reflected the melodies of a more certain age. Albert Edsor, Jeffreys' pianist, explained: "We believe in letting people sing music that is in their ears and has a nice familiar sound. We don't go in for any wild jazzy stuff, but anything pleasant that happens to be in the air might be adopted for a hymn.'"[52] Music was regarded as an essential component of the alternative framework of emotional and spiritual rewards designed to defy the drawing power of music assumed to be "carnal," in the Pauline sense of "worldly." It undoubtedly worked. For Landau, singing was an outstanding feature of all the meetings: "Nothing seemed to make them so happy as singing . . . revelling in the physical enjoyment of 'letting themselves go.'"[53] The *Daily Express* took a more jaundiced view: "Again and again—the same verse. It was a species of trance creation. Hysteria seemed at hand. They were lashed and urged by massed melody into an unearthly joy."[54]

49. Stevenson, *Penguin Social History of Britain 1914–45*, 366.

50. *EE*, 1 May 1928, 132.

51. Ibid., 143.

52. Hudson. "Schism and its Aftermath," 115.

53. Landau, *God Is My Adventure*, 128.

54. *EE*, 1 May 1928, 134.

In his book, *God is My Adventure* (1935), Rom Landau, writing from an agnostic perspective moderated by a sympathetic detachment, picked other elements in the ministry of Jeffreys that enhanced his popular appeal.[55] His interest in Jeffreys had been initially aroused by the billboards on display throughout London, inviting passers-by to meetings in the Royal Albert Hall on Easter Monday, 1934. He succumbed to his curiosity to witness at first hand "a religious movement powerful enough for its supporters to hire the Royal Albert Hall year after year." Contrary to the nature of his research into the other ideologues, he recognized that this visit was to an event "that seemed organised for people with very little critical faculty."[56] When Landau arrived at the venue on the Monday morning, he was surrounded by "a jumble of taxis, bath chairs and even ambulances in the street outside. In the crowd there were people on crutches, men and women with deformed limbs or with bandaged heads or eyes, mothers with sick children in their arms."[57] The 10,000 people who filled the huge arena had come primarily to listen to one slightly-built man in his mid-forties. As the evangelist approached the microphone to pray, Landau began to understand why ten thousand people had come to listen to him: "He was not a high priest but simply one of the people. Between them and their God there stood no altar of mystery; there was no priest in sacramental vestments; there was no complicated ceremony. This primitive form of self-realization is an important factor in mass movements."[58]

Landau was surprised people could stand the strain of a full day of "such concentrated religion." One of the evangelistic team explained: "Meetings like this are the greatest impulses in the life of these people. . . . They are the greatest joys of their lives. . . . Most of these people feed on the fare given them to-day when they return to their dreary surroundings in some London slum, to their work in factories, in the black towns of the Midlands. During all those months at work, they will have something to look forward to next Easter at the Albert Hall."[59] Hudson pointed to the significance of enhanced mobility offered by public transport, which enabled people to travel to the major meetings: "Of particular significance were the annual meetings in London, which besides being of spiritual benefit, inculcated a sense of being part of a wider 'family.' Churches travelling together to an event many miles from their home also strengthened the relationship ties of the local church. Particularly for those from the provinces, many would have never had the chance to visit London apart from these opportunities presented by Jeffreys."[60] In Ireland, railways were the most efficient way for Band members to travel around the province, and it was not entirely adventitious that all the main centers of Elim in Ulster

---

55. Landau, *God Is My Adventure*, 122–24. The book gave short pen-pictures of eight "modern mystics, masters and teachers." Besides Jeffreys, the list included Jiddu Krishnamurti, (theosophy), Frank Buchman (Moral Rearmament) and Rudolf Steiner (Anthroposophy). Landau saw his subjects as spiritual pathfinders with the potential to introduce spiritualties or ideologies, which reflected the *zeitgeist* of the inter-war years.

56. Ibid., 119. The annual meetings were to run in the Royal Albert Hall from 1926 to 1939.

57. Ibid., 120.

58. Ibid., 125 & 126.

59. Ibid., 128–29.

60. Hudson, "Schism and its Aftermath," 111–12.

were on or near the railway network. The Christmas Convention season in 1921 lasted a fortnight with no less than three centers, Belfast, Ballymena and Lurgan, to be serviced by members of the Elim Evangelistic Band. Band members were not slow to miss an opportunity to witness. On one occasion, they spoke to three strangers in their compartments "about eternal things" and as they neared Lurgan they began to break into singing choruses. It is not surprising that "people pass the windows and gaze in with a curious expression on their faces of mingled interest and pity!"[61]

The sociologist Bryan Wilson, in his study of the Elim movement, noted that an examination of photographs taken at the large campaigns showed that women formed a clear majority, comprising up to three-quarters and never much less than two-thirds of the audience. Also, of the printed testimonies to healing, women feature with twice as many claims as men.[62] That women predominated in this area lends support to the contention that they are more prone to, or more declarative of, psychosomatic and nervous disorders. Except in the early days, women played little part in the formal organization of the church, barring their periodic dominance in numbers on the mission field. The attraction of Elim to women rested on grounds other than feminism. Wilson places the appeal to women on the ability of Pentecostal fellowship and worship to provide "possibilities of self–expression." Scenes where emotion was uninhibitedly displayed were not unusual, be they "tears, heavy-breathing, groans, utterances of joy and rapture, and, of course, tongues."[63] At revival meetings working-class women were released from mundanity into an alternative world of color and excitement that vied with the music-hall and cinema. While men had the football match, the pub and the trade union meeting, godly, often housebound, wives were presented with an opportunity to forge a sense of corporate identity that was appreciably broadened by travel to national and regional rallies, and conventions.

On another occasion, Landau set out to watch Jeffreys in action at a healing service. This time the venue was in a hall with two or three thousand in attendance. His intention was to observe the evangelist at close quarters to detect whether he used a special formula when he laid hands on the sick, specifically to determine if Jeffreys saw his healing ministry coming from within himself or recognized himself as an instrument or "medium" for a superior power.[64] Several hundred people, sitting or kneeling, occupied the front rows. As Jeffreys moved among them, his mind "as concentrated as ever," he would often laugh aloud when exclaiming "Hallelujah." When he placed hands on heads, Landau could hear every word. He noted that Jeffreys never repeated the same words twice running, though some of them occurred with greater frequency than others. His most frequent petitions were laced with the commands, "Pray to the Lord" or "Glory" or "In the name of the Lord." When stooping down to the sick he would say: "You are shut in with God" or

---

61. Robinson, *Pentecostal Origins*, 198.

62. Wilson, *Sects and Society*, 102.

63. Ibid., 103.

64. Landau, *God Is My Adventure*, 137–40. Quotations in this paragraph and the next are selected from these pages.

"Concentrate on Jesus Christ" or "The power of God is within us" or "The power of God is here to heal."

Landau was left in no doubt that Jeffreys had no deep knowledge of his own performance, and was merely a channel of divine power. In comparison with the Albert Hall service, people collapsed more often the moment Jeffreys' hands touched their head and they dropped "like felled trees, as though their bodies had lost all strength." One of the fallen told him: "The moment the Principal had approached me and had laid hands upon me, I was struck by such a powerful shock that though I was perfectly conscious I could not help falling down as if dead." While most remained motionless on the floor for many minutes, they were then able to get up without seeming the least dizzy. Once eyes opened, they rose with a smile or even a grin, seemingly conscious of their surroundings, and, in most cases, they uttered "Hallelujah" or "Glory." At the same time, two or three men remained on the floor corpse-like for over ten minutes. A sense of joy again permeated the scene, mostly short-lived for the occasion, only trumped by the expectation of a life-enhancing release from a debilitating medical condition.

For an uncommitted observer, Landau's appraisal of the whole service was balanced:

> One could not judge how real or how lasting the effect of the healings was. Yet for most of the people concerned these moments were the highest of their lives. It was all very well to criticize the primitiveness of this religion, its crudeness, its lack of discrimination and to feel superior to people who believed in miracles; but in reality it mattered little whether the basis of the healings was the power of the healer, the faith or even the hysteria of the followers. We are as yet unable to offer clear rational explanations for miraculous healings—a purely intellectual criticism cannot therefore do them justice. . . . The decisive factor, in an estimation of Jeffreys, seemed to me the support of thousands of people who had found proofs of their faith through him, and that those who had knelt down on the floor with frightened and anxious faces, full of expectation, had got up and walked out with faces that radiated joy.[65]

He deemed that "the whole philosophy of Jeffreys was neither emotional nor intellectual—it was just biblical. . . . It seemed that the Scriptures had become the very lifeblood of George Jeffreys." It is a remarkable tribute, not only for its thoughtful assessment, but also because Jeffreys was the only Briton on his list of spiritual "gurus." Even more striking is the detail that the Pentecostal /Charismatic spirituality that Jeffreys represented was the only one of those discussed in the book that by the end of the century was truly global in its range.[66]

Outside of histories of British evangelicalism, it is one of the stranger lacunae of British social and religious history that little or no mention is made of the Jeffreys brothers or Pentecostalism in general. Stevenson refers to some of the smaller sects that continued to show slow growth in the period and names Jehovah Witnesses, the Society of

---

65. Ibid., 138–39.

66. Starting virtually from scratch in the first decade of the twentieth century, the Pentecostal/Charismatic constituency by the year 2002 accounted for 8.6 percent of the world's population, larger than the percentage of all Buddhists, and composed a quarter of all Christians. The last figure is estimated to rise to 31 percent by 2025.

Friends, Christian Science, the Salvation Army, and the Seventh Day Adventists.[67] None of these grew to an extent that outmatched the growth of Elim that started from scratch in 1915, and even that was in rural Ireland. It is doubtful if any of the other named groups had the self-assurance displayed at the Easter Conference in 1934 when a telegram from the King's private secretary, sent in reply to a loyal message from the Conference, was read out to great applause. Such an act played to the key objective of Jeffreys throughout his ministry, namely, the ever pressing need to establish the credibility of the Elim movement. It was with considerable satisfaction that in his end-of-the-year survey for 1927 he could point to many areas of growth. He rejoiced that

> during the year the greatest Revival Campaigns ever known in our beloved country along Pentecostal lines, have been conducted under the auspices of Elim. The largest and most commodious halls in the British Isles have been packed from top to bottom. . . . Signs and wonders are without a shadow of doubt taking place in our land, miracles just as wonderful as when our Lord walked the earth, are being seen in our midst. Many who last Christmas were upon beds of suffering, in wheeled chairs, on spinal carriages and others who dragged themselves along on crutches to our services, are today praising God because they have been healed. Deadly cancers, tumours, and growths of all kinds, have withered up before the power of the name of Jesus. Blind eyes have been opened, and paralysed limbs made whole.[68]

A self-assured Jeffreys was left to ponder, "Is it to be wondered that multitudes are flocking to the feet of the Saviour? Is it to be wondered that souls are saved?"

Itemizing the raft of activities instituted by the latter half of the 1920s, Jeffreys recorded that the Elim Bible College "has been a real beehive of activity. The Bible College Correspondence School had established itself with world-wide reach. The Elim Publishing Office and printing press were hard-pressed to cope with demand, with the *Elim Evangel* having reached "a startling figure" and the new *Young Folks Evangel* firmly launched. He recalled the words of Cunningham Pike, the late Principal of All Nations Bible College, spoken from an Elim platform: "I believe you are twentieth century representatives of New Testament Christianity. . . . You are pioneers of the latter rain, going forward boldly and freely, without waiting for human sanction or applause, to preach and practice as a church everything that the Bible enjoins." As for the oft-parlous state of financial sufficiency, Jeffrey's response was "we have our testing times." In effect, the denomination relied heavily on the income raised in the larger campaigns held in the major cities, and the abstemious life style of the Revival Party.

Once Elim moved into the 1930s, tensions began to increase to such an extent that Jeffreys resigned from Elim in 1940 to found the Bible-Pattern Church Fellowship. By that time he was a sick man and, though he continued to campaign, the successes of the former years were not perpetuated. The reasons for the split are complex and can only be summarized insofar as his healing ministry was involved. The heart of the problem lay in the fact that throughout the period of the 1920s and 1930s, Jeffreys had become the public face of Elim, the unifying force behind the growth of the movement. A de-

---

67. Stevenson, *British Society*, 371.

68. *EE*, 10 December, 1927, 1–2.

pendency culture permeated Elim in that its numerical success hinged on Jeffreys. It was something that he recognized, and there is little evidence to indicate that he discouraged it. Such dependency was unsustainable because as the number of assemblies increased, a bureaucratic structure commensurate with their growth was needed. From 1923, an administrative machine based in London and masterminded by the highly efficient E. J. Philips was issuing directives to pastors. In 1934, full administrative control passed to an executive council of nine men, to which Jeffreys appointed three, while the ministerial conference was the supreme governing body.

As the centralization of the movement increased apace, Jeffreys grew more frustrated and fought to establish what he called "the sovereignty of the local church," seeking to establish the congregational principle in church polity. The majority within the executive board and the ministerial conference feared that his decentralist position was a gambit to cover his real intention which was to use his rhetorical gifts "to persuade rank and file members to adopt British Israelism as a normative belief."[69] There was a real concern that Jeffreys would set out to win round individual Elim churches to British Israelism and effectively neuter the Conference in any decisions it might come to reach on this subject. The split left many disheartened during the 1939–45 war years.

The ripple effect of this dispute on the healing ministry of the Elim movement was considerable. It was foreshadowed in 1925 when three prominent pastors all suggested that they should be involved in healing campaigns. Jeffreys reacted by expressing disquiet about any multiplication of healing ministries. He explained that he was concerned lest the emphasis on healing by too many healing evangelists would be harmful to the work as a whole. On theological grounds, he defended his hesitancy by drawing a distinction between the ministry of the evangelist and the pastor. He set out his rationale in *Pentecostal Rays* (1933), the essence of which was to draw a distinction between Mark 16:15–20 and Jas 5:14–15 in the mode of healing. The command and promise of signs in the Mark passage, he argued, "applies more to the work of evangelism when the message of the gospel calls for confirming evidence. The Scripture in Mark makes manifest the love of God towards those who are out in the world. The evangelist is sent forth with the message to the outsider, and on the authority of these verses he lays hands on the sick, regardless of the particular person's faith or obedience, and the signs follow." However, the situation is different when healing is administered in an already established church. In this case, the gift of healing is permanently set, and the believer is clearly taught to comply with certain conditions if he expects to be healed.

> Unlike the outsider, he is in the home, he is a member of the family, and his Heavenly Father expects the child to render continual obedience to His Word. Sometimes this is not forthcoming, and, as Father, He has to chastise and permit the disobedient one to be afflicted. The purpose for which this special kind of affliction is allowed would be lost, if the child was granted healing without ceasing to be disobedient. If healing services are on campaign lines outsiders may continually come to be prayed for and not be healed, for the simple reason that the gift of healing, set in the Church, should

---

69. Hudson, "George Jeffreys, Revivalist and Reformer," 147.

be administered along church lines, and not expected as a sign which seems to be given to confirm the evangelistic message.[70]

Jeffreys defined his understanding of "obedience" in terms of the observance of the sacraments of water baptism and the Lord's Table, and worked out in a sanctified life style.

Hudson suggests that the differentiation between the two modes of healing carried an eisegetical subtext, that is Jeffreys imposed in Mark 16 and James 5 texts his own ideas. With access to Elim archives, Hudson opens the possibility that behind Jeffreys' denial for others to engage in an itinerant healing ministry lay his anxiety that his own opportunities would be impaired, and his healing success diluted, if there were too many Elim healing evangelists. During 1925, he expressed concern that his name had not been placed sufficiently prominently on a revised letter heading. He argued that there was nothing "in the eyes of the public that links me with Elim except as an ordinary worker and any work run on these lines will not succeed."[71] He insisted, in a letter to E. J. Phillips, the secretary-general of Elim, that it was "God's purpose to build a movement around 'a channel he chooses' and that future developments would see the work being 'built around one man's name. If I do not take steps now to preserve my own work the work with me will suffer.'"[72]

A case could be made for the view that Jeffreys, though reserved and private by nature, could be high-handed. A. W. Edsor recollected that it was not unusual for Jeffreys to summon him in a quite peremptory manner to drive him to South Wales to visit his sister, journeys made all the more inconvenient by the considerable distances involved.[73] Phillips, who was hardly a neutral observer in his assessment of Jefferys at the time of the schism, expressed his exasperation in some unpublished thumbnail notes he used for a talk at the Ministerial Conference in Ireland in 1941: "G. J. knows the power of his personality and builds up the whole of his methods on it. . . . Never happy unless in absolute control. Insisted on always being made much of, demanded photo in every *[Elim] Evangel* [with] healings through other Pastors in small type. Stopped campaigns when reached point of success. Often wrote up his own meetings and praise of himself. . . . We partly to blame for making him the idol of the Elim people."[74]

Any attempt to understand Jeffreys' motivation in the period leading up to the schism is fraught with difficulty. Hudson takes the view that a factor behind the schism lay Jeffreys' sense of insecurity, coupled with the "vanity of one who feared that he may be eclipsed by others."[75] Others are less critical, seeing him as a man fulfilling his God-given destiny, fully aware of the needs of a new movement. On the immediate issue of the reconciling the Mark and James texts, two observations can be made in Jeffreys' favor. First, he was more cautious in his interpretation of the texts than has so far been allowed. In his undogmatic summation of the two modes of healing, he wrote "but it

70. Jeffreys, *Pentecostal Rays*, 142.

71. Hudson. "A Schism and its Aftermath," 57.

72. Letter Jeffreys to Phillips, undated but around the end of 1925.

73. Personal interview conducted 16 April 1997 at Mitcham, London.

74. Hudson, "Schism and its Aftermath," 345, with some rearrangement of sentences: emphasis added.

75. Ibid., 58.

does *seem* as if the people should conform to the church pattern when it is decided [*by the assembly*] that the campaign aspect is over."[76] Second, it can be argued that his exegesis is sound. The Mark passage is a dominical command ("preach the good news to all creation," v. 15), while James directs the church to "call the elders," (v. 14). The earlier radical healers put great weight on holiness of life in those seeking healing. A. B. Simpson observed, "We find that God is dealing with men and women through their very sickness and we want to be careful first to get them into harmony with His will and spiritually prepared for the blessing of healing."[77] A later interpreter, Donald Gee, made a similar point: "In the early church it seems that the grace of healing could be experienced *within* the church, and also manifested *without* the church as a powerful agent in evangelistic work and witness. In the first case certain conditions had to be fulfilled, although these are not specified as far as the outside world is concerned. It is a mistake to confuse healing in the context of evangelism with normal Christian experience."[78]

On the wider issue of the centralization policy, it may well be, as Wilson maintains, that it was inevitable, because if Jeffreys had not had "the spontaneous, unorganised and naïve desire to convert the nation," then the congregational/ independent form of church government would have been an option. However, a movement with a charismatic leader burdened with large vision would have found it difficult to settle for being nothing more than a loose federation of independent churches."[79] Gee also recognized the inevitability about the polity that Elim, *contra* Jeffreys, was taking: "The majority of Elim Assemblies came into existence through the instrumentality of one man's spiritual gifts, and looked to one personality as their founder. To them, therefore, a unified form of central government was natural, logical, acceptable and successful."[80] What has baffled historians of Elim ever since the schism is the consideration that Jeffreys was showing a centralist mindset as early as the Elim Constitution, drawn up in 1922. In the early 1920s, a sizeable number of new assemblies born of the Pentecostal advance in England and Ireland became wary of Jeffreys' push for a merger under one Pentecostal umbrella. They feared such a union would divest them of their ability to run their own affairs. Such churches formed themselves into the Assemblies of God, a loose federation organized on congregationalist lines in 1924. The possibility of a united Pentecostal movement in Britain and Ireland was, in the event, thwarted.[81]

Despite the hurt on both sides engendered by the split and the privations of World War II, Jeffreys persisted in his healing evangelism in the post-war years with considerable success on the continent, notably in the Nordic countries, France, and Switzerland.[82] The Bible-Pattern Church Fellowship attracted only a minority of the Elim churches to join it. Its early leadership was drawn from the Revival Team who remained loyal to their

76. Jeffreys, *Pentecostal Rays*, 142 (emphasis added).

77. King, *Moving Mountains*, 145.

78. Kirby, *Question of Healing*, 21–22.

79. Wilson, *Sects and Society*, 58.

80. Gee, *Wind and Flame*, 110.

81. For a fuller discussion, see Robinson, *Pentecostal Origins*, 148–60.

82. Edsor, *"Set Your House in* Order." The writer was Jeffreys' pianist, car driver, and private secretary.

leader, and a small number of Elim ministers. As a church, it lacked sustained growth, and was not helped by Jeffreys introducing into his public teaching the highly controversial theory of British-Israelism, which large numbers of Pentecostals found an unacceptable interpretation of biblical prophecy. Elim settled into a period of steady growth in the post-war years that helped to bury the barren controversies of the past.[83]

It is perhaps befitting to leave the story of Jeffreys to a complete outsider, A. L. Lloyd, a member of the British Communist party. In the 1940s he was a journalist with popular weekly magazine, the *Picture Post*. His regular partner on the magazine was the celebrated photo journalist Bert Hardy, and "the two Berts" created many acclaimed features. In 1943 the magazine, noted for it left wing sympathies, reached a print run of 1.95 million copies. The relevant article, illustrated by Hardy's camera shots, appeared in May 1946. When Jeffreys speaks, reported Lloyd, he "can take the Albert Hall and pack it . . . and it is an intimate affair, everyone feels he is just talking to them alone. And without a lift of his voice he can rock them more surely than any other evangelist of the time. It isn't a subtle technique even. It is just a natural gift. But it can shake congregations. It can shake them into tongue-speaking trances and into dead faints. And sometimes it can shake them out of incurable illness into health, according to his own testimony."[84] Lloyd attributed to Jeffreys the transposition of early Pentecostals from "their huddles in little halls and backrooms [where] the whole thing was in a state of anarchy" to setting their movement on its feet. He classed Jeffreys as the "most assiduous and probably the most successful faith healer of our time . . . the whole thing done without mumbo-jumbo." Unlike many healers, Jeffreys is praised for his acceptance of medical science with doctors doing "the same job on the natural plane as he does on the supernatural."

George Jeffreys has been cast as the finest and most successful British evangelist since the time of Wesley and Whitfield. The harrowing events that darkened his latter years give rise to the "what-if" speculation. Left unresolved is the outcome of these scenarios, each within the bounds of possibility: What if George and his brother Stephen had continued evangelizing in harmony; what if George had not been diverted from healing evangelism and the pioneering of new churches instead of expending his energy on matters of church polity and the promulgation of British-Israelism; what if he had won the confidence of the whole British Pentecostal movement and become a recognized early leader of national standing in a post-war Britain open to new forms of religious expression.

SMITH WIGGLESWORTH

The ministries of Wigglesworth and Jeffreys overlapped by some forty years, yet they had quite limited personal contact. There are only seven mentions of Wigglesworh in the *Elim Evangel* in the years 1919–31. All but one of the seven was cursory. The longest was a half-page report of a week-long campaign in Clapham, London, sponsored by Elim. In temperament and in the practice of healing they were quite different personalities, as will be examined later.

---

83. Gee, *Wind and Flame*, 182.
84. *Picture Post*, 11 May 1946, 10.

The background to Wigglesworth's involvement in the healing ministry in the Bradford area was provided in the second volume of this trilogy up to the point just prior his entry into the Pentecostal experience.[85] This took place in October 1907 while on a short visit to Sunderland, at a time when T. B. Barrett, the Methodist minister from Norway, was paying a return visit to All Saints'.[86] In a letter written to A. A Boddy a month later he reprised the event that took place on Tuesday 28 October at 11 a.m. at All Saints' Vicarage. When Mary Boddy laid hands upon him, he recorded that "the fire fell and burned in me till the Holy Spirit clearly revealed absolute purity before God," followed by a revelation of the cross and the regnant Christ. The intensity of the vision was such that "I could not find words to express, when an irresistible power filled me … till I found to my glorious astonishment I was speaking in other tongues clearly."[87] The astonishing statistic applicable to Wigglesworth is that he was hardly known outside his home town of Bradford until he reached the age of forty-eight in 1907. He was not to know then that he would have a Pentecostal ministry of another forty years in front of him.

The first battle he had to face was to convince his wife Polly of the credibility of his experience. In a sermon he preached many years later, he recalled the event:

> When I arrived home my wife said to me, "So you have received the baptism of the Holy Ghost and are speaking in tongues?" She said, "I want you to know I am baptised as much as you." She said for twenty years I have been the preacher (I could not preach; I had tried many a time). … My wife said, "Next Sunday you go on to the platform by yourself—and I'll see if there is anything in it." I had been under great pressure what I was to speak about, and as I went on to the platform Jesus said to me (Luke 4) "The Spirit of the Lord is upon thee." I don't know what I said—but my wife got up, she sat down—she got up—she sat down—she said, "That is not my husband." No man can be filled with the Holy Ghost and be the same man. He is turned into another man.[88]

In November 1908, Boddy was able to report that both husband and wife had ministered in London in three locations. One of them was at the home of the Cantels, the leaders of the Zion work in Britain. Another was the home of Catherine Price who was the first person in Britain to speak in tongues in January 1907. The Price home in South East London was considered the first Pentecostal meeting place in Britain.[89] The third place visited was Bethel Hall, the first Pentecostal church, as such, sometimes known as

85. Robinson, *Divine Healing, 1890–1906*, 98–104.

86. Barratt first heard about the Pentecostal message while visiting America through reading about the Azusa Street revival from its newspaper, *The Apostolic Faith*, first published in September 1906. After lengthy correspondence with Azusa Street, he eventually received his Spirit-baptism on 15 November 1906. By January 1907, the Pentecostal revival had broken out in Oslo. In July 1907 he was forced to resign from the Methodist Episcopal Church, and from then on he launched into a new career as a Pentecostal revivalist, editor, statesman, author, theologian, and hymn writer as well as the founder of the Filadelfia Church in Oslo, where he remained pastor until his death in 1940. Boddy visited him in Oslo and urged him to travel to Sunderland, which he did in August 1907. During his stay of seven weeks, Mary Boddy and their two daughters received their Spirit-baptism: Boddy had to wait until December 1907.

87. Taylor, *In the Steps of Smith Wigglesworth*, 78.

88. Cartwright, *Real Wigglesworth*, 40.

89. Chapman, *Searching the Source of the River*, 19.

"the black man's church" because its pastor was the Ghanaian T. Brem Wilson.[90] Soon Smith became so well known that he was in constant demand as a speaker, particularly at conventions held at Easter, Whitsun and New Year. It was at the Whitsun Conference Sunderland in 1913 that he first met the youthful George Jeffreys, thirty years his junior. Thus, both Wigglesworths became deeply embedded into Pentecostal culture, taking most of the Bowland Street Mission, Bradford, with them.

It soon became clear that Wigglesworth's ministry was of wider compass than Bradford, extending his range to take in the national and international scene, in effect to become the first "world evangelist" of the Pentecostal movement. After his Spirit-baptism, his widening ministry began to affect the running of his plumbing concern and he came to the decision to devote himself to the ministry, leaving his eldest son to run the business. A major precipitating factor that led to his full-time call to healing evangelism was the sudden death of his beloved Polly in January 1913 at the age of fifty-two, after thirty years of marriage. It was an especially heavy blow for a man of great faith who, even at this stage, had seen healings of people who were near death.

Polly's sudden death had the effect of releasing him for a worldwide ministry. As he explained nine years after her death, he felt God speak to him at that time "to rise up and come away. I told him if he would give me a double portion of the Spirit—my wife's and my own—I would go and preach the gospel. ... I sail the high seas alone. I am a lonely man, and many a time all I can do is to weep and weep."[91] Fortunately, his daughter Alice was able to accompany him on his travels with the help of her husband James Salter (1890–1972), who intermittently took time out from his pioneer mission work in the Belgium Congo with the Congo Evangelistic Mission, which he and William Burton founded. The enigma surrounding Wigglesworth's healing ministry lies in the circumstance that he, as a man who was gifted to witness numerous dramatic healings, witnessed his wife suffer a premature death, his daughter Alice endure lifelong deafness in both ears, his son George die at the age of nineteen and his own eyesight deteriorate—all such blows striking an evangelist who claimed that he had seen three dead people raised to life, hearing restored to the deaf and sight to the blind.

Wigglesworth's first overseas venture was to North America in 1914, where he linked up with Boddy who had been invited to speak at the large camp-meeting site at Cazadero, California, a redwood setting north of San Francisco. George and Carrie Judd Montgomery were also in attendance. Boddy reported in *Confidence* that Wigglesworth was like "a victorious warrior, and all were thanking God for his ministry both in word and healing the sick."[92] In a letter to Boddy, dated 24 November 1914, Wigglesworth provided details of one of the more dramatic healings that followed laying on of hands:

> I laid hands on the [breast] cancer, cast out the demon, and the cancer which had up
> to then been bleeding dried up. She received a deep impression through the Spirit
> that the work had been done, and closely watched the healing process with a lady

90. Cartwright, *Real Wigglesworth*, 42.
91. Wilson, *Wigglesworth*, 9.
92. *Confidence*, December 1914, 223.

friend. The cancer began to move from its seat, and in five days dropped out entirely into the protecting bandage. They were much interested and full of joy, and, looking to the cavity whence the tumour had come, they saw to their amazement and surprise that not one drop of blood had been shed at the separation of the cancer. The cavity was sufficiently large to receive a small cup and they noticed that the sides were of a beautiful reddish hue. During the next two days, while they were watching closely they saw the cavity fill up with flesh and a skin formed over it, so that at last there was only a slight scar.[93]

At two subsequent meetings the woman held up a glass vessel containing the cancer, praising God for her healing.

In the period 1920–21 Wigglesworth paid visits to countries in northwest Europe, including Switzerland, France, Denmark, Norway, and Sweden. By this time he had become relieved of ministry responsibility of Bowland Street Mission, explained in part to

Smith Wigglesworth

tensions within its leadership that resulted in the building being sold to become a Memorial Hall to honor the dead of the Great War. In April 1921, he paid his first visit to Sweden. He conducted meetings mainly in the YMCA and the Auditorium, opened in 1910 as the capital's major concert hall. He had the support of Lewi Pethrus, a former Baptist minister, who became one of the world figures of the Pentecostal movement. In his *Spiritual Memoir* (1973), Pethrus referred to the widespread attack from the entire press, the medical profession and the leaders of the Lutheran state church, who all took exception to praying for the sick in a public place. Such was the furore that both Wigglesworth and Pethrus were apprehended by the police, the latter by the Criminal Investigation Department. Pethrus' inquisitors worked on the assumption that this form of healing was hypnotic, and quizzed him about

Wigglesworth's practice of anointing handkerchiefs with oil and praying over them. His response was to direct their attention to the biblical precedent in Acts 18:11–12.[94]

After a week had passed the Chief Constable referred the matter to the Medical Board, which in turn decided that no action should be taken against either man. However, Wigglesworth's application for an extension of his visa was refused, though the order was mitigated to allow him to remain for a final rally in a central park on Whit Monday on the condition that he did not lay hands on supplicants. It seems that behind the scenes one of the nurses in the King's household, who had been healed of a problem with her

93. Ibid., 228–29.

94. "God wrought special miracles by the hands of Paul: So that from his body were brought unto the sick handkerchiefs or aprons, and the diseases departed from them." He once declared that he had used the same cloth 200 times (Wacker, *Heaven Below*, 94).

leg during a Wigglesworth meeting, had informed the King of her healing. The monarch indicated that he was fully aware of the evangelist's activities and expressed his view that Wigglesworth be escorted from the country voluntarily, rather than risk being deported.[95]

Wigglesworth agreed to the stipulation about not laying hands on the sick, believing that God was not limited to this observance. With an estimated 20,000 people before him, he sought divine guidance, whereupon, as Pethrus recalled, "God revealed to him exactly what to do: Hundreds had raised their hands indicating that they needed healing. He felt a clear leading from the Lord to deal with one specific person who was standing on a rock. He asked her to detail her needs and she said that she was in great pain all over her body, which made life impossible for her. Wigglesworth prayed for her from where he stood on the platform and immediately she was delivered and began to dance and jump and shout for joy."[96]

Hundreds claimed to be healed as Wigglesworth prayed, and hundreds more professed faith in Christ. This practice of telling the sick to lay hands upon themselves as he prayed for them became a feature of his crowded meetings throughout his subsequent travels. Wigglesworth was to return several times in later years to Sweden, a country which witnessed a great expansion of Pentecostalism throughout the country. Pethrus was the driving force behind the following projects—the Filadelfia Publishing House (1912); the Filadelfia Bible School (1915); the periodical *Evangelii Harold* (1916); the Kaggeholms Folkhogskola (a secondary school) (1942); a national daily newspaper, *Dagen* (1945); a savings bank (1952); and IBRA, a worldwide radio network (1955).

In 1922 and again in 1923–24 Wigglesworth paid his first visits to Australia and New Zealand. He met some of his stiffest opposition in New Zealand. In Auckland during 1923, one evangelical minister, Joseph Kemp, preached a warning of "the Irvingite delusion, an hour of peril, monstrous, and blasphemous claims, a solemn warning regarding subtle delusions." The same week he took as his subject, "Miracle Evangelism of Modern Days, Is it of God or the Devil?"[97] About six weeks later Wigglesworth was in Blenheim, preaching in the Town Hall. The report in the local *Marlborough Express* awarded him the sobriquet the "Wordy Evangelist," describing him as "a big brusque Yorkshire man, who preaches a sermon like an endurance test. He commenced his discourse on the 'Four Square Gospel' before 7.30 last evening, and he was still at it at 9 o'clock. Much of this sermon was tedious repetition and much of it was arrant nonsense, but there was a certain oratory about the man which did something to relieve the tedium of his long discourse." Despite his offhand perspective, the journalist was prepared to write a straight report of a healing; "There was one case which was rather remarkable. It was that of a woman who had been suffering for three years with a bad leg and other ailments. She hobbled before the missioner on a stick, but before he had finished with her she was able to walk erect and to run, agilely enough, up and down the hall. It was a convincing demonstration as far as it went, and the lady testified that she was cured."[98]

95. Wilson, *Wigglesworth*, 145.

96. Whittaker, *Seven Pentecostal Pioneers*, 33–34.

97. Worsfold, *History of the Charismatic Movements*, 149.

98. Ibid., 153.

The subject of divine healing here as elsewhere prompted controversy. Joseph Kemp maintained his opposition in an article in the *New Zealand Baptist* in which he complained that

> campaigns of healing have been and are being held in various cities and hundreds of thousands of people have been treated in the meetings. All sorts of propagandists are abroad and not a few display marked skill in playing upon the emotional nature of the people, and others with great hypnotic influence fling a spell over the susceptible and unwary. . . . The "Pentecostal Gift of Tongues Healing movement" has been described as a deliberately cooked up frenzy of religious emotionalism of the most marked type, abandonment to which does incalculable harm.[99]

A divergent view was expressed by an Auckland doctor in a newspaper. Under the heading "The Church, Signs of Renewal and Association with Medicine," he pointed to the "many years the medical profession has been satisfied to see the Church slip in only to bury medicine's failures and mistakes. Now that the church is openly taking a hand in something more than that, faith is the fee for relief from disease and perhaps 'voluntary contribution.' From what I know of my own profession, it will lose heavily by the growth of faith and goodness."[100]

Wigglesworth's globe-trotting years came to an end with the clouds of war breaking in 1939, the year of his eightieth birthday. His travels were restricted to Britain during the war years. The daily mail, laden with requests for prayer, continued to arrive at his Bradford home. Each request was prayed over, and an anointed handkerchief distributed. His death in 1947 had a certain precision about it. Back in 1932 when he suffered greatly from kidney stones (see next paragraph), he asked God for fifteen more years in which to serve him. He was saddened in the last month of his life when he opened his mail: "Today . . . I had an invitation to Australia, one to India and Ceylon, and one to America. People have their eye on me. Poor Wigglesworth. What a failure to think that people had their eye on me. God will never give his glory to another; He will take me from the scene."[101] Though he was one of the most well-known of the thaumaturgic healers of the twentieth century, it was not for that he wished to be recognized. He told some students in 1927: "Don't go mad on preaching healing. You will be lopsided." In New Zealand he stated he would rather one soul was saved than ten thousand healed.[102] Nevertheless, and with this qualification in mind, an investigation of his unique style of healing calls for examination, looking at how it compared with other healing evangelists of the period

Wigglesworth and Dowie Compared

It is at this point, the questionas to the extent Dowieism influenced Wigglesworth's ministry can be returned to—a topic left in abeyance from Book 2 of the trilogy.[103] The question

99. Ibid., 155.

100. Ibid.

101. Liardon, *God's Generals*, 223.

102. Cartwright, *Real Wigglesworth*, 104.

103. Robinson, *Divine Healing, 1890–1906*, 98–104.

is one that cannot be resolved with confidence since significant dated primary sources are not available. What is demonstrable is that Wigglesworth was emphatically committed to an understanding of the healing ministry that resonated in ways with that of Zion. At the time when his life was threatened by appendicitis, he and Polly made a pledge of Dowieite intensity: "[We] saw that we could not go just half-measures with God. If we believed in divine healing, we would have to be whole-heartedly in it; so we pledged ourselves to God and then to each other. . . . We looked into each other's faces and said, 'from henceforth no medicine, no doctors, no drugs of any kind shall come into our house.'"[104] This decision was very personal, and there was no insistence that others should deny themselves medication. The vow to desist from the use of medical expertise carried a price. When he was in his seventies, an X-ray plate revealed the advanced stage of a kidney stone problem. He was warned by his doctor that without an operation death would ensue. His response was immediate, "Doctor, the God who made this body is the one who can cure it. No knife shall ever cut it so long as I live."[105] For six long drawn-out years he suffered bouts of excruciating pain, which never hindered his program of public meetings. Eventually the stones, numbering some hundreds, were expelled and retained in a glass bottle. He emerged from this test with a faith firmer than ever and with fifteen more years of active service.

His son-in-law, James Salter, who often accompanied him throughout these years, said of him, "He aspired to be like Job—someone in whom God would glory over the Devil."[106] Wigglesworth saw praying for the sick in cosmic terms as a contest between God and the devil: "I have no word for rheumatism only 'demon possessed.' Rheumatism, cancers, tumours, lumbago, neuralgia, all these things I give only one name, the power of the devil working in humanity. When I see consumption, I see demon-working power there. All these things can be removed."[107] Satan, for him, was the ultimate source of "all the discord and evil, and everything painful" that afflicts humankind. Therefore, in the light of Christ's victory over all the works of the devil, no Christian need ever accept an oppression caused by Satan: "There is healing through the blood of Christ and deliverance for every captive. God never intended His children to live in misery because of some affliction that comes directly from the devil."[108] This notion of praying for the sick as an act of spiritual warfare helps account for his rough handling of people in his earlier ministry. Such rough treatment was enough to deter some people from coming forward for healing. His advice to the hesitant was brusque: "If you are afraid to be touched, don't come to me to pray for you. If you are not prepared to be dealt with as God gives me leadings to deal, keep away. But if you can believe God has me for a purpose come and I will help you."[109]

104. Frodsham, *Smith Wigglesworth*, 21.

105. Ibid., 137.

106. Ibid., 139.

107. Dorries, "Smith Wigglesworth", 22–23.

108. Wigglesworth, *Ever Increasing Faith*, 43.

109. One Australian pastor commented that though Wigglesworth seemed "rough and ready, none ever complained. But at the same time he could be gentle. And he never said no to the sick, day or night" (Chant, *Heart of Fire*, 52).

At times, Wigglesworth would rage against malign forces using physical force, slapping or punching the afflicted part of the sufferer's body when rebuking or casting out the disease. A report in the *Marlborough Press* in New Zealand described how he "dealt a frail old lady such a smack in the stomach as might have doubled her up [in calling] in stentorian tones on the evil spirits . . . to come out."[110] In Australia, he prayed for a large woman suffering from cancer, which provoked him to rail against Satan and his works. Alarmed at such a barrage of angry words in front of a large audience, the woman called out repeatedly, "You're killing me," before falling to the floor. When attendants lifted her to her feet, the verbal onslaught was resumed, this time with the same result. Wiggleworth had a distinct feeling the third time he prayed for her that healing was complete. As the woman began to walk away, a large cancer fell from her body and she found herself completely healed. The reality of demonic activity was a belief that likewise provoked Dowie to stridency. The question whether or not such *modus operandi* was initiated or reinforced by Zionist influence in Britain is unanswerable at this distance.

On another occasion a young man who, Wigglesworth recounted, was "a slave to alcohol and nicotine came along with his wife to see if I could heal him. They stated his case, and I said, 'Yes, I can heal you in Jesus' Name.' I told him to put out his tongue, and I cursed the demon power of alcohol and cast out the demon power of nicotine. The man knew that he was free."[111] Tobacco and alcohol were established evangelical taboos, but none excoriated them with such ferocity as Dowie, nor did many others berate them so forcibly as demonic in origin. Wigglesworth's aversion to pig meat was one shared with Dowie. When asked to say grace at a meal with a roast pig the delicacy of the day, he uttered a prayer of discreet ambivalence, "Lord if you can bless what you have cursed then bless this stinking pig. Amen."

In terms of personality traits, Wigglesworth and Dowie were similar in a number of ways. They were *sui generis*, unconventional and unpredictable. They could adopt a severity of manner that was offensive to most conservative believers, born, as it was, of a self-assurance that what they were doing carried the seal of divine approval. When Boddy was on the train to Zion City in 1912, he had a talk with a railway official who had got to know Dowie on his travels. He described Dowie as "a smart man, pleasant enough unless you crossed him and then you better look out."[112] When asked why he struck people when praying for them, Wigglesworth retorted, "I don't hit them, I hit the devil," a corollary of his belief that one "will never reach a place where God will be able to use you until you get angry with the devil."[113] To "act faith," he would often make those whom he had just prayed for run up and down aisles, and even out into the street. Neither man stood on ceremony, nor suffered modish fashionistas gladly. "What sort of women are those," asked Dowie, "who go down the street with loud attire, and outrageous feathers in their hats, with mincing walk, and impudent smiles at strangers, and as they go seem

---

110. Cartwright, *Real Wigglesworth*, 117. The date of the report was 10 December 1923.

111. Ibid., 65–66.

112. *Confidence*, February 1913, 33.

113. Wilson, *Wigglesworth*, 83.

to say, 'Behold me?'"[114] Wigglesworth, during a meeting in the lounge of the Elim Bible College in Clapham, London, which was attended by a number of women wearing hats tufted with large feathers, fetched a pair of scissors and while they were kneeling in prayer, snipped off the feathers.

Both Dowie and Wigglesworth shared preaching styles that kept audiences hooked. Boddy said of Wigglesworth's delivery: "Bro. Wigglesworth has an earnest, fiery delivery, and unhesitatingly and freely uses the Chairman and others on the platform to illustrate his remarkable stories. This is highly entertaining to the audience and surely keeps up the interest, for no one knows what may happen next, or whose turn it may be to be embarrassed by being made use of as an object lesson."[115] "Unique" was the term Gee used: "When preaching he became entangled in long involved sentences. Then he would relieve our perplexity by speaking angelically in tongues that he always interpreted himself. It was all part of the sermon. Explain it how you will there were some remarkable flashes of revelation. The preacher himself probably little understood the sheer theological depth and insight of his own words. Wigglesworth was a Pentecostal phenomenon."[116]

One of Dowie's critics, J. M. Buckley, defined his voice as "clear and strong. . . . His speech is forcible and occasionally ornate; his wit, according to his mood, is refined or coarse, his oratory impressive or grotesque. To his canny shrewdness as a Scotchman he adds the warmth of southern Italy, and the fountain of his tears overflows readily."[117] The two men were adept at drawing a response from their listeners; neither were they restrained from weeping openly when they encountered people suffering from distressing ailments. They also placed the need for conversion above healing. Wigglesworth maintained that "there is only one thing that you will never go lopsided on, and that is the preaching of salvation."[118] Dowie also affirmed the primacy of conversion in his statement that "we have always taught that you can't get healing without salvation."[119]

Wigglesworth and Jeffreys Compared

Wigglesworth and Jeffreys were much more contrasting characters. Both men were at their peak in the 1920s and 1930s, but were quite different in most other respects. Jeffreys began his ministry as a young man in his twenties; Wigglesworth was forty-eight when he launched out on own. By temperament Jeffreys was a reserved man outside the pulpit, who never married.[120] By contrast, Wigglesworth was a tough, forthright son of Yorkshire, stockily-built, direct in manner and uncompromising in contention.[121] While Jeffreys was gentle with the sick in praying for them, Wigglesworth, as shown, could be decidedly

114. *LH*, 13 March 1896, 331.

115. *Confidence*, September/October 1917, 73.

116. Gee, *These Men I Knew*, 90.

117. Buckley, "Dowie Analysed and Classified," 928. Buckley was editor of the Christian Advocate, the recognized organ of the Methodist Episcopal Church.

118. Cartwright, *Real Wigglesworth*, 133.

119. Dayton, *Theological Roots*, 137.

120. Walker, *Restoring the Kingdom*, 259.

121. Hywel-Davies, *Life of Smith Wigglesworth*, 17.

aggressive. At Glad Tidings Tabernacle in New York City, after he had struck an Irish immigrant woman who had gone forward for prayer, she immediately drew back her fist and shouted, "Begorra, if it's a fight you want, it's a fight you'll get!" Both men had limited early education, and whereas Jeffreys developed, in Professor Savory's words, "a charming style and choice of the most perfect vocabulary ever," Wigglesworth's literacy was basic. What he learned he attributed to his wife Polly: "She saw how ignorant I was, and immediately began to teach me to read properly and to write; unfortunately she never succeeded in teaching me to spell."[122] In his preaching Jeffreys was engagingly fluent, whereas Gee, as noted earlier, described Wigglesworth's preaching at times becoming "tangled in long involved sentences."[123]

From his early days as an evangelist, Jeffreys' comportment in his ministry was one of order and restraint. It was not that emotion was dismissed, but rather that it was not allowed to run to self-gratification, and sink to levels where it became vacuous and unseemly. Even at this early stage, a note of wariness about emotional overreaction was being aired, an indicator of his becoming increasingly assured that he was the answer to his own prayer. In the first statement of doctrine of the nascent Elim movement, the fourth article was worded, "We can expect the onslaught of the enemy to be furious, in his seeking to counterfeit and to produce extravagances, which we must be careful to avoid, by continuing steadfastly in God's precious word."[124] In a tribute to his long-time friend, A. W. Edsor commented that Jeffreys in his preaching "never attempted 'to play to the gallery,' but pressed home his messages with authority and power. He exercised remarkable control over meetings."[125] In later years, the masthead of the *Elim Evangel* carried the watchword, "[Elim] condemns extravagance and fanaticism in every shape and form. It promulgates the old-time gospel in old-time power."[126] Employing a nautical metaphor to illustrate the lessons derived from church history, Jeffreys concluded: "The once powerful spiritual liner [of revival can] become a wreck upon the rocks of excrescences and extravagance and the end means disaster to all."[127]

Jeffreys' disposition to present the Pentecostal message within an ordered and restrained framework has featured strongly in the Elim church throughout its history. In particular, a consistently cautious line within Elim was taken against evangelists considered controversial. Aimee Semple McPherson was one of the few "outsiders" engaged to preach at an Elim big event. In 1926, she shortened her visit to the Holy Land to stay in London for four days to speak at the Easter Convention in the Royal Albert Hall. Even

122. Frodsham, *Smith Wigglesworth*, 11. The books attributed to Wigglesworth that continue to remain as best sellers, notably *Ever Increasing Faith*, are largely sermons committed to print and edited by others.

123. Gee, *These Men I Knew*, 90. The early printed sermons indicated the point when tongues were uttered, but later editors instead incorporated seamlessly the interpreted tongues as part of the sermon. Wigglesworth was more upfront about tongues than Jeffreys, who was less adamant about tongues as the evidential sign of Spirit-baptism, allowing for the acceptance of other different charismatic gift, as evidence.

124. The doctrinal statement was titled *What We Believe*, and was drawn up by Jeffreys in 1916 at the request of the oversight of the first Elim assembly, Hunter Street, Belfast.

125. Edsor, "*Set Your House In Order*," 42–43.

126. See, for example, *EE*, 25 December 1929, 547.

127. Jeffreys, *Pentecostal Rays*, 148.

so, when she visited London again, the media attention she attracted caused Elim considerable discomfiture. Her upbeat femininity did not have the same appeal to the more conservative British temperament, and caused some of Jeffreys' closest associates to urge caution about overt collaboration with her ministry.

Elim, similarly, was critical of some of the methods employed by Wigglesworth, and for a time would not allow him to minister in Elim churches. Concern revolved around Wigglesworth's style of ministry. His brusque manner forced the Elim leaders to think twice about inviting him to address their convention meetings. They were unconvinced about his custom of "wholesale healing," by which the sick were asked to stand and lay hands on themselves. At other times, he encouraged "congregational healing," whereby all would be invited to pray with him for a particular individual in order to see the demonstration of God's power. One close associate in Jeffreys' evangelistic team, William Henderson described as "absolutely tommyrot" Wigglesworth's periodic practice of asking the minister of the local church to repeat the words, parrot-like, which he had just heard. Henderson also indicated that he had warned Wigglesworth to tone down his words, otherwise he "would have carried on and frightened the people."[128]

Whereas Jeffreys founded and built up a denomination, only to be severed from it, Wigglesworth deliberately remained unattached to any denomination throughout most of his ministry, a reflection in a way of the multiplicity of religious influences on his early life from Anglican to Brethren. He refused to be limited by denominational barriers, and on at least three occasions he conducted special meetings for Anglican ministers. One such was W. H. Stuart-Fox, vicar of St. Saviour's, Crouch Hill, North London, whose son had been healed through Wigglesworth's ministry. Writing in 1928 of the ten-day mission held in a tent adjacent to the church, Stuart-Fox reported that the great truths of "a full redemption for body, soul and spirit through the Atonement came with extraordinary freshness. . . . One of the striking features of the mission was the large number of men, old and young, which came forward to confess Christ, while there were many cases of healing."[129] Occasionally, he would worship with the Salvation Army, and he maintained a warm feeling for the Anglican Communion service.

A strong reason for Wigglesworth's desire to remain independent of denominational ties can be traced back to a regrettable incident in 1915.[130] In that year he became a member of the Council of the Pentecostal Missionary Union (PMU), only to be forced to resign in 1920. In 1915 he had been a widower for seven years, during which he had developed a friendship with a Miss Amphlett. He informed her that he was drawn towards her by a feeling of "spiritual affinity," a term that was an in-phrase in some religious quarters at the time. It implied a special relationship with a person of the other sex that was on a higher, more spiritual plane than fleshly attraction.[131] Miss Amphlett wrote a letter of complaint

---

128. Hudson, "Schism and its Aftermath," 56.

129. Whittaker, *Seven Pentecostal Pioneers*, 37–38.

130. For the years 1924–29 he was an accredited minister of the American Assemblies of God, a status that had little practical bearing on his activities.

131. Spiritual Affinity carried echoes of the concept of Sympneumsta advocated by the spiritualist mystic, Laurence Oliphant (1829–88). The theory held that the spiritually complete individual cannot be wholly male or female, and to be complete must eventually become biune (two in one) through the interaction, both

against Wigglesworth to Cecil Polhill, the President of the PMU, who suggested that he resign from the Council and retreat for "a period of godly, quiet living, showing works meet for repentance."[132]

Wigglesworth, against whom no charge of impropriety was ever substantiated, felt bitterly disappointed by Polhill's response to an allegation that threatened to destroy his ministry. Upset by the tone of Polhill's letter, he wrote to T. H. Mundell, the missionary secretary of the PMU, in his unversed spelling and unpolished grammar, "I think Mr Polhill has Steped over the Boundry this time[.] They making things to appear as if I had committed Fornication or Adultery[.] I am innocent of thease things[.] I have done and acted folishley & God has Forgiven me[.]"[133] Boddy was not at the Council meeting when the issue of resignation was raised. He was of the opinion that Wigglesworth had been badly treated and showed his confidence in him by publishing accounts of his activities in *Confidence*. Mundell, a senior solicitor, was prepared to sign papers for Wigglesworth to validate his standing as a "missionary evangelist" that enabled him to claim discount on boat tickets. It is more than likely that the whole incident persuaded Wigglesworth to go freelance; only this time he took whenever possible his daughter Alice Salter and her husband to accompany him. The whole episode emboldened him to minister beyond Britain more extensively than Jeffreys, and work outside the constraints of denominational endorsement.

Jeffreys' lasting legacy remains in Elim as a denomination, Wigglesworth's more as a motivating force in the reverberations of healing evangelism up to the present. It is a matter for some wonderment that a man who began his ministry in his late forties and only ceased with his death at the age of eighty-seven in 1947 should have an ongoing impact at all. He once told an audience, "I am here before you as one of the biggest conundrums in the world. There never was a weaker man on the platform."[134] He founded no movement, had no denominational structure to back him, no official publication to endorse him, no wife for thirty-four years to reassure him, no academic qualifications to accredit him, and no superficial charm to ingratiate himself with others. What he did have was the dedication that R. A. Torrey attributed to D. L. Moody: "He belonged wholly, unreservedly, unqualifiedly, entirely, to God."[135]

Despite his limited formal attainments, his overriding desire was to be used of God in the power of the Spirit. For such a daunting task, he declared the exacting need of divine disciplining: "Before God could bring me to this place, He has broken me a thousand times. I have wept, I have groaned, I have travailed many a night until God broke me. It seems to me that until God has mowed you down you never can have this long-suffering

---

in mind and body, with the opposite sex. The idea distressed the Holiness advocate, Hannah Whitall Smith who proclaimed Oliphant's views "pure adulterous trash." (Strachey, *Remarkable Relations*, 104.

132. Lairdon, *God's Generals*, 220.

133. Cartwright, *Real Wigglesworth*, 93.

134. Dorries, "*Smith Wigglesworth*," 21.

135. Henry Varley, a friend of Moody, loved to recount the story of when he said to him, "It remains to be seen what God will do with a man who gives himself up wholly to Him," to which Moody said to himself: "Well, I will be that man."

for others."[136] His own experience of Spirit-baptism brought him to such a heightened sense of joy and power that he longed that other believers would be aroused from spiritual lethargy into a life that manifests victory: "I must have every man filled with the Holy Ghost, must have a message from heaven, that will not leave people as I found them." He believed profoundly that through the redemptive work of Christ, a new order of supernatural life and blessing awaited those whose faith was stirred by the outworking of this reality: "There is something that you have to wake up to; where you will never allow disease to have you, or sin to have you, or a weak heart to have you, or a pain in the back. You will never allow anything that isn't perfect life to have anything to do with you."[137] His watchword was "There is nothing impossible with God." It became the theme of the ditty reiterated at his meetings: "Only believe, Only believe, /All things are possible, / Only believe." His stress on faith earned him the title "Apostle of Faith" but it was at a price: "Great faith is a product of great fights. Great testimonies are the outcome of great tests. Great triumphs can only come after great trials."[138] On the "already/not yet" dichotomy understanding of the arriving of the kingdom of God, he came down heavily on the "already."

The Legacy of Wigglesworth

The influence of Wigglesworth remains far-reaching. In this section, attention will be directed to the following: his contribution to the promulgation of the Pentecostal message; the standing of his views on faith, medical means and satanic oppression; his rough handling of persons seeking healing; an assessment of his role as a model for the Word-Faith /Prosperity Gospel movement?

Contribution to the Promulgation of the Pentecostal Message

Though Wigglesworth resisted any desire to form a denominational structure around himself, his campaigns, and their global distribution led to the formation of new Pentecostal churches. It is estimated that nine churches were founded in Switzerland in the aftermath of a visit. From his two visits to New Zealand in 1922 and 1923–24, his campaigns were a factor in establishing the unified Pentecostal Church of New Zealand. The beginning of the work in South Australia followed the immediate healing of a man with a poisoned hand. The man, his wife and about forty other members of their church joined the newly formed Pentecostal church in Adelaide. From this nucleus, new assemblies developed.[139] While visits were paid to the Indian sub-continent in 1926 and South Africa in 1937, it was North America that was the most frequented in his overseas travels outside Europe. Carl Brumback, historian of the Assemblies of God in America, quoted an item of glowing praise paid to Wigglesworth: "No other person exerted more influence over the Assemblies of God with regard to faith for supernatural confirmation of the Word than this one-time illiterate English plumber. His book, *Ever Increasing Faith,* sold over

---

136. Wigglesworth, *Ever Increasing Faith*, 151.

137. Dorries, "Smith Wigglesworth," 22.

138. Frodsham, *Smith Wigglesworth*, 91.

139. Chant, *Heart of Fire*, 53–54.

100,000 copies."[140] Some ten years later the revised edition of the book appeared, with its cover page announcing "nearly a million copies in circulation: A legacy of love and faith from one of the great spiritual leaders of modern times." It was through his published sermons that Wigglesworth still speaks to the post-1945 generation. He continues to hold an enduring fascination in some circles, particularly in America. The popular appeal of his two books *Ever Increasing Faith* (1924) and *Faith that Prevails* (1938) lies for many in the dramatic stories of healing found in the pages, all of which raise an expectation of continual displays of supernatural power.

Why Wigglesworth's books should achieve such popularity deserves to be set in historical context. As discussed in earlier chapters, in the aftermath of the 1914–18 War and through the 1920s, America witnessed in a heightening of interest in healing evangelism through the impact of such luminaries as F. F. Bosworth, Aimee Semple McPherson, and Charles S. Price. Their appeal was widened by playing down the Pentecostal distinctives of evidential tongues, satanic oppression and the undesirability of seeking medical attention. For a variety of reasons, the period from 1930s to the latter half of the 1940s proved to be the lean years of public awareness of divine healing. In 1939 a number of articles in the Canadian *Pentecostal Testimony* posed the question "Have We Lost Divine Healing?" One writer expressed the fear that "it will recede and become an abstract teaching of a theory, and will be acknowledged as the same if it is not practiced."[141]

Immediately after World War II, a sea change took place in Pentecostalism in North America. The war sowed the seeds of a desire for change. Some Pentecostal leaders began to question the isolationism of the movement in the previous generation. A number had received commissions as chaplains and served on the battlefront in a pastoral capacity. Many Pentecostal denominations, especially the Assemblies of God, provided practical and social help for servicemen of all faiths and none. Just as significant was the move of a number of major Pentecostal denominations to join the National Association of Evangelicals (NAE) in 1943.[142] Donald Gee, his editorial antennae ever sharp to pick up trends, wrote an article in *Pentecost* in 1949 under the heading "Renewed Emphasis upon Divine Healing." He drew attention to the renewed emphasis on divine healing evangelism in North America: "Various preachers are conducting immense meetings on the lines that older friends will connect with such names as Mrs. Woodworth-Etter and others. After a forced and much needed rest, William Branham is back in active ministry on this line, and is stated to be 'a new man in body, spirit and vision.' . . . There are many testimonies to miraculous cases of divine healing through his ministry."[143] Branham was

---

140. Brumback, *Suddenly from Heaven*, 272.

141. Courey, "Real Issue in Pentecostalism," 21.

142. For an account of this period, see Nicol, *Pentecostals*. 208ff. The NAE was one of the institutions that formed part of the coalition that shaped neo-evangelicalism in the post-war years. It became a significant player on the American religious, social and political life, once it was seen to act as a counterweight to anti-intellectual aspects of Fundamentalism. In the early years of the NAE, Pentecostal leaders were unsure of their standing in the institution, but with the growth of their movement from the 1960s onward Pentecostals came to form the largest bloc within it.

143. *Pentecost*, September 1949, 14. This periodical was a quarterly review of world-wide Pentecostal missionary and revival activity, edited and published by Gee at the request of the World Conference of

to prove among the first crop of healing evangelists who were to advance the message globally.[144] With the arrival of the Charismatic Movement in the 1960s, divine healing was renewed in its prominence, and set on its way to reach a level that was unprecedented in the history of Christianity.

At this point Wigglesworth fits into the story. The fear of many of the older Pentecostals after his death and those of Aimee Semple McPherson (1944) and Charles Price (1947) was that the Spirit's anointing on the Pentecostal movement had been buried. Velmer Gardner (1913–93) recalled the day when he learned of the deaths Charles Price and Wigglesworth:

> I went down in the basement of the church and cried my heart out. I thought of all the sick, twisted, deformed, broken bodies. And then I thought of how few men were praying for the sick and had a compassion for the suffering. I cried until it seemed I couldn't stop. Both of these men had been such a help to me. I cried, "Oh, God why did you take them? The world is filled with sickness and disease. The World needs the faith of Wigglesworth and the preaching of Price, but now they're dead and their message gone."[145]

Such dismay turned out to be unfounded. It was but natural to think that Wigglesworth, noted for his "bold faith, colourful preaching, controversial methods, and the remarkable testimonies that followed his ministry and made him legendary," was irreplaceable.[146] In fact, the year of his death (1947) coincided with the renaissance of healing evangelism which came with astonishing force, of which Gardner was an early practitioner.

After the wilted years on the 1930s and the lacuna of the war years, the need of the hour was leaders and models of spiritual power. Though dead, Wiggleworth spoke through the two books written under his name. It was not so much their doctrinal content, minimal at best, that moved readers as their stories of spectacular healings that grabbed attention. Little wonder then that the sale figures for the books reached such an impressive number. His books inspired a new cadre of figures who rose to prominence in the post-war healing and charismatic revivals, notably in North America, and from there in truly global outreach. In one of his editorials, Gee contended that the deaths of Price and Wigglesworth within a few days of each other early in 1947 "certainly fired many pure young hearts with a holy desire to pick up the torch of their ministry and carry it forward to new achievements."[147] He noted that the vast crowds far exceeded those of the former generation of evangelists. As a result, the mammoth campaigns helped to raise the profile of the movement, making it one of the most potent religious forces of its time.

Pentecostal Churches. It is worth noticing that 1947 was the first year of its publication.

144. Names that come to mind include T. L. Osborn, A. A. Allen, Oral Roberts, Moris Cerullo, John Wimber, Benny Hinn, and Reinhard Bonnke (b. 1940). Bonnke, late in 2000 during his campaign in Lagos, Nigeria, drew a total of almost six million people, including 1.6 million in a single night. Every day millions throughout the world who tune into the "God Channel" will hear some reference to healing, and many will claim healing through its programs.

145. *Voice of Healing*, September 1952, 6.

146. Harrell, *All Things Are Possible*, 20.

147. *Pentecost*, June 1956, 17.

If Wigglesworth's writings served as a guide for the next generation of revivalists, then the question has to be raised as to how open they were to be questioned by the post-1945 generation. In other words, did some of his views on healing perpetuate idea which more theologically astute, Pentecostal scholarship would later come to question, even dismiss. Three of the positions taken by Wigglesworth that have been challenged are examined below:

HIS VIEW ON FAITH

A case in point was his stress on faith, famously captured in his *aperçu*, "I am not moved by what I see. I am moved only by what I believe."[148] He made a clear distinction between natural, human faith and the faith that rests in the faith of Christ which indwells the believer. His view of faith was more nuanced than is commonly appreciated. For believers to enter the rest of faith—"Faith always rests"—they must know God of the Bible:

> We must be able to go in and hold converse with God. We must also know the mind of God toward us, so that all our petitions are always on the line of His will. As this like precious faith becomes a part of you, it will make you so that you will dare to do anything. How shall we reach this plane of faith? Let go your own thoughts, and take the thoughts of God, the Word of God. If you build yourself on imaginations you will go wrong. You have the Word of God and it is enough. . . . It is supernatural in origin, eternal in duration, inexpressible in value, infinite in scope, regenerative in power, infallible in authority, universal in interest, personal in application, inspired in totality. Read it through. Write it down. Pray it in. Work it out. And then pass it on."

Frodsham's labelling of Wigglesworth as "apostle of faith" and the emphasis on the word in the titles of the two books under his name, *Ever Increasing Faith* and *Faith That Prevails,* turned the theme of the chorus "Only Believe" into something of a mantra that oversimplified the original intent.

The question can be raised as to whether the "only believe" mantra helped to sustain the belief that faith was the veritable *sine qua non* to receive healing? At the World Pentecostal Conference in Toronto in 1968, Leonard Steiner criticized those contemporary healing evangelists who spoke in such a way as to make God their servant, and avoided the limitation expressed in the Lord's prayer "Thy will be done." Colin Dye in his book *Healing Anointing* (1997) conceded that without an appreciation of God's sovereign purposes "the cross does not guarantee us automatic physical healing in this life, even if we are fully obedient and full of faith"—a statement that warns against tying healing too fixedly to faith. [149]

The Pentecostal theologian, Keith Warrington, holds that "the statements 'just have faith' and 'only believe' are almost meaningless, because faith requires an object; faith in itself has no power. . . . The assumption that God works to a formula that will inevitably result in action on his part is to be questioned."[150] In an earlier book, *Healing & Suffering*

---

148. Wigglesworth, *Ever Increasing Faith*, 21.

149. Warrington, *Pentecostal Theology*, 285 & 275.

150. Ibid., 276.

(2005), Warrington rejected any suggestion that an insufficient amount of faith could restrict Jesus is wrong on two counts: "Firstly, the teaching of Jesus concerning faith related to its existence, not to its quantity. . . . Secondly, the belief that a person's faith can be developed to achieve a greater level of success is a distortion of the NT teaching concerning faith. It undermines the majesty, wisdom and love of Jesus, making him a servant of the 'faith' by which he may be coerced or enabled to function."[151] Any such presumption must be forestalled by giving a proper recognition to the pre-eminence of the will of God. Faith is not to be regarded as a package of claims to which God must lend assent, "irrespective of his better judgment."[152] Frank Macchia summed up cogently the role of faith, recognizing that there is a creative tension between the hidden meaning of faith and the visible signs of its efficacy: "This tension should not be resolved through a reduction of faith to either hidden meanings or to visible triumphs over suffering. If the former, faith can become passive, glorifying suffering without any resistance or hope for any visible healing in the here and now. If the latter, faith can become triumphalistic, with no capacity to comfort those who live unavoidably in a state of serious need or suffering."[153]

His View on Medical Means

The fact that faith and the refusal to employ medical means were so closely related in radical healing circles had a decided bearing on Wigglesworth's resolve in the early 1930s to suffer the excruciating pain of kidney stones rather than submit to surgery. It was a view, here somewhat cautiously expressed, on which his preaching on healing was premised: "One thing God is showing to me which causes me to deal very faithfully with the sick people is this: If the first remedy that you have taken from the doctor's bottle had healed you, you would not have been here; so you are only giving God the next chance. If we would be as faithful to God as we have been faithful to doctors, we would all have been healed. But we have been unfaithful and there is need of repentance. Some people, after they have been healed, go back to medicine."[154] He stiffened the resolve of his hearers to rely on faith when he pronounced, "If you ask God seven times for the same thing, six times are in unbelief."[155] When a man with failing eyesight asked him if he should without glasses, Wigglesworth replied: "Put your glasses on. For when your faith is perfected you will not require any glasses, and when God perfects your faith your glasses will drop off. But as long as you have need, use them." He was not against doctors, believing that "they have a great suffering world of trials and sickness and sorrow to help."[156] In general, his views on medical intervention have faded in advanced societies, with their profusion

151. Warrington, *Healing and Suffering*, 32.

152. Ibid., 162–63.

153. Macchia, *Baptized in the Spirit*, 148.

154. Wigglesworth: The Ultimate Collection, (CD-ROM). The quote is taken from a sermon preached in California in the 1920s.

155. Hollenweger, *Pentecostals*. 478.

156. Wilson, *Wigglesworth*, 132–33. That he could not be entirely obdurate about the issue was exposed, to the amusement of his audience, when he was caught fumbling with his glasses while soliciting help from his deaf daughter.

of medical services inspiring the adoption of a perspective on healing that aims to be more biblically substantiated. Kay found that 94 percent of sampled Pentecostal pastors in Britain agreed with the statement, "I believe modern medicine is a God-given blessing."[157] Anyone who took Wigglesworth's views seriously would still be inclined to judge modern medicine as second best.

HIS VIEWS ON SATANIC OPPRESSION

Wigglesworth was of the view that 90 percent of diseases were satanic in origin, with cancer at the top of the list. Animated by a burning anger towards Satan, he would sometimes strike the afflicted person where their pain was seated as if he were actually hitting the devil. Two issues arise from this position—the prominence he gave to Satan in disease, and his treatment of the sick, dealt with below. The view expressed by Grant McClung that "no clarified doctrinal on demonology and exorcism exists among major Pentecostal bodies. . . . Exorcism has been practiced but not formally theologised" is surprising in that this topic has defined the movement in popular thinking.[158] Demonic activity, commented Hollenweger, is "an unsolved problem in Pentecostal belief and practice."[159] At one end of the ever-widening spectrum of Pentecostal belief is the view that identifies demons with virtually every ailment. Wigglesworth placed blame for "all the discord and evil, and everything painful" visited upon humankind on the devil, the common enemy of God and mankind.[160] His response to such oppression was to assert the authority of Jesus' name. The key to healing is not in our own resources, but in the unlimited power of Jesus indwelling us: "No man is capable of standing against the wiles of the devil by himself, but when you get Jesus in you, you are equal to a million devils." He sensed that Satan has deceived most Christians into thinking that bodily oppressions such as sickness and disease are given to serve some divine purpose. Such deception must be broken by believers refusing to accept such oppressions as coming from God. Believers do not have to be victimized by Satan's methods.[161]

At the other end of the spectrum are academics with Pentecostal sympathies like Keith Warrington and J. Christopher Thomas who have subjected the topic to detailed exegetic analysis. Both hold a worldview that accepts the factuality of the whole realm of spirit beings, both angelic and demonic, but have no desire to give the demonic a place that goes beyond biblical statement. Warrington is of the opinion that, for many Pentecostals, the popular view of demons owes too much "to medieval art and popular fiction." He noted that in the ministry of Christ "few illnesses were related to demonic activity, whilst in the rest of the NT such an association is absent", thus providing a useful perspective for modern thought.[162] Andrew G. Walker accepts that while the Gospels portray Jesus as clearly believing in demons, he did not see "all sickness and evil under

---

157. Kay, *Pentecostals in Britain*, 100.

158. McClung, "Exorcism." In Burgess, *IDPCM*, 624

159. Warrington, *Pentecostal Theology*, 297.

160. Dorries, "Smith Wigglesworth" 22.

161. Ibid., 23.

162. Warrington, *Healing & Suffering*, 80.

devilish control, and he shows no interest whatever in the minutiae and mechanisms of the demonic realm."[163] Thomas calculated that only around 10 percent of infirmities in the NT are attributed to Satan: therefore "it would seem wise to avoid the temptation of assuming that in most cases an infirmity is caused by Satan and/or demons. Such a realization . . . could serve to bring a degree of moderation through biblical critique to an area that has been and continues to be sorely abused."[164] Evidence suggests that the New Testament writers "did not always attribute infirmity to Satan, but worked with a more dialectical worldview: a world where God could also inflict. Such an understanding suggests that God is not only able to use suffering indirectly to accomplish his purposes, but he can also take a direct role in this activity."[165]

His Rough Handling of the Sick

What hampered Wigglesworth's appeal within sections of the Pentecostal and wider evangelical constituency, though more so in his early years than later, was his rough treatment of people who sought prayer for healing.[166] The question arising from this side of his practice is its bearing as a model for healers who succeeded him. Did his practice help to popularize the idea that God's power is most effectively deployed through shows of human militancy, however well meant. As was pointed out, his reaction to diseases like cancer was to oppose them, in Gee's words, "with a blaze of holy anger" against what he saw as a work of Satan that had to be forcibly ejected by rebuke and physical force. An explanation for Wigglesworth's vehemence in these situations can be found in aspects of Jesus' ministry and in his own innate weaknesses.[167] The verse that came to him at the time he was healed from chronic bleeding haemorrhoids was Matt 11:12 KJV ("From the days of John the Baptist until now the kingdom of heaven suffereth violence and the violent take it by force"). He interpreted this as a call to exercise violent or forceful faith—to storm the throne of grace—in order to overcome this trial in his body. It would appear that he took this verse as a template for his ministry. Another verse he leaned upon was Isa 58:6 ("to loose the bands of wickedness, to undo the heavy burdens, and to let the oppressed go free"). His attitude to severe disease, explains his biographer, "was never

163. Walker, "Devil You Think You Know," 89.

164. Thomas, *Devil, Disease and Deliverance*, 317.

165. Ibid., 300. His study found that Matthew and Luke/Acts reflected most on the role of the devil in sickness, while other NT writers provide little evidence for the idea.

166. Charismatic Catholic healers, according to Csordas, were "dismayed by those who feel it is necessary to 'shout' at evil spirits." The phenomenon was attributed to inexperience or the influence of "Protestant" deliverance style (Csordas, *Sacred Self*, 176).

167. The theme of "holy anger" was not alien to the ministry of Jesus (John 11:33) portrays Jesus being "deeply moved (Gk. *embrimaomai*) in spirit and troubled." Various commentators have sought to capture the sense of the Greek: "angry in spirit" (G. R. Beasley-Murray); "outraged" (D. A. Carson); "inexpressible anger" (Warfield). Calvin wrote that Jesus approached the tomb like "a champion who prepares for conflict." While death was the proximate occasion of his wrath, its main target was its source, Satan, the oppressor of human kind (Milne, *Message of John*, 165).

that of a child stroking a kitten, but rather of one who tore the prey out of the mouth of the dragon."[168]

In his vigorous handling of sick persons, Wigglesworth on one occasion was left exposed to blackmail. A woman, ostensibly crippled, who attended a large rally was prayed for by him in his usual robust manner. A week later a letter came from the woman's lawyer claiming damages for injuries sustained through his conduct. A doctor's certificate was obtained and legal action initiated. The claim was bogus, but to forestall court action, the sum demanded was paid to avoid injurious publicity. However, at no time did Wigglesworth display the level of violence reached more recently by healing evangelist, Todd Bentley, in Florida, though his *Wikipeda* entry suggests otherwise. It reads: "Bentley was criticized in mainstream media and on internet blogs for occasional violence done to participants, in the tradition of Smith Wigglesworth." Bentley exulted in telling the story of striking a Chinese man, which led to his spitting out a tooth, a ferocity that drew the aside, "Now we are talking Holy Ghost Revival." The same healer testified to choking the devil out of a man, and banging the damaged leg repeatedly of a woman against the floor before being directed, supposedly by the Spirit, to kick her face. The outcome was that he grazed the end of her nose with his biker boot.[169]

Jack Coe (1918–56), an ordained minister of the American Assemblies of God, was expelled from the denomination because of his methods and teachings. He thrived on controversy and was noted for his rough handling of supplicants. Like Wigglesworth, he was a fearless healer, recklessly so said his critics, who was not loath to take on hard cases. At a meeting in Birmingham, Alabama he lined up 103 people in wheelchairs and crutches. As he walked down the line he would lift people up from their wheelchair. If they fell, he would tell them that they did not have enough faith. Evidently sixty-three did because they got up and walked away from their wheelchair.[170] When he appeared on television, the viewer experienced the frisson that almost anything could happen. In one incident, Coe's photographers filmed him praying for a woman who had a back problem. After his prayer, Coe put his knee into her back, grabbed her shoulders, and pulled her backwards. Wayne Warner wrote that Coe was rough, believing that he was battling the devil, "a method possibly picked up from the legendary Smith Wigglesworth who would often punch the sick with his fist to drive out the devil."[171] Others of that ilk would destroy medicines, break canes and crutches, and use a saw to remove body plaster casts, while thousands in the tents cheered and TV viewers gulped.

Such rebarbative activity at the hands of Wigglesworth is hard to defend, and its effects are amplified by those who, in replicating similar means, use Wigglesworth's reputation as justification. Wigglesworth was fully aware of the criticism directed at him on this score but refused to change his method, perceiving that he acted under divine authority. He acknowledged that "there are some times when you pray for the sick and you are apparently rough. But you are not dealing with a person; you are dealing with

---

168. Frodsham, *Smith Wigglesworth*, 13.

169. Bentley, "Todd Bentley's Violent Ministry." You Tube Video clip.

170. Harrell, *All Things Are Possible*, 59.

171. Warner, *Kathryn Kuhlman*, 15.

the satanic forces that are binding the person. Your heart is full of love and compassion to all, but you are moved to a holy anger as you see the place the devil has taken in the body of the sick one, and you deal with his position with a real forcefulness."[172] What is difficult to deny are reports from eyewitnesses of healings that proved successful following such muscular handling. A side of Wiggleworth's personality was touched on by Wilson in his biography, which might prove helpful in understanding the temperament of Wigglesworth. The biographer identified three innate weaknesses revealed in the early life of Wigglesworth—"his volcanic temper, impatience and tactlessness." They were brought under control in the early days of his conversion, but erupted again in his backslidden period. Of that period, Wigglesworth confessed: "I used to go white with rage and shake all over with temper. I could hardly hold myself together."[173] His transformation can be viewed in classical psychoanalytical terms as an instance of sublimation, the redirection and refinement of instinctual impulses into ways that are socially acceptable, though regression to the aggressive behavior of an earlier stage of life remains a possibility.

Opinion remains divided as to the outworking of this side of Wigglesworth's ministry. As for his "impatience" and "tactlessness," he was noted to the contrary for his benign chairmanship of convention meetings. William Hacking, a Pentecostal pastor who knew him well, described him as "rugged and refined at the same time. Of his preaching he said, "There was always a poise, a reverence, a dignity of demeanor in his presentation."[174] He only became steely when he detected the misuse of spiritual gifts. Then he had no hesitation in telling offenders to sit down and keep quiet if he thought they were not in the Spirit.[175] Wigglesworth has to be taken for what he was—"unique, original and illimitable." This was Frodsham's assessment, who added that "he was too sincere to be a mimic and too transparent to be imitated. There were those who sought to borrow his innovations, but they found that these imitations were as incongruous to them as Saul's armour was to David . . . as revealing as the seven sons of Sceva who sought to cast out demons in the name of the Christ whom Paul preached."[176] Authority and confidence in God were qualities he had in abundance. He was the man for the despairing seeker, less so for the sensitive and the refined. The "shock" element in his rougher handling of the sick must have triggered, possibly in medically understood terms, some mental/somatic change that enabled the seeker to perform an action of which they felt incapable. His tactless, unconventional utterances changed mindsets more profoundly than emollient blandishments. His approach to the Godhead was equally direct, even seemingly blasphemous, as when asked how quickly he was moved by the Spirit, he replied, "Well, you see, it is like this. If the Spirit does not move me, I move the Spirit."[177] Such remarks require knowledge of their immediate context, and some appreciation of his limited grasp of the English language. His simplistic biblicism trampled on exegetical refinement because he

172. Dorries, "Smith Wigglesworth," 23.

173. Wilson, *Wigglesworth*, 29.

174. Whittaker, *Seven Pentecostal Pioneers*, 39.

175. Gee, *These Men I Knew*, 90–91.

176. Frodsham, *Smith Wigglesworth*, 85.

177. Lairdon: *God's Generals*, 216.

worked on the premise that he had a God-given authority to go for the jugular of evil forces—to command, in biblical terminology, the movement of mountains.[178]

At the personal level, Donald Gee found him to be "one of God's gentlemen" with "a fascination for the cultured." Wigglesworth may have spoken in the broad accent of a blunt Yorkshire man, but dressed like a gent. When he entered the ministry he promised God that he would obey him implicitly, but laid down the condition that his shoe heels must never be a disgrace, and his trousers never have their knees out: "I said to the Lord, 'If either of these things takes place. I'll go back to plumbing.'"[179] Noting how he had mellowed with time, Gee told of an incident when he had to leave early from an Easter Convention to fulfil another, pre-arranged engagement elsewhere. Wigglesworth reprimanded him "very tartly." Shortly afterwards, however, he sought Gee for forgiveness, "and apologised in a way that just broke me down."[180] As a guest at their home, Mrs Gee regarded him as "delightful—unselfish, courteous, generous and filling the home with the aroma of the presence of God."[181] Frodsham, in an obituary tribute to his long-standing friend, recalled the gentler side of his nature. Wigglesworth must have noticed from their shabby clothing that Frodsham and his wife were strapped for cash. He accompanied them to a shop selling new outfits. Frodsham recalled: "He was just overwhelmed with joy at being able to perform this kindness to two folk he loved, and I remember that in one of the stores, like Joseph, 'he sought where to weep.' I noticed that he went into one corner of the store, where he hoped no clerk could see him, wiping the copious tears from his eyes."[182]

A ROLE MODEL FOR THE PROSPERITY GOSPEL?

This complex movement appeared on the radar in the 1970s and has since grown globally. The message of healing and financial prosperity came to be combined through an act of positive confession. The idea behind the latter is that words spoken in faith are regarded as "objectifications of reality, establishing palpable connections between human will and the external world."[183] Faith is seen as a force that actuates words through "positive confession." Based on this faith formula, one need only speak words of faith, that is, make a positive confession regarding whatever one desires. The spoken word, coupled with creative faith, initiates the process of obtaining the desires of one's heart. In effect, it allows one to write their own ticket with God by saying it, doing it, receiving it, and telling it. Such audacious thinking works on the premise that all the spiritual and material blessings of the Abrahamic covenant are deemed to have been extended through Christ (Gal 3:14). Such blessings are unlocked by a *rhema* ("word" *Gk.*). In Word of Faith theology, a rhema word is a specific prophetic word for a particular moment. It may come as portion of

---

178. Matt 17:20 (NIV): "If you have faith as small as a mustard seed, you can say to this mountain, 'Move from here to there' and it will move. Nothing will be impossible for you."

179. Frodsham, *Smith Wigglesworth*, 33.

180. Gee, *These Men I Knew*, 91.

181. "Culture" was not quite his scene. When attending a performance of Handel's Messiah, his bellow of "Hallelujah" reverberated round the whole theatre at the end of the Hallelujah Chorus.

182. *RT*, 11 April 1947, 2.

183. Coleman, *Globalisation of Charismatic Christianity*, 8.

Scripture that the Holy Spirit directs to a current situation or meets a particular need for guidance. Its biblical warrant is taken from a verse such as Rom 10:8 ("The word is near you; it is in your mouth and in your heart, which is the word of faith we are proclaiming"). As the argument goes, the term *rhema* applies to particular needs and times, neither of which is plainly disclosed in the fuller revelation of Scripture, which provides generalized direction to all Christians—sometimes referred to as the *logos* ("word" Gk.).[184] The *rhema* word may be a sudden consciousness that a particular verse or passage, irrespective of its context, should be applied to a current circumstance. If the *rhema* revelation is positive about a specific act of healing, and is received with faith, then it must take place. In that situation the believers must avoid "negative confession" by ignoring the symptoms of "sense knowledge." For the sick person, the outcome of acting on such a *rhema* word ensures healing, thus obviating the need to ask repeatedly for prayer for the same matter.

Kenneth Hagin (1917–2003), generally regarded as the father of the Word of Faith movement, challenged sufferers to defy their symptoms. Echoing Kenyon's phraseology, Hagin stated, "When 'sense-knowledge truth' contradicts 'revelation truth,' or the Word of God, then I start walking by revelation truth. . . . That which is in the spiritual realm is made real in the natural realm through faith."[185] Gloria Copeland offered this advice to those seeking healing:

> Make this confession of faith before God: "Father, in the name of Jesus, I have accepted Jesus as my Lord and Savior, so now I accept Him as my healer. I say now with my mouth that my body is healed—from the top of my head to the tips of my toes. I determine now to walk in the light of healing in my spirit, in my mind, and in my body. I believe that just as surely as Jesus bore my sins, He also bore my sicknesses. I stand now, in Jesus' name, and proclaim that I am free from the bondage of Satan." If you have sickness in your body right now, then speak to it now: "Sickness, I resist you in Jesus' name. I refuse to allow you in my body any longer. I command you to leave. Satan, you'll not lord it over me. In Jesus' name, your work has been destroyed!" Now rejoice in what God has already done for you through Jesus and what He is continuing to do in you at this moment![186]

---

184. Linguistic usage, as in 1 Pet 1:23–25, shows the words are interchangeable: "Having been born again, not of corruptible seed but incorruptible, through the word ("*logou*") which lives and abides forever. . . . The grass withers, and its flower falls away, but the word (*rhema*) of the Lord endures forever. Now this is the word (*rhema*) which by the gospel was preached to you" (1 Pet 1:23–25).

185. Hejzlar. Pavel. "Two Paradigms for Divine Healing," 94. Even though Kenyon was involved in the ministry of healing and had contact with Pentecostal leaders, he kept his distance from the Pentecostal movement. The distinction he made between "Sense Knowledge" and "Revelation Knowledge" led him to disdain the Pentecostal quest for corporeal manifestations of the Spirit, such as tongues. More generally, the Pentecostal churches have been critical of the Prosperity movement. In 1980, the General Council of the AoG criticized the doctrine of positive confession, by noting examples of negative confessions in the Bible where Biblical figures express fears and doubt, yet had witnessed positive outcomes. For example, see Luke 7:7, for the healing of the centurion's servant.

186. Copeland, Gloria. "Reaping a Harvest of Healing." Online. Kenneth Copeland (b. 1937) and his wife Gloria are leading proponents of the prosperity gospel. Between them they have written over fifty-eight books, and head an international television ministry.

There is certain inevitability that Wigglesworth's name should become associated with Word-Faith theology, even if his intent, in contradistinction to his influence, cannot be proved. The origins and tenets of the movement are a source of controversy. D. R. McConnell in his *A Different Gospel,* and Hank Hanegraaff in *Christianity in Crisis* have claimed the movement as heretical or cultic, originating in New Thought metaphysics, with E. W. Kenyon (1867–1948) the earliest proponent of the modern movement. Others argue that the primary influence upon Kenyon was not New Thought metaphysics, but rather leaders of the Higher Life and Keswick Holiness movements, such as A. J. Gordon, A. B. Simpson, A. T. Pierson, Oswald Chambers, and others. Paul King takes the view that most of Kenyon's thought kept within the bounds of orthodox evangelical teaching, as represented by the Keswick/Higher Life movement, although admittedly some of his ideas stretched the limits of orthodoxy. He asserted that Hagin, while drawing the majority of his teaching from Kenyon, also acknowledged the influence of evangelical and Higher Life leaders such as Muller, Spurgeon, Simpson, and the Pentecostal leaders John G. Lake and Smith Wigglesworth.[187]

Derek Vreeland takes the view that Word of Faith teaching is not a heresy, but "a theologically premature movement that needs significant reconstruction. Word of Faith theology is within the bounds of orthodoxy because of its historical roots in Holiness/Pentecostalism and its exaltation of the biblical authority. These elements provide a sufficient theological foundation to absorb correction."[188] He held that Faith theology has a strong root in Pentecostalism, citing Wigglesworth as having "a substantial impact on Hagin and his theology." A quotation from Hagin's book *The Believer's Authority* exemplifies his regard for Wigglesworth: "I base my faith on what the Word says. Some people's faith is not based on the Bible; however, it's based on a manifestation. . . . As Smith Wigglesworth often said, 'I'm not moved by what I feel. I'm moved only by what I believe.' So stand your ground." Hagen argued that Wigglesworth's theology parallels that of Kenyon with its distinction between sense knowledge and revelational knowledge. Faith, he regarded, acts on divinely inspired disclosure and is prepared to defy the evidence of the senses, an understanding referred to as "acting faith" in earlier days. In his *Ministering to the Oppressed* (1983), Hagen again referred to Wigglesworth in pointing to the advantage of the sick in attending a service where healings are in evidence: "We can get faith into people by teaching them, but they also need to get into services where God is moving and manifesting Himself. Smith Wigglesworth said that if God doesn't manifest Himself, it is doubtful whether the Holy Spirit is really there"—a statement that betrays an unduly restricted view of the *modus operandi* of the Trinity.[189]

Rodney Lee ("Rod") Parsley (b. 1957) is a prominent advocate of the prosperity gospel, a television host and evangelist. He is senior pastor of World Harvest Church, a 5,200-seater, 12,000-member, Pentecostal church in Columbus, Ohio and founder and president of the Center for Moral Clarity, a right-wing Christian pressure group. He is

187. King, "Theological Roots," 1–2. Classical Pentecostal healers did not believe "that words are the containers of the force of faith, nor that those words can create reality."

188. Vreeland, "Reconstructing Word of Faith Theology," 297.

189. Hagin, *Ministering to the Oppressed*, 30.

also founder of *Breakthrough*, the television outreach ministry of his church. Raised a Free Will Baptist, he came under the influence of Lester Sumrall (1913–96), the Indiana-based Pentecostal evangelist, missionary, and broadcaster who was a friend of Wigglesworth. Sumrall became the youthful Parsley's spiritual mentor, the two often traveling together on mission. A forceful speaker, noted for his extreme phraseology and emotive gesticulations, Parsley has been dubbed "the Raging Prophet" who, in the words of one secular critic, "barks and grimaces and struts on stage, pretending to cure sickness and constantly demanding pledges of money from working-class Ohio parishioners."[190] The charge of pecuniary excess does not trouble Parsley as it epitomizes the "prosperity" side to Word of Faith teaching. He admits: "Let me be very clear—I want your money. I desire it. The church deserves it." Ownership of a house valued at over one million dollars and a private jet, a $500,000 seven-passenger, Hawker-Siddeley, is sustained by the tithes of his extensive Christian support base. Tithes and other offerings are described as "seed" that will produce a bounteous return: "It's selfish not to expect the hundredfold return [on the seed sown in the financial realm]. . . . The anointing is on the seed. If you will divest, God will invest."[191] Charges of misuse of church funds mounted against the leadership by former employees have all been successfully defeated in the courts.[192]

Parsley stands by standard Pentecostal healing practices, though with a brio and certitude, which are fading within the educated sector of advanced societies. Two assertions exemplify this: "Jesus is not sick—I don't have to be sick," and "Let's settle the matter once and for all, God doesn't want you sick." He promotes an understanding of healing that widens its scope to encompass lustful appetites, homosexual desires, bankruptcy, itchy scalp conditions, extremities plagued with rashes, brain fluid seepages, lack of the experience of Holy Ghost baptism (complete with *glossolalia*), breast tumors, infertility, lack of the desire to do Christian foreign missions' work, and over-excitement in a recovered diabetic's dog—all of which featured over a few months on televised *Breakthrough*, and all acclaimed as instantly remedied or alleviated. Typical glossy packets mailed to enquirers enclose a "miracle prayer cloth" with the directive: "Receive this prayer cloth as your point of contact. Place this prayer cloth in the envelope provided and believe God to receive your miracle. . . . As you send me your prayer cloth and your most generous gift toward our Breakthrough ministry, I will send you my 3-tape audio cassette series, 'Releasing the Anointing. . . . Your Breakthrough to Victory.'"[193]

Parsley ascribes his ability to perform both direct and distance healings to a straight link to the Holy Spirit. This link is attributed by Parsley to "a special connective 'impartation' that was first established between God and Smith Wigglesworth, subsequently relayed to Howard Carter, and then transferred to his own mentor Lester Sumrall before becoming transmitted to him."[194] Parsley frequently explains that he can pass on this "im-

190. Posner, *God's Profits*, xi. American Africans form 45 percent of the church membership.

191. Fisher, "Rod Parsley: The Raging Prophet," Online.

192. Hedges, *American Fascists*: 166.

193. Wise, "Con of the Month." Online.

194. Gunn, "Rewired Pentecostalism," 352. Howard Carter (1891–1971) was a British Pentecostal leader and teacher, who from 1921 to 1948 was Principal of Hampstead Bible School in London. He traveled

partation" or "anointing" to those who become his covenant partners (invariably financial supporters), or attend his World Harvest Bible College. He undoubtedly captures something of the audacity of Wigglesworth but exercises it in a fashion more accommodative to the brashness of contemporary consumerist culture, which makes it far more incautious about maintaining the standards of conduct that remain embedded in the older Holiness tradition.

That Wigglesworth's influence extends to wider communities is borne out by three research projects outlined here. Catherine Bowler carried out ethnographic research on the storefront African American Word of Faith Church, Durham, North Carolina. The church practices healing within the Prosperity Gospel tradition. Though the congregation had access to medical care, it mistrusted medicine as inferior to faith, partly because the healthcare system had failed to provide the members with color-blind treatment. The pastor in one of his sermons preached against resigning oneself to death. He reminded his listeners that famous healers like A. A. Allen and Smith Wigglesworth had raised the faithful from the dead.[195]

Arlene Sánchez Walsh found in her study of Maranatha, a Puerto Rican Pentecostal denomination based in Chicago, that the church revered not only Hagin and other Word of Faith teachers but also "certain Anglo-Pentecostal pioneers, notably Smith Wigglesworth and A. A. Allen.[196] The appeal of the two men lay both in their anti-denominationalism and their stance on faith healing, which made them appealing to cross-cultural churches. The denomination's shop and online bookstores continue to sell Wigglesworth's books.

Paul Gifford found that it would be hard to find an African Pentecostal church that "is entirely untouched by the global Word of Faith movement."[197] He made particular study of one denomination, the Living Faith Church Worldwide, founded in Lagos in 1983 by David Oyedepo. By the year 2000 it had branched out into thirty-eight African countries. Its Lagos church, seating 50,400 people, makes it the largest church auditorium in the world. Oyedepo published a 649-page blockbuster *Signs and Wonders Today: A Catalogue of the Amazing Acts of God among Men* (2006). He readily admits that his commission is a Word of Faith ministry. Nor is he reticent to admit his main debt to Hagin, and Kenneth Copeland, adding the names of Oswald J. Smith, T. L Osborn, and Smith Wigglesworth. This small sample is representative of a trend that gives credence to the

extensively as a preacher and conference speaker. In the 1930s, Carter and Sumrall journeyed 150,000 miles together visiting many countries (Carter, *Howard Carter*, 125–26).

195. Bowler, *Blessed Bodies*, 98.

196. Walsh, "Santidad, Salvación, Sanidad, Liberación," 159. Alan Alenso Allen (1911–70) was renowned as "the boldest of the bold" independent healing evangelists, who thrived on praying for the hard cases. He was regarded as the leading specialist in driving out demons. However, he ran into trouble with his denomination, the Assemblies of God, in the mid-1950s over his questionable claims to miracles. He was among the first to appeal for financial support, tying it to blessing for the giver. His battle with alcoholism ended with his death from sclerosis of the liver.

197. Gifford, "Healing in African Pentecostalism," 257. Oswald J. Smith was the famed pastor of the People's Church in Toronto from 1928. Earlier, he led a CMA church in the city. He invited the Bosworth brothers to conduct missions that attracted enormous crowds with their healing evangelism (Opp, *Lord for the Body*, 153).

conclusion that Wigglesworth is a bigger name today in global terms, even more so than he was in his lifetime.

Wigglesworth would have been vexed if he had lived to see the level to which healing evangelism had degenerated in places. Most disturbing for him would have been the number of current perpetrators who find aspects of his ministry a model for theirs. That he, unwittingly, had paved the way for them would have grieved him greatly. He would have found himself bracketed with those who, in Curtis' words, "rejoice in the fact that faith in the Great Physician remains so strong in the postmodern world, yet bewail the flamboyant performances of some popular evangelists and wince at the tendency of certain prominent figures to link the 'promises' of physical rejuvenation and financial success."[198] His personal probity remains unquestioned, especially when it came to money about which he was a stickler for honest dealings. Above all, he declared: "What God wants is a people that are full of truth."[199] For him, conversion remained his foremost priority, more so than healing. At the same time, he was as much prepared to attend a sick individual, no matter how inconvenient, as address a large gathering. Not for him, the requirement list of a speaker invited to address a meeting in Texas a few years back. It included a five-figure honorarium, a $10,000 gasoline deposit for the private jet, a hairstylist, a luxury car from airport to hotel and Perrier water warmed to room temperature.[200] But then, the present zeitgeist would continue to be a source of puzzlement to the erstwhile Yorkshire plumber, just as much as his incomprehension of the fame attached to his name today in all continents.

Two significant figures in British Pentecostalism were prepared to vouch for the credibility of Wigglesworth. A. A. Boddy and Donald Gee knew him well and, though they were aware of his foibles, they continued to hold him in high esteem.[201] Boddy recorded his activities and sermons up to the final editions of *Confidence*. In the penultimate issue in 1925, he published an extract from Wigglesworth book, *Ever-Increasing Faith*, which included the dramatic healing of an elderly lady in Belfast whose fractured thigh bone had not set after five months in a plaster cast. It is inconceivable that the account of her immediate healing would have been printed if Boddy had any doubts about the veracity of Wigglesworth's testimony.[202] Gee agreed with the homage paid to Wigglesworth at his funeral that he "was not an ordinary man, but extraordinary, and it was his faith that made him so."[203]

Gee in his booklet *Trophimus I Left Sick* presented one of the best short statements on divine healing written by a Pentecostal teacher. In it, he expressed the view that "we make our own problems of divine healing because of an inveterate tendency to push any

---

198. Curtis, *Faith in the Great Physician*, 206.

199. Wilson, *Wigglesworth*, 81.

200. Grady, *Holy Spirit Is Not For Sale*, 116.

201. Gee was widely regarded as a Pentecostal statesman. He was a dominant figure at the Pentecostal World Conferences, for which he edited *Pentecost-* a quarterly review of world Pentecostalism from 1948 to 1966.

202. *Confidence*, May 1925, 3–4.

203. Gee, *These Men I Knew*, 92.

truth revealed to us to extremes."[204] His knowledge of healing ministries extended from of Maria Woodworth-Etter, Aimee Semple McPherson, Charles Price, through Smith Wigglesworth and the Jeffreys brothers, to the new breed of American healing evangelists in the 1950–60 years. He was never slow to express his misgivings about trends in healing evangelism that were unbalanced. It was possible, he thought, that the rapid expansion of Pentecostalism in the post-war years might foster "the real menace" of a shallow spiritual-ity that neglected "teaching on the deeper life."[205] Attempts to make foolish and exagger-ated claims to healing, for him, were inexcusable. He was no pushover when it came to assessment of character. His opinion that "whatever his faults, Smith Wigglesworth was a man of God" has to be respected.[206]

General Overview: Assessing Claims of Healing

In a write-up of Harrell's *All Things Are Possible*, the reviewer commented that "there is something beguiling about faith healers. Exuberantly larger than life, they are a jumble of warring contradictions—prophet, entrepreneur, miracle worker, con man. No one knows for sure just how much is supernatural, how much psychosomatic, how much magic and sham."[207] It is a patently justifiable statement and carries the implication that the claims of neither healer nor healing movement should bypass scrutiny. Wigglesworth's healings cannot be excluded. Some of his miracles as recorded are so astounding that they beg-gar belief, especially those that appear to match, even threatening to exceed, any in the Gospel records. The healings ascribed to Wigglesworth are brought into high relief when set beside the issues raised by the canonization of John Henry Newman (1801–90). In 2010, the ratification of a second miracle necessary to attain to sainthood was taken a step closer. The proof of a miracle requires a Catholic panel of doctors to rule that the healing is inexplicable to scientific scrutiny, while theologians consider whether it occurred as the result of the intercession of the nominee. This situation highlights the huge incongruity in the paucity of organic healings at the hands of Newman, a complex man who left a potent spiritual legacy, compared to the number of them attributed to a minimally educated, ageing Yorkshire plumber. That said, it is an incongruity that Christianity can recognize and uphold (1 Cor 1:26–29).

Two of the stories of healing attributed to Wigglesworth are inexplicable by any standard. A two-year-old child with deformed feet was left, it was reputed, at the evan-gelist's feet and kicked by him into the group of onlookers. The child landed on his feet and ran off down the aisle. In another case, an Anglican curate who walked with the aid of two artificial legs entertained Wigglesworth overnight at his home. After supper, Wigglesworth told him to buy a new pair of shoes in the morning. Next morning in the shop, the bemused assistant, when asked for shoe size 8 and color black, looked at the artificial legs and said, "I don't think we can help you." The curate persisted and removed

---

204. Gee, *Trophimus I Left Sick*, 26.

205. Gee, *These Men I Knew*, 92.

206. Ibid., 92.

207. Anon, *Kirkus Reviews*. Online. Harrell's book is a scholarly account of the Charismatic healing movement in America in the period 1947–75.

his artificial legs when the correct shoes were brought. He placed one stump in the shoe. Instantly the leg and foot formed, to be repeated for the other leg. The goggle-eyed staff watched the man walk out of the shop.[208] The first story is said to be based on eyewitness accounts, while the second is of unknown or unpublished provenance. Specific details about the persons involved and the where and when of the healing are not documented in any manner, therefore thwarting accredited corroboration. No mention is made of these particular miracles in any of his published sermons or other writings, such as his letters, a fact which must throw considerable, if not outright, doubt on their authenticity. It is not unknown for myths to embellish heroes of any stamp.

While the authenticity of such stories must be queried, that does not necessarily make many of them apocryphal, figments of minds prepared to accept rumor as reality and tale as truth. Two considerations need to be borne in mind. First, Wigglesworth was a man of integrity, unafraid to declare that "as long as I live, I shall never exaggerate. Exaggeration is lying.[209] He claimed only three cases of persons being raised from the dead, even though one writer claimed to have known of fourteen. That alone is evidence of myth-making, and of claims made without his knowledge. Second, many healings were performed in private, not in the public arena. There was no reason why they should feature in a press generally sceptical of such claims. Even some of Wigglesworth's larger public meetings went unreported. When in Washington, DC around 1934, he conducted a series of meetings the venues of which had to shift from the sponsoring Gospel Tabernacle to the Masonic Temple to accommodate the 800 or more attenders. James Taylor, a visitor from Massachusetts, wrote a report of one crowded afternoon meeting. The healing that most moved Taylor concerned a young girl, who had never walked before without crutches was able to dispose of them. At the evening meeting her uncle confirmed that the girl had walked up the stairs at her home without assistance. Many others claimed healing at the two meetings. Despite such scenes, Taylor ended his article by telling how he had combed through the many local papers the next morning to see if any had carried a report "either in a headline or even some other place. There was not a word to be found anywhere."[210]

The press, for Wigglesworth, was an enemy. When Lester Sumrall, arrived for the first time at the Wigglesworth home in Bradford, he had a Bible in one hand and a newspaper tucked under the other arm. He was curtly informed, "I don't permit these lies into my house. In my house there is only truth."[211] Consequently, he had no publicity machine, such as the one around George Jeffreys that welcomed press reporting as a means to advance his cause. The healings Wigglesworth ministered to were so recurrent as to render them almost commonplace. A reference of one of Wigglesworth's meetings even stated, "There is no need for me to describe the meeting; we all know Brother Wigglesworth!"[212]

---

208. Madden, *Wigglesworth Standard*, 17–18. Wigglesworth was always more surprised when a miracle did not take place and was anxious to explore why. If no healing was discernible, he took the view it had taken place, but because of inactive faith it had yet to manifest itself.

209. Wilson, *Wigglesworth*, 81.

210. Cartwright, *Real Wigglesworth*, 150.

211. Sumrall, "My Relationship with Smith Wigglesworth." Online.

212. Cartwright, *Real Wigglesworth*, 147–48.

One of the claims to restoration of life is said to have taken place in a working-class home in Belfast in 1926, to which reference in the local press has still to be found.[213] His verbatim account of the incident concluded, "I told this story in the assembly. There was a doctor there. He was sceptical. He saw her. She said it is all true." It is not unexpected that majority medical opinion would be ill-disposed to the claim. By any standard, the onset of death is difficult for a lay person to determine, even if the woman could testify, "I saw countless numbers all like Jesus. He pointed and I knew I had to go [back to earth]."[214]

Medical opinion would find it difficult to verify a happening such as this last one. The *Kirkus Review* chided Harrell for keeping "a safe historical distance, letting doctors and theologians hassle over what finally comes down to faith-claims." It is the problem that all those who research this area have to face. When George Marsden, a doyen of evangelical history, was posed the question about miracles being a sticking point for Christian historians, his reply was, "Miracle stories raise some hard questions. You want to acknowledge that miracles can happen, but . . . you ought to make some distinction between how you treat miracle stories that you find credible and those about which you find some evidence of deception. So I think it is appropriate to be critical of certain religious claims to miracles. . . . The general rule in the academy is not to criticize anyone's story. You talk about their experience and leave it at that."[215] The British Pentecostal historian, Timothy Walsh, recognizes as imperative any historiographical treatment of pioneering figures and the roles they played in the growth of fledgling Pentecostalism. Scholarship must adhere "to creditable conventions if it is to be taken seriously by a wider readership."[216] Walsh notes a problematic feature about the literature fuelling the Wigglesworth legend. He sees the pieces as "persistently episodic and anecdotal. . . . Many consist largely of a conglomeration of narratives, rarely documented, and often stretching credulity toward, if not beyond, the outer limits of its boundaries. It is not fanciful to suggest that these writings display notable characteristics of the 'pious legend,' carrying a pronounced tendency toward "a certain uncritical exuberance."[217]

Under the heading "Revivalist as Showman and Shaman—Wigglesworth," Walsh proceeded to subject Wigglesworth to a measure of academic suspicion, largely in the form of verbal barbs. Wigglesworth's repeated attribution of sickness to devilish attack was "another integral if *inflammatory* feature of his ritual . . . akin to a form of *Manichean dualism.*"[218] Wigglesworth, convinced of his empowerment to be more than a match for satanic forces, "reveals something of the self-perception of an individual who felt himself called upon to enact such "*dualistic theodramas.*"[219] Not only did Wigglesworth introduce

---

213. The account of the incident is to be found in a verbatim account from Wigglesworth himself lodged in the archives of the Assemblies of God in America.

214. Hywel-Davies, *Life of Smith Wigglesworth*, 90.

215. Marsden, "The Link: Christian History Today," 50–54.

216. Walsh, *To Meet and Satisfy a Very Hungry People*, 15.

217. Ibid., 12–13.

218. Ibid., 145.

219. "Manichean dualism" was a religious system with Christian, gnostic, and pagan elements, founded in the third century. It was based on the belief of a primeval conflict between light and darkness, which

Pentecostal rhetoric to a wider audience, "but he also translated and dramatically conveyed this into a *seemingly* incontrovertible experimental reality." For Boddy to display a longstanding loyalty to Wigglesworth is regarded as "*curious.*" The fact that *Confidence* in its declining years kept on printing Wigglesworth's sermons serves, for Walsh, "as a vivid indicator of the esteem in which the *high priest* of English Pentecostalism held its most visible prophet or *shaman.*

Walsh makes rather much of the role of shaman, describing Wigglesworth "as something of a *revivalistic shaman.*" He takes his definition of "shaman" from I. M. Lewis, anthropological text *Ecstatic Religion* (1940), viz., a figure "appearing to possess, among other attributes, privileged access to supernatural powers, capacities of discernment and diagnosis, and the ability to convey or prescribe the appropriate spiritual remedy." This profile Walsh regarded as "readily observed in the expanding ministry of the plumber from Bradford."[220] The term "shaman" in the context of Wigglesworth's ministry is not particularly helpful, while coupling it with "showman" casts a shadow over Wigglesworth mission.

On Lewis' definition, Paul and other charismatically gifted Christians would fill the bill, with Jesus something of a Grand Shaman.[221] The term as used by Walsh provides little explanatory purchase in assessing the validity or otherwise of Wigglesworth's thaumaturgic feats. It can be maintained that there is a link between shamanism and Pentecostalism. One explanation for the rapid growth of Pentecostalism in traditional, especially animistic, cultures where shamanism is practiced, is the resonance between the two in that they are both alert to the spirit world. Both bear witness to healing and the casting out of demons, though a polarity exists in Pentecostalism's affirmation that there is only one Holy Spirit.[222] Keener draws a lesson from South Korea where an emphasis on divine healing pervades mainline Korean Protestantism, which, "in keeping with indigenous Korean culture and in *competition* with shamans and Buddhist monks, rejected the cessationism of the earlier Western missionaries."[223]

---

presented Evil as coeternal with God. Satan was seen to have stolen particles of light and imprisoned them in the human mind. It was the task of Jesus, Buddha, the Prophets, by mobilizing the whole physical universe, to bring about the release of the light particles. To assist release, Manicheans were strict vegetarians, believing that such a diet, through the digestive system, released light. They became one of the most persecuted heresies under Christian Roman emperors. It has been placed by some as "the first deliberately conceived religion."

220. *Oxford English Dictionary* defines "theo-drama" as "a drama in which the actors are gods."

221. The complexity surrounding the word "shaman" is discussed in a lengthy entry by D'Anglure in Bernard, *Encyclopaedia*, 504–7. The article notes that Clifford Geertz in 1966 asserted that shamanism was "a dry and insipid category with which ethnographers of religion had devitalized their data." In the era of postmodernism, the revival of shamanic studies sets out to evince their affinities with "pre-Socratic thought, irrationalism, esotoricism and the great systems of non-Western thought such as Daoism." To link Shamanism with charismatic Christianity, as is oft done with the ministry of Korean pastor, Paul Yonggi Cho,, for Gifford, "is too simple" (Gifford, "Complex Provenance," 63, n.2).

222. Miller, *Global Pentecostalism*, 24–25.

223. Keener, *Miracles*, 290–91 (emphasis added). The emphasis on healing emerged first among Korean Presbyterians, despite the cessationist views of their American Presbyterian missionaries. In 1923, the Korean Presbyterian Church officially overturned the doctrine that miracles had ceased. One of its native preachers reported 10,000 healed during his ministry. A Commission designated in 1923 to evaluate the claims astonished the missionaries "by confirming genuine miracles had occurred."

At base, the issues raised by thaumaturgic healings reveal conflicting worldviews. For adherents of philosophical naturalism such phenomena, if duly confirmed, can be safely left to the future, to await scientific breakthrough to explain them. In this view, any recourse to extramundane belief or presupposition will be outmoded, and any expression of them discredited. For the Christian theist, all things are possible to a God whose creative energy pervades and upholds the cosmos. Nonetheless, even among theists there is a wide spectrum of belief, which extends from the theologies represented by Bultmann to that of Wigglesworth. Bultmann maintained that "to revive or perpetuate the demonology of the New Testament in the modern world is to incur the charge of obscurantism and superstition. The church should do all in her power to root it out, for it can only stultify her proclamation."[224] The contrast in views was wittily demonstrated in the response the Pentecostal leader. At the other extreme, Wigglesworth contended that in his dealing with cancer, one has to "recognise that it is a living evil spirit that is destroying the body."

In response to the valid criticism of some modern healing ministries, new voices are stirring, which, like Gee, are prepared to challenge unsustainable theology and errant practices found in some modern healing, particularly where it is associated with televangelism. One such is J. Lee Grady, the editor-in-chief of *Charisma,* who in his *The Spirit Is Not for Sale* (2010) addresses some of the dubious state of affairs touched on above.[225] He calls for an end to the "foolishness" of preachers who hit, slap, or push others during prayer, treating bodies as commodities to be pushed and tossed around the room. Television ministries must cease and all manipulative fundraising tactics should be eschewed. Giving platforms to ministers who make outlandish claims of supernatural financial returns should cease, especially when Scripture is twisted, deadlines are imposed and the poor are exploited. Fakery should be exposed and an end put to such practices as these: the sprinkling of glitter to suggest God's glory is upon the leader; fake jewels hidden under the floor to prove an anointed ministry, and chicken feathers placed up sleeves to simulate the presence of angels. There should be an end to those "lone rangers" who refuse to be accountable to competent others of patent integrity. While spiritual warfare is a reality, charismatics must stop blaming everything on demonic principalities—people are usually the problem. Grady holds an influential position in that the sympathies of *Charisma* lie with contemporary streams of charismatic Christianity.

224. Bultmann, *Kerygma and Myth,* 120.

225. *Charisma* is a monthly magazine with an extensive readership among Pentecostals and Charismatics. R. T. Kendall ranks Grady with Martin Luther who in his day "exposed the wickedness of leaders who led innocent people to buy indulgences to get them out of purgatory" (Grady, *Holy Spirit,* 14).

The Developing Healing Scene in North America

RELIGIO-CULTURAL BACKGROUND

WORLD WAR I HAD a far-reaching impact on American life. The Progressive Era, generally recognized as lying between the Depression of 1893 and the American entry into the War in 1917, was seen as a period of social activism and political reform. A revived dynamism led Americans to press for major post-war societal change about which the inventor Thomas Edison voiced the opinion: "We've stumbled along for a while trying to run a new civilization in old ways, but we've got to make this world over."[1] A major attempt was made to eliminate the corruption attached to party machines. One means to this end was to call for the prohibition of the sale alcohol that was often bought in saloons run by local politicos. Women's suffrage was eventually won in 1919, much against the opposition of brewers and distillers who feared (correctly) that enfranchised women would vote for prohibition. Another drive was towards the pursuit of greater efficiency, which set out to eliminate waste in all areas of the economy and society, and encourage best practice across all disciplines. In medicine, the Flexner Report turned medicine toward a firm scientific foundation and raised standards of education and practice in the profession. It is estimated that up to a quarter of the 168 North American medical schools may have been closed or merged because of an unsatisfactory assessment by Flexner.

In the event, the war that was heralded as a crusade to make America safe for democracy failed to usher in a time of societal harmony. Disharmony within the Christian community hardened, while evangelicalism entered into a period of internal strife and experienced diminishing rapport with the prevailing culture. Frivolity, fed by economic growth, and social ferment distinguished the 1920s, only for the former to be stifled in the Depression years of the 1930s. The zaniness that characterized the decade earned it the tag "the Jazz Age." The Great War destroyed the last vestiges of Victorian prudery, particularly among the young. Young women reveled in a new sense of freedom. They shocked the older generation with their short bob hair style, short skirts, and skimpy beach wear that often got the Flappers, as they were dubbed, arrested for indecent exposure. When not dancing or kissing, the carefree flapper and her boyfriend were commonly depicted seated in an automobile, another salient cultural image of the Jazz Age. It

---

1. Thompson, *Dictionary of Modern American History*, 328.

is in this context of overt sexuality that the ministry of Aimee Semple McPherson brought her inviting charms to good use. Her femininity, which freed her to adopt the modish styles of the time, will be considered later, as will the girl healing evangelists inspired by the razzmatazz surrounding her.[2]

The military victory of the Great War proved not to be the auspicious prelude to post-war tranquillity. The bloodletting of the War not only muffled the easy optimism of Progressive America but also lent impetus to healing evangelism. During the war, the youthful Raymond Richey (1893–1968), who was later to become a major healing evangelist, established the "United Prayer and Workers' League" for the distribution of literature. He erected a gospel tent near an army camp in Houston, Texas, and hundreds of conversions of doughboys (infantrymen) were reported.[3] During the War, a fervent patriotism was rampant, only to turn sour once hostilities ended. Any persons regarded as unpatriotic—conscientious objectors, draft dodgers, German-Americans, immigrants, Communists—were all suspect. The so-called "Red Scare" (1919–20), focused on suspected communists, was intense but short-lived. "Red hunting" became the national obsession, and thousands were harassed and blacklisted without due recourse to law. Adding to a growing insularity were the passing of restrictive immigration laws, the resurgence of the Ku Klux Klan, and the introduction of Prohibition in 1920 that proved so unenforceable that it ended in 1933. The big winners from Prohibition were the nation's gangsters. Living in splendor in Chicago, Al Capone was said to be pocketing in the mid-1920s some $100m a year, a sizable proportion from illegal nightclubs.

If liberal opinion was disturbed by the restriction of personal freedom, the growing body of fundamentalists within American evangelicalism found much that was supportive of their cause. Prohibition implemented their long-term commitment to temperance. Restriction of immigration kept out the non-Protestants, notably Jews and eastern Europeans whose naturalization, it was feared, would further diminish the WASP [White Anglo-Saxon Protestant] majority, and dilute its cultural and religious hegemony. The Ku Klux Klan reached its peak of three million members in 1923. Claiming explicitly to be a defender of Protestantism, the Klan drew tacit support from such figures as Alma White and Aimee Semple McPherson. The journalist-pundit, Walter Lippmann, accused Fundamentalism of being entangled "with all sorts of bizarre and barbarous agitations with the Ku Klux Klan."[4] Furthermore, with dispensationalist premillennialism finding credence within their ranks, fundamentalists believed their eschatological position on the imminence of the *parousia* was confirmed by the outbreaks of civil disturbance that fed the widespread perception of moral decline. Feeding on such diverse scraps, they were prepared to do battle over the issue of evolution that was to reach its apogee in 1925 in the seminal Scopes trial. The outcome of that episode proved only to further indict

---

2. Loud,. *Evangelized America*, 321.

3. Richey received a miraculous healing from tuberculosis in 1919, and began his healing ministry the following year. In 1923, 11,000 conversions were reported in Tulsa, OK. Those who had received healing paraded through the streets with "a truck piled high with discarded crutches" (*IDPCM*, 1022).

4. Marsden, *Fundamentalism*, 191.

the movement of obscurantism, and force it into greater marginalization in the life and culture of the nation.

America's entry in 1917 into the Great War in Europe exposed the German-American citizenry to harassment out of fear of sedition within its ranks. Many German-language newspapers were closed down. Public schools stopped teaching German and, in the name of patriotism, musicians no longer played Bach and Beethoven. German biblical scholarship, also, was attacked for undermining the authority of the Bible by implying the purely human authorship of Scripture. This was something of a longstanding charge, only to be exacerbated by the War. In 1926, the fundamentalist *Crusader's Champion* had complained that thirty years earlier five men, believed to be of German origin, had met in Boston to form a conspiracy "to secretly and persistently work to overthrow the fundamentals of the Christian religion in this country."[5] Such a dating is an indication that the roots of Fundamentalism can be traced to developments in the nineteenth century. In 1919, Griffith Thomas, the English-born principal of Wycliffe College in Toronto, accused nineteenth-century German scholarship of denying "the supernatural element, first in the Old Testament, then in the New Testament, and now, most serious of all, in the Person of Christ Himself. . . . What is more serious is that the German spirit has dominated our theological seminaries . . . with the result that there is abundant spiritual powerlessness in many churches."[6] It was this sense of powerlessness that disturbed radical evangelicalism most.

It was, therefore, no chance occurrence that as the War drew to its end the World's Christian Fundamentals Association was established. It was conceived in 1918 by the leaders of the Bible School and Prophetic Conference movement under the guidance of the Baptist pastor, William B. Riley. It developed into a movement of social and religious protest against the threats of modernity to traditional Christianity. One of their weapons was to disseminate widely the three million copies of twelve booklets titled *The Fundamentals,* published in the period 1910–15. The booklets were designed to defend elemental Christian truths, generally identified as biblical inerrancy, the deity of Jesus, the virgin birth, substitutionary atonement, and the bodily resurrection and physical return of Christ. Believing in the doctrine of plenary inspiration of the Bible, Fundamentalists rejected the tenets and practices of higher biblical criticism that downplayed the supernatural element in Scripture.

The term "Fundamentalist" was coined in 1920 by Curtis Lee Laws, Baptist pastor and editor, for those willing to do "battle royal for the Fundamentals." The Fundamentalism of the 1920s developed into "a federation of cobelligerents opposed to centralizing authority."[7] The schismatic tendency of the movement can be explained by a number of factors. On doctrine, for example, while fundamentalist Presbyterians, like their Baptist counterparts, set great store on biblical inerrancy, they disagreed with them on the issue of dispensationalism. Neither of them brooked the more experiential orientation of

---

5. Marsden, *Fundamentalism,* 190.

6. Thomas, "German Moral Abnormality," 103.

7. Hatch, *Democratization,* 214.

Pentecostals and Holiness advocates. They, in turn, clashed over their differing views on Spirit-baptism.

The ramifications of the spread of the so-called "Fundamentalist-Modernist Controversy" deepened the conflict within and between the Protestant churches that spilled over into the public arena. At issue for militant fundamentalists was the threat from a modernism poised to undermine the Christian heritage of the nation, thereby calling into question America's historical destiny to act as a "City upon a Hill."[8] The conflict came to a pitch in 1925 with the Scopes "Monkey Trial" in Dayton, Tennessee, over the issue of the teaching of evolution in schools. The battle waged over the literal reading of the Genesis account of creation as against the Darwinian postulate. The court case reinforced a persistent stereotype of fundamentalists as obscurantist backwoodsmen. The climactic confrontation of the Scope's trial left Fundamentalism with an increasingly restricted place in the life of the nation. Fundamentalist denominations found they were unable to change either the content of scientific education or curb critical scholarship except in the institutions they controlled. Fundamentalism was forced in retreat—only to recover, somewhat spectacularly, in the post-war period in the substantially modified form of neo-evangelicalism.[9] The latter adopted a more irenic posture towards the world in general, as typified in the ministry of Billy Graham.

It is a measure of the growth of Pentecostalism in these years that it became in the post-war years a valued member of the NAE [National Association of Evangelicals], and over time become its largest constituency. The ministry of the healing contributed greatly to the increase. Fred Bosworth was but one of a number of healing evangelists, either Pentecostal or with charismatic sympathies, who established an independent ministry in the 1920s in the USA and Canada. The well-known other campaigners were Charles S. Price, Paul Rader and Raymond T. Richey, while Aimee Semple McPherson in Los Angeles, John G. Lake in Spokane, and Maria Woodworth-Etter in Indianapolis (d. 1924) maintained settled healing ministries. These named laid the groundwork for the new generation of healing evangelists to come in the post-World War II years. The healing ministry, needless to say, was not confined to the mammoth crusades held by these noted evangelists. In the small towns and backcountry, particularly in the Southern states, fervent prayers were being uttered for healing in numerous Wesleyan Holiness churches in the more sacramental mode explored in Kimberly Alexander's thesis, and discussed in chapter 2. In this setting, the laying on of hands, anointing with oil, the use of anointed handkerchiefs, and even the ceremonial giving of a cup of water in the name of the Lord had emerged as important and regular practices.

Because space is limited, detailed study is limited mainly to F. F. Bosworth and Aimee Semple McPherson. Before coming to McPherson, the contribution of two promi-

8. The phrase was used in a sermon preached by Puritan John Winthrop in 1630. He admonished the future Massachusetts Bay colonists that their new community would be a "city upon a hill" (Matt 5:14), a godly, shining template for the old world to follow.

9. Ahlstrom, *Religious History of the American People*, 914–15. Ahlstrom missed out on the marked expansion of fundamentalist academic institutions within all the diverse groups from the 1930s onwards, which continue to provide vibrancy up to the present to American Fundamentalism.

nent fundamentalist pastors will be examined, to allow McPherson's moderating role to be appraised.

F. F. BOSWORTH: THE PENTECOSTAL CONTRIBUTION

Fred Francis Bosworth (1877–1958) was reared on a farm in Utica, Nebraska. Early in life, he showed a natural gift for music that, as a coronet player, led to his playing in the Nebraska State Band. At the age of sixteen, he was converted during a local Methodist mission. Shortly after, he developed a lung problem that plagued him for eight years to the extent that he was regarded as beyond medical help. After wandering into a Methodist meeting, his rasping cough attracted the attention of the leader, Mattie Perry, who offered to pray for him. Within days his healing was complete. From that point, he was totally convinced of the reality of divine healing. Early in the 1900s the whole Bosworth family moved to Zion City, established by John Alexander Dowie, to join the Christian Apostolic Church, noted for its heavy emphasis on divine healing.[10] Dowie set great store by music, and Bosworth was quickly promoted to leadership of the Zion Band. When the Zion community fell into disarray in 1906, Charles Parham seized the opportunity to introduce it to the Pentecostal message. A sizable number of Zionites accepted the message, and it was there

F. F. Bosworth

that Bosworth received his Spirit-baptism in October 1906. Subsequently, he visited Azusa Street to appraise the newly-fledged Pentecostal movement, followed by a visit to Chicago where he first met E. W. Kenyon.

For a short period Bosworth assisted Cyril Fockler, another ex-Zionite, in evangelistic healing missions, before branching out independently to introduce Pentecostalism to Dallas, Texas, in 1909. For three years he faced many trials, one of the more serious being a brutal beating by white racists for convening racially mixed meetings. His reputation was enhanced when news of a revival, stirred up during the five-month mission of Maria Woodworth-Etter in 1912, was circulated. With the declining influence of the Azusa Street Mission, the view began to be aired that Dallas was the up-and-coming, new focus of the Spirit's power.

In 1914, Bosworth aligned himself with Assemblies of God (AoG), the newly constituted denomination formed by believers drawn largely from the Reformed/Higher Life tradition. Unlike most other Pentecostal groups that evolved from the Wesleyan Holiness tradition in local settings in the South, the AoG appealed to many from a Reformed background such as Chicago-area independents, and those with ties to the CMA and Zion City. Despite an early preponderance of southerners, the new body emerged specifically

10. For Dowie and Zion, see Robinson, *Divine Healing 1890–1906*, 47–76.

to meet the needs of a nationwide constituency that over time made it the largest classical Pentecostal denomination in the USA. Following his resignation from the AoG in 1918 over the initial evidence issue, Bosworth presented his case in a booklet titled *Do All Speak with Tongues?* Rather than foment further dissension, he withdrew his allegiance and joined the CMA, a body that was more congenial to his view on tongues in eschewing the necessity of the evidential function of tongues, without succumbing to a blanket rejection of tongues and/or Spirit-baptism.

Following the death of his first wife in 1919, Bosworth started on what turned out to be a lifelong ministry as an itinerant healing evangelist. He began with a mission in Pittsburgh, where 5,000 conversions were claimed and many hundreds healed. During his mission in Lima, Ohio, the following year, he determined to give greater prominence to healing in his ministry as a means of gaining the attention of greater numbers to the gospel message. He argued: "If Christ and his apostles could not draw the multitudes without miracles, does he expect more from us?" Thirteen years later, he could reflect that preaching this facet of the gospel "in a bolder and more public way" led to more conversions in a week than he ever saw in a whole year of more conventional evangelism.[11] Together with his brother Burt and their respective wives, he held most of his impressive campaigns in the USA and Canada in the 1920s. These were reported by the CMA in many articles in its *The Alliance Weekly*. In 1924, his perennial *Christ the Healer,* in effect a collection of his sermons, was published in response to the pressing requests of leaders working in cities where his revival campaigns had been conducted. It was published the same year as Torrey's *Divine Healing* and *The Power of Prayer,* and S. D. Gordon's *Quiet Talks on the Healing Christ.* None of the three authors was aligned with Pentecostal denominations. Hence, they bear further evidence of the acceptance of divine healing within the wider fundamentalist movement. The years 1927 and 1928 found Bosworth sharing in several revival campaigns with Paul Rader in the latter's Chicago Gospel Tabernacle (CGT). Rader was a nationally known preacher, distinguished by his colorful background. Well over six foot tall and sixteen stone in weight, he described himself as an "ex-bellboy, ex-cowboy, ex-prospector, ex-football player, and ex-pugilist." In the last role he had acted as a sparring partner for two world heavyweight champions, Bob Fitzsimmons and Jim Jeffries.

F. F. Bosworth and Paul Rader in the 1920s

In the period 1915–21, Rader pastored Moody's Church in Chicago, during which he succeeded A. B. Simpson as President of the CMA from 1920 to 1923. His elevation to leadership of the CMA led to his resignation from the Moody Church pastorate to concentrate for a short period on his presidential duties. However, June 1922 found him back in Chicago, invited to hold a six-week campaign in a specially erected large steel-framed structure that evolved into the Chicago Gospel Tabernacle (CGT), with Rader its leader for the next eleven years. Meetings were held almost nightly, and a series of special programs was designed for outreach to young people, single working girls, and diverse ethnic groups. Such was the popularity of the Sunday afternoon services that one

---

11. Bosworth, *Christ the Healer*, 71.

regular attender reminisced that it was "like going to the ballpark."[12] Rader's return to Chicago stirred up lingering pique within his former charge, the Moody Church. His over-hasty departure and present drawing power did not go down well with them. Decidedly more rigid than Rader, they opposed the CGT's welcoming of mildly charismatic revivalists such as Aimee Semple McPherson and the Bosworth brothers. The brothers by their musical brilliance added to the upbeat atmosphere that pervaded the tabernacle. It was Rader's policy to attract some of Chicago's most talented gospel musicians and evangelists to his staff. A former Salvationist led the Tabernacle band in its medley of hymns, gospel choruses, light classical pieces and Sousa marches. Occasionally, special pageants and cantatas attracted large crowds. In 1932, one such drew a total attendance of 40,000 to its Christmas special.

Paul Rader and Aimee Semple McPherson at Angles Temple

Perhaps the most significant venture of all to emanate from the CGT took place on June 17, 1922 when the mayor of Chicago, William Hale Thompson, invited Rader to broadcast several programs over the new radio station, WBU, owned by him. It was among the first religious radio broadcasts in the history of the new medium, and turned the CGT into a major broadcasting center, whose output reached from the Eastern seaboard of the USA to Western Canada. The broadcasts carried huge appeal and by the time of Rader's leave-taking from the CGT in 1933 over a quarter of a million pamphlets and printed sermons had been distributed to listeners who requested them. This response was much greater than the number of requests received by the Federal Council of Churches for its preaching series over the entire NBC network.[13] In 1929, a short-lived program called *Healing Hour* was aired, carrying both the message of its title, and prayers for the sick. The program was directed towards those listeners who had "followed the course of preparation" for divine healing.[14] It was possibly the first broadcast of this type, the first step in a revolution that in other hands and different times would bring the healing message to the ends of the earth.

12. Carpenter, *Revive Us Again*, 127.

13. Ibid., 128. Formed in 1926, the National Broadcasting Corporation (NBC) is the oldest major broadcast network in the USA.

14. Hagen, *Redeeming the Dial*, 53.

One of Rader's distinctive contributions to the ministry of healing was his evocative chorus "Only believe. . . . All things are possible, only believe." It was sung repetitively in communal settings where prayer was offered for the sick. It became the theme song in the ministry of William Branham (1909–65), who played a leading role in the post-WWII healing revival. In his sermons Branham referred many times to Paul Rader, and in one of his sermons he mused: "I wonder if Paul, in glory, hears that old song being sung by the thousands and thousands, and by the different languages. How did he know . . . that God would let me take that song around the world?"[15] In a voice that matched his vigor, Smith Wigglesworth led his listeners into the chorus at the fitting moment. "Over and over in his services and in those of other evangelists," instanced Gary McGee, "the words of this song brought hope to the suffering by telling them that 'All things are possible, only believe.'"[16] In one of his sermons, Wigglesworth remarked: "There is something very remarkable about this chorus. God wants to impress so deeply on our hearts that we may get so engrossed in this divine truth that we will know all things are possible. . . . Beloved, let me tell you, this chorus will help you."[17] The chorus chimed deeply with his core theme of faith. As his friend Donald Gee observed: "His favorite and almost his only subject was faith. No matter what the text, we all knew where he would arrive."[18]

Bosworth and Rader had much in common. They were of similar age, with Bosworth the older by two years. Both, at some time, had direct links with the CMA, and maintained sympathies with the movement when they became independent evangelists. They remained open to charismatic phenomena and maintained links with restrained Pentecostalism. King speaks of a "resurgence of charismatic life" in the CMA during the period 1920–24 when Rader was its President.[19] It reflected his conviction that "the fight of our day is supernaturalism against naturalism; the answer to materialism is a supernatural Christ."[20] Bosworth's son praised his father's major contribution "in returning supernatural power to [God's] church."[21] They shared a similar style of preaching that played down rampant emotionalism. Rader's daughter contrasted her father's style to that of his friend, the Presbyterian evangelist, Billy Sunday. Of the latter, she recalled him "running all over the place, breaking chairs and what not." Rader, though he was a forceful, straight-talking preacher, was also fully aware that "excitement and high emotional reaction are not to be mistaken for soul-winning. . . . The nature of man must be changed, not merely the emotions stirred."[22] His folksy language and warm personality attracted enthusiastic listeners to his radio slots. Bosworth, similarly, was restrained in his preaching. A CMA pastor wrote of the mission in Detroit in 1921 that "the meetings were generally very quiet, with few expressions of any kind from the audience. Even the familiar 'Amen' was

15. Anon. "Audio file of William Branham." Online.

16. McGee, "The Revival Legacy of Smith Wigglesworth." 1998.

17. Warner, *Smith Wigglesworth: Only Believe*, xiii.

18 Ibid., back cover.

19. King, *Genuine Gold,* 195.

20. Rader, Paul. "At Thy Word." *Alliance Weekly,* Nov. 20, 1920, 532.

21. Bosworth, *Christ the Healer,* Foreword.

22. Rader, Paul. "Power From On High." Online.

heard only occasionally. There was no attempt upon the part of the evangelist to produce an effect or to urge anyone to hasty decisions by emotional appeals."[23]

The studied downplaying of emotional intensity by both men widened their appeal to folk of all, and no, church connection. Rader on his visit in December 1930 to Belfast, terminated his mission in the Assembly Hall, the central auditorium of the Presbyterian Church in Ireland, the largest Protestant denomination in Ulster. The press reported that the evangelist had gained so much in the affections of the people on account of the "genial personality of the preacher, always dignified in a profound simplicity and the fidelity of his message to the original."[24] John Scruby, the publisher of Perkins' early biography of Bosworth, spent a week attending the Detroit mission in an attempt to assess the evangelist. He formed the impression that "no religious service has ever been attended by a more thoroughly cosmopolitan crowd. . . . Roman Catholics, who are more ready to believe in supernatural power than is the average Protestant, seem as happy to be present as any others, and 'happy' is the correct adjective too. The regular denominations of Protestants and irregular kinds, such as Christian Science, New Thought, Unity, Mysticism, Vedantism, Bahaism, and Theosophy, humans of all or no creeds are represented more or less in these meetings." [25]

Rader was the pioneer of evangelical religious broadcasting, though Bosworth was not far behind.[26] Between 1925 and 1930, Rader's Tabernacle was one the most important users of the religious airwaves. Its all-day Sunday broadcasts over WHT, and later WJBT ("Where Jesus Blesses Thousands"), were the first major experiment to provide regular religious programs through the purchase of air-time funded largely by its listeners. In 1930, Rader's daily "Breakfast Brigade" became the first independent fundamentalist program to be broadcast over the national Columbia Broadcasting System network.[27] The same year saw the first advertisement in the Bosworth magazine, *Exploits of Faith*, for Bosworth's own radio program. His revival campaigns at the CGT in the years 1927 and 1928 must have deepened his appreciation of the importance of the new medium. Prior to 1930, there are indications that some of his sermons featured on Rader's station. Bosworth's first self-financed radio program was called "The Sunshine Hour," and scheduled for 9 a.m. in the Chicago area.[28] Soon after, he established the National Radio Revival Missionary Crusaders as a non-profit corporation in Illinois. Soon its programing superseded that of Rader after the CGT ran into financial difficulties. Bosworth, by contrast, continued to broadcast well into the 1940s.

23. Perkins, *Joybringer*, 141.

24. Anon. "Ephemera of Daniel Paul Rader—Collection 38." Online.

. One of the noted converts at his mission held in Los Angles in 1926 was the thirteen-year-old Richard Nixon, who went on to teach a Bible class at Whittier Friends Church, California, some 42 years before his election as President.

25. Perkins, *Joybringer*, 149–50.

26. Calvary Episcopal Church, Pittsburgh, is considered to be the first to broadcast a service on Jan. 2, 1921.

27. Eskridge, "Paul Rader." In Larsen, *Biographical Dictionary*, 534.

28. Aimee Semple McPherson used the same title for her live broadcast at 7.00 a.m. each morning from early 1924.

Bosworth's daily radio preaching enabled him to cut down on his travels in the 1930s, though his healing meetings were not discontinued altogether. The severe Depression of the early 1930s made it very difficult to travel far from home, so most of his activity was concentrated on the Chicago area. During the downturn years, he settled in River Forest, Illinois, outside of Chicago where he recorded his programs in a studio at his home. The October 1931 edition of *Exploits* encouraged listeners who had been healed in body to write to the radio station, "telling what the Lord has done for them in messages that can be read over the air, and made a blessing to others. All who write are promised a souvenir in return."[29] By the time he retired from radio ministry in the 1940s, Bosworth had received over 250,000 letters from those who had been stirred or healed through his preaching.

What Rader started in the early 1920s had an enduring influence on the shape of the evangelical movement. In effect, Rader was among the first to harness the power of communication technology in the service of evangelism. His successful broadcasting laid the foundation for the eventual dominance of evangelical broadcasters within the "Electronic Church."[30] From the Tabernacle's creative cauldron issued a new, radio-inspired, ministry promoted by Clarence Jones, one of the most able of his assistants. Jones in the late 1920s developed a missionary radio station in South America that aimed to reach the entire continent. As Robins has pointed out, "regardless of what was happening among the intellectual elite, the influence of historicism, scientific naturalism, and philosophical relativism had not so permeated popular culture as to seriously hinder the prosperity of a new edition of old-time religion, particularly one so keenly tuned to the sociological and technological dimensions of the modern age."[31]

In the twenty-first century, a technology that began with rudimentary gadgetry and patchy range has turned into a massive, technically sophisticated enterprise. In the early days radio was regarded in some fundamentalist circles with suspicion. One hurdle that had to be crossed was radio's pull towards entertainment and its potential to create celebrities, thus elevating the self. The founder and Dean of the Bible Institute of Los Angeles (BIOLA), T. C. Horton and R. A. Torrey respectively, had their misgivings about the Institute's decision in 1923 to proceed with its own station. They argued that the airwaves were the realm of Satan, described in the Bible as "the prince of the power of the air" (Eph 2:2).

Others, however, spoke more than they could ever have foreseen. Evangelist William Foulkes in 1937 wrote that "radio waves" might create another "Pentecost—a potential Pentecost at least." Forty years later, a former executive of National Religious Broadcasters could write that radio and television had "restored conditions remarkably similar to the early church."[32] Undoubtedly, the current rapid growth of Pentecostalism at the global scale owes much to its appetite for using, even pioneering, the appliances of technological breakthrough. Allan Anderson makes the point that "the mass media, beginning with the use of periodicals and newsletters, followed by a ready acceptance of new technologies—

29. Barnes, Roscoe III. "F. F. Bosworth," 44.

30. Eskridge, "Paul Rader," 534.

31. Robins, *Pentecostalism in America*, 59.

32. Schulte, "Evangelicals' Uneasy Alliance with the Media," 69.

first radio and then television and internet—tourism and pilgrimages to mega-churches, ubiquitous voluntarism, and an international economy, combined to create conditions conducive to the spread of a globally friendly religion like Pentecostalism."[33]

Bosworth's Healing Missions in the 1920s

Bosworth is generally regarded as one of the most successful campaigners to emerge from the small coterie of American independent healing evangelists in the 1920s. One of his youthful admirers who received healing at his hands wrote that in the late 1920s "the Bosworth revival had electrified dozen of cities in the United States and Canada and the work of this man had already had a profound impact on an entire generation of Americans."[34] A case can be made that Pentecostalism rejuvenated revivalism in North America in a period of history when classic revivalism was in decline. The Bosworth brothers were among those who rekindled it to striking effect. Their ministry was such as to draw the support of interdenominational audiences, and the support of non-Pentecostal churches. Their campaign in Ottawa in January 1924 drew unexpected support from at least three of the city's doctors. One of them informed the Ottawa *Citizen* that he was aware of the cure of six cases of deafness, and one bore witness to his improvement of eyesight.

An invitation to hold a mission in Toronto in the late spring of 1921 was extended from Oswald J. Smith (1889–1986), who was in the process of starting a new work associated with the CMA in the city. Driven by a passion for evangelism, Smith developed a strategy to attract people to his church by lining-up famous preachers and musicians capable of adding color to the services. The Bosworth brothers fitted the bill with their music, Fred playing the cornet and Burt acting as song leader and trombonist. The local *Star* newspaper suggested that Fred, dressed in his fashionable "sack suit," gave the appearance of "a master salesman explaining his art to a class of eager students."[35] Such was the success of the five-week campaign that the decision was taken to hire the prestigious 3,400-seat Massey Hall. A report of the mission in the *Alliance Weekly* indicated that many were "seeking for either salvation, the baptism with the Holy Ghost, or healing." The writer assured readers that there was "no special excitement or outward demonstrations in the services." The demand for the extra workers to deal with "anxious souls" and the anointing of the sick was such that the arrival from Detroit of five women helpers–dubbed by Fred the "Five Wise Virgins"—was welcomed. Bosworth's methodology was labor intensive in that meetings typically ended with three types of invitation—one to the converted, one to those seeking Spirit-baptism, and one for those requesting healing. The three groups were then separated, and workers spread amongst them for counselling and guidance.

33. Anderson, *To the Ends of the Earth*, 255–56.

34. Harrell, *All Things Are Possible*, 15.

35. Opp, *Lord for the Body*, 152. The "sack suit", was an unfitted, loose, and informal lounge suit with no darts, regarded at the time as posh, Ivy League, student wear.

It was, however, the healings that contributed to the fascination of both audience and press. Five weeks into the campaign, one newspaper declared that some 7,000 people had sought healing, doubtless encouraged by the evangelist's reiterated conviction that "it is God's will to heal every afflicted person in Toronto of their afflictions." Hopes were roused sky-high by stories of healings. Bosworth recounted one that he considered "the most remarkable that ever happened as a result of implicit faith." It referred to a woman in Pittsburgh, whose name and address were supplied. She had suffered for eight years from the loss of one kidney removed by operation, and the other "eaten away by cancer." Her condition left her subject to "uric convulsions" and, towards the end, dependent on sixty grains of morphine each week. Her doctors declared that her living with these conditions was more remarkable than even a cure would be. She attended a service one Saturday evening and "the following Tuesday at 1.30 in the afternoon, she became perfectly normal. Later, her doctors attested she had miraculously received new kidneys."[36] Adding to the veracity of the testimony, Bosworth intimated that the woman's sister had sat in the front row of the audience the previous evening.

Bosworth was keen that printed testimonies to healing were subject to verification by the healed person providing their name and precise address, such as that provided by Tranum Burgan, who lived at 2436 Ashland Avenue, Indianapolis. In a testimony to his complete recovery from rheumatism during the Bosworth mission in January 1923, Burgan wrote that he had lived in the city for thirty-five years "and can give any number of references, friends and relatives, who can vouch for the truth of this testimony." During the same mission it was noted that "one meets folks here from nearly every social strata, among them the business man, the professional and the lawyer." The last-named was praised for basing "his conclusions only upon sound evidence and the facts."[37]

Especially welcome at the Toronto Campaign was the backing he received from two well-known church figures in the city. The first was Prof. P. S. Campbell of McMaster University, a Baptist foundation. He recounted:

> Some twenty years ago, owing to the severe illness of my wife, I was compelled to study the very subjects that are being brought to your attention from this platform by our brother, Mr Bosworth and, although prejudiced myself at the time, I was compelled to find out the truth of the matter and investigated Old and New Testament teachings on the subject. . . . Now, our dear brother here, who has been holding services is bringing truths before us constantly which are to be found in accordance with the Word of God. Not a word has escaped his mouth since I have been here that anyone could not endorse. I bless God for the remarkable healings that have taken place.

The other witness was John (Jock) Inkster, minister of the imposing Knox Presbyterian Church in the heart of Toronto. Born in the Orkney Islands, he migrated to Canada in 1889 to minister in Vancouver, from whence he received a call to Toronto in 1921. Of Bosworth he wrote: "I can endorse every word he says. I know God can heal all manner of disease. I have seen it and have experienced it, and have had testimonies of the most

---

36. *Alliance Weekly*, May 7, 1921, 122.
37. *Ibid.,* January 17, 1925, 42.

wonderful kind—more wonderful than anything I have heard Brother Bosworth speak of to-night. . . . It rejoices my heart to see work like that going on, and I am willing to lend my little influence to that end. I hope that the influence of these meetings will extend far beyond this building and shake Toronto."[38]

During Bosworth's highly publicized mission to Ottawa in 1924, support was provided by some local physicians. Dr Leonard Derby informed the *Ottawa Citizen* that "he knew of six cases of deafness that had been cured, some cases of weak eyes, and varicose veins had also been cured." Two other doctors, R. M. Cairns and C. T. Bowles, shared the platform with the Bosworth brothers. Bowles attested to an improvement in his eyesight following anointing with oil. Bosworth's response to the criticism of four local clergy in the capital who were dubious about claims of healing was to devote a service to rebutting their charge. Prior to the service, he arranged for about 500 seats on the ground floor to be reserved. Before beginning his address, he invited any who had been healed over the past weeks to come forward and occupy the reserved seats. Such was the number coming forward that the aisles became blocked and many had to return to their gallery seat. The sight was enough to make the audience "go wild with applause, which was renewed from time to time as those who had been healed kept on coming in streams from all directions."[39] Such an spectacular sight ensured the event made the headlines in the local press.

Such was the impact of the mission that a crowd of 6,000 gospel-harmonizing songsters assembled at the Union Station before the brothers' departure. A final assessment of the mission estimated that 12,000 had been converted, roughly half of this number had come forward for healing, and over 1,500 testimonials of healing by those who had been anointed had been received. In a soured reaction to the whole event, one correspondent to the *Citizen* gave vent to his irritation:

> So if any young man is undecided as to the choice of a profession, let him take up faith healing. With a fair amount of assurance and an insensibility to ridicule and contempt, he cannot fail. No matter how absurd his pretension. No respectable paper will dare say a word against him, and medical men so far from opposing him will actually give their aid. As for the general public—well there is one born every moment, two or three in Ottawa.[40]

The 1920s were the peak years of Bosworth's ministry, though he was not short of detractors. During the Ottawa campaign, the four clerics who opposed him numbered three Catholic priests and a Presbyterian minister. Despite the fact that about 800 Catholics attended the meetings, one of whom was a nun whose healing from back pain was widely publicized, the flow of criticism was not staunched. Canon Fitzgerald warned his flock that to attend them was "a grievous sin." As to the eighty-six-year-old nun's healing, he pointed out that though she still wore a nun's habit, she had ceased to be one thirty years earlier. In the press Father Laflamme was quoted as saying, "they are not miracles, but an imposture and a fake," while his colleague, the Rev. J. J. O'Gorman, maintained that

---

38. *Alliance Weekly,*

39. *Alliance Weekly,* August 2, 77.

40. Opp, *Lord for the Body,* 154–55.

the so-called healings were only a form of "religious Coueism."[41] The minister of Erskine Presbyterian Church, the Rev. Dr Wylie, disclosed that he had attended the mission meetings several times, and "had gone away heart-sick, and that in no case had he seen any healing or any improvement." In response, Bosworth, during a service, sought the support of his listeners in asking for the papers that published the criticisms to publish his reply. At this suggestion, "instantly the audience rose *en masse*, and clapped with prolonged vigor." The sequel was that "hundreds of Roman Catholics were filled with glee" when they read the press reports the next day. The reply had enabled those Catholic friends who had not heard Bosworth "to read the great truths and logical statements which no unbiased mind could gainsay."[42]

The Ottawa detractors were as nothing compared to May Wyburn Fitch, one of Bosworth's former helpers, who voiced her concerns in her booklet *The Healing Delusion*.[43] Her charge was that the teaching of healing evangelists was "pernicious," a stricture that rested on her first-hand knowledge as a team member at Bosworth's campaign in the early 1920s. Prior to joining the team, she had for twenty years lent support to her husband in the running of the McAuley Water Street Mission, New York—the first rescue mission to be opened in the USA, dating from 1872. After his death she succeeded her husband as superintendent of the Mission for two years, before resigning to join the Bosworth party. The decision to join was made at a time when, in her own words, "sorrow ruled my life. My heart was very tender, and perhaps more susceptible to the message which was put in a very appealing way."[44] Her own experience of healing when she recovered from septicaemia following child-birth had confirmed her belief in God's healing power, a position she continued to maintain: "I object to no preacher or evangelist praying for the sick but I am objecting to the harmful way in which it is being taught and done."[45]

Once her initial hesitancy was quelled, she entered fully into the work of the early campaigns: "I have attended fourteen healing campaigns, ranging from two to nine weeks in length, and was a member of the party in nine. I have attended between three hundred and three hundred and fifty meetings, in most of them being on the platform where I could observe all that was taking place. I have dealt with hundreds of sufferers before and after they were anointed and prayed for, and I have assisted the evangelists as they anointed and prayed for the sick."[46] The conclusion she finally reached from her close observation of the healing scenes was brutally dismissive: "*I have never seen any evidence of healing. If there were healings they were of an internal character and not visible to the eye. Of the hundreds, yes, I believe I could safely say anointed, I have never seen one healed or even definitely improved.* There have been a few, a very few, who have said they could

41. Coueism was introduced into America about 1920 as a method of self-help that stressed the value of autosuggestion by the French psychotherapist Emile Coué. It featured the slogan, "Every day, in every way, I am getting better and better."

42. *Alliance Weekly*, August 2, 77–78.

43. Fitch, *Healing Delusion*. The booklet was published in the second half of the 1920s.

44. Ibid., 15.

45. Ibid., 31–32.

46. Ibid., 12–13.

hear 'a little better' or see 'a little better,' but at the end of the campaign they were not improved."[47] When, either by sign-language or written note, the dumb were encouraged to repeat "Praise God" or "Praise the Lord," their pitiful attempt sounded "Ugh! Ugh! Ugh!," in an attempt regarded as passable to convince large audiences that the person had spoken. To Fitch, the whole scenario came "pretty close to blasphemy."[48]

Doctrinal Issues

Besides the exaggerated claims to healing, Fitch extended her criticism both to the doctrine of healing promulgated by Bosworth, and his healing methodology. The fundamental flaw that affected all the healing evangelists of whom she had personal knowledge was to base their claim for healing as an atonement-won entitlement. Fitch was heavily dependent on two other figures, I. M. Haldeman and Arno C. Gaebelein for presenting the case against this particular doctrine.[49] While they argued that the Matthew passage ["Himself took our infirmities and bare our sickness"] can be taken literally to mean physical healing, it referred to Jesus' healing ministry while he was alive. This was stated in Fitch's quote from a pamphlet penned by Haldeman: "In every single case of healing recorded of Him it was while He was alive." This interpretation looked at the context of the Matthew passage, which tells of the occasion when the demonized and sick were brought to Jesus who healed them all that "it might be *fulfilled* which was spoken by Isaiah the prophet." Thus, the fulfilment spoken of in the prophecy was being actualized in Jesus' act of healing some three years within his death on the cross.

The Pentecostal theologian Keith Warrington takes a similar view. He contends that the Matthew texts do not have Jesus' death in view. To associate healing of a supernatural nature exclusively with the death of Jesus is invalid: "Healing depends on God, not an event in time." He urges caution about seeing the commission in Matt 10:8 and parallel texts as fully applicable to present practice since they "had relevance only for the Twelve." Indeed, to take the record of Jesus' healings as a prototype for current healing practice would be "inappropriate, unless the uniqueness of the ministry of Jesus is first recognized." His healing powers were essentially a pointer to the authenticity of his divine nature. The continuing ministry of healing is dependent on two notions: Jesus' ministry of initiating the kingdom, and believers, empowered by the Spirit, while continuing to advance the kingdom by means that presuppose biblical warrant.[50]

47. Ibid., 31. Italics in text.

48. Ibid., 44.

49. Isaac Massy Haldeman (1845–1933) was the long-serving pastor of Calvary Baptist Church, New York. A noted, fundamentalist polemicist, he attracted large crowds in his railings against "worldliness." Arno Clemens Gaebelein (1861–1945) was a prophetic Bible teacher, and dispensationalist analyst of current affairs whose ideas were spread through his periodical *Our Hope*. His *Healing Question* (1925), together with Biederwolf's *Whipping-Post Theology* (1934) were two of the influential works that strongly opposed the healing-in-the-atonement doctrine. The fact that Fitch's booklet was published by the Loizeaux Brothers, a long-established Plymouth Brethren Publishing house, is a further indication of the cessationist stance that lay behind her confession that during her time with the Bosworths, "I was going against my conscience all the time" (15) [Biederwolf, *Whipping-Post Theology*, 1934].

50. Warrington, *Healing & Suffering*, 52, 65, 74. For kingdom and healing, see Matt 19:9: "Heal the sick

The other doctrinal position to which Fitch took exception was, in her eyes, Bosworth's degrading of the sacraments by turning the Lord's Supper into "a healing Clinic, and likewise the sacred ordinance of baptism."[51] She considered Bosworth's teaching on the Lord's Supper demeaning in its claim that "you can be healed when you put the bread in your mouth . . . by discerning the Lord's body."[52] In *Christ the Healer*, Bosworth took the view that the sacrament "is more than an ordinance, because we may partake of Christ while we are partaking of the emblems of his death and the benefits thereof."[53] He took as one of his proof texts 2 Chr 30:10, which instanced Hezekiah and the people being healed at the celebration of Passover. In 1 Cor 11:30 Paul held that spiritual ills can have physical outcomes because of the failure of the Corinthians to rightly "estimate the body"(Weymouth's translation) of 'Christ our Passover' as the reason why many among them were "weak and sickly." The implication is that those who come to the table in the right spirit have satisfied a prerequisite for healing. However, Fitch indicated that she had never known any of the evangelists to hold a communion service in their public meetings, which raised the question as to why they did not practice it. If they had, she surmised, they would make "a public exhibition of such a mockery" that would entice only hundreds of people."

Bosworth's position on this issue was familiar both in historical and contemporary practice. In his book *Body and Soul* (1909), the Anglo-Catholic cleric Percy Dearmer (1867–1936) argued that the interaction of sacrament and miracle was so close that at times an act of grace could extend to physical healing. The reality of the active presence of God was now ministered through the sacraments, and in so doing they serve as a tangible reminder to both saint and sinner of divine truths. To saints, sacramental healings are signs that "sickness is not the will of God; because God is the author of health, and the spreading of his power is the quenching of sickness." To sinners, divine healing can offer assurance "that religion is not a mere probability, nor faith a passive acceptance of conjectures; that prayer is a power producing results, that grace is real."[54] To buttress his view that the Eucharist and Unction with the laying-on of hands have proved efficacious, he cited four cases from the historical record. In sequence, they are: Augustine (426 AD), Catherine of Siena (1373 AD), and in the nineteenth century both the Russian Orthodox Father John of Cronstadt and an eighteen-year-old Irish girl, Miss Lalor (1823). In the Lalor case, her local rector wrote a letter to his Bishop stating that he had administered the sacrament to her, whereupon "instantly she heard, as it were, a voice distinctly saying to her, 'Mary, you are well.'" On her way home, the street was thronged with people, "gazing with wonder at this monument of power and goodness of Almighty God."[55]

Baptism was the other sacrament that raised a problem for Fitch because she regarded the way it was handled as manipulative. As mentioned above, those seeking prayer

---

who are there and tell them, 'the kingdom of God is near.'"

51. Fitch, *Healing Delusion*, 52.

52. Ibid., 61.

53. Bosworth, *Christ the Healer*, 16.

54. Dearmer, *Body and Soul,* 1909, 321.

55. Ibid., 370; the others named in order 239, 354, 381.

for salvation, Spirit-baptism (without tongues) and healing were divided into separate groups. According to Fitch, those sufferers seeking healing had to attend at least three services. At the conclusion of the first service, all had to go to the inquiry room to receive a colored card to sign, indicating that they were seeking healing and were either already a believer or had come forward that particular evening. They were then directed to attend another meeting on a designated night set aside each week for teaching on healing, at the end of which the colored card was exchanged for a white one. If the questions on the card were answered to satisfy the conditions set out on the bottom two lines of the card, then O.K. was jotted on it.[56] The final step was to join the line for anointing and prayer.

---

1. Are you saved or "born again"? . . . .

2. Are you living in obedience to God's will? . . . .

3. Have you any restitution to make or any wrongs to right? . . . .

4. Are you harboring an unforgiving spirit toward anyone? . . . .

5. Do you read the Bible and pray every day? . . . . .

6. Are you convinced that it is God's will to heal you? . . . .

7. Is your faith based exclusively upon the promise of God? . . . .

8. If you are healed will you be willing to give or write your testimony? . . . .

On the reverse side space is allowed to answer the question, "What is your trouble?"

Questions 1, 2, 5, 6, 7, and 8 must be answered in the affirmative, 3 and 4 in the negative

---

The Colored Card

Particular emphasis was laid by Bosworth on the sacrament of adult baptism, with the added inducement voiced that "all sorts of diseases have been left in the baptismal tank. . . . People have gone down into the tank with cancer, goiter, diabetes, tuberculosis, fallen arches, and all sorts of conditions, and have come up without them." During the Ottawa campaign, 7,000 people attended the largest baptismal service ever held in the city. Out of that number, 130 were immersed and 2,800 men, women and children sought healing. Impressive as the scene was, Fitch was perturbed at the coercive linking of baptism with healing: "The great majority of these people go down into the baptismal

---

56. Fitch, *Healing Delusion*, 29. Fitch indicates that the method described here prevailed up to her departure in December 1925, adding "I have no knowledge of its having changed."

tank, not because they are convinced that it is the proper form of baptism, but because they want to be healed. *They will do anything, and believe anything, to get healed.*"[57] Those seekers who met all the printed conditions were told their failure to be healed was due to their disobedience in not following the Lord in baptism.[58] Fitch, as well, was aware of some conscientious individuals who delayed filling in their card until they had met the condition in question 4 that they had sought to be reconciled to others with whom relationships had soured. Even so, after having met all these conditions and been prayed for, they returned *"from the platform in just the same condition as when they mounted it.*"[59]

Later Ministry and Legacy

In contrast to the 1920s, the 1930s were the quieter years of Bosworth's ministry. Pentecostalism grew apace in the 1930s at the same time as the mainstream denominations entered a period of stagnation in the era of the great Depression. A. J. Tomlinson could exult, as far as his new denomination was concerned, "This is our time."[60] In the period 1926–36 the AoG tripled its membership from 50,000 to 150,000. By the end of the 1930s, probably the total American Pentecostal constituency had reached half a million. As membership expanded, so did institutionalism, and the calibre of its professionalism. Within the diversified range of denominations the process of routinization was well advanced with centralized authority structures in place to administer the denominational nerve centers. Concomitant with this growth was an escalation of intra-Pentecostal rivalries. By contrast, Bosworth and other healing evangelists played a significant role in cross-denominational ecumenism in attracting support from the wider Christian constituency. Charles S. Price, after his mission in Victoria, Vancouver Island, was pleased to receive the resolution of the city's Ministerial Association, which commended his "deeply sympathetic attitude towards the various churches, as well as towards all persons who might in any way differ from him in doctrinal belief."[61] By the 1930s, Bosworth concentrated mainly on radio evangelism in creating the "National Radio Revival Missionary Crusaders." Within a few years, this ministry handled more than 250,000 letters. His change in direction away from the great campaigns was partly forced on him by growing health problems. The campaigns of the twenties were held before public address systems came into general use with the result that his preaching to vast audiences and praying for thousands of people began to take its toll.[62] His chronic diabetic condition was a further handicap to continuing large-scale mission activity. He celebrated his seventieth birthday in 1946, and by that stage he had semi-retired.

---

57. Ibid., 62–63, emphasis in original.

58. Bosworth took the verse "He that believeth and is baptized shall be saved" as a clear demand, and a sacrament that stands for "total surrender and obedience." Since "faith always implies obedience," and baptism is commanded, the rite clears the path for the blessing of healing.

59. Ibid., 30, emphasis in original.

60. Robins, *Pentecostalism in America*, 62.

61. Price, *And Signs Followed*, 66.

62. *Voice of Healing*, April 1948, 4.

If his days had ended at that point, they would have rounded off a fulfilled life, and left him with a creditable legacy. In the event, instead of winding down, he came to play a significant part in one of the most arresting periods of healing evangelism in North America. The period between the end of WWII and 1960 witnessed a revival that won the religious backing and financial support of millions of American citizens. It was pre-eminently a healing revival, launched by a number of independent evangelists who in the main shared a common Pentecostal background. In particular, three who were to become household names drew encouragement through their direct contact with Bosworth. They were Oral Roberts, T. L. Osborne, and William Branham. The first two built up multimillion dollar organizations that depended heavily on the personal charisma and sustained financial backing of each evangelist for their survival. It is a format that continues to sustain much of the popular religiosity of America in the era of televangelism

Bosworth's friendship with Branham, the most enigmatic and mystic of the three evangelists, was to prove the closest of the three. William Marrion Branham (1909–65), despite his lack of formal education, became a national healer who had a whole article devoted to him in *Time* magazine in 1947. He was susceptible to seeing visions that left him open to ridicule from his school friends. Later, two visions were to define his ministry. In 1933, he heard the angelic message that he would be the forerunner of the second coming of Jesus, as John the Baptist had been of the Messiah. Thirteen years later, he claimed to have received the commission from an angel to pray for the sick throughout the world. To equip him for this task, two "signs" would distinguish his practice of healing. The first was an ability to identify diseases by vibrations in his left hand when it grasped the right hand of a sick person seeking prayer.[63] The other, and greater, was a faculty to detect the "secrets of the heart" of the sufferer, a competence that some later evangelists recognized as the charism of the "word of knowledge."[64] The most publicized healing was that of Congressman William Upshaw, a cripple for fifty-nine of his sixty years, who in a letter sent to all fellow congressmen recounted his healing. Branham estimated that 35,000 persons received healing during the first year of his healing ministry. There developed a consensus at the time that the preternatural manifestations of signs and wonders in Branham's ministry exceeded anything any previous healing evangelist had ever accomplished. As the revival grew by leaps and bounds in his world-wide travels, Branham became universally acknowledged as "the pacesetter, 'the father' of this last work before the second coming."[65]

Just as he was gaining global recognition, Branham cried off his scheduled meetings in 1948, giving mental and physical exhaustion as the reason. He blamed his campaign

63. Bosworth explained the pulsations in Branham's arm resulting from the "afflicting sprit" coming into contact with the healing charism. As a result, it sets such up a physical reaction that it becomes visible in his hand, and "so real it will stop his wristwatch immediately."(Weaver, *Healer-Prophet*, 75)

64. The esteemed historian of Pentecostalism, Walter Hollenweger, acted as interpreter for Branham during his stay in Zurich. He commented on the evangelist's ability "to name with astonishing accuracy the sickness, and often also the hidden sins, of people he had never seen." Hollenweger declared that he was "not aware of any case in which he was mistaken in the often detailed statements he made." Hollenweger, *Pentecostals*, 354.

65. Weaver, *Healer-Prophet*, 45.

team for acceding to requests for prayer that stretched far into the night. After a break of six months his recovery was complete. One of the first decisions he took was to recruit Gordon Lindsay to serve as his publicist and campaign manager.[66] With an eye to publicizing Branham's campaigns, Lindsay published the first issue of *Voice of Healing* in April 1948. The magazine developed into the primary voice of the worldwide healing revivals and gave a collective and ecumenical identity to an otherwise heterogeneous assemblage of ministries. About the same time Branham persuaded Bosworth out of retirement to become part of his evangelistic team. The Bosworths by that stage had retired to Miami, Florida, but they took the opportunity to attend the Branham's mission when it was held in Miami. Bosworth was so impressed by what he saw that he conceded that "although God has given me meetings of tremendous magnitude, yet, I have never witnessed miracles taking place with such consistency so early in the campaign. In my campaigns I often have to labor for several weeks, before faith had risen sufficiently high for outstanding miracles to occur. But I see in Brother Branham's meetings, such miracles were taking place the first night."[67] It was the beginning of a bond between the two men that was maintained throughout the remainder of their lives, even when Branham later became sidelined because of his doctrinal eccentricities—a situation sadly reminiscent of the latter years of J. A. Dowie.

Bosworth's prolonged career stretched from Dowie to Branham. Branham in Harrell's reckoning, received "inspiration and instruction in Pentecostal doctrine and campaigning technique" from Bosworth.[68] Chappell buttresses this view in affirming that "Bosworth added enormous prestige to Branham's ministry."[69] Starting with Branham's crusade in Miami in January 1948, Bosworth remained a loyal supporter, and his presence lent enormous prestige to the team. He acted not only in an advisory capacity but he also played an active role in preaching. On occasions, he, along with other team members, led morning and afternoon services, tailored to raise the faith of the listeners in anticipation of Branham's ministry in the evening. There were occasions when Branham became so exhausted after spending hours in prayer for the sick that he had to be physically carried off the platform. In that situation, Bosworth stepped in and pressed on with the healing ministry until well after midnight. Before his retirement, Bosworth had never ministered outside North America, but his contact with Branham motivated him to evangelize outside America. In 1951, both men took the healing message to South Africa. Fired by this experience, and despite being in his late 70s, Bosworth gave the last six years to the work of mission in mainly in Africa.

While working with Branham, Bosworth's healing methodology adjusted in two distinct but related ways. He had always emphasized the role of faith in healing, but he increasingly came to the view that the healing process begins only to operate when the

66. Lindsay's parents were members of Dowie's Zion City community. He was converted under Parham's ministry, and was strongly influenced by John G. Lake, joining in his healing and evangelistic campaigns. He was pastor for a short time in Ashland , OR, before handling Branham's ministry.

67. Lindsay, *William Branham:* Online.

68. Harrell, *All Things Are Possible,* 15.

69. Chappell, "William Branham." In Lippy, *Twentieth-Century Shapers,* 45.

faith of the seeker increases to a certain level. The sick were pressed to pray for faith, even to seeking the charismatic gift of faith. One way to inspire faith, particularly in services thronged by the sick, was to orchestrate the prayer line. Bosworth saw a certain virtue in the healing line, in contending that early healings among those near the front of the line acted as a stimulant to faith among those at the tail. It was, therefore, his prayer that God would confirm his message with two or three faith-inspiring miracles at an early stage. Faith would be stirred among the wider audience, enough to spread healing *en masse*. The idea began to grow that mass faith produces mass results on the grounds that it was less demanding to pray a single prayer for all the sick attending a mass rally than to pray successively for the individuals in the prayer line. It was a step that proved a practical solution to the problem which developed when the healing evangelists brought their message to vast open-air gatherings, notably in Africa. The concept came to Benny Hinn (b. 1952) at the start of his ministry at Willowdale, Ontario, when in May 1975 he claimed to have received a supernatural "word of knowledge" that allowed him to identify people's ailments before they were communicated to him, and publicly declare them healed on the spot, without the need to join a line.

In his own ministry, Bosworth first applied this policy in South Africa, possibly following a discussion with T. L. Osborn during a crusade in Flint, Michigan, in 1949 when Osborn was filling in for Branham. Osborn recalled that Bosworth

> was concerned about suffering people who waited in long prayer-lines for someone's special prayer when they could embrace God's healing promises as soon as they heard them and be healed. He often discussed this with us. For some mysterious reason, God chose Mr Bosworth to seed us with these and many other biblical reasons for faith to help multitudes to be healed at the same time. We had no way of knowing that we would face teeming multitudes of sick people in mass crusades all over the world. God was using this dear old veteran of the healing ministry to prepare our young hearts for greater and more vast healing ministry than had ever been experienced in the history of humankind.[70]

Osborn, apparently, first applied the policy at Flint. He called all who were totally deaf in one or both ears to come forward. Fifty-four persons responded. He prayed earnestly in the belief that if he had power and authority over all devils, then in his own words, "I could cast all 54 out at one time as easy as one." All but three received their hearing immediately. By the next day they, too, had recovered. The episode was sufficient to confirm his belief that "mass prayer, mass faith, mass healing was the answer to demonstrating the Gospel on a mass evangelistic scale."[71] Barnes is possibly correct in his conclusion that "while the practice of healing *en masse* was first used, and indeed, popularized, by Osborn, the *concept* actually originated with Bosworth."[72] What is certain is the regard Osborn held for Bosworth. He reminisced in 1972: "Old F. F. Bosworth used to share a lot of secrets with us. . . . I always loved to talk with him." When Bosworth died in January 1958, at the age of eighty-one, he was one of the few charismatic evangelists in the nation

70. Barnes, *Bosworth: The Man behind 'Christ the Healer.'* 65.

71. Osborn, *Healing "en Masse,"* 4–5.

72. Barnes, *Bosworth: The Man behind "Christ the Healer,"* 65.

who had participated in both the expansive phase of the 1920s and the highly charged revival of the immediate post-war years.

A degree of inevitability hangs over this particular mass healing stratagem in the light of the rapid expansion of the Christian faith in parts of the developing world. It was taken up by African evangelists such as Nicholas Bhengu in South Africa, Benson Idahosa in Nigeria and the German evangelist Reinhard Bonnke. During the 1980s Bonnke's campaigns attracted some of the largest crowds in the history of mass evangelism. In November 2000, during his campaign in Lagos, Nigeria, it is estimated some 1.6 million people attended its single largest meeting. Healings throughout the vast crowds were reported at all his rallies. The internal report of the first service in Lagos carried the news that "cancer and hernias disappeared which made the crowd hilarious."[73] A downbeat assessment of Bonnke's ministry comes from Roswith Gerloff: "When Reinhard Bonnke makes ten thousand people speak in tongues in half a minute or when he stages miracle after miracle in his services, then religion is marketed like a new shampoo or a disco song."[74] Nevertheless, it is difficult to see without the "*en masse*" approach how Bonnke could report, "since the year 2000 more than 58 million people made decisions for Jesus and documented what they had done by completing decision cards. These cards are used in the follow-up work and help to ensure that people are integrated quickly and smoothly into local church fellowships."[75]

Other aspects of Bosworth's heritage need to be mentioned. The most constant is the continued appeal of his book *Christ the Healer*. First published in 1924, it had undergone eight revisions by 1992. The 1922 edition carried on its cover the line "More Than 150,000 Copies in Print!" One of the leading healing evangelists in the 1960s, Velmer Gardner, a favorite speaker of the Full Gospel Businessmen's Fellowship, in a letter to Bosworth, described the book as the "greatest and most enlightening book ever published on the subject of healing. . . . Your book is just what I want to leave with the people to keep their faith. Send me another 200 copies at once."[76] As a measure of the book's influence, it was said that most mid-century revivalists began to preach with the book tucked under their arm. Some historians have sought to link Bosworth with the writings of E. W. Kenyon, who laid the theological, metaphysically inflected, foundation of the modern Prosperity Gospel movement. Simmons adjudges that the two men first met shortly before 1910, the year Bosworth left Chicago for Dallas. Kenyon's teaching on positive confession so impressed Bosworth that in the 1948 edition of *Christ the Healer* he stated at the end of chapter 10, (titled "Our Confession,") that the ideas it conveyed were "brought together, by permission, from the writings of Rev. E. W. Kenyon."[77] The thought and language of the Prosperity Gospel are reiterated in *Christ the Healer*: "Healing is always in response to faith's testimony. Some fail when things get difficult *because they lose their confession.*

---

73. Bonnke, "Great Gospel Campaign in Lagos, Nigeria." Online.

74. Hollenweger, *Pentecostalism*, 364. Roswith Gerloff was founding director of the Centre for Black and White Christian Partnership, Birmingham, UK.

75. Anon, "Evangelist Reinhard Bonnke." Online.

76. A commendation printed in one of the editions.

77. Simmons, *Kenyon*, 295.

Disease, like sin, is defeated by our confession of the Word. Make your lips do their duty; fill them with the Word. Make them say what God says about your sickness. Don't allow them to say anything to the contrary."[78]

In turn, *Christ the Healer* became a major influence on the theology of Kenneth Hagin (1917–2003). The book was also something of a textbook for the scores of healing evangelists whose ministries proliferated during the 1950s, thereby helping to ensure Kenyon's lasting impact. Others have emphasized his influence on the so-called Prosperity Gospel movement that began to flourish in the 1980s. Based much on Kenyon's teachings, the Word of Faith movement emerged in the 1970s, placing an emphasis on the Christian's authority to claim healing and material prosperity. Hagin, the father of the modern Word of Faith movement, made *Christ the Healer* a required text for his school, Rhema Bible Training Center, founded in 1974. Rhema centers are to be found in thirteen other countries, including Germany, Peru, India, and South Africa. By 2010, almost 25,000 Rhema alumni had planted over 1,500 congregations worldwide. Their health and wealth message has spread like wildfire throughout the globe with its powerful appeal to both aspiring and marginalized people, notably in Africa, Latin America, and East Asia, to the chagrin of more conventional Pentecostals and mainstream church leaders. One Anglican bishop bewailed its spread within the Anglican Communion in Nigeria, likening it to "a virus that is taking us over."[79]

THE FUNDAMENTALIST CONTRIBUTION

At a superficial glance, it would seem improbable that divine healing could be practiced within some hard core fundamentalist settings. A resolution passed at the 1928 World's Christian Fundamentals Association [WCFA] convention, presided over by W. B. Riley, conveys the degree of negativity towards Pentecostalism found within the ranks of American Fundamentalism:

> The present wave of Modern Pentecostalism, often referred to as the "tongues movement," and the present wave of fanatical and unscriptural healing which is sweeping over the country today, has become a menace in many churches and a real injury to the sane testimony of fundamentalist Christians,
>
> BE IT RESOLVED, That this convention go on record as unreservedly opposed to Modern Pentecostalism, including the speaking in unknown tongues, and the fanatical healing known as general healing in the atonement, and the perpetuation of the miraculous sign-healing of Jesus and His apostles, wherein they claim the only reason the church cannot perform these miracles is because of unbelief.[80]

One of the more formidable fundamentalist critics of Pentecostalism was Isaac M. Haldeman (d. 1933), minister of the prestigious First Baptist Church of New York. Fellow believers were warned by him that "no one who loves the Lord Jesus Christ in sincerity and

---

78. Bosworth, *Christ the Healer*, 145. Bosworth acknowledged that his chapter 10 ("Our Confession,"), drew upon nine of Kenyon's writings.

79. Anon, "Prosperity Gospel in Nigeria. Online.

80. King, *Disfellowshipped*, 129.

truth should . . . attend meetings where this preaching and teaching [of divine healing] may be heard."[81] Adding to the deterrent effect, he sensationalized behavior attributed to a Pentecostal meeting: "Men and women flung prostrate upon the floor, on their backs, rolling over; men and women in indescribable positions, giving utterance to expressions like those who are on the threshold of madness, insane folly, hysteria and close neighbor to the worst of erotics [sic]."[82] Alongside the charge of fanaticism, fundamentalists took exception either to tongues downright—the tempestuous Carl McIntire described them as "one of the great signs of the apostasy"—and as evidence of Spirit-baptism. Criticism of divine healing was directed mainly to its staging in the public arena by contemporary healing evangelists. The arch-critic of Pentecostalism, Arno Gaebelein, denounced Pentecostal healers as "a special menace" because they preached "a good deal of the truth of God, the gospel, prophetic truths and others [that appealed to] the untaught and unsuspecting in the household of faith."[83]

Fundamentalists, *contra* modernists, were supernaturalist, and gave a high place to biblical miracles. Even though the majority of them were cessationist, there was a minority in their ranks who were open to the practice of divine healing. This helped Pentecostals to think of themselves as "fundamentalists plus," a term coined by David McDowell at an AoG executive meeting in 1924. In an article penned by the editor of the *Pentecostal Evangel* soon after the disfellowshiping of the Pentecostal movement in 1928, Stanley Frodsham wrote: "Although we Pentecostal people have to be without the camp, we cannot afford to be bitter against those who do not see as we do. . . . [Our] business is to love these fundamentalists and to unitedly pray, 'Lord, bless them all.'" He was keen to point out that a number of fundamentalists like R. A. Torrey did "recognize that the gospel of Christ has in it salvation for the body as well as the soul."[84]

Besides Torrey, other fundamentalists were receptive to the ministry of healing. One of them was none other than W. B. Riley, who as President of the WFCA acted as chairman of the 1928 meeting that passed the divisive resolution. It has not been generally noticed that this resolution failed to get a unanimous vote. The motion was adopted by a majority of only four votes. Riley in the debate pushed for the idea that the issue was not one the WFCA should touch at all "since the fanatical advocates of tongues and of healing are not opponents of the doctrine of the inspiration of the Bible, or the deity of Christ, or any other of our declarations."[85] A degree of irony is attached to this episode because fifteen years later Pentecostals became foundation members of the NAE under which banner Billy Graham evangelized from 1948 onwards.[86] Carl McIntire's American Council of

81. Haldeman, *Did our Lord Jesus?* 31.

82. Ibid., 26.

83. Gaebelein, *Healing Question,* 69.

84. *Pentecostal Evangel,* August 18, 1928, 7.

85. Poewe, *Charismatic,* 115.

86. Synan takes the view that the break with Fundamentalism in America in 1928, and compounded later in 1943, "turned out to be a blessing that freed the rising Pentecostals from the dead cultural and theological baggage of a discredited movement and opened up the way for unparalleled influence and growth in the last half of the twentieth century" (Synan, "Fundamentalism," 658).

Christian Churches [ACCC] became the home from 1943 of hard line Fundamentalists who retreated into limited engagement with the wider culture. Fundamentalist rigidity led one journalist to write that the difference between an evangelical and a fundamentalist is that the latter is "an evangelical who is angry about something."[87]

WILLIAM BELL RILEY

W. Bell Riley (1861–1947) graduated from the Southern Baptist Theological Seminary at the age of twenty-seven. He ministered to three Baptist churches before becoming the pastor of the First Baptist Church in Minneapolis in 1897, a post he held for well-nigh the next fifty years. Described as "perhaps the most important fundamentalist of his day," he was both the founder and the leading figure in the WFCA.[88] A man of boundless energy with a keen sense of humor, he ranked among the most effective debaters in the American anti-evolutionist controversy. At the denominational level, he was a recognized leader of the Baptist Bible Union, the fundamentalist pressure group within the Northern Baptist Convention. He turned out numerous articles, pamphlets, and books for the fundamentalist cause, as well as editing two fundamentalist magazines. His greatest success lay, arguably, in his time as President of the non-denominational Northwestern Bible and Missionary Training School, an institution that was to become the center of what has been dubbed "Riley's Empire." In 1930 at least ninety-four Northwestern-trained ministers served in the Upper Midwest, a total that rose to 172 in 1940. Many were recommended by Riley to rural churches, all custodians of the fundamentalist message. Northwestern's role in its region helps to support the thesis that such Bible Institutes were crucial to the survival and growth of Fundamentalism in the interwar years, only to blossom in the post-war renascence of American evangelicalism in all its various strands.[89]

Riley was under pressure to address the subject of Pentecostalism following its arrival in Minneapolis in 1907, especially after he had declined an invitation to greet the new arrival. He had to tread carefully in his response because Pentecostals largely espoused premillennialism, and tongues, both of which he accepted as featuring in the New Testament. As a man of the Book, he could not dismiss tongues as an aberration, since he concurred to the idea that the *charismata* "were intended for all ages." Though receptive to the idea of tongues remaining extant, his problem with Pentecostalism lay in its association with tales of "contortions, trances, and babble." Nevertheless, he exhorted those who truly possessed the gift to exalt God "as an additional evidence of the enduement of the Spirit." To dismiss tongues was, for him, tantamount to limiting God's power at a time in history when a worldwide revival was expected, during which the Lord would show his arm in wonders. "Power" was every much a desideratum for Fundamentalists as for Pentecostals.

---

87. Ostling, "Jerry Falwell's Crusade," 48. Jerry Falwell subsequently adopted this witticism, while George Marsden popularized it.

88. Trollinger, "Riley's Empire," 199.

89. Before his death, Riley persuaded Billy Graham to take over as President of Northwestern, which he did for a short time.

Such greater openness of some leading fundamentalists to Pentecostal thinking was not pervasive in fundamentalist circles. As King points out, "it was hardly the case that every fundamentalist was scurrying to a Pentecostal healing service, but there were enough to arouse solicitude. Their churches were leaking members, and occasional splits occurred where healing was emphasized, such as at United Presbyterian in Albany, Oregon in 1929. Fundamentalists struggled with balancing the spark of renewal within their churches while dousing Pentecostal fires from without." In attempts to square this circle, it was "little wonder that they strove against the healing 'fakirs,'" as Gaebelein branded them.[90]

In four sermons that he preached in November 1909, Riley presented his views on divine healing. One of them tackled the live issue of Christian Science that was at the peak of its influence in North America at the time. He was convinced that had the orthodox churches "stood for what the Scriptures had to say on the subject of healing, the misty and uncertain teachings of Christian Science . . . would have received no attention whatever."[91] His view of healing was similar to such pre-Pentecostal stalwarts as A. J. Gordon and A. B. Simpson. The success of these men had for him one overriding explanation — "they were men who *believed* God."[92] The biography of fellow Baptist, Charles Spurgeon, written by Russel Conwell, was cited in support of his position. Conwell wrote, "There are now living and worshiping in the Metropolitan Tabernacle, hundreds of people who ascribe the extension of their life to the effect of Mr Spurgeon's personal prayers. They have been sick with disease, and nigh unto death; he has appeared, kneeled by their beds and prayed for their recovery."[93] Riley admitted that claims of healing made by proponents of Theosophy, Spiritualism and Christian Science cannot be denied, but "we say this, that any system that does not conform its teaching to the truth in God's Word, must explain its healing upon some other ground than that of the intervention of the Divine One."[94]

Through his contact with a Spiritualist healer who claimed success in healing, Riley's response was to attribute such power to Satan because "God has never given this to mortal man." In support of his denial, he drew on a surprising source: "The newspapers used to speak of Dr Dowie, 'the Divine Healer'. They used to apply a kindred term to Dr Cullis, 'the Faith-cure'. . . . But such men as love the Scriptures reject instantly and almost with insult, having any such abilities assigned to them."[95] With Dowie's death two years earlier and his reputation in shreds, for Riley to call him in defense of his position was puzzling, and was bound to provoke annoyance in some quarters. Early in his Minneapolis pastorate, he found himself at loggerheads with some members. Among the areas of dispute were his

---

90. King, *Disfellowshiped*, 108. Gaebelein's *Healing Question* (1925) was written to address the situation that arose "during the last few years when a veritable craze in healing of diseases by faith seems to have taken hold of thousands of professing Christians." The book was aimed to alert "the household of faith and guard them against one of the most subtle delusions of our times."

91. Riley, *Divine Healing and Christian Science*, 24.

92. Riley, *Divine Healing*, 14.

93. Ibid., 13–14.

94. Ibid., 15.

95. Ibid., 14.

belief in divine healing, and his qualified support of J. A. Dowie.[96] Grumbling over the issue continued throughout his ministry, particularly his stance against the widely accepted view that suffering was God's means of testing and sanctifying the believer. His reaction to such a position was sharp: "Personally, I have not found it to be a means of grace, and I do not believe it to be from God, and hence I have no hankering for unhealth."[97] Speaking from hard experience, he recognized that to preach as scriptural what long has been disregarded is to bring upon the speaker "criticism, and often even rebuke."[98]

Riley lent heavily on Jas 5:14–16 for biblical support, though it would appear that not all members of the church agreed over the anointing of the sick person with oil as enjoined in verse 14. Two questions raised about unction, and which still remain live issues, were addressed by Riley: "Was the oil used as a medicine?" and "Did the oil carry sacramental connotations?" The idea that the oil referred to in James 5 was used for medicinal purposes was widely advanced at the time. This interpretation was proposed by such popular commentators as Albert Barnes (1798–1870), American Presbyterian divine, whose *Notes on the New Testament* had sold more than a million copies by 1870. Barnes' comment on the James 5 passage reads: "The custom of anointing the sick with oil still prevails in the East, for it is believed to have medicinal or healing properties."[99] A current website makes the same point in citing Luke 10:34: "The oil and wine were poured into the man's wounds. That is, they were used as medicine. . . . Oil and wine were two common cure-alls in scripture for wounds, sores, and diseases."[100] The dispute over the use of oil as a medicine arose from the response of those sufferers who declined the use of medicaments. For them to accept the Barnes' view would undercut the radical position that to avail oneself of such help would be a denial of the efficacy of faith, the very means by which healing comes. Those who supported the Barnes' saw no inconsistency in seeking both medical help of any kind, and prayer for healing. To take the opposite view would risk the prolongation of unnecessary suffering, and even lead to death. On this issue, it would appear Riley's congregation were divided.

Riley contested the Barnes' view, holding that the oil in James 5 is the symbol of the Holy Ghost; and is applied as such. He contended that the oil in the healing context is unlikely to be medicinal, for if God is any sort of a physician, "he is not a quack who would prescribe oil for all diseases. . . . The fact that the elders, and not physicians, were to apply it, makes this view the more reasonable, and the additional words, 'And the prayer of faith shall save the sick', puts beyond dispute the thought that the oil had any other significance than symbolizing the Spirit."[101] He found support from at least one of the early Baptist fathers, Hanserd Knollys, (d. 1691) who, "when attacked by illness, discarded

96. Russell,. "William Bell Riley" 19.

97. Riley. *Divine Healing*. Pamphlet, No. 2, 7.

98. Ibid., 3.

99. Barnes supported the New School side in American Presbyterianism that backed revivalism and social reform. Online. http://barnes.biblecommenter.com/james/5.htm.

100. Anon. "What Is the Purpose?" Online.

101. Riley, *Divine Healing*, 10–11.

medicine, and resorted to anointing and prayer."[102] Any suggestion of a sacramental tinge was dealt with more summarily by taking a quotation from the commentary on Mark's gospel by Johann Peter Lange (1802–84), whom Riley regarded as "one of the greatest of Bible students and scholars." He cited Lange's comment on Mark 6:13: "Oil in this context is simply a symbolic medium of the miraculous work, and the anointing was a symbol of the bestowing of the Spirit as a prerequisite condition of healing."[103]

Riley was passionate about divine healing but was strangely silent about his practice of it. In all the works consulted there is no reference to any actual healing having taken place. One explanation for this is his rigorous adherence to the directive given in Jas 5:14 on the role of the elders. As he read it, they "are not to hunt out the sick, but are to respond to the request of the sick."[104] The calling upon the elders at the behest of the sufferer would suggest individual ministration in the sequestered setting of a home or medical/care institution. For Riley, so long as "the one hundred and one texts that teach the doctrine" continue, then "my marching orders are too clear for me to refuse this service to any man who asks it; and the meaning of the Word is so evident that when the prayers go unanswered I will suspect my own faith rather than deny the truth of this Bible doctrine, or call in question the faithfulness of my covenant-keeping God."[105] The importance of the doctrine, for him, was such that, though he was dismissive of Christian Science, yet by teaching it at all, it had turned the attention of an unbelieving world, and a faithless church, "to a long neglected Scripture truth." If the churches' had stood up for the scriptural teaching on healing, they would have denied Christian Science its rapid growth, and strengthened "the foundations of the 'faith as it is in Christ.'"[106]

While there is no direct statement in Riley's writings about the disputed issue of medical intervention, there can be little doubt that his sympathies lay more with unction and prayer than physicians: "When once we get the idea that our bodies are temples of the Holy Spirit we will seek to keep them clean, to conserve their energies, to concentrate their powers, and by the very process we will prove that righteousness is medicinal beyond all that *materia medica* has yet discovered."[107] Though mildly critical of the Emmanuel movement, he was quite prepared to accept the effectiveness of suggestion, the therapeutic technique favored by Emmanuel practitioners. "From a scientific standpoint," he opined, "I have no doubt that by mental suggestion a man can be made sick: neither have I any question that by mental suggestion many people can be made well." Despite its claim to embrace divine healing, the weak spot in Emmanuel methodology lay, for him, in confining its hopes in the human power of psychotherapy to alleviate nervous functional disorders. By contrast, Christ did not confine himself to "superficial diseases,"

102. Newport, "Hanserd Knollys." Online.

103. The verse reads; "[Jesus] anointed with oil many that were sick, and healed them." Lange (1802–84) was Professor of Theology in the University of Zurich, then in Bonn. He began this commentary series in 1857, the 25 volumes of which were issued in English in the period 1865–80.

104. Riley, *Divine Healing*, 10.

105. Riley, *Christian Science*, 23–24.

106. Ibid., 24.

107. Riley, *Divine Healing and the Emmanuel Movement*, 22.

open to mental suggestion, but was also equal to the healing of the deaf, the blind, even to "the raising of the dead."[108] Christ, for Riley, was "not only the Healer; he is health; not for repair of the body only, but for preservation as well." Unable to convince those in his own congregation, he made the plea that they would come in confidence to the Christ of the Roman centurion in Matt 8:8 centurion who pleaded, "Speak the word only and it shall be done."[109]

JOHN ROACH STRATON,

J. R. Straton (1874–1929), like Riley, was a prominent Baptist fundamentalist leader. Born in Evansville, Indiana, into a Baptist preacher's home, he grew up in the Deep South. Following his time at Mercer University, Macon, Georgia, he trained at the Southern Baptist Theological Seminary. After serving in a number of churches in the South, he received a call in 1918 to Calvary Baptist Church in New York City, where he ministered for eleven years before his premature death at the age of fifty-four. Straton quickly became a public figure in New York, noted for his attacks on vice and corruption, which, he alleged, had turned the city into a modern Babylon awaiting divine wrath. In castigating the lewdness of its shows, he turned Broadway into one of his prime targets An article in the *New York Times* listed his shibboleths that included card-playing, theatre and nude art, evolution and theological modernism. In the face of such rife irreligion, Straton was convinced that the mainstream churches in the city were presenting a pale imitation of the faith that he derided as "rag-time religion." Scorn was poured on one Manhattan church that had hired a professional musician to divert its congregation by whistling hymns, while another had engaged a Mr Reef, "the banjo king," to perform his repertoire with organ accompaniment.[110] In short, the city suffered from an "amusement culture" that betrayed its past civilized mores.

One of the two big names in Stratton's sights was Harry Emerson Fosdick, pastor of the liberal minded and influential Park Avenue Baptist church from 1925. His sermon "Shall the Fundamentalists Win?" so clearly expressed the liberal case of the time that it received publicity in a widely distributed pamphlet. Straton's response was to orate, "Yes, we all owe a debt of undying gratitude to devout scholarship, but we need not be unduly exercised by this swaggering, self-assertive, boastful 'new learning,' which arrogates to itself superior insight and which sneezes every time a German sceptic takes snuff. . . . I would like to raise the question: 'Shall the Funnymonkeyists win' for that is really what the issue of today is: Is man a child of God or a descendant of the monkeys?"[111] His spirited denunciation of modernism peaked in 1926 when he withdrew from the Northern Baptist Convention, which earned him the sobriquet "The fundamentalist Pope." His other tussle was with Al Smith, the Democratic candidate for President in 1928. He attacked Smith's affiliation to the Democratic Party and its association with the electoral malpractice its powerful Tammany Hall arm, as well as its anti-Prohibition stance. Straton's premature

---

108. Ibid., 17–18.

109. Ibid., 20. Reference to Matt 8:8.

110. Gigge, *Faith in the Market*. 77.

111. Straton, "Shall the Funnymonkeyists Win? Win?" Online.

death from a stroke on 29 October 1929 spared both men from his castigation. It coincided with the beginning of the worst crash of the stock market, which proved to be the harbinger of the Great Depression. The church was left with a staggering debt of more than $2 million that resulted from an ill-timed church property project.

Unlike Riley, Straton was more open about his acceptance of divine healing and his practice of it. In acknowledging that there was "great interest in the religious world today in divine healing," he found it astonishing that he had completed his theological training "without even so much as hearing that there was such a truth as that of divine healing." A series of events pressed him into acceptance. His own healing and that of one of his cousins during his earlier pastorates, he revealed, "satisfied my heart and conscience on the healing issue by praying for the sick, both publicly and privately, as a part of the regular round of pastoral duties and, I am afraid, without very much hope or faith that anything

Uldine Utley

out of the ordinary would really happen." His heart was further stirred in Baltimore by "several instances of direct answer to believing prayer, when the officers of the church came together on their own initiative for combined and earnest intercession on behalf of sick brothers." These events led him, step by step, to the conclusion that the Christian churches are remiss in leaving healing to Christian Scientists, psychologists, as well as "any mercenary charlatan or self-appointed 'evangelist' who may elect to use divine healing to draw crowds."[112]

His ministry was given a fillip in 1926 by a number of revivalist campaigns with city-wide appeal. He described the meetings as "deep and profoundly spiritual," led by the thirteen-year-old evangelist Uldine Utley, about whom more below. Straton was bowled over by the diminutive Uldine, admitting that "little Uldine's life and ministry have influenced me, but I am by no means ashamed to confess it. I am glad, indeed, that Jesus has seen fit to use this devoted little disciple of His to bring blessings—not only to my own life but to the members of my family, as well as to many friends, who have been touched with divine power

through her gracious and Christ-like ministry."[113] During the mission, his wife testified to relief from pain after prayer by the young girl. She also attributed her Spirit-baptism "to the young prophet, declaring that under the experience she fell to her knees and wept in gratitude and humility before the Lord."[114]

Though not formally identified as a Pentecostal, Uldine had been converted in a Pentecostal setting, while her periodical *Petals from the Rose of Sharon* was identified

112. Straton, *Divine Healing*, 7–8.

113. Ibid., 8.

114. Loud, *Evangelicals*, 351.

as Pentecostal at the time. Her influence on Straton's son, Warren, seems to have played a major part in his encounter with the Holy Spirit. The *Pentecostal Evangel* reprinted a newspaper report that Warren "lay prone on the floor during a Monday night young people's meeting at Calvary Baptist in June or July 1927," though there was no mention of Utley being present. According to his parents, Warren sang in an unknown tongue "in a most beautiful way" while his face appeared "illuminated by joy."[115] These events led to the resignation of five deacons in protest, who saw it all as a move to the pentecostalization of Calvary Baptist Church.

Straton was quite prepared to give due recognition to the influence of "this devoted little disciple," as he termed Uldine, on his ministry. He acknowledged that "his conviction that it is both the privilege and duty of the churches today to obey the commands of the Master about healing" reached its culmination during her mission in 1926. As an outcome, he instituted a weekly healing service in his church. His sermons on the topic were published the following year under the title *Divine Healing in Scripture and Life*. In the fall of 1927, he conducted healing services, which the American Association for the Advancement of Atheism sought to stop by charging him with "practicing medicine without a license."[116] About the same time, he began prayers for healing on radio, which led to a confrontation with the city's health commissioner, who denounced him as a possible menace to public health. Two Pentecostal periodicals supported him in his position on healing—the *Pentecostal Evangel* printed his sermon on God's "Conditional Covenant to Heal his People," while the *Latter Rain Evangel* welcomed his defense of healing as a "manifestation of the power of God [that] will . . . destroy unbelief far more than arguments or debates ever could."[117]

Straton's theological position on divine healing was much on the lines of the nineteenth-century radical stalwarts in the Higher Life tradition, notably A. B. Simpson and A. J. Gordon. His book was dedicated to the former, acknowledged as "a true knight and concentrated crusader of the Fourfold Gospel." Gordon was lauded as "one of our greatest Baptist teachers and scholars . . . who laid due emphasis on this truth of divine healing."[118] In terms of the healing triad of atonement-faith-medical means, Straton stood with them. He upheld healing in the atonement as a present reality, not "a doctrine that belongs merely to extremists or fanatics."[119] On faith, he stressed that "the salvation of the soul and the healing of the body . . . are the one thing, so far as faith is concerned."[120] As to medical means, he looked back to the morning of his immediate and complete restoration of health from a nervous breakdown. His first act was to dump "all the medicine out."[121] He took the view that any person taking medicine cannot trust Christ as fully and freely as the one who lays aside all remedies and trusts in God alone. He was impressed by Uldine in

---

115. *Pentecostal Evangel*, 9 July 1927, 9.

116. King, *Disfellowshiped*, 133.

117. Ibid., 133.

118. Straton. *Divine Healing*, 109.

119. Ibid., 111.

120. Ibid., 39

121. Ibid., 49.

allowing sufferers the opportunity "to follow the directions laid down in the fifth chapter of James."[122] From this, it can be taken that the administration of healing was within the church, with the participation of elders and attention directed to the individual sufferer.

Never afraid to speak his mind, Straton defended the case for healing against "one of our distinguished city pastors, greatly beloved, and a great expositor of Scripture, but a man seemingly constitutionally antagonistic to divine healing in the full sense."[123] The allusion was to Arno Gaebelein whose published diatribe, *The Healing Question,* Straton had read with "pain and real distress of mind and heart." Gaebelein attacked him on three fronts—healing-in-the-atonement doctrine, dispensational cessationism, and the authenticity of healing claims. For Gaebelein, the reference to Christ carrying our diseases in Matt 8:17 means only that "Jesus bore our sicknesses when He was alive, at Capernaum." Straton countered this interpretation by holding that when Scripture asserts that Christ was the "Lamb slain from the foundation of the world" (Rev 13:8), then "just as Jesus settled sin by anticipation before He hung upon the cross, so He also bore our sicknesses before He hung upon the cross."[124]

Gaebelein was one of the leading advocates of dispensational premillennialism in America, which he promoted through his periodical *Our Hope,* and as a consulting editor of the *Scofield Reference Bible* (1909). The doctrine closed his mind to divine healing in the present dispensation, the so-called church age, and deferred it to the age to come when the covenant nation of Israel was held to enter its promised heritage, at which point all of God's promises to Abraham and his seed will be literally fulfilled. Among the promises is healing (q.v. 2 Chr 6:28–30). Straton argued, to the contrary, that though the letter of James, with its pivotal passage on healing in chapter five, was addressed to "the twelve tribes," it was also inclusive of Gentiles as both Jews and Gentiles were integral to the church when the epistle was written.

When it came to the issue of medical intervention, both men were forced into trading statistics taken from recent surveys. Straton took a jaundiced view of Gaebelein's book for its coverage of an inquiry carried out by a committee, which investigated the healings claimed during the Charles Price campaign in Vancouver in 1923. The committee consisted of eleven ministers of various denominations, eight well known Christian physicians, mostly specialists, three university professors and a well-known member of the legal profession. The majority report contended that Price used hypnotic suggestion. Of the 350 cases of those who professed healing, they found that thirty-nine of those anointed, and pronounced cured, had died; five were declared insane; 301 remained sick, even though "they had been hypnotized into the belief that they were cured." The five cases of definite healing had suffered from "certain nervous diseases" of a type amenable to medical treatment, and thus they were clearly functional and not organic.

Unhappy with the attitude taken in the report, two dissatisfied members of the investigating committee produced a minority report that took issue with the majority on

122. Ibid., 9.

123. Ibid., I22.

124. Ibid., 122–23. On Stratton's reading of the texts, sin and suffering are inextricably intertwined, which leads to the unsustainable conclusion that total forgiveness and total health are the believer's blessings.

a number counts. They objected that the 350 cases investigated were drawn largely from those who were disappointed because they had not been healed, and was poorly representative of the 6000 that had been anointed. They pointed to the official statistic that the death rate had declined slightly from the corresponding period in the two preceding years. Another flaw was the committee's reliance on information collected from parties other than the individual concerned. This charge was backed up by a highly publicized letter from two ministers, one of whom had a daughter who been cited in the report as being cured by mental suggestion. The charge made was that if the investigators had been in direct contact with the young woman they would have found that her condition, agreed by all medical opinion, was one of curvature of the spine, shortening of the leg and bending of the foot at the ankle caused by infantile paralysis. It could not possibly have responded to mental suggestion. The city's Ministerial Association received both the majority and the minority reports at a tense meeting called especially for their acceptance or rejection. Such was the division of opinion that the Association voted neither to endorse nor reject the two reports. Though copies were given to the press, the decision was taken not to have them printed for distribution. It turned out that not all the opponents of Price could be classed as liberal, nor were all his supporters clearly identified as conservatives.[125]

Straton, in his response to the controversy, turned to a similar type of survey carried out by William Keeney Towner, who during his time as pastor of the First Baptist Church of Oakland, California, had invited Aimee Semple McPherson to conduct a mission that witnessed many conversions and healings. Shortly afterwards, he sent a questionnaire to all who had signed prayer cards, asking them to assess the impact of the healing ministry in their lives. Over 2,500 people returned the questionnaire by post. They replied to the following statements (in italics), "Yes'" or "No," with results provided:

> 1. "*I was immediately and completely healed.*" Six percent answered in the affirmative.
> 2. "*I was immediately and partially healed and have continued to improve ever since.*" Eighty-five percent replied in the affirmative.
> 3. "*I experienced no change in my condition, either for better or worse.*" Fewer than twenty answered this in the affirmative.
> 4. "*The ministry of anointing, and prayer for healing was a great spiritual uplift to me and strengthened my faith.*" Only ten out of the 2,500 failed to reply to this statement in the affirmative, thus showing that independent of its effect upon the body, the ministry of prayer for the healing of the sick is a means of spiritual grace, inspiration and comfort.[126]

When Towner moved to the Baptist church in San Jose, California, he continued his healing ministry. In his four years there, he baptized 1,700 candidates.

As for the converts at Price's three crusades in the city, they showed little sign of being deterred by the negative report of the investigating committee. By 1925, several thousand had left existing Protestant churches in Vancouver, and formed eight new Pentecostal congregations, adding to the two existing ones. The 1931 census indicated that Pentecostalism in British Columbia had increased tenfold from 1921, with its great-

125. Burkinshaw, "Strangers and Pilgrims," 155–56.
126. Ibid., 148.

est concentration in the Vancouver area. Continued rapid growth in succeeding decades led, by 1951, to proportionately more Pentecostals in British Columbia than in any other province from Quebec westwards.[127]

Overview of Fundamentalist Healing

The fact that leading figures, even if a minority, in the fundamentalist movement advocated divine healing suggested to Baer, in his Yale doctoral thesis, that two points were worth making. First, the influence of the healing contribution of Higher Life worthies such as A. B. Simpson and A. J. Gordon remained much stronger in fundamentalist circles than previously recognized. Through the 1920s, numerous prominent fundamentalists followed their teachings to a differing degree. Second, Pentecostal healers of the 1920s significantly impacted fundamentalist thought and spirituality.[128] While there were leaders like Gaebelein who rejected Pentecostal healers on dispensationalist grounds, others were also attuned to the shared heritage of late nineteenth-century Holiness spirituality. Even a critic like Gaebelein was not against healing in maintaining that "all true ministers of the Gospel . . . pray with the sick and can tell of many answered prayers." He spoke of visiting the sick hundreds of times, and "many times we have seen His gracious answers in the raising up of the sick."[129] If many fundamentalists rejected the flamboyance of Pentecostal healers and their more extreme teachings, they still held to the belief that God hears and answers prayer for every need.

The onset of the 1930s saw the beginning of a steady decline within fundamentalism of support for divine healing, as the dispensational cessationist view won over the fundamentalist rank and file.[130] Baer submits that the most significant reason was generational, as many of those who were advocates of divine healing, and whose spirituality had been shaped by the Higher Life movement, died in the 1920s into the mid-1930s—such as R. A. Torrey in 1928 and J. R. Straton in 1929. The younger generation of fundamentalists who entered the scene in the 1920s and later, had no direct experience of the radical healing movement of the 1880s. Instead, dispensational premillennialism and Keswickian caution on the subject shaped their thinking. The new generation of fundamentalists had reason to be antipathetic to healing as they understood it practiced by Christian Scientists, Emmanuel-endorsing liberal Protestants, and Pentecostal Holy Rollers, along with the discredited J. A. Dowie. The scandals surrounding Aimee Semple McPherson, coupled with the alleged excesses of other healers in the 1920s like Bosworth, Branham

---

127. Burkinshaw, "Conservative Protestantism and the Modernist Challenge in Vancouver, 1917–1927." Online. This article provides an accessible contextual study (see web) of the impact of the Fundamentalist-Modernist controversy behind the events. James Opp devotes the best part of his chapter 7, "Exposing the Body," to the ramifications of the three Price missions in Vancouver in his *The Lord for the Body*, 176–95.

128. Baer, "Perfectly Empowered Bodies," 324.

129. Gaebelein, *Healing Question*, 123.

130. Besides Gaebelein, a new figure appeared on the fundamentalist scene. Harry A. Ironside (1876–1951) was appointed pastor of the Moody Memorial Church in Chicago. He promoted dispensational cessationism, arguing, "All the Christian's blessings are spiritual, in contrast to Israel's, which were of an earthly character. Ours are in heavenly places, not in the land of Canaan."

and Price also sullied divine healing for those who missed out on the precedent set by the radical healing movement of the previous century. Even Higher Life advocates like Torrey became more guarded with the rise of Pentecostalism.[131]

More so than Fundamentalism, American Pentecostalism enjoyed impressive numerical growth throughout the 1920s and 1930s. By contrast, the decade, marred by the economic Depression, saw a worrisome stagnation within the mainstream churches as secularism and institutional malaise began to bite.[132] If one were to follow the mainstream media, it would appear the Scopes Trial had succeeded in burying the fundamentalists and "Holy Rollers" for good. The reality, however, was quite different. "Despite public humiliation at the hands of critics like H. L. Mencken," writes Robins, the "fundamentalists and their alienated Pentecostal kin flourished in the years that followed. Indeed, a triumphant A. J. Tomlinson could hardly contain his euphoria over the success that buoyed his branch of the movement in the 1930s. 'I do not understand why people want to go back to the early church. I admit those were great days . . . but look what we are and what is just ahead.'"[133] By the end of the 1930s, it is estimated that America's Pentecostals numbered half a million.

Where Pentecostals felt they had the edge over other conservative evangelicals in facing a culture of doubt-sowing modernism lay in their belief of the renewal of miracles and supernatural powers as recorded in the New Testament. A glowing sense of confidence filled many a Pentecostal breast. William Booth-Clibborn, the Pentecostal evangelist, and grandson of Salvationist William Booth, during his visit to Vancouver in 1925 wrote of the fundamentalists' refusal to accept the Pentecostal outpouring of the Spirit wrote: "I pity the poor fundamentalists. God help them. They have certainly got a hard time of it. I pity any man who is attacking the evil forces of this age without the full armour of God upon him."[134] Representative of the attraction Pentecostalism had for some evangelicals was the story of Vancouver's Free Methodist pastor, H. B. Wilson. Despite the displeasure of some of his own members, hundreds from other churches were attracted by the new emphasis and enthusiastic worship that he encouraged. Among the influx was the entire membership of the young women's prayer circle from the nearby Mount Pleasant Methodist Church, many of whom had been converted during the Price campaigns.[135] Adding to the denominational mix in Vancouver in 1928 was the arrival of the International Church of the Foursquare Gospel, whose founder was the intrepid Aimee Semple McPherson.

AIMEE SEMPLE MCPHERSON; EVERYBODY'S SISTER

A casual passer-by approaching McKendree Methodist Episcopal Church in Washington, DC on a Thursday afternoon in April 1920 would have been startled by seeing two figures

---

131. This paragraph draws heavily on Baer, "Perfectly Empowered Bodies," 324–25.

132. The Depression made it harder to finance revivals with the effect that large healing campaigns and nationally known healing evangelists reduced in number. Radio remained a viable means of witness.

133. Robins, *Pentecostalism*, 62.

134. Burkinshaw, "Strangers and Pilgrims," 158–59.

135. Ibid., 159.

clambering into the church by a rear window. One was its minister and the other was a short, stocky thirty-year-old woman dressed not unlike a nurse with her white uniform draped by a blue cape. Once inside, the couple shouldered their way through a dense crowd before reaching the platform to face an auditorium packed by 2,000 people. The main entrance of the church was blocked by an equally large crowd outside, which had forced the couple to make their unconventional entry. The center aisle of the church was littered with up to 500 sick people, many on camp beds, and some who had travelled hundreds of miles. Once the minister had handed the meeting over to the guest, she led the singing "The Great Physician now is here, the sympathizing Jesus." She then introduced a Mrs Jackson from Baltimore who testified to the restoration of her tubercular-damaged vertebrae. For the period of four months previously, she had been encased in a plaster cast that extended from her armpits to her knees.

Mrs Jackson proceeded to tell of her son bringing home an anointed handkerchief from a healing service in Baltimore conducted by the speaker. It was pressed under the cast to rest against her damaged spine. Within several prayer-filled days, she was able to take her the first steps in her complete recovery. Following this prelude aimed to bolster faith, and a call for sinners to repent, ushers arranged for the invalids to approach the altar in clusters of thirty, where they were anointed and briefly prayed for. Comparable services continued until the following Sunday. By that time it was estimated that more than 1,000 crippled and sick had been prayed for, and 50,000 had heard the gospel preached "with signs following." Hardbitten journalists had cause for concern, not just because healings were occurring more rapidly than they could be recorded, but they could not detect a hoax. Indeed, "a hoax would have been more miraculous than the healings."[136]

Welcome to the captivating world of Aimee Semple McPherson, the self-styled "Everybody's Sister," of whom it was said, "Once you come beneath the spell of her personality you're lost."[137] Charlie Chaplin, following his visit to her Angelus Temple, Los Angeles, told her admiringly, "Whether you like it or not, you're an actress."[138] The Mexican American actor, Anthony Quinn, who for a time played in the Angelus band, said of her "I have known most of the great actresses of my time, and not one of them could touch her." Another likened her to a siren of "magnetism such as few women since Cleopatra have possessed." Epstein spoke of "her erotic energies as a source of power."[139] As is to be expected, she was not short of critics. The Dean of Denver Bible Institute, Clifton Fowler, wrote of her healings that "outside of perhaps Mrs Eddy [Mary Baker], there has not been so dangerous a teacher in the United States in the past two hundred years."[140] Robert ("Fighting Bob") Shuler, minister of Trinity Methodist Episcopal Church in Los Angeles, preached a series of sermons on "McPhersonism" in which he denounced her as "neither honest nor genuine." While acknowledging that her personality was "winsome and at-

136. Epstein, *Sister Aimee*, 177–84. These paragraphs draw heavily on Epstein's work, which presents a composite picture of Aimee in action in her early itinerant ministry.

137. Barfoot, *Aimee Semple McPherson*, 232.

138. Blumhofer, *Aimee Semple McPherson*, 230.

139. Epstein, *Sister Aimee*, 116.

140. Sutton, *Aimee Semple McPherson*, 19.

tractive," he attributed her success to her "almost unbelievable . . . hypnotic powers [that played on] every chord of emotionalism that is left in human nature."[141] R. A. Torrey had her in mind when he criticized those leaders who exploit their "magnetic powers" with a propensity to "thrive on controversy and scandal."[142] Aimee was not lacking in scandal, with her three divorces and one alleged "kidnapping" in 1926, which most judged a cover for her affair with the operator of her KPSG radio station.

Space restricts a fuller coverage of Aimee and her ministry. Attention will be confined to the following outline. Some facts about her background will be presented, followed by an appraisal of her healing ministry. The modification of her views on the place and practice of healing will be examined, together with a consideration of the factors behind the reshaping of her standpoint. This will require a perusal of her position on the Fundamentalist-Pentecostal issue. Finally, her legacy will be appraised, both in the era of the flapper and beyond, to the point that one recent book (2013) perceives her as a candidate for a freshly defined twenty-first century apostolate.

Background

Aimee Elizabeth McPherson (*née* Kennedy) (1890–1944) grew up on a farm near Ingersoll, Ontario. Her father was a Methodist, while her mother was committed to the Salvation Army. She was converted through the Pentecostal ministry of a young Ulster immigrant, Robert Semple, who was born in Magherafelt, Co. Tyrone. They married in 1908, with Robert nine years her senior. The following year, the couple moved to Chicago, where both were ordained by William Durham before setting off for missionary work in China. Shortly after their arrival in Hong Kong, Robert died of malaria, leaving a pregnant widow, not yet twenty years old. Aimee Semple and her new-born daughter, Roberta Star, returned to New York to join her mother Minnie in the Salvation Army. Her short-lived marriage to a young entrepreneur Harold McPherson ended quietly in divorce in 1921 in the main because Harold expected a

Aimee cuts her Angelus birthday cake

conventional home life with their two children, his son Rolf and stepdaughter Roberta. Aimee had no aspiration to fulfil a conventional domestic role. Rather, the pull to evangelism never left her from her days with Robert, the only man she ever truly loved, and whose memory was a constant inspiration for her ministry.

141. Ibid., 36.

142. Robinson, *Divine Healing 1890–1906*, 81.

Assisted by Minnie, Aimee launched into an itinerant evangelistic and healing ministry in the years 1915–23. Between 1919 and 1922 she worked at times as an evangelist with the AoG; otherwise she was freelance. At the beginning she concentrated on revival meetings on the eastern seaboard from Maine to Florida. Late in 1918 she moved her base to Los Angeles and for the next four years she crossed the country repeatedly. Most of her crusades were a stunning success. Clergy of all denominations regularly offered their support, and their presence added luster to her platform. Those who sought Spirit-baptism were directed to smaller, separate meetings. Even so, fellow Pentecostals were disquieted that she did not permit the utterance gifts of prophecy and tongues in the larger meetings. On 1st January 1923 the 5,300-seated Angelus Temple, sited in Los Angeles, and modeled on the Royal Albert Hall, London, was dedicated. Much of the finance was garnered from the period of the great campaigns. The following year she opened her dedicated radio station, a step that made her the first woman to preach a sermon over the radio. The year 1925 saw the completion of a Bible School, which over the years prepared thousands of keen students for diverse forms of ministry. Many of them found their way into leadership of her new denomination, which was incorporated in 1927 as the International Church of the Foursquare Gospel. The notorious kidnapping storyline took place in 1926, which in a way was to prove the prelude to her troubles. Her defense against the charge of perpetrating a hoax of her disappearance sapped her energy and lost time before the charge was dropped. In 1930 she suffered a nervous breakdown, while her hapless four-year marriage to David Hutton ended in divorce in 1935. In the same decade she became estranged from both her mother and daughter Roberta. Despite her setbacks, she never entirely lost either her verve or the affection of multitudes of her plain-folk supporters.

The early seven years of Aimee's itinerant life brought to light her extraordinary gifts under optimal conditions. They were years of relative freedom, which allowed her to develop her potential as both evangelist and healer. She probably addressed four thousand audiences spaced from coast to coast, and traversed the north American continent six times in a second-hand car with her mother and two children in tow. She maintained contact with her followers through the pages of her monthly magazine *Bridal Call,* introduced in 1917. Opening any issue at random, the reader would regularly learn of conversions, Spirit-baptisms and healings. The January 1921 copy carried reports of her three-week mission in Montreal, which was sandwiched between her visits to Philadelphia. The mission in Montreal was held in St. Andrew's Presbyterian Church, and was initiated by the Pentecostal evangelist Charles Baker, who first came to the city in 1916. One of the two printed reports was contributed by "J. M. B.," the Art Editor of the Montreal *Standard*; the other report was supplied by Assistant Pastor C. Swann. The first writer intimated that, in his forty years of attending remarkable missions, none of them matched "such mighty outpourings of the Holy Spirit in such soul-cleansing and life-giving torrents" as during the McPherson revival.[143] He surmised that if each of the Montreal churches "could catch a fraction of the pentecostal power so remarkably manifested," the city would be regener-

143. J. M. B. "Miracles of Healing," 15.

ated. Pastor Swain was equally exhilarated. The city had been "stirred from its center to its circumference. The revival flame has swept the city like a cyclone."[144]

Aimee lacked a formal theological training. Such tuition as she received was at the hands of Robert Semple, who taught her that salvation and Spirit-baptism should be preached side by side, and was part of the normal Christian life. She saw it as her duty "to educate the church universal about the universality of Spirit-baptism with speaking in tongues."[145] Swann wrote that "never have we heard anyone bring forth the message of the Baptism in such clear, concise, convincing and convicting manner, as our dear Sister McPherson." A *Montreal Gazette* article reported that Aimee's address on Spirit-baptism "was delivered with a readiness and command of language and an earnestness of manner that it carried the audience by its very vehemence. There was no criticism of the churches and no denunciation of the world at large."[146] The basement of St. Andrew's acted as a prayer-room for those seeking Spirit-baptism, frequently during the time of the main service in the auditorium. The intensity of the process is caught in Baker's description: "Men and women rich and poor alike, with great tears rolling down their cheeks, some kneeling, others lying prostrate under the power of God, tarrying to be endowed with power from on high. God's presence was real the moment you entered the place, the air being charged as it were with His Spirit."[147]

Healing Ministry

Press reports played a major part in the dissemination of incidents of healing. Baker, the Pentecostal pastor who initiated the Montreal mission, beamed his delight that journalists were so taken by what they saw that they almost forget their task and found themselves among the many that were swept along with astonishment. Healing services were held on Thursdays, and at the final event hundreds of sick people packed the church, while outside policemen were at times almost overpowered by the rush. Inside, the piteous sight of the many blind, halt and maimed was tempered by "the sight of those who were completely delivered walking back and forth over the platform, praising God for what He had done." Even Aimee was surprised at the instantaneous nature of a few healings. One notable case was that of a woman burdened by the weight of a tumorous growth on one of her legs. While she was being prayed for, the tumor "suddenly disappeared as if it had been a punctured toy balloon."[148] Swain was able to report that "letters are pouring in daily of people claiming complete deliverance."[149] Aimee would appear to have got off lightly from harsh criticism during this particular mission; rather, to Baker's relief, ministers "confessed that this was nothing else than the real 'old time religion,'" which left them "feeling their need of more power." J. M. B. set such scenes in a wider context by recalling

---

144. Swann, "The Revival Flame in Montreal." Vol. 4.8, Jan. 1921, 16.

145. Michel, "Aimee Semple McPherson and the Reconfiguration of Methodism," 183.

146. Di Giacomo, "'Shot in the Arm' for French-Canadian Pentecostalism," 162.

147. *The Bridal Call*, Vol. 4.8, Jan. 1921, 13.

148. Ibid., 15.

149. Ibid., 17.

the church's long history of healing. He drew attention to its persistence in the Greek Orthodox Church, and the American Episcopal Church restoring healing "to the place it occupied in the Prayer Book of 1549."[150]

Epstein, in his *Sister Aimee* (1993), reflected that the healings associated with Aimee presented "a monstrous obstacle to scientific historiography [in which] there is no place in scholarly or scientific history for recurrent miracles."[151] In the case of Aimee, there was no solid evidence of fakery to undermine claims to healing. Not all were healed and there were those who relapsed within a short time, a circumstance that holds equally true about claims to conversion. So strong was the desire to expose fraudulence during her San Francisco mission in August 1921 that those prayed for were seized upon by journalistic hawks, who proceeded to grill them. Posing as *bona fide* investigators, they set out to destroy the credibility of claims to healing. Unbeknown to the organizing committee, a group of doctors from the American Medical Association investigated covertly some healings. Their report, disclosed a week later, confirmed that healing was "genuine, beneficial and wonderful."[152] This also was the drift of the plethora of press clippings, testimonials, and private correspondence that bore witness to healing. Aimee's personal accounts of the healings were presented with an absence of pretension, which contrasted with the sensationalized accounts spread by the press. As the young Anthony Quinn recollected from his view in the orchestra pit of the Angelus, her handling of the sick was distinctly low-key:

> Suddenly a figure with bright red hair and a flowing white gown walked out to the center of the stage. In a soft voice, almost a whisper, she said, "Brothers and sisters, is there anyone here who wants to be cured tonight?" Long lines formed to reach her. She stood center stage and greeted each one. One man said, "I can't see out of one eye." She asked, "Do you believe, brother?" And suddenly, the man cried, "Yes, sister, I can see, I can see!" And the audience went crazy. To a woman dragging herself across the stage on crutches she said, "Throw away that crutch!" Suddenly, the woman threw away her crutch and ran into Aimee's open arms.[153]

Little wonder that he exclaimed, "I left that service exhilarated, renewed."

Despite her renown as a healer, Aimee was not particularly comfortable with being cast in that role. It was not one she actively sought, and she became over time quite purposive in modifying its practice to accord with a deeper, more holistic, understanding of her ministry. The first early sign of change took place in Baltimore during her mission in the Lyric Theatre, December, 1919. She described its impact as "a turning point not only in my own ministry but in the history of the outpouring of Pentecostal power."[154] A number of happenings disturbed her. The mission was sponsored by a secular businessman as a commercial venture in renting a city theatre. Early on, the garish advertising, glowing press write-ups, invitations to society grandees, and the push to drum up ministerial

150. Ibid., 15.

151. Epstein, *Sister Aimee*, 111.

152. Ibid., 233.

153. Quinn, Anthony. *Original Sin*, 152.

154. McPherson, *This Is That*, 179.

support all unsettled her. She confessed, "I was never so frightened in all my life. Taking one look at the throng of sick people, I ran down the stairs, buried my face in a chair in the corner and began to weep: 'Oh Lord . . . there are all those sick folks upstairs and thine handmaiden never felt so helpless!'"[155] With her reputation as a healer preceding her, public expectation was high, but equally failure hovered in the wings. Success would be attributed to the glory of God; failure would be heaped on her. It was an unenviable position in which to be placed, and not immediately assuaged by what "seemed a strange message from the Lord, and for a time I could not understand it." The message revealed, "You are not fishing for minnows; you are fishing for whales."[156]

It soon became clear who and what the "whales" were. She was elated to report that "night after night, ministers, Doctors of Divinity, Jewish rabbis, medical doctors, and the best people of the city sat in the orchestra and boxes of this their finest theatre for which we were paying over three hundred dollars a day rental, in order to 'fish for whales.'"[157] The problem was that she was regarded as a Pentecostal evangelist, and it became clear that the two terms were in certain ways incompatible if she was to fulfil her calling. An incident in the theatre threatened to get out of hand when a woman walked towards the platform shouting that she wanted to speak. Pentecostals in the audience would have assumed that the woman was seeking to exercise a spiritual gift, whether prophecy or tongues/ interpretation. For Aimee, this was the turning point when her resolve was about to be tested. She started the congregation singing, and called on her team to remove the woman. Her fear was that for non-Pentecostals such a scene would only lend substance to the commonly held poor image of Pentecostalism. As she put it: the impact of her preaching would only diminish "if the devil can but make some misguided soul rise and do some foolish, fanatical, outlandish thing under the pretence of the Spirit's leadership and power."[158]

Aimee recognized that while Baltimore numbered "Pentecostal saints, precious people" among its residents, there were a few people who were "largely given to fleshly manifestations [that] had brought bitter reproach upon the work." Their training had led them to believe that "wherever there was power there must be continuous noise and loud outcry. . . . Our task, therefore, was to represent these glorious Bible truths in such a way as would win the respect and confidence of the churches and people."[159] This, for her, was the time to deflect from narrow-minded minnows of overheated Pentecostalism, and aim for the big catch of whales within mainline churches. She was pleased that the ministers supporting the mission had gently laid those under the power on the floor; and "bade us not to worry as they had often seen such things in the earlier days of Methodism, in the United Brethren, and other churches."[160] Those prayed for sometimes began to speak in tongues, and the fact that the nearest person near to them was a denominational minister meant "they could not blame us." She was assured that denominational Pentecostalism

155. Ibid., 175.
156. Ibid., 174.
157. Ibid.
158. Ibid., 177.
159. Ibid., 174.
160. Ibid., 175.

did not have a monopoly on charismatic experience. Once, when asked by a journalist if she was a member of the AoG, she replied, "No, I am not a member of that sect. . . . I have done everything in my power to curb the apparent wildness of the Pentecostal believers."[161] Her sights were set high, nothing less than a drive "to reinvigorate twentieth-century mainstream churches by embodying the religion of their forbearers before their very eyes."[162]

This task Aimee undertook by aligning herself with the expositional preaching style and strong biblicism of conservative Baptists and Methodists, but at the same time assisting them to overcome their emotional inhibitions in worship, and maintaining an openness to the charismatic dimension. At various times in her itinerant period, she was formally accredited to minister in the AoG, as well as holding a Methodist exhorter's license and a Baptist preaching license, requirements that made her acceptable to some of the more fundamentalist-minded members of the latter two communions. Even so, she retained her Pentecostal mindset, but pared it down to its core, at the same time moulding a less heated, more ecumenical form of evangelicalism that, as she told fellow ministers, carried a concern for "the passer-by, the butterfly, the atheist, the society girl, the movie people and the sinner."[163]

Modification of View on Healing

Her experience in Melbourne, Australia, in late 1922 revealed her newly honed priorities. Some healings had taken place, but "the Lord gave us a very decided check in spirit" not to continue with the healing ministry because of the undue weight given to it in the advertising of the meetings prior to her arrival. The conviction grew on her that the battle here had to be won on "the merits of the Word and Blood." On the few occasions during the mission when she was disposed to break the "invisible restraint" on healing, the Spirit hindered and revealed the greater emphasis to be placed on the other three of her Fourfold Gospel, viz., Jesus as Savior, Baptizer in the Spirit, and Coming King. Earlier in the same year, she had conducted a short mission in Arkansas City. The local newspaper touched on the way the congregation had been enthralled by her talk, adding that "the sick waited for the moment when she would pray for them alone." It was not to be. At the end of her address, Aimee asked for a show of hands of those who wanted to become a Christian. Five hundred raised their hands. When she retreated from the scene, the sick ones were stunned. "Over the faces of the sick," the report continued, "unfolded an expression that would have aroused the sympathy of a stone-hearted person."[164] Evidently, Aimee was exhausted, but the Aimee of old was known to pray for hours and, with short breaks only, was able to weather her exhaustion. Her refusal to pray in this situation probably reflected her growing apprehension about the nature and role of healing in her ministry.

161. Sutton, "Refrigerator," 175.

162. Ibid., 173.

163. Sutton, *Aimee Semple McPherson*, 44 & 77.

164. Barfooot, *Aimee Semple McPherson*, 345.

Aimee did not bring any new insights to the theology of divine healing as borne out by her only book, *Divine Healing Sermons* (1923), which was devoted to the topic.[165] Healing was regarded as part of "God's great plan of redemption, salvation for the soul and divine healing for the body in holy matrimony."[166] She believed conversion to Christ was paramount, seeing it at the necessary antecedent to faith for healing: divine healing is but "the handmaiden of the Gospel." She explained: "Many have been not a little surprised and filled with questioning, when, in our meetings we have made a complete surrender to Jesus, a change of heart and a bright salvation experience, among the conditions under which we would pray for the healing of the sick and afflicted.[167] Healing she regarded, was antithetic to any attitude that was little more than the plea: Heal my broken body, so that I may go out to better enjoy the world; heal my eyes that I can the better see the moving pictures; open my deaf ears that I may enjoy the devil's jokes and gossip; heal my crippled hands that I can play cards or work for my own selfish ends; my feet that I might dance and run in worldly paths,"—all activities anathema to Holiness fundamentalists.[168] Once converted, the sufferer was advised, "Come with radiant, active faith . . . nothing doubting and you will feel His mighty hand upon your life."[169]

Aimee's attitude to doctors and medicine was at times raised with her. Her answer was to praise the profession, telling that many doctors were among her "most blessed Christian friends; some kneel and pray with their patients. . . . Splendid physicians and surgeons have sat with us on the platform in our meetings, have brought patients for prayer, and written letters praising God that He had accomplished that which their skill and power could not do."[170] She took the view that doctors should be the last people to oppose the power of Christ. Among those she prayed for were people whose condition had worsened through mistaken treatment by doctors. In two cases, one had lost eyesight, in another a man all his toes, both treated by ill-judged medication. Dope addicts were frequently prayed for, their condition caused by constant hypodermic injections following an operation. The prevailing message of *Divine Healing Sermons* is that the believer should seek God for healing, while absent is any advice that would dissuade them from seeking medical help. With regard to her own health, she did not abstain from medical intervention. Her death at the age of fifty-four was attributed to an overdose of sleeping pills to help overcome her chronic insomnia.

Aimee's change of mind about healing continues to intrigue her biographers. Barfoot thinks that although the healing side of her ministry had made her famous, it increasingly was the one part of her ministry she found least appealing. In April 1922, when she was asked at a pre-campaign press conference if she planned any all-day healing services, she

165. The book was printed on the same presses as the *Fundamentals,* the twelve-volume booklets that were orchestrated and financed by Lyman Stewart (d. 1923) maintained a neutral stance towards the growing influence of Pentecostalism, particularly McPherson.

166. McPherson,. *Divine Healing Sermons,* 34.

167. Ibid., 60.

168. Ibid., 61.

169. Ibid., 64.

170. Ibid., 93.

protested: "I say very definitely, right now, that I do not wish the lame, the halt, the blind, and the cripples to crowd my meetings. That is the portion of my work to which I am least attracted."[171] It was an impulsive remark expressive of a deep-seated frustration, but it needs to be interpreted in context. All-day exclusive healing services made up entirely of the sick, except in special cases, never featured greatly in her campaigns, and even then were limited to distinct days and times. Even in such circumstances, the gospel was preached first, followed by the healing line. This created a problem, which must have exercised her in that some made conversion a cover for joining the healing line.

In terms of results, the healings associated with her were among the most impressive in late modern history, yet, in Barfoot's assessment, hers "was a spiritual gift that increasingly mystified and baffled her as well as wore her out—a gift she could not quite comprehend or understand. It was thrilling, yet an uncomfortable gift and burden. Always some were healed, but many were not. With the passing of time she would be known more as a preacher than a healer. For Aimee, in the end, soul-winning rather than healing was "the one big business of the church."[172] To those who thought of her only as "the miracle woman," her reply was to deny the appellation and then primly put them in their place. Indulging in a bit of mock humility, Aimee maintained she was "only a simple little body whom the Lord has called from a milk-pail on a farm, bidding her tell the good news of a Savior who lives and loves and answers prayers."[173] Healing remained part of her ministry, but it was played down. She was content to have other ministers share in the prayers for healing. Sometimes the healing services were apportioned to assistants, convened apart from the main evangelistic meeting. By early 1922, she had begun to interest clergy and laymen in the idea that they, like her, had the same privilege to pray for the sick. Following her San Francisco campaign, she left behind a group of regular clergy whom she encouraged to put into practice her theology of "the Great I AM."[174]

Taking the Middle Path

In the era of the Modernist-Fundamentalist controversy, Aimee was a reconciler though not with Modernism. Reflecting her fundamentalist background, she never wavered from her schooldays' aversion to evolutionary theory and the exercise of "higher criticism" to biblical studies. Her energy was channelled more into playing a mediating role within mainstream conservative Protestantism. When she was asked to explain her own position, she often used the analogy of walking in the middle of a road with banks on either side, which carried the label Formalism and Fanaticism, otherwise expressed as between "the Refrigerator and the Wild-fire."[175] Hers was not an easy option, especially as her main opposition came from the two sides with which she had much in common—harder-edged fundamentalists and over-the-top Pentecostals. The fundamentalists numbered among

---

171. Bahr. *Least of All Saints*, 168. This quote is without attribution to a source.

172. Barfoot, *Aimee Semple McPherson*, 346.

173. Epstein, *Sister Aimee*, 223.

174. Dicken, "Take Up Thy Bed," 142.

175. Sutton, *Aimee Semple McPherson*, 44.

them dispensationalists, stern upholders of cessationism. For them, it was anathema to stretch the virtue of the atonement to healing, because it seemed to impose on God's will, and it failed to deal with the problem of unanswered prayer for healing. A doctrinaire mindset and a legalistic spirit characterized some churches she singled out as "cold, backslidden and dead." On the other hand, she shuddered at the "wild-mirth-provoking, ridiculous, jumping, screaming, egotistical, unteachable, impractical, reproach-bringing something which some mistakenly call 'Pentecostal.'"[176] It is clear that with Aimee any idea of a clean-cut separation of Fundamentalism from Pentecostalism must be queried. At grass-roots level, as a result of her endeavors, thousands of non-Pentecostal churches and people eagerly sought to be involved in Pentecostal revivals.

The events that gave her the greatest satisfaction were those similar to the three-day conference held in Trinity Episcopal Church, Oakland, California, which aimed to integrate evangelistic outreach in the Golden Bay area. Seventy-five denominational ministers and evangelists were enrolled on the first day. Among those addressing the conference were representatives from the Congregational, Baptist, Methodist, Presbyterian and Episcopal churches. Included in the topics discussed were "The Ministry of the Spirit" and "The Ministry of Healing." Attention was directed to the gifts and fruit of the Holy Spirit. Times of prayer saw a rector weeping and praying with heartfelt earnestness, and a Presbyterian pastor praying that "unbelief, higher criticism, worldliness and pride may be swept from all of the churches of the land, and the old-time power of the Holy Spirit falls as it did on the day of Pentecost."[177] What is novel about her grand stratagem was her attempt to make the old-time religion palatable to the sensual tenor of the age. If it had not been for her reputation becoming sullied by the innuendo surrounding her disappearance in 1926, her project might have come to greater fulfillment.

Legacy

Aimee's legacy has been acknowledged in a number of quarters. Blumhofer holds that Aimee's place in the roll of American evangelists is secure, and solidly within the American revival tradition. One of her least noticed legacies is to be found in her native Canada. Her missions to Montreal and Quebec in the early 1920 made a lasting impact in the francophone province of Quebec. Michael Di Giacomo summed up her contribution arising from the Montreal mission in 1922: "[It] not only gave wings to the [Pentecostal] movement in Quebec but reversed the tide of the French-Canadian evangelical movement to make it one that has experienced continual growth ever since. . . . [She] encouraged her converts to join the church of their choice, and did not turn her AoG membership into an icon. In other words, she was preaching Pentecost and not Pentecostal denominationalism and sectarianism."[178]

Aimee's forte lay in the way she seized on the techno-cultural fixations of the time, exploiting them—radio, theatre, film, and music—as instruments of revival. She demon-

176. McPherson, "The Narrow Line," 10.

177. McPherson, *This Is That*, 492.

178. Michel, "Aimee Semple McPherson," 181.

strated that even the most fundamentalist faith could be enlivened by their usage. Her use of the media placed her at the cutting edge of the evangelical quest to keep the presentation of the gospel robustly effectual. Among her publicity coups was the scattering of thousands of flyers from an airplane, also her invitation to watch her pray for the healing of a sick lion at the zoo. Her illustrated sermons were exemplars of stagecraft. Animals were frequently used. In one incident, a camel was directed to squeeze through a narrow gate built on the stage to illustrate the message of the eye of the needle pericope (Matt 19:24). Aimee unburdened the beast of a number of bags, carrying labels such as "Worldly Pleasure" and "Indifference to the Poor," until all the burdens were removed to allow the camel to pass through the gate. All this effort engaged a small group of artists, electricians, decorators, and carpenters who built the sets for each Sunday's service. An orchestra enlivened all services with its repertoire, which stretched to playing arrangements of sacred operas.

Civic recognition was given when the Angelus Temple entered floats in the *Tournament of Roses* parade in Pasadena, California each year.[179] In a number of ways, Aimee was the harbinger of the post-war Charismatic movement. Her drive to dispel the crass side of manifestations in some contemporary Pentecostalism, which marked the lowly social status of some adherents, was pitched to enable the merits of its doctrinal singularities to be given biblically-reasoned consideration. She proved it was possible for Christians from all social strata to possess the power and grace of the charismatic gifts. Events have shown that such an outcome is clearly attainable. The sociologist, Margaret Poloma, compared a sample of 1,275 AoG members with a national sample of Protestants and found that members had slightly higher than average earnings and were more likely to be college graduates.

Though, in many ways, the years after 1927 are considered to be anticlimactic, it would be incomplete to neglect the widening range of her activities beyond her commitment to the Angelus Temple. During the 1930s Great Depression her commissary (food bank) met the physical needs of over 1.5 million people of all social classes. She became politically engaged in the fight for higher wages and against organized crime. Her visit to Europe in 1936 alerted her enough to publicize the dangers associated with the rise of Stalin, Hitler and Mussolini. When America entered World War II she actively participated in raising money for war bonds. Sutton evaluates Aimee's influence as follows:

> Her blend of faith and activism marked the beginning of Pentecostalism's advance from separatism to engagement, from the margins of American Protestantism to the mainstream . . . while her defiance of traditional gender norms broke new ground for women. McPherson's integration of politics with faith established a model that subsequent Pentecostals have used to move themselves from the outer reaches of sectarian separatism to the inner circles of power. . . . Indeed, from her location in Hollywood, Aimee Semple McPherson reshaped and redefined the old-time religion in the United States, in effect resurrecting Christian America.[180]

179. Blumhofer, *McPherson*, 391.
180. Epstein, *McPherson*, 280.

Two of the most prominent Pentecostals to become involved in political life in modern times have been Pat Robertson and John Ashcroft. Roberson, a Yale graduate, unsuccessfully sought the Republican nomination for the presidency of the USA in 1988, even though he had the support of three million registered voters who signed to support his candidacy financially and with prayer. Ashcroft, the son and grandson of Pentecostal pastors, was a Senator in Congress before he was confirmed USA Attorney-General in 2001.

Nothing became the ministry of Aimee more than her relationship with the girl evangelists who operated in the flapper era of the 1920s, for whom she was the inspiration. Flappers were the new breed of young Western women in the Jazz Age who flouted the social and sexual mores of the period. In a decade fascinated by the quirky and novel, the involvement of children in activities that older generations had assigned to adults became acceptable. Child prodigies performed in concert halls, while others lectured on atheism and evolution, "shaking their fists at God with the same vigor that little girl evangelists shook their fist at the devil."[181] Never out of step with the times, Aimee established a school to train teenagers in their hundreds—400 in 1923—over the summer months, with the initial intent to evangelize their own generation, only for them to be snapped up for adult meetings. Among other lecturers were Dr Lilian Yeomans, who offered classes on divine healing, and Frank Thompson, a retired Methodist minister, famed for his Thompson *Chain Reference Bible* (1908).[182] Readers were advised by Yeomans to color in biblical references to healing in her Bible study course. As shown earlier, Stratton was greatly impressed by little Uldine Utley, to the extent of having her preach at Madison Square Garden to 14,000 people. Some of the more promising students were dubbed by the press "flapper evangelists," who even arch-critic Bob Shuler admitted were "swaying large audiences."

A number of girl evangelists practiced divine healing, sometimes making it a regular feature of their campaigns. Uldine Utley, at age eleven declared: "The main points of my commission are three in number: Salvation, divine healing and baptism of the Holy Spirit." In her magazine, *Petals from the Rose of Sharon*, there were regularly reports on prayer for the sick at her campaigns. Eleven-year-old Mary Ann Weitgraven, the daughter of an ordained minister, prayed for the sick at every service, with her father to support her. In general, it was those girls brought up in the Pentecostal tradition who made healing a part of their ministry. Since their audiences were mostly interdenominational, speaking in tongues was usually avoided.

By the 1930s the flapper phenomenon was beginning to fade. An article in the AoG *Pentecostal Evangel* displayed distaste for the fashion of trying to attract the unsaved, not by the power of the gospel, but by "the bizarre." The writer was thankful that the trend was moving away from "a fad" or "craze," quite dependent on "crowd curiosity." While the majority of girls continued their ministry into adulthood, Kathryn Kuhlman for one, others either married a preacher and combined their ministries or remained unmarried and

---

181. Robinson, "Out of the Mouths of Babes," 37.

182. Yeomans was a qualified physician who became seriously addicted to prescription drugs in an effort to relieve stress. Detoxification programmes and Christian Science failed, and her healing came through the ministry of J. A. Dowie.

often teamed up with another woman evangelist. The remainder dropped out of public life. Udine Utley in her early twenties was ordained in the Methodist Episcopal Church. Her marriage to Eugene Langkop, a footwear salesman, ended in divorce. She died in 1995 in a mental health institution.

Hirsch and Catchim in a recent book named a heterogeneous group of famous Christians, whom, improbable as it would seem, they consider have something in common. Those named are: St. Paul, St. John, St. Patrick, Count Zinzendorff, John Wesley, William and Catherine Booth, and Aimee Semple McPherson.[183] The authors selected those named as representative exemplars of those who, in their generation, played the role of an apostle to the wider church. The authors set out to make a case for revisiting the concept of an apostolate, which is fitted to meet the stiff challenges of the twenty-first century. Those named above, they maintain, had the essential attributes needed to fulfil the work of an apostle for coming generations. The qualities that they suggest are to be found in part or whole in the people listed, and remain of lasting importance. They include: a missional impulse; a focus on expansion; style that is adventurous, prepared to take risk; decisive, strategic leadership style; over-riding concern in decision-making, directed to increase of capacity for mission; planning for expansion within and beyond cultural boundaries; maintaining the health of the movement by ensuring consistency with core ideas.[184] A good case can be made for the girlhood milk-maid from Ontario to feature within the apostolate, at least on the terms delineated in *The Permanent Revolution.* Her arch-critic, Robert Shuler, after her death almost did, when he wrote: "Personally, I can never understand why God used Aimee to start such a movement. But I can easily understand why He is using the army of preachers and workers who will now carry on. They are nearer akin to the army with which Wesley started than we Methodists would rejoice to concede."

---

183. Hirsch, *Permanent Revolution,* xxvi & 52.

184. Ibid., 51–52

Conclusion

THE ONE BIG ISSUE left to be addressed is how central is the healing message to contemporary Christianity on the global scale. If the opinion of the learned Calvinist theologian, B. B. Warfield, is accepted, the status of contemporary divine healing is negligible. In his book devoted to the subject, *Counterfeit Miracles* (1918), he wrote: "Had any miracles perchance occurred beyond the apostolic age, they would be without significance; mere occurrences with no universal meaning." The ground on which he reached this conclusion was the cessationist position: "Because all revelation and redemption alike are summed up in (Christ), it would be inconceivable that either revelation *or its accompanying signs* should continue after the completion of that great revelation with its accrediting works."[1]

In his own way, as a boy at the age of ten, C. S. Lewis reached a similar conclusion on the death of his mother. When her case (of cancer) was pronounced hopeless he remembered what he had been taught, that "prayers offered in faith would be granted. I accordingly set myself to produce by will-power a firm belief that my prayers for her recovery would be successful. . . . When nevertheless she died I shifted my ground and worked myself into a belief that there was to be a miracle. The interesting thing is that my disappointment produced no results beyond itself. The thing hadn't worked, but I was used to things not working, and I thought no more about it." Her death was a blow that removed from him "all settled happiness, all that was tranquil and reliable. . . . It was sea and islands now; the great continent had sunk like Atlantis." It was with the insight of Christian maturity that he came to recognize that in his boyhood mental picture of the miracle he was seeking, God had appeared "neither as Savior or Judge, but merely as a magician," who would restore the *status quo*.[2]

To show that Warfield's view is contestable, and Lewis' sense of failure is not inescapable, is the substance of this chapter. The sequence of coverage is as follows: the changing distribution of global Christianity, and the related large numerical increase in Renewal (or Pentecostal/Charismatic) believers; the factors accounting for the growth of Pentecostalism; the role of healing based on representative studies taken from Latin America, Africa, and Asia. It will become clear that some of the major changes in global Christianity would not be to the taste of Warfield, who was dismissive of early Pentecostalism. For him, the "Welsh excesses" of the 1905 Revival were "as nothing,

---

1. Warfield, *Counterfeit Miracles*, 27–28 (emphasis added).
2. Lewis, *Surprised by Joy*, 22–23.

however, to what befell . . . in the summer of 1907 (*sic*) when the so-called Pentecost Movement shook with its full force."[3]

CHANGES WITHIN GLOBAL CHRISTIANITY

Changing World Distribution of Christian Believers (Percentage of Christians rounded)

	1900	2010	2050
Africa	1	22	33
Asia	4	15	19
Latin America	11	23	21
Oceania	1	0.1	1
Europe	69	26	17
North America	14	13	10
	100	100	100
Population (millions)	558m	2,291m	3,188m

The table above indicates the massive change in the distribution of Christian believers among the continents between 1900 and the estimated figures for 2050. It becomes clear that today they are more evenly distributed around the world than they have been at any other time in the past 2,000 years. This greater parity has been brought about by a major transfer of Christian numbers away from Europe and North America, the "North," and toward Africa, Asia, and Latin America, the "South." While Europe and North America remain major players in terms of their wealth, missionary-sending past, Christian and educational heritage, they no longer remain unchallenged. Alternative cores have sprung up among them Brazil, Nigeria, and South Korea, with others waiting at their edges. If present trends continue to 2050, the predominance of the South will become more marked. Africa will have around one-third of all Christians, with Latin America overtaking Europe for second place. Rapidly secularizing Europe is set to show the most dramatic decline from seven-tenths to less than two-tenths of the world Christian population. By 2050, only about one-fifth of the world's Christians will be white, if Latin American Hispanics are excluded.

With the centre of gravity for Christendom now centered in the western half of sub-Saharan Africa, the era of a dominant western Christianity has passed within present lifetime. It is a situation that raises major issues for the future of Christianity. Many of the newer churches of the South, as Philip Jenkins points out, "preach deep personal faith and communal orthodoxy, mysticism, and puritanism, all founded on clear scriptural authority. They preach messages that, to a Westerner, appear simplistically charismatic, visionary, and apocalyptic. In this thought-world, prophecy is an everyday reality, while faith-healing, exorcism, and dream-visions are all fundamental parts of religious sensibility. For better or worse, the dominant churches of the future could have much in common

3. Warfield, *Perfectionism*, 333.

with those of medieval or early modern European times."[4] Evidence of conflict in the offing can be seen over the issues surrounding gender and sexuality within the Anglican Communion. With a growing acceptance in the more liberal West of gay-marriage and the ordination of women as bishops, Anglicanism faces the possibility of schism over such matters. In the words of a Kenyan archbishop, "Our understanding of the Bible is different from them. We are two different churches."

The other notable feature in the changing face of global Christianity lies most recently within the Prosperity Gospel constituency. Today fewer than 5 percent of Christians in Europe are Renewalist (Pentecostal/Charismatic) but more than 25 percent of all Christians in Africa are Renewalist, rising to more than 30 percent in Asia. Pentecostalism has been described as the most successful social movement of the past century, the same period that witnessed the demise of Communism and Fascism as global ideologies. The rate at which this has happened has left the churches largely unprepared for the challenge of absorbing the new influx. In Africa, Renewalist Christianity is spreading faster than Islam, expanding twice as fast as Roman Catholicism and three times as fast as other forms of Protestantism. Almost one out of every three Renewalist Christians in the world is an African. The second largest grouping is found in Latin America, with Asia close behind. Renewalists on the 2010 figures constitute 8.5 percent of the world's total population—larger than the number of strict Buddhists—and 26.7 percent of the world Christian population. At 13 percent, evangelicals are short of half that number.[5] By 2050, Renewal will probably embrace well over one third of all Christians. With such unparalleled growth, the future of divine healing being preached and practiced to all corners of the earth is assured.

Key Factors in the Growth of Pentecostalism

The Pentecostal/Charismatic movement has multidimensional reasons for its proliferation. Complete agreement about the nature and significance of the factors contributing to such rapid expansion is not possible because of the sheer diversity of socio-cultural environments contributing to its advance. The ideological lens through which researchers survey the topic is another consideration. In any case, Pentecostalism is not a monolithic construct, but is better considered as an array of variant Pentecostalisms. Even so, it is possible to identify those features that are shared across the global movement. Matthias Deininger, in his research travels, found the service in a Pentecostal church in Soweto, South Africa, reminded him of one he had attended in Tampa, Florida. Despite the minor differences in their intensity of experiencing the Holy Spirit—Tampa stressing holy laughter; Soweto healing through exorcism—"the emphasis and centrality given to the presence of the Holy Spirit were alike." Likewise, his visits to Indonesia and Singapore allowed him to observe similar patterns of Pentecostal worship. In general, a common Pentecostal spirituality can be detected around the world, be it Chinese Pentecostal manifestations in Sydney, among migrant African Pentecostals in London or Philippine Charismatics

---

4. Jenkins, *Next Christendom*, 10.

5. Anon. "Demographic Portrait of Renewalists." Pew Research Center. Online.

in Hong Kong.[6] The movement is a good example of a global and localized ("glocalized") religion, with its ability to adapt itself to diffuse local conditions while maintaining its distinctive hallmarks.

Before the rise of historical enquiries, sociological studies used class analysis and theories of deprivation to understand the movement's appeal. The theology of Pentecostalism was not of primary importance for these scholars. The prevailing view was that Pentecostalism flourished because it compensated for its adherents' lowly social status, typifying it as a religion of the oppressed. The majority of converts were seen as people at the lower end of the social scale, many displaced from an impoverished rural background, and forced by circumstance to seek work in crowded mega-cities, only to find themselves trapped in poverty and reduced to a state of anomie. For them, Pentecostalism offered "ecstatic escape, hope for millennial redress, and an egalitarian environment in which everyone is eligible for the highest rewards (i.e., salvation and gifts of the Spirit.)"[7] From a more positive perspective, it is not that anomie and alienation do not exist, or are labels rather than explanatory in substance. The problem is that as concepts they are not smart enough, and so explain "too much too soon."[8]

Wacker, too, warned of a tendency to reductionism in earlier studies of Pentecostalism, which aimed to explain its appeal. Any interpretations that attribute religious enthusiasm to the anxieties surrounding status and multiple deprivations "almost always reduce the enthusiast in some way. Accounts of this sort effectively suggest that enthusiasts are not fully responsible agents, that they do what they do not because they rationally choose it, but because they are in some sense victims. This diminishes the dignity of the choice and, more important, strips away accountability for the choice."[9] Also the statistics show that this viewpoint is not universally true. The Pew Report in 2006 found that those with lower incomes were not necessarily more prevalent within Renewalist groups. For example, in Brazil, Kenya, Nigeria, South Africa, the regions of India surveyed, the Philippines and South Korea, Renewalist populations did not include a disproportionately high number of lower-income people. In Nigeria, Pentecostals are much more likely than the public as a whole to have obtained at least some post-secondary education.[10]

For the anthropologist, Joel Robbins, foremost of the reasons for the rapid growth of Pentecostalism is the paramount importance its churches place on evangelization. Spirit-baptism is regarded as the source of power for witness to others. The Spirit is expected to sustain and direct evangelists and missionaries to go out in faith, asking for no funding, and inspired to succeed by building churches supported by tithes. An egalitarian ethos pervades much of the movement, based on the assumption that the gifting of the Spirit in its diversity is accessible to all for use in multifarious ministries. With emphasis placed on each adherent to advance in Spirit-gifting, members are encouraged to serve in some capacity. In the AoG church in Belem, Brazil, Chesnut found that almost three-quarters of

6. Deininger, *Global Pentecostalism,* 1–2.

7. Robbins,. "Globalization," 124.

8. Martin, "Undermining the Old Paradigms," 18–38.

9. Wacker, "Taking Another Look," 19.

10. Anon. "Spirit and Power." Pew Research Center. Online.

his informants held a designated role in the church, with women only about ten percent below the level of men.[11] Another researcher, Emilio Willems, marveled that in Brazil and Chile after a full working day, more than 5,000 had found the time and energy to defy the distance and the appalling transportation system to attend the services.[12] An egalitarian rationale drives its outreach to the poor and marginalized, and within its churches to break down the barriers raised by class, race, gender or ethnicity. One of the assumptions made is that leaders do not need a costly, academic education to preach or form a congregation. Training received through the apprenticeship of working as a street pastor, as happens in Chile, ensures that preaching is never above the heads of listeners, nor empathy with their plight glossed over.

Where Pentecostalism distinguishes itself from other forms of Christianity is its openness to engage with the spirit world. The late, eminent Nigerian scholar, Ogbu Kalu, wrote of that world in its African context: "Affliction is a pivotal issue in the theology of the African primal world. . . . It has been shown through a survey of the Igbo of southeastern Nigeria that 615 spirits occupy their religious ardor, though different culture theatres in Africa prioritize which deities are central for their needs."[13] Nigerian politicians are not immune from attempts to manipulate the spirits to procure their ambitions. In 2013, the outspoken poet/playwright and Nobel Laureate, Wole Soyinka, spoke on this custom when he stated: "Give me the name of any Head of State who hasn't been consulting marabouts [Muslim mystics] and prophets and so on, sacrificing goats, animals in the dead of night to remain in office and so on."[14] Pentecostals, taking from the New Testament their warrant of a spirit world portrayed as antagonistic to the kingdom of God [Matt 12:27–35; Acts 8:9–11; Eph 6:12], also believe in such a world. Where they differ from animistic cultures rests on their affirmation that the Holy Spirit has been given to destroy the works of the evil one, and bring release of the captives.

Harvey Cox identifies Pentecostalism with a recovery of primal spirituality, comprising primal speech (tongues), primal piety (trances, dreams, and visions), and primal hope (miracles, supernatural interventions, and the *Parousia*). What was unleashed at Azusa Street was a kind of "primal spirituality that had been all but suffocated by centuries of western Christian moralism and rationality" that has now re-emerged with meteoric thrust. Its resurfacing in cultures not embedded in Enlightenment rationality helps to explain why the movement has gathered speed apace.[15] It can incorporate into its spirituality various kinds of local customs, beliefs, and rituals. Thus, African Pentecostalism is in "constant interaction with the African spirit world much in the same way that Latin American Pentecostalism conceptually encounters folk Catholicism and Brazilian spiritism, and Korean Pentecostals have made use of shamanistic traditions in their culture."[16]

11. Chesnut, *Born Again in Brazil*, 115.
12. Bomann, *Faith in the Barrios*, 96–97.
13. Kalu, *African Pentecostalism*, 177–78.
14. Agazue, *The Role of a Culture of Superstition*, 48.
15. Cox, *Fire from Heaven*, 101–2.
16. Kärkkäinen, .*Pneumatology*, 172.

The globalization of Pentecostalism has inevitably brought about contact with other religions. This has raised questions about how Pentecostals should engage with other faiths, whether at the two extreme positions of conflict or dialogue. A number of Pentecostal theologians of religions are supportive of the proposition that dialogue is both legitimate and laudable. Indeed, Kärkkäinen maintains that Pentecostalism's primal spirituality is a wonderful asset because of its marked similarities with Hinduism and Buddhism in their resistance to modernity's "reductionist, over-rationalistic, and at times dualistic worldview."[17] He foresees the missiological rewards of exploring "the meaning of suffering and the release from its power in the Christian and Buddhist traditions for doing Pentecostal mission in a Buddhist environment."[18]

THE CONTRIBUTION OF DIVINE HEALING

Renewalist Christianity has become the major carrier of divine healing in today's world. The Pew Forum 10-Country Survey of Pentecostalism, titled *Spirit and Power* (2006) singled out divine healing as the feature that distinguished Renewalists from all other Christians.[19] The Survey found in every one of the ten countries, large majorities of Pentecostals say they have experienced or witnessed a divine healing of an illness or injury. Indeed, with the exception of the USA and South Korea, more than 70 percent of Pentecostals claim to have experienced or witnessed miraculous cures. Such experiences also are fairly well-known among Charismatics. In South Korea, charismatics are just as likely to have experienced divine healing as Pentecostals. In three other countries, Guatemala, Kenya and India, majorities of charismatics say they are familiar with divine healings. Though non-Renewalist Christians have generally less experience of divine healing, yet more than half of this group in Nigeria and India say they have experienced or witnessed miraculous cures. For many Renewalists, knowledge of the supernatural extends to exorcisms. This is particularly true of Pentecostals in Latin America and Africa, where large majorities in every country surveyed have witnessed evil spirits being driven out. First-hand familiarity with exorcisms is less common among Pentecostals in Asia and the USA.

In 2000, *Christianity Today* reported that in the rapidly growing church in Nepal 40–60 percent of the Nepalese Christians had become believers as the outcome of a miraculous healing.[20] Further growth is to be expected as the Pentecostal message becomes increasingly globalized through satellite television and the internet. West African healing evangelists are noted for saturating private TV and radio stations with back-to-back programming. Dag Heward-Mills, the African-born grandson of a Swiss missionary is famed as the "doctor-turned-healer." As founder of a Ghanaian megachurch with numerous branches in Africa and Europe, he has established an organization named the "Jesus

---

17. Kärkkäinen, "Pentecostal Pneumatology." In Kärkkäinnen, *Spirit in the World,* 179.

18. Richie, *Toward a Pentecostal Theology,* 111–12.

19. Anon. *Spirit and Power.* Online. The countries are: USA; Brazil, Chile, Guatemala; Kenya, Nigeria, S. Africa, India, Philippines, and South Korea.

20. Noll, *New Shape of World Christianity,* 140.

Healing Crusade," announced as "a ministry that carries the gospel of Jesus Christ to the world through massive evangelistic crusades accompanied by healing signs and wonders." The website claims that "these crusades present the full gospel in powerful preaching, divine healing, free medical outreaches [and] distribution of clothes to the poor."[21]

Latin America: Brazil

BRAZIL (percent)	Witnessed divine healings	Received divine revelations	Experienced/ witnessed exorcisms
All Christians	38	35	34
Pentecostals	77	64	80
Charismatics	31	28	30
Other Christians	32	29	26

Andrew Chesnut, a leading research specialist in Latin American religion, has highlighted the place of divine healing in the growth of Protestantism in Latin America. In fact, it is the central emphasis of his whole analysis. Research findings in Chile and Argentina respectively found that a majority of converts had come to faith through healing. In Haiti, three-quarters of the Pentecostals in one survey had converted through healing, either their own or that of a relative. Haitian demand for faith healing is explained partly as a reaction to Voodoo, whose *lwas* (spirits) give vent to their resentment against Christian believers by inflicting them with illness. Two recent studies in Guatemala found sickness and alcoholism, a type of illness, to be primary factors in conversion to Pentecostalism. In his research into the Pentecostal boom in Brazil, the nation with the world's largest Charismatic Protestant population, Chesnut found that over one-half of his informants in the Amazonian city of Belem had come to faith in their search for healing. He also discovered, as in Guatemala, that it was primarily the desire to stop abusing alcohol that led the Belem males to affiliate with the Pentecostal churches. Finally, the largest survey ever conducted on Latin American Protestants found that 55 percent of the sample of 921 evangelical believers living in Rio de Janeiro had come to faith during a period when facing a serious problem, in most cases one related to sickness.[22]

The healing message is introduced at front-door level by hundreds of thousands of Pentecostal pastors and lay persons throughout the continent. In the AoG, lay women evangelists, called *visitadoras* (visitors) proselytize not only door to door but also in hospitals where the sick are predisposed to listen to their message. Theirs is a holistic message to the poor, who face the major problems of debilitating sicknesses in societies where access to medical care is denied by the prohibitive cost of treatment. After sickness, it is behavior associated with *machismo* (aggressive masculine self-esteem) that most often draws women to seek divine help. Alcohol addiction and related physical abuse, infidelity

---

21. Währisch-Oblau, "Material Salvation." In Brown. *Global Pentecostalism*, 70.

22. Chesnut, *Competitive Spirits*, 45.

and gambling, on the part of husbands/partners constitute the main hardships that draw distressed womenfolk towards healing in its widest sense.

For men, who make up about one-third of converts, this particular conversionist religion offers a transformative way out from such a lifestyle under the guidance of a supportive church community. Chesnut found that two-thirds of his male informants in Brazil mentioned the renunciation of "vice" as the most important change in their life since conversion. Their new life allowed them "to reclaim and maintain their health through their rebirth into a salutary new environment that is largely devoid of the demons of the street."[23] In Brazil, it is said that there are only two institutions that function in the *favelas* (slums)—organized crime and Pentecostal churches.

Brazil has one of the largest numbers of Charismatic believers in the world. They constitute 42 percent of the total population of 186 million. The breakdown of the Christian numbers is as follows: 45 percent traditional Catholic, 30 percent Charismatic Catholic, 12 percent Protestant Renewal, and 3 percent Protestant Evangelical.[24] The Roman Catholic Church had a monopoly on religious power in the continent for 450 years up to the mid-twentieth century. The apparently impregnable bastion of Catholicism tumbled in a manner reminiscent of the Berlin Wall. However, it would be wrong to think that Catholicism was in retreat. The mushrooming of Pentecostal religiosity in the latter third of the twentieth century galvanized the Catholic Church into remedial action, especially in its attitude to the poor who had been peripheral to the power structures of the church. The new emphasis placed on social justice found expression in the base community movement, through which the Catholic Church sought to present itself as a church *for the poor*. In this, it has been moderately successful, but not to the measure of Renewalist churches, which find their appeal in high-density urban areas as churches *of the poor*.

The Catholic Charismatic Renewal (CCR) movement began in North America in 1967, and quickly disseminated around the world, reaching Latin America in the early 1970s. The two North American promoters in the southern continent were Francis MacNutt and Edward Dougherty, respectively Dominican and Jesuit priests. It was MacNutt who thrust faith healing to the center of the CCR movement through his pioneering activity in its spread, and consolidated his position with the publication of his book, *Healing*, (1974). In the book he stated: "My experience speaking with groups in Latin America showed me that praying for the healing of the inner being will help as much as anything toward the creation of a just society. My friends working in the ministry of social justice have experienced the failure of so many dreams they had in the 1960s, and they wholeheartedly agree that more is needed than structural change. Friends working with the oppressed are the most open to learn about prayer for inner healing. They themselves see the widest range of its applications."[25]

A new dimension in the practice of healing was introduced within the CCR, a movement that carries its appeal to those of higher social class. Whereas healing practiced in

23. Ibid., 49.

24. Jacobsen, *World's Christians*, 207.

25. MacNutt, *Healing*, 21.

Pentecostal churches tends to focus on the healing of the physical illnesses that afflict the poor, the healing sought at CCR masses and assemblies in the 1980s more often involved the inner healing of painful memories and psychological traumas. In CCR thinking, illness falls into three causal types: emotional, physical, and spiritual. Physical illness arises from disease and accidents, while spiritual desolation stems often from personal sin and occasionally from demonic oppression. The methods of healing directed to emotional and physical illnesses are straightforward, the former requiring prayer for inner healing and the latter prayer for physical healing. Spiritual afflictions are regarded to have two distinct origins, personal sin and satanic oppression, each requiring a different method of treatment. The former requires prayers of repentance, the latter exorcism.

Since the late 1980s, competition with Pentecostalism has led to the formation of a team of CCR priests who specialize in "liberation" (exorcism) ministries. The demand for deliverance from demonic possession is so high that a number of priests celebrate "liberation masses" (*missas de libertacao*) on a weekly basis. Some CCR lay leaders also practice unofficial exorcism behind closed doors, which has drawn denunciation from a number of bishops who see such a ministry as a threat to their clerical authority. One archbishop excommunicated several members of a CCR for expelling demons without his approval, and exhibiting a "Protestant tendency" in ignoring the role of the Virgin. There is little danger that Pentecostalism will trump Catholicism. With the introduction of freedom of worship legislation in the 1950s and the growth of Pentecostalism from the late 1970s, Brazil has become "a hotbed of religious fervor and change."[26] Competition has sharpened Catholicism to the extent that today almost half the Catholics are religiously active, compared to a quarter half a century before.

West Africa: Nigeria & Ghana

NIGERIA (percent)	Witnessed divine healings	Received divine revelations	Experienced/ or witnessed exorcisms
All Christians	62	41	57
Pentecostals	79	64	75
Other Christians	75	46	62

The charismatization of established missionary churches is a feature of the globalization process. Ghana is a good example in the context of West Africa, especially in its Presbyterian church. With the pressing demand for healing being met by the Pentecostal and AIC (African Independent/Initiated Churches), the mainline churches felt compelled to incorporate divine healing in their churches. In 1963, the Presbyterian Church set up a committee to study the *charismata* in the mission of the church, particularly the gift of healing. One of its recommendations was the desire "to see the New Testament ministry of healing through prayer restored within congregations of the church." Similar findings emanated from the Catholic Church and the Methodist churches. The Methodist study

26. Jacobsen, *World's Christians*, 215.

rued that many of their societies were either stagnant or actually declining. The drift away was most marked among the young and women, while others retained their membership in Methodism, at the same time associating with Renewalist fellowships. One of the reasons given in the official report for both the decline and perfunctory attitudes found within the mainstream churches was "insufficient teaching on the manifestation of the gifts of the Holy Spirit."[27]

The Presbyterian committee challenged the synod to examine its theology, liturgy, practices, and ethos to make room for the *charismata*, or else there would be a drain to Renewalist churches. The earliest way Presbyterians accommodated to charismaticism was through the formation of the "Bible Study and Prayer Group of the Presbyterian Church of Ghana," which began in 1938 and was formally recognized by the church in 1966. The Catholic and Methodist churches established similar prayer fellowships, and it is through such bodies that charismatic teaching and practice were introduced to the extent that various mainline churches have become pentecostalized. Healing has found a ready place because it has always been part of the religious concerns within African culture in a way that was alien to the theological brief of most early Western missionaries. For example, the role of the diviners and traditional priests within the culture of the Akan people of Ghana was to diagnose and heal maladies that were frequently attributed to malignant spirits. With the introduction of Christianity, Akans expected their pastors to play a similar role.

The Akan concept of salvation is all-embracing, dealing holistically with both soul and body as shaped by the values of their community. Foremost in the mind of the Akan is the desire "to seek a harmonious relationship with all human beings and particularly with the mystical powers that control life and bestow it with vitality." All dimensions of life are involved, be it "healing and good health; the ability to ward off evil; protection against evil spirits and witches; financial and material prosperity; peace of mind; peace with God, the gods, ancestors, and fellow human beings; human and animal fertility; harmonious relationships with others and success in one's occupation; and abundant life."[28] It is a spirituality that helps to explain why the Prosperity Gospel movement has gained considerable currency in Africa. In Zambia it is so widely received that the former President, Frederick Chiluba (1991–2002) subscribed to its theology. Speaking at the annual conference of Swedish Pentecostal churches in 1994 he told the gathering: "Give one tenth of your money to [God] and see returns on your capital. . . . The benefits you will receive will astound you." He extended it even further; if you give to God, you will experience not only personal prosperity, but national prosperity.[29]

27. Omenyo, "New Wine," 239.

28. Ibid., 235.

29. Gifford, "The Complex Provenance," 65. After leaving office, the five-feet-tall Chiluba was investigated for alleged corruption, to be acquitted in 2009. It became known that a Swiss firm had produced over 100 pairs of size 6 shoes for him with two inch heels, many monogrammed.

China

Verifiable demographic statistics for China are notoriously difficult to come by. Current estimates state that 5 percent of its 1.3 billion people are Christian. The government maintains there are about 20 million Christians in the country; other observers put the figure at 150 million or more. A reasonable estimate calculates it around 65 million. Of this number, 12 million are Roman Catholic, c. 15 million Protestant and 35 to 40 million Renewal. The growth of the church in China has no parallels in history, of Protestant and affiliates from 3.1 million in 1949 to 47 million in 2000. China Christian Council estimates that probably about half of the new conversions of the last twenty years have been the outcome of divine healing, either that of one's own or family member or close friend.[30] Gotthard Oblau from his own random observations, was of the opinion that this figure may be as high as 80–90 percent.[31]

Oblau discovered that divine healing experiences were a regular and widespread phenomenon among Protestant Christians in China. His overall impression corresponded well with those of Chinese colleagues and other international observers.

> Strikingly, [healings] are not limited to particular denominations or specific Christian traditions. In China, one need not be a Pentecostal or Charismatic to believe in or experience divine healing. It permeates Protestant Christianity as a whole and appears to be a mainline phenomenon in official and unofficial churches, in registered and unregistered congregations, in rural and urban communities. Equally striking is the fact that, among China's Protestant Christians, prayers for the sick tend to be a democratic practice. All in all, no special healing gifts are perceived as needed, no particular healing ministries relied upon. Healing crusades are unheard of, and special church services for the sick appear to be uncommon.[32]

Besides prayer for healing in church, the sick are also comfortable about praying for each other in the privacy of the home. The Chinese take seriously the doctrine of the priesthood of all believers, a doctrine that gives rise to the consensus that any single believer can pray for the sick and expect healing. Many congregations organize a roster of people responsible for visiting the sick in hospital. Healing prayers, too, are made for non-Christians, neighbors and colleagues, though not usually unconditionally. As a rule, they demand from the sick person that he or she accept faith in Jesus. With publically advertised evangelistic meetings banned, most evangelism in China takes place at the personal level. It is in such encounters that Christ is witnessed to as both Savior and healer.[33]

Währisch-Oblau came to the conclusion that a major factor in the prevalence of divine healing in China, at the time of writing (2001), was to be found in the reform of the health care system. An earlier national, low-cost health care system gave way to full payment imposed on the majority who were outside officialdom. Especially in rural areas, where village health stations and county hospitals were denied state funding, medical

---

30. Währisch-Oblau, "God Can Make Us Healthy," 93.

31. Oblau, "Divine Healing in China." In Brown: *Global Pentecostalism,* 313.

32. Ibid., 308.

33. Währisch-Oblau, "God Can Make Us Healthy," 93.

care was often so expensive that those who could not pay might be left to die in the street. In this situation, prayer was the only recourse that many rural Christians could take to relieve the suffering around them. The evangelistic efforts of many Christians undoubtedly appealed directly to such expectations. While it is easy to criticize such pragmatism, the fact remains that it was by this means that Christians found a genuinely democratic, holistic and acculturated way to respond to the needs around them.[34]

CODA

Much more would need to be written to give a fuller, perhaps less positive, picture of the place of divine healing in the global church today. Space prohibits consideration being given to some of the issues raised by divine healing in many different countries and cultures. However, the aim of this chapter has been to challenge Warfield's view that any miracles that took place in the post-apostolic age "would be without significance; mere occurrences with no universal meaning." The evidence presented in this chapter would suggest otherwise.

The ministry of healing within Western Protestantism, pioneered theologically by Edward Irving almost two centuries ago, has now become an established feature in the global church. While its practice has become more muted among Western Pentecostals in recent decades, it has added new dimensions by the arrival of the Charismatic Movement with its appeal to the middle class, and the Prosperity Gospel with its attraction for the more marginalized. Thus, the nature of healing has expanded in the Charismatic Movement beyond that of bodily healing to include psychosomatic healing. As Amos Yong has pointed out: "These 'middle-class afflictions' highlighted the importance of having a multifaceted theology of healing—i.e., healing as a result of receiving the forgiveness of sins, healing of the body, deliverance/exorcism, and healing of the inner person, memories (often suppressed), or hurt emotions."[35] With the advancement of the Prosperity Gospel movement the view has grown that it is God's will for Christians to lead not only healthy but also materially prosperous lives. Healing has come to be seen as stretching across the domains of social, economic, and material life, and as such imparting to and through ordinary believers some of the promised blessings of biblical *shalom*.

34. Ibid., 94.

35. Yong, *In the Days of Caesar*, 261.

Bibliography

Adams Rev. J. W. *Miracles Today*. published privately, n.d.

Agazue, Chima. *The Role of a Culture of Superstition in the Proliferation of Religio-Commercial Pastors in Nigeria*. Bloomington, IN: Author House, 2013.

Ahlstrom, Sydney E. *A Religious History of the American People*. New Haven: Yale University Press, 1972.

Albanese, Catherine L. *A Republic of the Mind & Spirit: A Cultural History of American Metaphysical Religion*. New Haven: Yale University Press, 2007.

Alexander, Kimberley Ervin, and John C. Thomas. "'And the Signs Are Following': A Journey into Pentecostal Hermeneutics." *Journal of Pentecostal Theology* 11.2 (2003) 147–70.

Alexander, Kimberly Ervin. *Pentecostal Healing: Models in Theology and Practice*. Blandford Forum, UK: Deo, 2006.

Anderson, Allan Heaton. *To the Ends of the Earth: Pentecostalism and the Transformation of World Christianity*. Oxford: Oxford University Press, 2013.

———. *Spreading Fires: The Missionary Nature of Early Pentecostalism*. London: SCM, 2007.

Anderson, Robert M. *Vision of the Disinherited: The Making of American Pentecostalism*. Peabody, MA: Hendrickson, 1992.

Anon, "Prosperity Gospel in Nigeria. Online. http://jessezink.com/2011/06/21/prosperity-gospel-in-nigeria/

———. "Spirit and POWER: A 10–Country Survey of Pentecostals." Online. http://pewforum.org/Christian/Evangelical-Protestant-Churches/Spirit-and-POWER.aspx.

———. "Audio file of William Branham." Online. http://www.vrijezending.nl/english/branham/only-believe

———. "Burrswood: Christian Hospital." Online. http://communications.london.anglican.org/ministry matters

———. "Ephemera of Daniel Paul Rader—Collection 38." Billy Graham Center, Wheaton College. Online

———. "Evangelist Reinhard Bonnke." Online. http://www.bonnke.net/cfan/en/cfan/reinhard-bonnke

———. *Kirkus Reviews*. Online. https://www.kirkusreviews.com/book-reviews/paula-nelson-3/all-things-are-possible-the-healing-and-charism/

———. "Spirit and Power." Pew Research Center. A 10-Country Survey of Pentecostals: Demographic Portrait." Online. http://www.pewforum.org/2006/10/05/spirit-and-power/

———. "Spiritual Healing in the English Church." *British Medical Journal*, 19 January, 1924.

———. "What Is the Purpose Of Anointing with Oil in James 5?" Online. http://theonlyhope.net/?p=32

———. "Demographic Portrait of Renewalists." Pew Research Center. Online. http://www.pewforum.org/2006/10/05/spirit-and-power-a-10-country-survey-of-pentecostals5/#income

———. *Spiritual Healing: Report of a Clerical and Medical Committee of Inquiry into Spiritual, Faith, and Mental Healing*. London: MacMillan, 1914.

Anson, Harold. *Looking Forward*. London: Heinemann, 1938.

Anson, Harold. *Spiritual Healing: A Discussion of the Religious Element in Physical Health*. London: London University Press, 1923.

Arnold, Dorothea Musgrave. *Dorothy Kerin: Called by Christ to Heal*. London: Hodder & Stoughton, 1965.

Ash, Edwin Lancelot. *Faith and Suggestion*. London: Herbert & Daniel, 1910.

Baer, Jonathan R. "Perfectly Empowered Bodies: Divine Healing in Modernising America." PhD diss., Yale, 2002.

Bahr, Robert. *Least of all Saints: The Story of Aimee Semple McPherson*. Lincoln, NE: Universe, 2001.

Barclay, Oliver. *Evangelicalism in Britain, 1935–95: A Personal Sketch*. Leicester, UK: InterVarsity, 1997.

Barfoot, Chas. H. *Aimee Semple McPherson and the Making of Modern Pentecostalism, 1890–1926*. London: Equinox, 2011.

Barnes III, Roscoe. *F. F. Bosworth: The Man behind 'Christ the Healer.'* Newcastle-upon-Tyne, UK: Cambridge Scholars, 2009.

———. "F. F. Bosworth: A Historical Analysis of the Influential Factors in his Life and Ministry." PhD diss., University of Pretoria, 2009.

Bartleman, Frank. *Azusa Street.* South Plainfield, NJ: Bridge, 1980.

Bell, E. N. "Questions and Answers." *The Pentecostal Evangel,* August 19, 1922, 1–16.

Bentley, Todd. "Todd Bentley's Violent Ministry (WOTMR)" at Lakeland, Florida 2008. You Tube Video Clip.

Bergunder, Michael. "Constructing Pentecostalism: On Issues of Methodology and Representation." *JEPTA* 27.1 (2007) 52–71.

Bernard Alan and Jonathan Spencer, eds. *Encyclopaedia of Social and Cultural Anthropology.* London: Routledge, 1996

Biederwolf, William Edward. *Whipping-Post Theology or Did Jesus Atone for Disease?* Grand Rapids: Eerdmans, 1934.

Blethen, H. Tyler, and Curtis W. Wood. *Ulster and North America: Transatlantic Perspectives on the Scotch-Irish.* Tuscaloosa, AL: University of Alabama Press, 1997.

Blumhofer, Edith L. *Aimee Semple McPherson: Everybody's Sister.* Grand Rapids: Eerdmans, 1993.

———. *The Assemblies of God: A Chapter in the Story of American Pentecostalism,* Volume 1. 1941. Springfield, MO: Gospel Publishing House, 1989.

———. "Life on Faith Lines: Faith Homes and Early Pentecostal Witness." *AoG Heritage* 10 (1990) 10–12.

———. *Pentecostal Currents in American Protestantism.* Chicago: University of Illinois Press, 1999.

Boddy, Alexander A. "A Vicar's Testimony: 'Pentecost' at Sunderland, 1909." Online. http://www.scribd.com/doc/106290105/A-Vicars-Testimony.

Bomann, Rebecca Pierce. *Faith in the Barrios: The Pentecostal Poor in Bogota.* London: Lynne Reinner, 1999.

Bonnke, Reinhard. "Great Gospel Campaign in Lagos, Nigeria." Online. http://www.bonnke.net/cfan/en/events/africa-20062007/lagos.

Bosworth, F. F. *Christ the Healer,* Grand Rapids: Revell, 1973.

Boulton, E. C. W. *A Ministry of the Miraculous.* London: Elim, 1928.

Bowler, Kate. *Blessed Bodies: A History of the American Prosperity Gospel.* New York: Oxford University Press, 2013.

Brown, Candy Gunther "Chiropractic and Christianity: The Power of Pain to Adjust Cultural Alignments." *Church History* 79.1 (2010) 145–81.

———, ed. *Global Pentecostalism and Charismatic Healing.* New York: Oxford University Press, 2011.

Brown, Callum G. *Religion and Society in Twentieth-Century Britain.* Harlow, UK: Pearson Longman, 2006.

Brumback, Carl. *Suddenly from Heaven; A History of the Assemblies of God.* Springfield, MO: Gospel, 1961.

Buckley J. M. "Dowie Analysed and Classified." *Century Magazine,* October 1902, 928–32.

———. *Faith Healing, Christian Science and Kindred Phenomena.* New York: Century, 1892.

———. "Faith Healing and Kindred Phenomena (Supplementary Article)." *Century Magazine* 33, March 1887, 781–87.

Bultmann, Rudolf. *Kerygma and Myth.* New York, Harper, 1961.

Burgess, Stanley M. *[NIDPCM] New International Dictionary of Pentecostal and Charismatic Movements.* Grand Rapids: Zondervan, 2002.

Burkinshaw, Robert K. "Conservative Protestantism and the Modernist Challenge in Vancouver, 1917–1927." Online.http://www.google.co.uk/url?sa=t&rct=j&q=&esrc=s&frm=1&source=web&cd=3&ved=0CDkQFjAC&url=http%3A%2F%2Fojs.library.ubc.ca%2Findex.php%2Fbcstudies%2Farticle%2Fdownload%2F1344%2F1387&ei=Q19cUqi7Eo3KoAXWmYGgCg&usg=AFQjCNF06d2uei13GjBGno9uU1x704vvEQ&sig2=u7i41TI56jDs8H1XQlAirA&bvm=bv.53899372,d.d2k

Burkinshaw, Robert Kenneth. "Strangers and Pilgrims in Lotus Land: Conservative Protestantism in British Columbia, 1917–1981." PhD diss., University of British Columbia, 1988.

Carpenter, Joel A. *Revive Us Again: The Reawakening of American Fundamentalism.* New York: Oxford University Press, 1997.

Carter, John. *Howard Carter: Man of the Spirit.* Nottingham, UK: AoG, 1971.

Cartwright, Desmond. *The Real Wigglesworth: The Man, the Myth, the Message.* Tonbridge, UK: Sovereign World, 2000.

Cerillo, Augustus. "The Beginnings of American Pentecostalism: A Historiographical Overview." In *Pentecostal Currents in American Pentecostalism*, edited by Edith Blumhofer, 229–59. Urbana, IL: University of Illinois Press, 1999.

Chan, Simon. *Pentecostal Theology: A Systematic Study of the Christian Life*. Downer's Grove, IL: InterVarsity, 1998.

Chant, Barry. *Heart of Fire: The Story of Australian Pentecostalism*. Fullarton, Australia: Luke, 1973.

Chapman, Diana. *Searching the Source of the River: Forgotten Women of the British Pentecostal Revival 1907–1914*. London: Push, 2007.

Chappell, Paul G. "William Branham." In *Twentieth-Century Shapers of American Popular Religion*, edited by Charles Lippy, 44–48. Westport, CT: Greenwood, 1989.

Chavchavadze, Marina. *Dorothy Kerin As I Knew Her*. Published privately, 1995.

Chesnut, R. Andrew. *Born Again in Brazil: The Pentecostal Boom and the Pathogens of Poverty*. New Brunswick, NJ: Rutgers University Press, 1997.

———. *Competitive Spirits in Latin America's New Religious Economy*. New York: Oxford University Press, 2003.

Clayton, Allen L. "The Significance of William H. Durham for Pentecostal Historiography." *Pneuma* 32 (1979) 27–42.

Clinebell, Howard. *Understanding and Counseling the Alcoholic*. Nashville, TN: Abingdon, 1990.

Copeland, Gloria. "Reaping a Harvest of Healing." Online. http://www.kcm.org.uk/reaping-a-harvest-of-healing-by-gloria-copeland/

Corten, André, and Ruth Marshall-Fratini. *Between Babel and Pentecost*. Bloomington, IN: Indiana University Press, 2001.

Courey, David. "'Real Issue in Pentecostalism': Revival, Institution and the Quest for a Pentecostal Hermeneutic." *New Voices, New Visions: The 39th Annual Meeting of Society of Pentecostal Studies*, 1–35. CD-ROM. Springfield, MO: SPS, 2010.

Cox, Harvey. *Fire from Heaven: The Rise of Spirituality and the Reshaping of Religion in the Twenty-First Century*. Reading, MA: Addison-Wesley, 1995.

Craig, Borlase. *William Seymour: A Biography*. Lady Mary, FL: Charisma, 2006.

Crawford, Mattie. *On Mule Back Thru' Central America with the Gospel*. Indianapolis: Crawford, 1922.

Creech, Joe. "Visions of Glory: The Place of the Azusa Street Revival in Pentecostal History." *Church History* 65.3 (1996) 406–24.

Csordas, Thomas J. *The Sacred Self: A Cultural Phenomenology of Charismatic Healing*. Berkeley: University of California Press, 1994.

Cunningham, Raymond Joseph. "Ministry of Healing: The Origins of the Psychotherapeutic Role of the American Churches." PhD diss., Johns Hopkins University, 1965.

Curtis, Heather D. "'Acting Faith': Practices of Religious Healing in Late Nineteenth-Century Protestantism." In *Practicing Protestants*, edited by Laurie Maffley-Kipp, 137–58. Baltimore, MD: John Hopkins University Press, 2006.

———. *Faith in the Great Physician; Suffering and Divine Healing in American Culture, 1860–1900*. Baltimore MD: John Hopkins University Press, 2007.

———. "Houses of Healing: Sacred Space, Spiritual Practice and the Transformation of Female Suffering in the Faith Cure Movement 1870–90." *Church History* 75.3 (2006) 598–611.

Dayton, Donald W. *Theological Roots of Pentecostalism*. Peabody, MA: Hendrickson, 1987.

Dearmer, Percy. *Body and Soul: An Enquiry into the Effects of Religion upon Health*. London: Pitman, 1909.

DeArteaga, William. "A Wedge into Cessationism: The Anglican Tradition of Healing Prayer. Part 1." Online. http://anglicalpentecostal.blogspot.co.uk/2013/09/the-anglican-tradition-in-healing-part.html

Deininger, Matthias. *Global Pentecostalism: An Inquiry into the Cultural Dimensions of Globalization*. Hamburg: Anchor Academic, 2013.

Di Giacomo, Michael. "'Shot in the Arm' for French-Canadian Pentecostalism." In *Winds from the North*, edited by Michael Wilkinson and Peter Althouse, 151–68. Leiden: Brill, 2010.

Dicken, Janice. "'Take Up Thy Bed and Walk': Aimee Semple McPherson and Faith Healing." *Canadian Bulletin of Medical History* 17 (2000) 137–53.

Dickson, Neil T. R. *Brethren in Scotland 1838–2000*. Studies in Evangelical History and Thought. Milton Keynes, UK: Paternoster, 2003.

Dieter, Melvin E., ed. *Five Views on Sanctification*. Grand Rapids: Zondervan, 1987.

———. "Primitivism in the American Holiness Tradition." *Wesleyan Theological Journal* 30.1 (1995) 78–91.

Dorries, David W. "Smith Wigglesworth: The Making of His Message." *AoG Heritage* 12.4 (1992–93) 20–29.

———. "William J. Seymour." In *Encyclopaedia of Religious Revivals in America*, edited by Michael McClymond, 395. Westport, CT: Greenwood, 2007.

Edsor, Albert W. *"Set Your House in Order": God's Call to George Jeffreys as the Founder of the Elim Pentecostal Movement* .Chichester, UK: New Wine, 1989.

Edwards, Owen Dudley. "Doyle, Sir Arthur Ignatius Conan (1859–1930)." *Oxford Dictionary of National Biography*. Oxford University Press, 2004. Online ed., Jan 2011.

Epstein, Daniel Mark. *Sister Aimee: A Life of Aimee Semple McPherson*. New York: Harcourt Brace, 1993.

Ernest, Johanna. *Dorothy Kerin (1889–1963): Her Ministry of Healing*. Burrswood, UK: Dorothy Kerin Trust, 1987.

———. *The Life of Dorothy Kerin*. Burrswood, UK: Dorothy Kerin Trust, 1983.

Eskridge, L. "Paul Rader." In *Biographical Dictionary of Evangelicals*, edited by Timothy Larsen, 533–34. Downers Grove, IL: InterVarsity, 2003.

Espinosa, Gastón. "Ordinary Prophet: William J. Seymour and the Azusa Street Revival." In *Azusa Street Revival*, edited by Harold Hunter and Cecil Robeck, 29–60. Eugene, OR: Wipf & Stock, 2006.

Faupel, D. William. *The Everlasting Gospel: The Significance of Eschatology in the Development of Pentecostal Thought*. Sheffield, UK: Sheffield Academic Press, 1996.

———. "William H. Durham and the Finished Work of Calvary." In *Pentecost, Mission and Ecumenism*, edited by Jan Jongeneel, 85–95. Frankfurt: Lang, 1992.

Fisher, G. Richard. "Rod Parsley: The Raging Prophet." Online. http://www.pfo.org/parsley.htm

Fitch, May Wyburn. *Healing Delusion: Dealing with the Doctrine, the Methods Prevailing and the Claims Made in the Present-Day Healing Campaigns*. New York: Loizeaux, n d.

Flexner, Abraham. *Medical Education in the United States and Canada*. New York: Carnegie Trust, 1910.

Ford, David F. *The Future of Christian Theology*. Oxford: Wiley-Blackwell, 2011.

Frodsham, Arthur W. "The Sixteenth Chapter of Mark: How God Vindicates His Word in the Last Days." *Pentecostal Evangel*, April 28, 1923, 1–16.

Frodsham, Stanley Howard. *Smith Wigglesworth: Apostle of Faith*. London: AoG, 1949.

Frost, Evelyn. *Christian Healing: A Consideration of the Place of Spiritual Healing in the Church of To-day*. London: Mowbury, 1940.

Fuller, Robert C. *Alternative Medicine and American Religious Life*. New York: Oxford University Press, 1989.

Furlong, Monica. *Burrswood—Focus of Healing*. London: Hodder & Stoughton, 1978.

Gaebelein, Arno Clemens. *The Healing Question*, New York: Our Hope, 1925.

Garrett Clarke. *Spirit Possession and Popular Religion: Origins of the Shakers: From the Old World to the New World*. Baltimore, MD: Johns Hopkins University Press, 1998.

Gee, Donald. "Extremes are Sometimes Necessary." *The Voice of Healing*, April 1953.

———. *These Men I Knew*. Nottingham, UK: AoG, 1980.

———. *Trophimus I Left Sick: Our Problems of Divine Healing*. London: Elim, 1952.

———. *Wind and Flame*. Croydon: Heath, 1967.

Gevitz, Norman. *Other Healers: Unorthodox Medicine in America*. Baltimore, MD: John Hopkins University Library, 1988.

Gifford, Paul. "The Complex Provenance of Some Elements of African Pentecostal Theology." In *Between Babel and Pentecost*, edited by André Corten and Ruth Marshall-Fratini, 62–79. Bloomington, IN: Indiana University Press, 2001.

———. "Healing in African Pentecostalism: The 'Victorious Living' of David Oyedepo." In *Global Pentecostalism and Charismatic Healing*, edited by Candy Brown, 251–66. New York: Oxford University Press, 2011.

Gigge, John M., and Diane Winston. *Faith in the Market*. New Brunswick, NJ: Rutgers University Press, 2002.

Gleason, Willard. "Notes from My Journal while En Route for the City of the Great King." *Tongues of Fire*, 15 July 1898. Online. http://www.fwselijah.com/glassey.htm.

Goff, James R. *Fields White unto Harvest: Charles F. Parham and the Missionary Origins of Pentecostalism*. Fayetteville, AR: University of Arkansas, 1988.

———. "Initial Tongues in the Theology of Charles Fox Parham." In *Initial Evidence*, edited by Gary McGee, 57–71. Peabody, MA: Hendrickson, 1991.

Grady, J. Lee. *The Holy Spirit Is NOT For Sale.* Grand Rapids: Chosen, 1994.

Gunn, Ada Borkowski. "Rewired Pentecostalism: Rod Parsley's Link to the Spirit." Paper presented at the 30th Annual Meeting of the Society for Pentecostal Studies, 2001.

Hagen, Tona. *Redeeming the Dial: Radio, Religion, and Popular Culture in America.* Chapel Hill, NC: The University of North Carolina Press, 2002.

Hagin, Kenneth E. *Ministering to the Oppressed.* Tulsa, OK: Kenneth Hagin Ministries, 1983.

Haldeman, I. C. *Did Our Lord Jesus Christ by His Death Atone for Bodily Sickness?* New York, n.d.

Hardesty, Nancy A. *Faith Cure, Divine Healing in the Holiness and Pentecostal Movements.* Peabody, MA: Hendrickson, 2003.

Hardy, Alister. *The Spiritual Nature of Man: A Study of Contemporary Experience.* Oxford: Clarendon, 1979.

Harrell, David Edwin. *All Things Are Possible: The Healing and Charismatic Revivals in Modern America.* Bloomington, IN: Indiana University Press, 1975.

Hastings, Adrian. *A History of English Christianity 1920–1990.* London: SCM, 1991.

Hatch, Nathan O. *The Democratization of American Christianity.* New Haven: Yale University Press, 1989.

Hathaway, Malcolm R. "The Elim Pentecostal Church: Origins, Development and Distinctives." In *Pentecostal Perspectives,* edited by Keith Warrington, 1–39. Carlisle, UK: Paternoster, 1998.

Heckscher, Stephens. "Dorothy Kerin: Sign and Significance." *Journal of Christian Healing* 23.2 (2007) 1–19.

Hedges, Chris. *American Fascists: The Christian Right and the War on America.* New York: Free, 2006.

Hejzlar, Pavel. "Two Paradigms for Divine Healing: Fred T. Bosworth, Kenneth E. Hagin, Agnes Sanford, and Francis MacNutt." PhD diss., Fuller Theological Seminary, 2009.

Henson, Hensley. "Spiritual Healing." *The Hibbert Journal* 23 (1925) 385–401.

Hickson, James Moore. *Heal the Sick.* New York: Dutton, 1924.

———. *The Revival of the Gifts of Healing.* Online. http://webjournals.ac.edu.au/journals/HOM/hickson-james-moore/01-the-revival-of-the-gifts-of-healing/

Hirsch, Alan, and Tim Catchim. *The Permanent Revolution: Apostolic Imagination and Practice for the 21st Century Church.* San Francisco: Jossey-Bass, 2012.

Hollenweger, Walter J. *The Pentecostals.* London: SCM, 1972.

———. *Pentecostalism: Origins and Developments Worldwide,* Peabody, MA: Hendrickson, 1997.

Hood, Ralph W. and W. Paul Williamson. *Them That Believe: The Power and Meaning of The Christian Serpent-Handling Tradition.* Berkeley: University of California Press, 2008.

Hudson, Neil, and Andrew Walker, "George Jeffreys, Revivalist and Reformer." In *On Revival,* edited by Andrew Walker and Kristen Aune, 137–56. Carlisle, UK: Paternoster, 2003.

Hudson, Neil. "A Schism and Its Aftermath: An Historical Analysis of Denominational Discerption in the Elim Pentecostal Church, 1939–1940." PhD diss., King's College, London, 1999.

Hunter, Harold D., and Cecil M. Robeck, eds. *Azusa Street Revival and Its Legacy.* Eugene, OR: Wipf & Stock, 2006.

Hutchinson, Mark. "The Worcester Circle: An Anglo-Catholic Attempt at Renewal." Online. http://www.academia.edu/345662/The_Worcester_Circle_An_AngloCatholic_attempt_at_Renewal_in_the_1920s

Hywel-Davies, Jack. *The Life of Smith Wigglesworth.* Ann Arbor, MI: Servant, 1987.

J. M. B. "Miracles of Healing." *The Bridal Call* 4.8, Jan. 1921, 14–15.

Jacobsen, Douglas. *Thinking in the Spirit: Theologies of the Early Pentecostal Movement.* Bloomington, IN: Indiana University Press, 2003.

Jacobsen, Douglas. *World's Christians: Who They Are, Where They Are, and How They Got There.* Oxford: Wiley-Blackwell, 2011, 207.

James, William. *The Varieties of Religious Experience: A Study in Human Nature.* London: Collins, 1960.

Jeffreys, George. *Healing Rays.* Worthing, UK: Walter, 1985.

Jenkins, Philip. *Next Christendom: The Coming of Global Christianity.* New York: Oxford University Press, 2011.

Jones R. B. *Rent Heavens.* Welsh Revival Library, CD–ROM. Revival Library, Bishop's Waltham, SO32 1AA.

Jongeneel, Jan A. B., ed. *Pentecost, Mission and Ecumenism: Essays on Intercultural Theology,* Frankfurt: Lang, 1992.

Kalu, Ogbu. *African Pentecostalism: An Introduction.* New York: Oxford University Press, 2008.

Kärkkäinen, Veli-Matti. "Pentecostal Pneumatology of Religions." In *The Spirit in the World,* edited by Veli-Matti Kärkkäinen, 155–80. Grand Rapids: Eerdmans, 2009.

——. *Pneumatology: The Holy Spirit in Ecumenical, International and Contextual Perspective.* Grand Rapids: Baker Academic, 2002.

——, ed. *The Spirit in the World.* Grand Rapids: Eerdmans, 2009.

Kay, William K. *Inside Story: A History of the British Assemblies of God.* Mattersey, UK: Mattersey Hall, 1990.

——. *Pentecostals in Britain.* Carlisle, UK: Paternoster, 2000.

Kerin, Dorothy. *Fulfilling: A Sequel to "The Living Touch."* London: Hodder & Stoughton, 1963.

——. *The Living Touch.* Tunbridge Wells, UK: Courier, 1914.

Keener, Craig S. *Miracles: The Credibility of New Testament Accounts.* 2 vols. Grand Rapids: Baker Academic, 2011.

King, Gerald. *Disfellowshipped: Pentecostal Responses to Fundamentalism in the United States, 1906–1943.* Eugene, OR: Wipf & Stock, 2011.

King, Paul L. *Genuine Gold: The Cautiously Charismatic Story of the Early Christian and Missionary Alliance.* Tulsa, OK: Word & Spirit, 2006.

——. *Moving Mountains.* Grand Rapids: Chosen, 2004, 145.

——. "Theological Roots of the Word of Faith Movement." In *Society of Pentecostal Studies: Annual Papers 1982–2004,* 2004: 1–15. CD-ROM. Springfield, MO: SPS, 2004.

Kirby, Gilbert W. *The Question of Healing.* London: Victory, 1967.

Knight III, Henry H. "God's Faithfulness and God's Freedom: A Comparison of Contemporary Theologies of Healing." *Journal of Pentecostal Theology* 2 (1993) 65–89.

——. "Love and Freedom 'by Grace Alone' in Wesley's Soteriology: A Proposal for Evangelicals." *Pneuma* 24.1 (2002) 57–67.

Koenig, Harold G. *Handbook of Religion and Health.* New York: Oxford University Press, 2011.

Land, Steven J. *Pentecostal Spirituality: A Passion for the Kingdom.* Sheffield, UK: Sheffield Academic Press, 1994.

Landau, Rom. *God Is My Adventure.* London: Faber and Faber, 1943.

Larsen, Timothy. *Biographical Dictionary of Evangelicals.* Downers Grove, IL: InterVarsity, 2003.

Lewis, C. S. *Surprised by Joy.* London: Collins, 1959.

Liardon, Roberts. *God's Generals: Why They Succeeded and Why Some Fail.* Tulsa, OK, Albury, 1996.

Lindsay, Gordon. *William Branham: A Man Sent From God.* Online. http://www.williambranham homepage.org/mansent1.htm#masent16

Lippy, Charles H., ed. *Twentieth-Century Shapers of American Popular Religion.* Westport, CT: Greenwood, 1989.

Loud, Grover C. *Evangelized America.* New York: Ayer, 1928.

Macchia, Frank D. *Baptized in the Spirit: A Global Pentecostal Theology.* Grand Rapids: Zondervan, 2006.

——. "The Kingdom and the Power: Spirit Baptism in Pentecostal and Ecumenical Perspective." In *The Work of the Spirit,* edited by Michael Welker, 109–25. Grand Rapids: Eerdmans, 2006.

——. "Pentecost as the Power of the Cross: The Witness of Seymour and Durham." *Pneuma* 30.1 (2008) 1–3.

——. "Pentecostal Healing (Review)." *The Expository Times,* Dec. 2007, 145–46.

——. *Spirituality and Social Liberation: The Message of the Blumhardts in the Light of Wuerrttemberg Pietism.* Metuchen, NJ: Scarecrow, 1993.

MacNutt, Francis. *Healing.* Notre Dame, IN: Ave Maria, 1999.

——. *The Nearly Perfect Crime: How the Church Almost Killed the Ministry of Healing.* Grand Rapids, Chosen, 2005.

Macy, David, ed. *Dictionary of Critical Theory.* London: Penguin, 2001,

Madden, Peter J. *The Wigglesworth Standard.* New Kensington, PA: Whitaker House, 1993.

Maddocks, Morris. *The Vision of Dorothy Kerin.* Guildford, UK: Eagle, 1991.

Maffley-Kipp, Laurie, ed. *Practicing Protestants: Histories of Christian Life in America 1630–1965.* Baltimore, MD: John Hopkins University Press, 2006.

Maxwell, David. "'Networks and Niches': The Worldwide Transmission of the Azusa Street Revival." In *The Azusa Street Revival,* edited by Harold Hunter and Cecil Robeck, 127–40. Eugene, OR: Wipf & Stock, 2006.

Maillard, John. *Healing Faith and Practice.* Brixham, UK: Healing Life, n.d.

——. *Healing in the Name of Jesus.* London: Hodder & Stoughton, 1936.

——. *The Sacrament of Healing.* London: Morgan & Scott, 1925.

Mains, George Preston. *James Monroe Buckley.* New York: Methodist Book Concern, 1917.

Marsden, George, and John Woodbridge. "The Link: Christian History Today." *Christian History* 20.4 (2001) 50–54.

Martin, David. "Undermining the Old Paradigms." *PentecoStudies* 5.1 (2006) 18–38.

Martin, Larry E., ed. *The Topeka Outpouring.* Joplin, MO: Christian Life, 1997.

McClung, L. G. "Exorcism". In *New International Dictionary of Pentecostal and Charismatic Movements,* edited by Stanley Burgess, 624–28. Grand Rapids: Zondervan, 2002.

McClymond, Michael, ed. *Encyclopaedia of Religious Revivals in America.* Westport, CT: Greenwood, 2007.

McGee, Gary B., ed. *Initial Evidence: Historical and Biblical Evidence of the Pentecostal Doctrine of Spirit Baptism.* Peabody, MA: Hendrickson, 1991.

———. *Miracles, Missions & American Pentecostalism.* Maryknoll, NY: Orbis, 2010.

———. "The Revival Legacy of Smith Wigglesworth." *Enrichment Journal,* Autumn, 1998. Online: http://enrichmentjournal.ag.org/199801/070_wigglesworth.cfm.

McGrath, Alister. *Christianity's Dangerous Idea: The Protestant Revolution.* London: SPCK, 2007.

McPherson, Aimee Semple. *Divine Healing Sermons.* Nabu Reprints, n.d.

———. "The Narrow Line." *The Bridal Call* 6.5, October, 1922.

———. *This Is That: Personal Experiences, Sermons and Writings.* Los Angeles: Echo Park Evangelistic Association, n.d.

Mews, Stuart. "The Revival of Spiritual Healing." In *The Church and Healing,* edited by W. J. Sheils, 299–332. Oxford: Blackwell, 1982.

Michel, David. "Aimee Semple McPherson and the Reconfiguration of Methodism in America 1916–1922." In *Winds from the North,* edited by Michael Wilkinson and Peter Althouse, 169–90. Leiden: Brill, 2010.

Miller, Donald E., and Tetsunao Yamamori. *Global Pentecostalism: The New Face of Christian Engagement.* Berkeley: University of California Press, 2007.

Milne, Bruce. *The Message of John.* Leicester, UK: InterVarsity, 1993.

Miskov, Jennifer Ann. "Life on Wings: The Forgotten Life and Theology of Carrie Judd Montgomery (1858–1946)." PhD diss., University of Birmingham, UK, 2011.

Missen, Alfred F. *The Sound of a Going.* Nottingham, UK: AoG, 1973.

Morrow, Jimmy. *Handling Serpents.* Macon, GA: Mercer University Press, 2005.

Mullin, Robert Bruce. *Miracle and the Modern Religious Imagination.* New Haven: Yale University Press, 1996.

Newport, Kenneth G. C. "Hanserd Knollys." *Oxford Dictionary of National Biography Archive,* 1992. Online. http://www.oxforddnb.com/view/olddnb/15756.

Nicol, John Thomas. *The Pentecostals.* Rev ed. Plainfield, NJ: Logos International, 1971.

Noll, Mark. *The New Shape of World Christianity.* Downer's Grove, IL: InterVarsity, 200.

Numbers, Ronald L., and Darrel W. Amundsen. *Caring and Curing.* Baltimore, MD: John Hopkins University Press, 1986.

Oblau, Gotthard, "Divine Healing and the Growth of Practical Christianity in China." In *Global Pentecostalism and Charismatic Healing,* edited by Candy Brown, 307–27. New York: Oxford University Press, 2011.

Omenyo, Cephas N. "New Wine in an Old Wine Bottle?" In *Global Pentecostalism and Charismatic Healing,* edited by Candy Brown, 231–50. New York: Oxford University Press, 2011.

Opp, James. *Lord for the Body: Religion, Medicine & Protestant Faith Healing in Canada 1880–1930.* Montreal: McGill–Queen's University Press, 2005.

Ostling, Richard N. "Jerry Falwell's Crusade: Fundamentalist Legions Seek to Remake Church and Society." *Time* 126, September 2, 1985.

Overy, Richard. *The Morbid Age: Britain between the Wars.* London: Allen Lane, 2009.

Parham, Charles F. *Divine Health.* Baxter Springs, KS, n.d.

———. *Selected Sermons of the Late Charles F. Parham and Sarah E. Parham.* Baxter Springs, KS: Parham, 1941.

———. *A Voice Crying in the Wilderness.* Baxter Springs, KS: Apostolic Faith Bible College, 1910.

Parham, Sarah. *The Life of Charles F. Parham.* Joplin, MO: Tri–State, 1930.

Penn-Lewis, Jessie. *War on the Saints,* Kent, UK: Diasozo Trust, 1973.

Percy, Martyn. *Words, Wonders and Powers: Understanding Contemporary Christian Fundamentalism and Revivalism.* London: SPCK, 1996.

Perkins, Eunice M. *Joybringer Bosworth: His Life Story.* Dayton, OH: Scruby, 1921.

Poewe, Karla, ed. *Charismatic Christianity as a Global Culture.* Columbia, SC: University of South Carolina Press, 1994.

Pollock, J. C. *The Keswick Story.* London: Hodder and Stoughton, 1964.

Porterfield, Amanda. *Healing in the History of Christianity.* New York: Oxford University Press, 2005.

———. "Introduction: Forum on Sacred Spaces of Healing in Modern American Christianity." *Church History* 75.3 (2006) 594–611.

Posner, Sarah. *God's Profits: Faith, Fraud, and the Republican Crusade for Values Voters.* San Francisco: Polipoint, 2008.

Price, Charles S. *And Signs Followed.* Plainfield, NJ: Logos International, 1972.

Puller, F. W. *Anointing the Sick.* London: SPCK, 1910.

Quinn, Anthony. *The Original Sin: A Self-Portrait.* Boston: Little, Brown, 1972.

Rader, Paul. "At Thy Word." *Alliance Weekly,* Nov. 20, 1920, 532.

———. "Power From On High." Online. http://www.sermonindex.net/modules/articles/index.php?view=article&aid=27897.

Randall, Ian M. *Evangelical Experiences: A Study of the Spirituality of English Evangelicalism 1918–1939.* Studies in Evangelical History and Thought. Carlisle, UK: Paternoster, 1999.

Reynolds, David. *America, Empire of Liberty: A New History.* London: Penguin, 2009.

Richardson, Robert D. *William James: In the Maelstrom of American Modernism.* New York: Houghton Mifflin, 2006.

Richie, Tony. *Toward a Pentecostal Theology of Religions.* Cleveland, TN: CPT, 2013.

Riley, William B. *Divine Healing or Does God Hear Prayer for the Sick.* Online. http://cdm16120.contentdm.oclc.org/cdm/ref/collection/riley/id/4543

———. *Divine Healing and the Emmanuel Movement.* Transcript of sermon. Online: http://cdm16120.contentdm.oclc.org/cdm/ref/collection/riley/id/4533.

———. *Divine Healing and Christian Science.* Online. http://cdm16120.contentdm.oclc.org/cdm/ref/collection/riley/id/4403

Robbins, Joel. "The Globalization of Pentecostal and Charismatic Christianity." *Annual Review of Anthropology* 33 (2004) 117–43.

Robbins, Keith. *England, Ireland, Scotland, Wales: The Christian Church 1900–2000.* Oxford: Oxford University Press, 2008.

Robeck, Cecil M. *Azusa Street: Mission & Revival.* Nashville, TN: Nelson, 2006.

Robertson, Roland. "The Salvation Army: The Persistence of Sectarianism." In *Sects and Society,* edited by Bryan Wilson, 48–105. London: Heinemann, 1961.

Robins R. G. *Pentecostalism in America.* Santa Barbara, CA; Praeger, 2010.

Robinson, James. *Divine Healing: The Formative Years 1830–1890.* Eugene, OR: Pickwick, 2011.

———. *Divine Healing: The Holiness-Pentecostal Transition Years, 1890–1906.* Eugene, OR: Wipf & Stock, 2013.

———. "James McWhirter: Pentecostal Ecumenist." *JEPTA* 32.1 (2012) 87–98.

———. *Pentecostal Origin: Early Pentecostalism in Ireland in the Context of the British Isles.* Studies in Evangelical History and Thought. Milton Keynes, UK: Paternoster, 2005.

Robinson, Martin. "The Charismatic Anglican—Historical and Contemporary: A Comparison of the Life and Work of Alexander Boddy (1854–1930) and Michael C. Harper." M.Litt. diss, University of Birmingham, UK, 1976.

Robinson, Thomas A. "'Out of the Mouths of Babes': Pentecostalism and Girl Evangelists in the Flapper Era." *AoG Heritage* 37 (2013) 37–40, 42–45.

Root, Jonathan B. "A People's Religion: The Populist Impulse in Early Kansas Pentecostalism." MA diss., Kansas State University, 2006.

Ross, James Davidson. *Dorothy: A Portrait.* London: Hodder & Stoughton, 1958.

Russell, C. Allyn. "William Bell Riley: Architect of Fundamentalism." *Minnesota History,* Spring, 1972, 14–30.

Sanders, Cheryl J. *Saints in Exile: The Holiness-Pentecostal Experience in African American Culture.* New York; Oxford University Press, 1916.

Sanders, Rufus G. W. *William Joseph Seymour: Black Father of the 20th Century Pentecostal/ Charismatic Movement.* Sandusky, OH: Xulon, 2003.

Savige, Craig. "The King James Bible Only Position and True Pentecostalism." Online. http://www.bibleprotector.com/ KJBOandPENTECOST.pdf.

Schulte, Quentin J. "Evangelicals' Uneasy Alliance with the Media." In *Religion and Mass Media*, edited by Daniel Scott and Judith Buddenbaum, 61–73. London: Sage, 1996.

Schoepflin, Rennie B. *Christian Science on Trial: Religious Healing in America*. Baltimore, MD: John Hopkins University Press, 2003.

Scott, Daniel A., and Judith Buddenbaum, eds. *Religion and Mass Media: Audiences and Adaptations*. London: Sage, 1996.

Seymour, W. J. "Divine Mandates of the Azusa Street Revival." In *Azusa Street Revival*, edited by Harold Hunter and Ceceil Robeck, 363–64. Eugene, OR: Wipf & Stock, 2006.

Simmons, Dale H. *E. W. Kenyon and the Postbellum Pursuit of Peace, Power, and Plenty*. Lanham, MD: Scarecrow, 1997.

Smail, Tom, Andrew Walker, and Nigel G. Wright. *Charismatic Renewal: The Search for a Theology*. London: SPCK, 1995.

———. "The Cross and the Spirit: Towards a Theology of Renewal." In *Charismatic Renewal*, 49–70. London: SPCK, 1995.

Smith, Vicki. "Pastor Mark Wolford, Snake-handler, Dies of Rattler Bite." *Huffington Post* (UK Version) 16 January, 2013. Online. http://www.huffingtonpost.com/2012/05/31/veteran-snakehandling-pas_n_1559762.html.

Stevenson, John. *The Penguin Social History of Britain: British Society 1914–45*. London: Penguin, 1990.

Stewart, Adam, ed. *Handbook of Pentecostal Christianity*. DeKalb, IL: Northern Illinois University Press, 2012.

Strachey, Barbara. *Remarkable Relations: The Story of the Pearsall Smith Women*. London; Universe, 1982.

Straton, John Roach. *Divine Healing in Scripture and Life*. New York: Christian Alliance, 1927.

———. "Shall the Funnymonkeyists Win? Answer to Dr Fosdick's sermon on 'Shall the Fundamentalists Win?'" *Religious Searchlight* 7, October 1, 1922.

Sumrall, Lester. "My Relationship with Smith Wigglesworth." Online. http://abrahamblessings.blogspot.co.uk/2011/10/lester-sumrall-my-relationship-with.html.

Sutton, Matthew A. *Aimee Semple McPherson and the Resurrection of Christian America*. Cambridge: Harvard University Press, 2007.

———. "'Between the Refrigerator and the Wildfire': Aimee Semple McPherson, Pentecostalism, and the Fundamentalist-Modernist Controversy." *Church History* 72.1 (2003) 159–88.

Synan, H. V. *An Eyewitness Remembers the Century of the Holy Spirit*. Grand Rapids: Chosen, 2010.

———. "Fundamentalism." In *New International Dictionary of the Pentecostal and Charismatic Movement*, edited by Stanley Burgess, 655–58. Grand Rapids: Zondervan, 2002.

———. "Pentecostal Healing (Review)." *Pneuma* 29.2 (2007) 347–48.

Taves Ann. *Fits, Trances & Vision*. Princeton, NJ: Princeton University Press, 1999.

Taylor, Malcolm. "A Historical Perspective on the Doctrine of Divine Healing." *EPTA Bulletin* 14 (1995) 54–84.

Taylor, Philip. *In the Steps of Smith Wigglesworth*. Self-published. Philip Taylor, 2007.

Thomas, John Christopher. *The Devil, Disease and Deliverance: Origins of Illness in New Testament Thought*. Sheffield, UK: Sheffield Academic Press, 1998.

Thomas, W. H. Griffith. "German Moral Abnormality." *Bibliotheca Sacra*, January 1919, 84–104.

Tomberlin, Daniel. *Pentecostal Sacraments: Encountering God at the Altar*. Cleveland, TN: Pentecostal Theological Seminary, 2010.

Treharne, David. *Healing via Redemption*. London: Jarrold, 1913.

Trollinger, William Vance. "Riley's Empire: Northwestern Bible School and Fundamentalism in the Upper Midwest." *Church History* 67.2 (1988) 197–22.

Van de Walle, Bernie. "A Man for His Season: A. B. Simpson, the Fourfold Gospel and Late Nineteenth-Century Evangelicalism." PhD diss., Drew University, 2004.

Vreeland, Derek. "Reconstructing Word of Faith Theology." Paper presented at the 30th Annual Meeting of the Society for Pentecostal Studies, 2001.

Wacker, Grant. *Heaven Below: Early Pentecostalism and American Culture*. Cambridge: Harvard University Press, 2001.

———. "The Pentecostal Tradition." In *Caring and Curing*, edited by Ronald L. Numbers, 514–38. Baltimore, MD: John Hopkins University Press, 1986.

———. "Taking Another Look at the 'Vision of the Disinherited.'" *Religious Studies Review* 8.1 (1982) 15–22.

———. "Travail of a Broken Family." In *Pentecostal Currents in American Protestantism*, edited by Edith Blumhofer, 24–49. Chicago: University of Illinois Press, 1999.

Währisch-Oblau, Claudia. "God Can Make Us Healthy." *International Review of Mission* XC (January/April 2001) 87–102.

———. "Material Salvation: Healing, Deliverance, and 'Breakthrough' in African Migrant Churches in Germany." In *Global Pentecostalism and Charismatic Healing*, edited by Candy Brown, 61–80. New York: Oxford University Press, 2011.

Wakefield, Gordon. *Alexander Boddy: Pentecostal Anglican Pioneer*. Milton Keynes, UK: Paternoster, 2007.

Walker, Andrew. "The Devil You Think You Know." In *Charismatic Renewal*, edited by Tom Smail et al., 86–105. London: SPCK, 1995.

———. *Restoring the Kingdom*. Rev ed. Guildford, UK: Eagle, 1998.

Walker, Andrew and Kristin Aune, eds. *On Revival: A Critical Examination*. Carlisle, UK: Paternoster, 2003.

Walsh, Arlene Sanchez. "Santidad, Salvación, Sanidad, Liberación." In *Global Pentecostalism and Charismatic Healing*, edited by Candy Brown, 151–68. New York: Oxford University Press, 2011.

Walsh, Timothy B. *To Meet and Satisfy a Very Hungry People: The Origins and Fortunes of English Pentecostalism, 1907–1923*. Studies in Evangelical History and Thought. Milton Keynes, UK: Paternoster, 2012.

Walsh. H. Pakenham-Walsh. "Divine Healing: A Record of Missionary Study and Experience." *International Review of Missions* 11 (1922) 96–103.

Ward, Robert C. et al. *Foundations of Orthopractic Medicine*. Philadelphia: Lippincott, Williams, and Wilkins, 2002.

Warfield, B. B. *Counterfeit Miracles*. Reprint. Edinburgh: Banner of Truth, 1972.

———. *Perfectionism*. Philadelphia: Presbyterian and Reformed Publishing, 1971.

Warner, Wayne E. *Kathryn Kuhlman: The Woman behind the Miracles*. Ann Arbor, MI: Servant, 1993.

———. *Smith Wigglesworth: Only Believe*. Gainesville, FL: Bridge-Logos, 2005.

Warrington, Keith. *Healing and Suffering: Biblical and Pastoral Reflections*. Milton Keynes, UK: Paternoster, 2005.

———, ed. *Pentecostal Perspectives*. Carlisle, UK: Paternoster, 1998.

———. *Pentecostal Theology: A Theology of Encounter*. London: T. & T. Clark, 2008.

Wasserstein, Bernard. *Barbarism & Civilisation: A History of Europe in our Time*. Oxford: Oxford University Press, 2009.

Weatherhead. Leslie D. *Psychology, Religion and Healing*. London: Houghton & Stoughton, 1952.

Weaver, C. Douglas. *The Healer-Prophet William Marrion Branham: A Study of the Prophetic in American Pentecostalism*. Macon, GA: Mercer University Press, 1987.

Welker, Michael, ed. *The Work of the Spirit: Pneumatology and Pentecostalism*. Grand Rapids: Eerdmans, 2006.

White, Christopher G. *Unsettled Minds: Psychology and the American Search for Spiritual Assurance 1830–1940*. Berkeley: University of California Press, 2009.

Whittaker, Colin. *Seven Pentecostal Pioneers*. Basingstoke, UK: Marshal, 1983.

Wigger, John H. *Taking Heaven by Storm: Methodism and the Rise of Popular Christianity in America*. Oxford University Press, 1998.

Wigglesworth, Smith. *Ever Increasing Faith*. Springfield, MO: Gospel, 1924.

Wilkinson, Michael and Peter Althouse, eds. *Winds from the North: Canadian Contributions to the Pentecostal Movement*. Leiden: Brill, 2010.

Wilson, Bryan R., ed. *Sects and Society: The Sociology of Three Religious Groups in Britain*. London: Heinemann, 1961.

Wilson, Julian. *Wigglesworth: The Complete Story*. Milton Keynes, UK: Authentic, 2002.

Wise, Robert. "Con of the Month—Rod Parsley." Online. http://www.forgottenword.org/parsley-con.html

Worcester, Elwood, and Samuel McComb. *Religion and Medicine*. New York: Moffat & Yard, 1908.

Worrall, B. G. *The Making of the English Church: Christianity in England since 1800*. London: SPCK, 1991.

Worsfold, James E. *A History of the Charismatic Movements in New Zealand*. Wellington, NZ: Julian Literature Trust, 1974.

Yeomans, Lillian B. *Healing Treasury*. Tulsa, OK: Harrison House, 2003.

Yong, Amos. *In the Days of Caesar: Pentecostalism and Political Theology*. Grand Rapids: Eerdmans, 2010.

Index